1889

1889

THE BOOMER MOVEMENT, THE LAND RUN, AND EARLY OKLAHOMA CITY

Michael J. Hightower

UNIVERSITY OF OKLAHOMA PRESS : NORMAN

Also by Michael J. Hightower

Inventing Tradition: Cowboy Sports in a Postmodern Age (Saarbrücken, Germany, 2008)

Frontier Families: The Records and Johnstons in American History (Oklahoma City, 2010)

The Pattersons: A Novel (Oklahoma City and Charlottesville, Va., 2012)

Banking in Oklahoma Before Statehood (Norman, Okla., 2013)

Banking in Oklahoma, 1907–2000 (Norman, Okla., 2014)

Loyal to Oklahoma: The BancFirst Story (Oklahoma City and Charlottesville, Va., 2015)

This book is published with the generous assistance of the
Wallace C. Thompson Endowment Fund,
University of Oklahoma Foundation.

Library of Congress Cataloging-in-Publication Data

Name: Hightower, Michael J., author.
Title: 1889 : the boomer movement, the land run, and early Oklahoma City / Michael J. Hightower.
Other titles: Eighteen eighty-nine, the boomer movement, the land run, and early Oklahoma City | Boomer movement, the land run, and early Oklahoma City
Description: First edition. | Norman, OK : University of Oklahoma Press, [2018] | Includes bibliographical references and index.
Identifiers: LCCN 2018006260 | ISBN 978-0-8061-6070-2 (hardcover : alk. paper)
Subjects: LCSH: Oklahoma—History—Land Rush, 1889. | Public lands—Oklahoma—History—19th century. | Oklahoma City (Okla.)—History—19th century. | Frontier and pioneer life—Oklahoma.
Classification: LCC F699 .H54 2018 | DDC 976.6/03—dc23
LC record available at https://lccn.loc.gov/2018006260

The paper in this book meets the guidelines for permanence and durability of the Committee on Production Guidelines for Book Longevity of the Council on Library Resources, Inc. ∞

1 2 3 4 5 6 7 8 9 10

Titling books after watershed years (1177 B.C., 1492, 1688, 1776, 1789, 1876, 1918, and so forth) has become popular—so much so that historians are running out of widely recognized dates to commemorate in their titles. Maybe this one will draw attention to another seminal year, 1889, when a presidential proclamation opened central Indian Territory to homesteading and townsite development in the Run of '89. It is with that hope that I dedicate this book to the generation of 1889, whose experiences, for better and worse, form the bedrock of Oklahoma culture.

Contents

List of Illustrations ix

Preface xi

Part I. Indian Territory to 1885

    CHAPTER ONE Antecedents 3

    CHAPTER TWO Wars and Reservations 17

    CHAPTER THREE On to Oklahoma! 35

    CHAPTER FOUR Cattle Kings 55

    CHAPTER FIVE Boomers 74

    CHAPTER SIX Our Sorrow 95

Part II. The Run

    CHAPTER SEVEN A Big Boom 117

    CHAPTER EIGHT Endgame 139

    CHAPTER NINE Everybody at Sea 159

Part III. City Building

    CHAPTER TEN Born Grown 183

    CHAPTER ELEVEN Status Quo 203

    CHAPTER TWELVE 1890 226

    Postscript 246

Notes 261

Bibliography 303

Index 313

Illustrations

Figures

Sidney Clarke 13

Battle of the Washita 22

David L. Payne 36

Roundup on the Open Range 65

Capt. Payne Crossing the Line Going to Oklahoma 76

William L. Couch 83

Capt. Payne's Last Camp in Oklahoma 89

The Branding Chute 91

Waiting for the Beef Issue 92

Samuel Crocker 112

James B. Weaver 113

Indian Territory, 1885 119

Royal Ranch in Oklahoma 120

Ejecting an "Oklahoma Boomer" 122

Charles F. Colcord 137

G. William Lillie, "Pawnee Bill" 147

Oklahoma depot before the opening, April 1889 163

T. M. Richardson 164

The Rush for the Promised Land 167

Angelo C. Scott 169

Oklahoma (City), April 27, 1889 177

Henry Overholser 191

Oklahoma (City) in 1889, viewed from the Santa Fe depot . 191

Daniel F. Stiles 195

Main Street, Oklahoma (City), June 1, 1889 197

Santa Fe depot, Oklahoma (City), July 4, 1889 201

Men striking a deal near the Santa Fe depot. 213

Andrew J. Beale. 221

Charles G. "Gristmill" Jones 223

Indian Territory and Oklahoma Territory 229
   (excluding No Man's Land), June 1, 1890241 229

Oklahoma City, 1890 241

Street map of Oklahoma City,
   Indian Territory, February 22, 1890 257

Map

Unassigned Lands, or Oklahoma Proper, 1887 xiii

Preface

The story which has thus been obtained is not cheerful to contemplate.
It is a story of cunning deception and fraud. It is a story of rich men who
led poor men into distress to further lawless schemes for gain. It is a story
of patient endurance of great hardships in a cause that, though conceived
in fraud, was well nigh just—perhaps was altogether just.

New York Sun, *February 17, 1889*

1889 is the culmination of a deep dive into my native state's foundation
story, whose purpose is twofold: to illuminate the push for homesteading and
townsite development in central Indian Territory (known alternatively as the
"Oklahoma country," "Oklahoma Proper," or the "Unassigned Lands") that
escalated in the 1870s, crystallized in the 1880s, and ended with the Run of
'89; and to examine the first stirrings of urbanization in the 320-acre townsite
that became Oklahoma City. As a social historian with a view of history that
percolates up from the churn of everyday life, I have made liberal use of primary
sources such as newspapers, memoirs, oral history interviews, and correspondence that reveal Oklahoma's pioneers on a deeply human level. Although they
came from a wide array of backgrounds and ethnicities and occupied different
rungs on the socioeconomic ladder, the homesteaders and entrepreneurs who
converged on the two million–plus acres of Oklahoma Proper were united in
their optimism and steely-eyed determination to turn a profit.

To situate 1889 in the expansive literature on early Oklahoma history,
I posit Oklahoma Proper as a crucible of politics in the Gilded Age, when
time-honored assumptions about American exceptionalism—the shining "city
on a hill" that politicians like to resurrect whenever they perceive America's
self-confidence at low ebb—slammed into contradictions posed by population
growth, the rise of industrial giants, and revolutions in transportation and

communication. Wherever they stood in the social hierarchy and spectrum of opinion leadership, people swept up in the Oklahoma Question (always capitalized, as momentous issues are, to signify their standing as really big deals) were animated by the social, political, and economic issues of the day. At one end of the scale were businessmen whose cosmopolitan outlook rested on laissez-faire capitalism, an ethos of social Darwinism, and business boosterism. At the other end were farmers and merchants who saw in Oklahoma Proper their last, best hope for building better lives.

Oklahoma's foundation story coincided with the rise of prairie populism as a political force, briefly but powerfully vested in the Populist (or People's) Party in the early 1890s, whose most important themes were hostility toward remotely wielded power and rejection of political elites. As agrarian discontent gained traction in the Gilded Age, its spokespeople found legitimacy in the tradition of dissent and protection of individual liberties dating back to the nation's founding. Presidents Jefferson, Jackson, and Lincoln refined this tradition to provide late-nineteenth-century reformers with a value system that constituted nothing less than America's secular religion.[1] Oklahoma Proper was one of the Gilded Age's most contentious battlegrounds, literally and figuratively, in America's ongoing and, arguably, unfinished effort to define itself.

1889 divides rather neatly into three periods: (1) a decade-long protest against power structures known as the boomer movement; (2) the Run of '89 and the first stirrings of urbanization in Oklahoma City; and (3) the lingering effects of controversies that raged unabated through 1890 and beyond. One of the challenges in writing this book is that people who staked claims in Oklahoma Proper left a disproportionate share of records that survive as primary sources. Their nemeses—cattlemen who grazed their herds on the cheap in central and western Indian Territory and railroad owners with both eyes on the bottom line—did not leave as much of a trail. For the most part, cattlemen operated from benign self-interest and maintained the status quo for as long as they could, while railroad officials focused on business-building opportunities. The result is an abundance of material reflecting an inherent bias against corporate interests and a scarcity of counterarguments that would present a more balanced perspective of the eighty-niner story.

As pioneers put the Run of '89 behind them and built their cities, Oklahoma City's dominance was not a foregone conclusion. To think it was, historians know, is to commit the teleological fallacy—explaining historical processes by their outcomes rather than as open-ended narratives. Famously, Oklahoma City

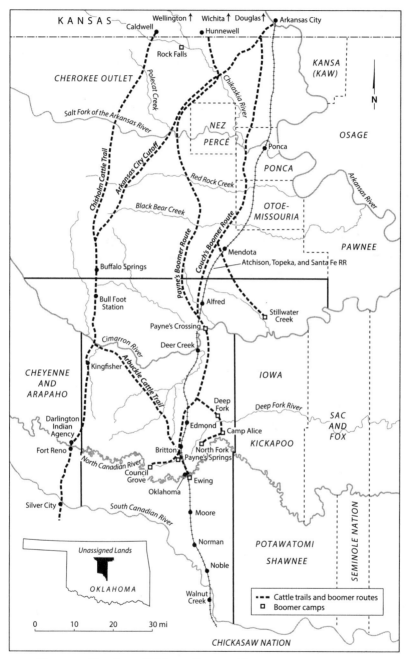

Unassigned Lands, or Oklahoma Proper, 1887. *Cartography by Bill Nelson.*

did not achieve capital status until 1910, when the wily governor Charles N.
Haskell (D; 1908–11) transferred the capital from Guthrie to his preferred city.
That happened three years after Oklahoma and Indian Territories (the Twin
Territories) were merged into a single state and more than two decades after the
Run of '89. From the pioneers' perspective, the big story was the stiff competition
between cities for commercial and political power. Oklahoma Proper was the
quintessential land of opportunity, and nobody had a crystal ball to see which
communities would thrive, which ones would merely survive, and which ones
would wither into ghost towns and die.

Readers will find in *1889* a story far more nuanced than a century-plus of
mythmaking has conditioned us to accept. In its survey of Indian Territory
history from the Five Tribes' forced relocation in the 1830s to the eve of the
Run of '89, the *New York Sun* in February 1889 advised readers (in the words
that form the epigraph to this preface) to brace for a shocking tale.

1889 opens in part 1, "Indian Territory to 1885," with a prequel on Indian
Territory's designation as a home for displaced tribes and freedmen, its division into tribal enclaves, Indian land cessions to the U.S. government, and
clarification of disputes pertaining to public lands policies. With this in the
way of background, I proceed to the period of wars and reservations (1866–90)
when Indian Territory became the red-hot center of disputes over public lands
policy and the dominant civilization's relationship with Indian tribes that stood
in the way of territorial expansion. Topics include the battles and massacres
that brought peace, however tenuous, to the southern plains; wars of words
waged in the frontier press to sway public opinion over opening Oklahoma
Proper to homesteaders; Captain David L. Payne's leadership of prospective
settlers, dubbed "boomers" in frontier vernacular, whose aims coalesced in
1880 as the boomer movement; boomers' incursions into Indian Territory and
expulsions by U.S. cavalry; cattlemen's tactics in keeping the grasslands for
themselves; and the competition among railroad corporations to control what
was sure to be a lucrative market in crops and cattle and, eventually, people.

Part 2, "The Run," begins with the presidential election of 1884 and ends on
Sunday, April 28, 1889, when homesteaders and urban pioneers celebrated their
first week of settlement with religious observances. Alternating between the
Oklahoma frontier and Washington, D.C., I describe the politics of settlement
and the first stirrings of development at tiny railroad depots along the Santa Fe

line. To capture the drama of the Run of '89, I rely on eyewitness accounts of a picture-perfect Monday afternoon in April when everything changed.

In part 3, "City Building," I chronicle the Oklahoma City story from Monday, April 29, 1889, through 1890. Milestones include the first election of municipal officers; the grandstand collapse during what was supposed to be a spectacular July 4 celebration; the creation of Oklahoma City's first businesses; the Frisco Convention, which ignited a firestorm over Guthrie's attempt to preempt Congress's responsibility to provide for territorial governance; the battle between townsites to woo the Choctaw Road from the coalfields in eastern Indian Territory; the ongoing crisis in city government, which culminated in an armed standoff between soldiers and the citizens they were sworn to protect; and the efforts to fuel industrial development that came to a standstill (but not for long!) in a failed canal project. All of these episodes unfolded in a political vacuum until Congress got around to creating a territory in the Organic Act of May 1890. Two months later, Wyoming followed North Dakota, South Dakota, Montana, Idaho, and Washington (all admitted to the Union in 1889) in affixing its star to Old Glory. Clearly, state building was progressing at a more rapid clip elsewhere in the West.

Historical highlights of Oklahoma as an official territory include ongoing mayhem in the city's ubiquitous saloons and gambling dens; former mayor William L. Couch's fatal shoot-out with a rival land claimant; the Organic Act of May 2, 1890, which ended Oklahoma Proper's thirteen-month experiment in frontier democracy and ushered in seventeen years of territorial governance; the first territory-wide elections and convening of Oklahoma Territory's first legislature; the conversion of land east of the Santa Fe depot from military to school use; battles, legal and literal, stemming from "soonerism" (a term fraught with contested meaning); black migration to the new territory; and the Indian war that never happened in December 1890, as distinguished from the massacre that did happen in a place called Wounded Knee.

Writ large, the Oklahoma story is a profoundly American story, and it has much to teach us about homesteading and nascent urbanization during the Gilded Age. Historians should ask not only what happened but why, and most of all, why it matters. This historian is no exception.

———————

After the dust settled from the Run of '89, Oklahoma Proper's urban pioneers launched businesses, built homes, and imported cultural amenities from back east as surefire antidotes to frontier scarcity. Seemingly overnight, tangible evidence of the Run of '89 was hard to come by. And as the generations passed, it disappeared altogether beneath a skyline of glass and steel. Likewise forgotten in the rush to modernize were the passions that lured pioneers to participate in a headlong race to claim town lots and homesteads.

Save for marketing slogans and paeans to hardy settlers, a city that has always prided itself on being "born grown" allowed the Run of '89 to vanish without a trace. Even the monuments just north of Interstate 40 and east of downtown Oklahoma City, magnificent as they are in depicting that wild scramble, commemorate what happened in the countryside, not the city. Urban pioneers marched to a quicker cadence, and they were embroiled in controversies beyond the ken of the yeoman farmers who frame our understanding of frontier settlement.

Thanks go to my partners in scholarship: archivists at the Oklahoma Historical Society in Oklahoma City and Western History Collections in Norman for preserving so many of the state's foundational documents; Kent Calder and Steven Baker at the University of Oklahoma Press for helping me shape the manuscript; and Professors Kenny Brown at the University of Central Oklahoma and Sterling Evans at the University of Oklahoma for their careful reading of the original draft and suggestions for making it better. Chuck Wiggin, organizer of the 89er Trail Fund at the Oklahoma City Foundation and developer of the 89er Trail in downtown Oklahoma City, deserves credit for sparking my interest in the Run of '89 and subsidizing my work. As always, I appreciate Judy Hightower's good cheer and wise counsel—both indispensable in a writer's solitary routine. Earl Walston, who expresses his passion for the American West in paint rather than words, read chapters in their formative stages, and for that I am truly grateful. I leave it to readers to determine whether I have done justice to one of the most interesting and, paradoxically, least understood chapters of American history.

MJH
Oklahoma City and Charlottesville
Spring 2019

PART I

Indian Territory to 1885

CHAPTER ONE

Antecedents

Every new farm that is snatched from the wilderness adds to the
wealth of the nation, while the monopoly of millions of acres
which are withheld from cultivation is a positive public curse.
Hon. George W. Julian, March 6, 1868

With the notable exception of trading outposts that served as conduits for
manufactured goods and promoted peaceful relations between Anglos and
Indians, Indian Territory before the Civil War was populated primarily by
tribes whose ancestral homelands stretched from the Mississippi River and Gulf
Coast to the Carolinas and Virginia. These tribes included Cherokees, Creeks,
Choctaws, Chickasaws, and Seminoles, and they are known condescendingly
as the "Five Civilized Tribes" (hereafter designated as the "Five Tribes") for
their gradual acceptance of European culture. Yet their adoption of foreign
customs and integration into an alien economy in the decades following
the American War of Independence made little difference to land-hungry
farmers and their advocates in the nation's capital. Accustomed to moving
when and where they pleased, pioneers settled in tribal territory convinced
that the land was theirs by right of conquest and, more to the point, part of
God's plan to spread Christian ways clear to the Pacific Ocean.

By the second decade of the nineteenth century, some Indians saw the
handwriting on the wall and migrated west, where white interlopers would be
less likely to bother them. The end of their trail put them in western Arkansas
Territory. Organized on July 4, 1819, Arkansas Territory stretched west from the
Mississippi River to the hundredth meridian, the present-day eastern boundary
of the Texas Panhandle. To the south were Louisiana and the Red River; to the

north were Missouri and the southern boundary of the future state of Kansas. The territory shed its western half in 1824, leaving its westernmost outpost at Fort Smith and present-day Oklahoma effectively beyond the reach of American laws and constitutional protections. The next year, the government created an Indian country, later known as "Indian Territory," whose original boundaries stretched north from the Red River to the Great Bend of the Missouri River and west from Arkansas and Missouri to the hundredth meridian.

Steeped in Enlightenment philosophy, opinion leaders in the early federal period were convinced that Indians could be "civilized"—that is, they could climb the social ladder and, with a little prodding from the dominant civilization, assimilate into mainstream American society. Eventually, tribal governments would be extinguished, and property would be distributed to Indians on an individual basis. But in the meantime, tribes removed to the Indian country could rest assured of two things: they would be undisturbed and free from rival claims of neighboring states; and nothing would be done without their consent.[1]

A trickle of Indian migration became a flood when President Andrew Jackson launched his jeremiad against Indians. History has branded Jackson as a racist and has saddled him with responsibility for the horrors that Native tribes endured during his administration. Yet a close examination of Jackson's Indian policy reveals that the president, although a die-hard Indian fighter, aimed not to destroy Indian culture, but rather to prevent his countrymen from doing so. He believed that removal to the trans-Mississippi West was the Indian's only chance of survival. Congress fell in line with the president's wishes when it passed the Indian Removal Act of May 28, 1830, thereby paving the way for the Five Tribes' cross-country migration.[2]

Most Indians had learned enough of Anglo ways to realize that resistance was futile. Over the course of two years, an estimated sixty thousand people made the harrowing trek westward. Along the way, one in ten died from disease and exposure.[3] At trail's end, survivors joined early immigrants and rebuilt their lives as best they could in a region deemed to be of no use to people of European descent. In vernacular aimed at assuring skeptical Indians that the Great Father in Washington, D.C., had their best interests at heart, they were promised independent governance and territorial integrity for as long as the grasses grew and the waters ran.

The U.S. government was bound by its treaties to supply the Five Tribes with meat, corn, and other staples to ease their transition to the trans-Mississippi West. What the transplanted Indians got was disappointment. In

September 1841, the War Department assigned Major Ethan Allen Hitchcock to investigate fraud and corruption on the part of contractors who were supposed to provide the Five Tribes with the wherewithal to survive, and what he saw did not augur well for Anglo-Indian relations. Nor did his report bolster confidence in the U.S. government's ever-evolving vision for Indian Territory: the development of tribal governments into a grand council that would enlist all the tribes in maintaining law and order; a permanent peace among all removed Indians; the eventual appointment of a territorial governor and secretary; the creation of an Indian confederacy that would function under Congress's watchful eye; and, perhaps most important, widespread emulation of the Five Tribes' "civilized" ways to the point that farming and raising stock would sweep nomadic ways into the dustbin of history.[4]

Hitchcock's report signaled a paradigm shift in the federal government's stewardship of Indian country. Acting on the assumption that Indian wars were essentially over, Congress in 1849 voted to move the Office of Indian Affairs (later, the Bureau of Indian Affairs) from the War Department to the newly created Department of the Interior. As Senator Jefferson Davis (D-Miss.; 1847–51, 1857–61) remarked when the proposed change arrived on the Senate floor for debate, wars and rumors of war characterized the Republic's early days, not its modernizing present.[5]

Just as the Five Tribes had once occupied distinct regions of the southeastern United States, so, too, did they occupy separate regions of what came to be known as Indian Territory: Cherokees in the northeast; Choctaws in the southeast; Creeks and Seminoles just west of the Cherokee Nation; and Chickasaws in the southwest. Known colloquially as "the Nations," these tribal enclaves stretched from the Red River in the south to Kansas (incorporated as a territory on May 30, 1854) in the north. Their western boundary was less certain, and it lay in the largely unexplored country that sloped gently toward the pre-1848 border with Mexico just east of the Rocky Mountains. Soldiers and overland freighters whose wagon trains snaked along the Santa Fe Trail between Missouri river towns and the Spanish settlements in New Mexico were among the only non-Indian visitors to that vast and uninviting terrain.[6]

Two of the Five Tribes were especially important to Oklahoma Proper's history: Creeks and Seminoles. In the eighteenth century, the Seminoles were affiliated with the Creeks, a loose confederation of ethnic groups and tribes in southern Georgia, northern Florida, and Alabama. During the late eighteenth century, a few villages on the middle Chattahoochee River cut their social and political ties with their neighbors and moved to northern Florida. The tribe's name, "Seminole," translates as "wild" or "those who camp at a distance," and it is equivalent to the white American's "frontiersman." Even so, their designation as Seminoles might have come from *cimarrón*, the Spanish term for runaways. Whatever their name, the Seminoles posed enough of a threat, real or imagined, to the slaveholding culture of the South to be swept up in Jackson's policy of pacification and forced removal to the trans-Mississippi West. Although they were never defeated in the so-called Seminole Wars (1817–18, 1835–42, and 1855–58), the Seminoles probably suffered more than any of the Five Tribes in their rough treatment at the hands of the U.S. Army. They might have taken grim consolation to know that the Seminole Wars cost the United States more in lives and money than any Indian war in its history.[7] Thousands recognized the futility of their cause and moved west on their own. By 1839, most Seminoles had made it to Indian Territory. Three years later, their population stood at 3,612.

The Seminoles arrived in Indian Territory with minority status in land controlled by their former neighbors, the Creeks. The U.S. government granted the Seminoles the right to self-government, but only if they adhered to Creek laws. Chafing under Creek dominance, some Seminoles lit out for Mexico in 1849. The ones who stayed were led by Chief John Jumper, who in 1856 signed a treaty with federal and Creek officials to establish the Seminole Nation. Then came the Civil War, and, like the rest of the Five Tribes, most Creeks and Seminoles cast their lot with the Confederate States of America.[8]

The Civil War ended for the Five Tribes some five months after Lee's surrender at Appomattox Courthouse when federal officials summoned tribal representatives to Fort Smith to announce what the triumphant Union had in store for Indian tribes. Indian Affairs commissioner Dennis N. Cooley presided over the council at Fort Smith, and he came with assurances that the president was "willing to hear his erring children in extenuation of their great crime" and make new treaties with them. Cooley's main message was less reassuring: although Indians who had remained loyal to the Union would be protected in their just claims, the nations as a whole had forfeited their rights to annuities and land.[9] On the second day of the council, commissioners presented specific policies that they aimed to incorporate in future treaties: (1) signatories would agree to permanent peace among tribal members and with other tribes as well as with the U.S. government; (2) tribes living in Indian country would aid federal authorities in convincing Plains tribes to keep the peace; (3) slavery would be abolished, and former slaves would be granted the rights and responsibilities of tribal citizenship; (4) the U.S. government would purchase sections of Indian Territory and reserve them for settling other tribes; (5) all tribes in the region would eventually be consolidated under a single Indian government; and (6) no people of European ancestry, with the exception of federal employees and contractors who worked on internal improvements, would be allowed to settle in Indian Territory unless they were connected to one of the established nations. In later years, railroad companies would cite references to internal improvement companies as evidence of their privileged status in Indian Territory.[10]

Promises and assurances notwithstanding, Indians who had fought on both sides of the Civil War were stunned. Some Indian delegates thought they had come to Fort Smith to make peace, only to discover that the federal government's real motive was to reduce their landholdings, realign their relationships with other tribes, and undermine their sovereignty, all in utter disregard of their wartime allegiances. Elias C. Boudinot, a Cherokee railroad attorney who was thoroughly socialized in white culture, was one of the few Native Americans who agreed with the policy overhaul, particularly with regard to consolidation of tribes in a territorial government. The Fort Smith negotiators adjourned with an agreement to meet in Washington, D.C., the following spring to hammer out agreements in what came to be known collectively as the "Reconstruction Treaties of 1866."[11]

Many of those same representatives, including Boudinot, journeyed to Washington to participate in the realignment of Anglo-Indian relations. Not surprisingly, a main topic of discussion was land cessions. Although representatives from the Five Tribes knew what to expect from negotiators who routinely broke their own treaties, none who gathered in the nation's capital to define Reconstruction in Indian Territory suspected that they were sowing the seeds of controversy destined to frame the final stage of America's westward expansion.

Large-scale settlement in the Great Plains was several decades in the future when lawmakers tried to figure out what to do with the continent's vast and uncharted territory. In the early years of the Republic, the U.S. government forbade settlements in the public domain and, in 1807, began to remove settlers who ventured there without legal sanction. By the time people began seriously to consider settling west of Missouri and Arkansas, Congress was loosening such restrictions and devising ways to facilitate the transfer of land from the public domain to private ownership.[12] Congress's motivations were twofold: in terms of bedrock ideology, lawmakers wanted to spread America's bounty to ordinary citizens; and in terms of fiscal responsibility, they perceived the nation's resources as an unlimited source of revenue to fund the federal government. Their deliberations resulted in two land laws that, in a later generation, fueled demands to open Indian Territory to homesteading.

The first of those laws was the Preemption Act of 1841. According to the rights of preemption, settlers could choose to establish homes on both surveyed and unsurveyed land. Small landowners of not more than 320 acres in any state or territory were entitled to purchase a quarter section (160 acres) for as little as $1.25 per acre. But there was a catch: to stymie speculators, buyers were required to use and improve the land rather than resell it. The next landmark law was the Homestead Act of 1862. Unlike the Preemption Act, the Homestead Act restricted settlement to surveyed land, and it required homesteaders to live on their claims for five years and make improvements before they could receive their titles. Settlers who wanted to improve their land immediately and avoid the five-year residence requirement had the option of paying $1.25 per acre to the federal treasury. As the law drew no distinction between genders, more women had an opportunity to acquire property in their own names in the West than in other parts of the country. The law further required claimants to be at least twenty-one years old unless they were heads of families, meaning that enterprising women could gain value by enabling underage husbands to acquire homesteads through marriage.[13]

The Great Plains had yet to entice very many settlers when Congress passed the Reconstruction Treaties of 1866, and those laws came at a pivotal moment in American history. Now that the Confederacy was vanquished, soldiers were deployed to pacify the frontier and protect westbound caravans. Meanwhile, former combatants could resume what had always been the nation's favorite pastime: business. In the North and South and increasingly in the West, empires of steel and petroleum and manufactured goods of all descriptions were transforming communities into outposts of consumerism. Business titans with names like Rockefeller, Carnegie, Vanderbilt, Gould, and Fisk were combining human capital and natural resources to propel Western civilization into the age of industry. Railroads were pushing into remote hamlets to bring consumer goods to the frontier and nature's bounty to centers of money and power, where factories received raw materials and converted them into consumer goods that generated demand for more of the same. Great fortunes were rising overnight, and they coexisted all too easily with pestilential poverty to brand the era between 1865 and 1900 as the Gilded Age—an age when tycoons gained status by flaunting their wealth; when corporations succeeded by buying their competitors or driving them into bankruptcy, and sometimes both; and when politics and business blended to create an ever-widening gulf between rich and poor. The battle lines were drawn as capital and labor settled in for decades of contention and, all too often, violent confrontations.

As homesteaders and entrepreneurs were rethinking their aversion to the Great Plains, lawmakers were putting the finishing touches on the Reconstruction Treaties of 1866. Those agreements included treaties with the Creek and Seminole Nations, and they effectively upended a half century of treaty making that began in 1803 when the U.S. government acquired title to Louisiana. When the Indian Removal Act of 1830 authorized the president to set aside certain areas for the Five Tribes' resettlement, the federal government began a decades-long process of relinquishing its exclusive title. Over the next few years, the original act was supplemented by various bargains and treaties that further defined Indian landownership and relations between the Five Tribes and Washington.

The process accelerated with a treaty signed on February 14, 1833, in which the United States conveyed to the Creek Nation an area of Indian Territory that included Oklahoma Proper. Not only did the 1833 treaty patent the land to the Creek Nation; it expressly provided that the land would be forever free from state or territorial laws. More than two decades later, a treaty of August 7, 1856, required the Creek Nation to convey Oklahoma Proper to the Seminoles. The treaty stipulated that the land could not be sold or otherwise disposed of without the consent of both Indian nations.[14] During a decade in which America was nearly rent asunder in the Civil War, Oklahoma Proper was held in partnership by Creeks and Seminoles. Their agreement remained undisputed until the Reconstruction Treaties of 1866.

Determined to punish Confederates in Indian Territory for their rebellious ways, U.S. negotiators initiated a thorough realignment of relations with the Five Tribes. Some provisions applied to each of them, including the relinquishment of rights-of-way to railroad companies. The clause that provided for an intertribal council referred to the proposed union of Indian nations as the "Territory of Oklahoma," a name suggested by Allen Wright of the Choctaw delegation. In his native Muskogean language, "Oklahoma" translates as "red people," and its usage marks the first time this moniker was used in an official U.S. document.[15]

The Treaty between the United States of America and the Seminole Nation of Indians, concluded on March 21, signed by President Andrew Johnson for the United States and Chief John Chup-Co for the Seminole Nation, and proclaimed on August 16, 1866, acknowledged the Seminoles as former enemies of the U.S. government. In keeping with other treaties with the Five Tribes, the treaty required the Seminoles to free their slaves, hereafter referred to as "freedmen," and to accept a land cession consisting of part of its present reservation. With specific reference to the treaty of August 7, 1856, requiring the Creeks to cede land to the Seminoles, article 3 of the treaty laid out the essential conditions of the federal government's new relationship with the Seminole Nation. Stripped to its essentials, it gave the United States the right to locate other Indians and freedmen on Seminole land, estimated at 2,169,080 acres, and required the United States to pay the Seminole Nation $325,362 for its land cession, a sum representing a bargain-basement rate of fifteen cents per acre.[16]

The entire domain included Oklahoma Proper as well as acreage to the east. Article 3 further required the Seminole Nation to buy back from the U.S. government 200,000 acres for its reservation for the sum of $100,000, or fifty cents an acre.[17] Leftover land was used for reservations for Potawatomis and other tribes that had been relocated to Indian Territory. Ultimately, the Seminole Nation received $225,362 ($325,362 minus $100,000) for its equity in Oklahoma Proper.[18] To ensure Creek compliance, a quit claim was obtained from the Creeks in a separate treaty in June 1866. Even though the Creeks received cash for their equity in Oklahoma Proper, they had no choice but to accept the possibility of more Indians and freedmen moving onto land that was supposed to be theirs for as long as the grasses grew and the waters ran.

It is hard to avoid the conclusion that the government's stated desire to locate other Indians and freedmen on former Seminole land was at best a stretch of the truth, and at worst a deliberate lie. On July 27, 1866—just four months after the Seminole treaty was concluded—Congress approved an act incorporating the Atlantic and Pacific Railroad Company (later reorganized as the St. Louis and San Francisco Railroad Company, better known as the "Frisco") and authorizing it to construct a railroad and telegraph line from

Missouri and Arkansas to the Pacific coast. The proposed route included a right-of-way through the land recently purchased from the Seminoles. Section 6 of the act granted odd-numbered sections of land for forty miles on each side of the tracks to the Atlantic and Pacific Railroad. That same section opened even-numbered sections along the route to preemption and homesteading. As far as prospective settlers were concerned, Indian title to large swaths of Indian Territory was thereby extinguished, and one had only to read section 2257 of the *Revised Statutes of the United States* to learn what might become of it: "All lands belonging to the United States, to which the Indian title has been or may hereafter be extinguished, shall be subject to the right of pre-emption under the conditions, restrictions and stipulations provided by law."[19]

It seems clear that the U.S. government bought the land from the Seminoles so that it could be given to the railroad. According to the *New York Sun*, "There is no doubt that could all the facts pertinent to the case be brought out in a court of justice the title in fee to Oklahoma proper would revert to the Creeks and Seminoles on the ground of fraud and misrepresentation in the transfer, but no such case will ever be heard in court."[20]

As pressures mounted after 1866 to compel a succession of U.S. presidents to open Oklahoma Proper to homesteading, activists cited presidential authority to allow settlers into what was clearly part of the public domain as a key plank in their argument. If the United States had purchased title to land that was assigned to no other tribes, then what, exactly, was the holdup? Further evidence of the federal government's ownership of the land and, by extension, the president's authority to open the public domain to homesteading came when surveyors arrived in Indian Territory to begin their work on land granted to the Atlantic and Pacific Railroad. Commissioning a survey was an obvious prelude to disposing of the land. If officials truly aimed to settle Indians and freedmen in Oklahoma Proper, then they would not have purchased the land for their use and then given it to non-Indians (in this case, a railroad company) against Creek and Seminole wishes. "The Creeks and Seminoles still have an equity in justice, the Indians say, in Oklahoma proper," concluded the *New York Sun*, "whether they have [it] according to the letter of the law or not."[21] Critics of the government's alleged deceit had a final argument in their arsenal: if U.S. negotiators were truly intent on justice, they would not have forced Seminoles and Creeks to sell their land for a pittance while allowing white Confederates in the Deep South to remain on their property.

For a glimpse into debates over public lands policies that culminated in the Run of '89, we turn to the Honorable George W. Julian (FS-Ind.; 1849–51 and R-Ind.; 1861–71). Appointed to the chairmanship of the House Committee on Public Lands in late 1863, Julian was relentless in defending the rights of settlers against speculators and giant corporations. Like Jefferson, he believed that men had an inalienable right, and maybe even an obligation, to bring forth the earth's bounty. Yet preemption and homestead laws were threatened from two directions: some wanted to pay off government debts by selling federal land; and others wanted to give land to schools and colleges. But for Julian, the gravest threat came from railroads. Aided and abetted by speculators, they received enormous land grants that cheated the government out of productive wealth and citizens out of homesteads. Julian's land policy, reflected in a series of proposed legislative measures, was founded on the principle that public lands should be given exclusively to settlers under preemption and homestead laws.[22]

Julian clarified his position on public lands policies in a speech on March 6, 1868, under the no-nonsense title, "Our Land Policy—Its Evils and Their Remedy." Julian was speaking in support of House Bill 370, whose aim was to prevent the sale of public lands except as provided for under the Preemption and Homestead Acts and laws pertaining to townsites and mineral properties.[23] Although the congressman did not mention Indian Territory specifically, his blistering denunciation of U.S. land policy (to be remedied, of course, by his bill) takes us straight to the dawn of Oklahoma history, when disagreements over landownership crystallized in opposing ideologies, fueled endless disputes that sometimes turned violent, and culminated in the Run of '89. It is of more than passing interest to find a copy of Julian's speech in the papers of Sidney Clarke, a onetime congressman-at-large (R-Kans.; 1865–71) and chairman of the House Committee on Indian Affairs during the Forty-First Congress (1869–71). Following his six-year stint in Congress, he was elected to the Kansas State House of Representatives and served as its speaker. As arguments over public lands policies escalated in the 1880s, Clarke advocated tirelessly for opening Oklahoma Proper to non-Indian settlement. He served as provisional mayor of Oklahoma City in the fall of 1889 and, until his death in 1909, guided his adopted city's early development.[24]

Congressman Julian's two cardinal principles are simply stated: (1) the U.S. government had a moral obligation to make land as productive as possible;

Sidney Clarke.
Courtesy Oklahoma Historical Society, Oklahoma City, 15012.1.

and (2) maximum productivity could only be achieved on small holdings tilled by their proprietors. This was the America that Jefferson envisioned as he gazed westward from the heights of Monticello: a land of small farmers, self-sufficient and supremely productive, whose progeny would tame the wilderness and carry the nation's promise from coast to coast. To imbue his vision with the force of law, Jefferson devised a framework for orderly settlement that was codified in the Land Ordinance of 1785. Most importantly, Jefferson's ordinance established the requirements for survey and created a grid of meridians and baselines from which to hew privately owned land parcels from the wilderness.

Clearly, there was no need to encourage migration. Long before the Treaty of Paris brought the War of Independence to a close in 1783, settlers were already flooding across the Alleghenies. The challenge was to channel public lands laws in accord with republican principles. Frontiersmen aiming to carry their families into the western wilderness needed to know that there was a path to inclusion in the national polity and that they and their descendants would eventually become U.S. citizens. In essence, the ordinances conceived by Jefferson and made permanent by the Confederation Congress (1783–89) defined the western domain as a sacred trust whose endurance as a cornerstone of public lands policy depended on the federal government's willingness to deliver the fruits of America's bounty to its citizens.[25]

To support his argument, Julian included in his speech passages not from Jefferson, but from Europe's most renowned philosophers—John Locke, John Stuart Mill, and others who would have been familiar to his erudite listeners—who extolled the virtues of a free and independent peasantry. "They are the voice of reason and justice," intoned Julian, "affirming, in different forms of speech, the scriptural truth that the earth belongs 'to the children of men.'"[26] Tangible evidence that small farmers were the backbone of a sound economy could be found throughout Europe, where landowners with tiny acreages routinely outproduced great proprietors and their downtrodden tenants. As one of Julian's authorities wrote after his travels in France, "Give a man the sure possession of a bleak rock, and he will turn it into a garden; give him a nine years' lease of a garden, and he will convert it into a desert."[27]

But there was a serpent in America's garden, and it slithered into the Gilded Age in the form of monopolists and speculators. According to the commissioner of the General Land Office, approximately thirty million acres of public land had been sold to speculators since the foundation of the Republic. As Julian deftly explained to his fellow lawmakers in the epigraph to this chapter, by aligning itself with speculators, the federal government not only cheated farmers but also robbed the national treasury. Viewed from Julian's perspective, U.S. public lands policies were nothing less than "legalized landlordism" with roots in Old World feudalism. Julian continued, "Instead of flourishing towns and villages, small homesteads, and an independent yeomanry, with the attendant blessings of churches and free schools, it consigns the fertile plains of the West to the tender mercies of the monopolist, whose greed alone is his law." In an age when captains of industry were gaining heroic status, Julian's real heroes were settlers who were prepared "to encounter either wild beasts or savages in exploring our distant borders." By keeping settlers from public land that was rightfully theirs under preemption and homesteading laws, the U.S. government was assuming the mantle of King George, who, in Jefferson's immortal words, had "endeavored to prevent the population of these States."[28] Julian's listeners needed no reminding that King George's policies had spawned a revolution.

Julian reserved special opprobrium for railroads in the South and West to which Congress had granted an astonishing fifty-seven million acres, thus subordinating the rights of settlers to soulless monopolies. Although railroad grants resulted in avenues of commerce that accrued to the common good, they also inflicted "great mischiefs upon the country" insofar as they discriminated against settlers. Julian estimated that railroad corporations controlled a third of the public domain. For evidence of the pernicious effects of the nation's public lands policies, Julian cited acquaintances from Kansas who blamed railroad land grants for making it nearly impossible to secure a homestead. Frustrated in eastern Kansas, many farmers had migrated farther west, only to find their prospects compromised by railroad agents.

Equally ruinous to settlement in the West was the creation of Indian reservations. No sooner did those lands become off-limits to settlers than monopolists and speculators showed up to bend legislation to the contours of their pecuniary interests. "I believe the time has come to sound the cry of danger," thundered the congressman from Indiana, "and to demand, in the name of our pioneers and producers, a radical reform in the policy of the Government as to any future grants it may make in aid of these enterprises."[29]

Like other opinion leaders of his generation, Congressman Julian waxed biblical to hammer home his message. Just as frogs had once rained pestilence on Pharaoh, so, too, were public lands laws perverting the national character, poisoning social life, and encouraging people to congregate in cities that were already teeming with criminals and tenements. In closing, Julian invoked the Declaration of Independence to urge Congress to reform preemption and homesteading laws and thereby "extend the borders of our civilization, increase our national wealth, curb the ravages of monopolists, satisfy the earth-hunger of the multitudes who are striving for homes on our soil, and thus practically reassert the right of people to life, liberty, and the pursuit of happiness."[30]

When Congressman Julian delivered his rant against public lands policies in March 1868, a war-weary nation was shifting its attention from blood-soaked battlefields to the vastness of the trans-Mississippi West, where opportunities beckoned and socioeconomic distinctions mattered less than pluck and ingenuity. To accommodate a rising tide of westward migration, the federal government saw to it that soldiers would be available to mitigate conflicts and offer protection against Indian depredations. Seemingly overnight, military forts, farms, and settlements extended from Texas to the Dakotas and western Missouri to the foothills of the Rockies, and they were linked by expanding networks of transportation and communication. For all intents and purposes, Manifest Destiny was on the verge of fulfilling its promise to obliterate the frontier and extend American civilization across the continent.

But there was a hole at the southern end of all those forts and farms and settlements, where millions of acres were occupied by a hodgepodge of Indian nations in the east and nomadic tribes in the west. It was also a place that was off-limits to anyone without Indian ancestry. That anomaly was of little consequence in 1868. A decade later, it was beginning to fester as a breeding ground for Gilded Age inequities. A decade after that, it was front-page news in a rising clash over Americans' concept of fairness and a powder keg of conflicting ambitions set to explode in ways Congressman Julian's listeners could never have imagined.

CHAPTER TWO

Wars and Reservations

I do not want to settle down in the houses you would build for us.
I love to roam over the wild prairie. There I am free and happy.
When we sit down, we grow pale and die.

Satanta, October 1867

Under a full moon in late April 1880, twenty-five men rendezvoused in southern Kansas and pointed their wagons in a southerly direction. None doubted that they were embarked on a dangerous mission. U.S. cavalry might show up at any moment to put a quick end to their travels. They would then be branded as trespassers in Indian country and, if President Rutherford B. Hayes (R; 1877–81) was to be taken at his word, arrested and prosecuted to the full extent of the law. Worse yet, Indian trouble was possible, maybe even inevitable. Pushed from their ancestral hunting grounds to make way for westbound migrants, Plains tribes had no reason to welcome a convoy of armed white men as they passed through their reservations. A third threat came from cowboys as they prodded herds of longhorn cattle from Texas to northern railheads and allowed them to gorge on lush prairie grasses along the way. Determined to keep the grasslands for themselves, cattlemen and the pistol-toting cowboys who worked for them bristled at the prospect of sharing nature's bounty with anybody, let alone "nesters," so named because their clearings, with brush stacked in circular patterns to protect crops from range cattle, resembled giant birds' nests.[1] Wagons laden with farming implements signaled that something new was in the wind. Firmly entrenched in Gilded Age networks of power and privilege, cattlemen would want to put a stop to it before things got out of hand.

Tensions mounted as the invaders crossed the Kansas line en route to the North Canadian River, where they aimed to establish a colony. Perhaps, as the caravan wound its way through Indian Territory unchallenged by soldiers or Indians or cowboys, its leader was mulling over a name for the capital city he wanted to build in the middle of a region that was drifting into frontier vernacular as "the Oklahoma country." Maybe that is when he decided to call the capital city "Ewing."

Ewing did not survive. Oklahoma City did.

The spring 1880 intrusion into the Oklahoma country and establishment of the stillborn capital of Ewing in present-day Oklahoma City were still a dozen years in the future when, in October 1867, U.S. peace commissioners summoned tribal representatives to Medicine Lodge Creek in southwestern Kansas for the last great gathering of free Indians in the American West. The U.S. government was represented by Lieutenant General William Tecumseh Sherman, commander of the Military Division of the Missouri, whose methods of keeping the peace in Georgia in the waning days of the Civil War were a topic of conversation around frontier campfires.

Confident that the great council would capture headlines in the white man's talking leaves, thousands of mounted tribesmen arrived at the campground in full battle regalia, complete with red-painted faces and war bonnets and gay battle streamers. Government negotiators watched as the warriors concentrated into a wedge-shaped mass and whipped their horses into a full gallop. Without breaking stride, they reformed themselves into the shape of a huge wheel about a mile short of the campground and charged their audience in a circular pattern that came nearer with each revolution.

And then, within a hundred yards of what were surely some apprehensive commissioners, the great whirling and glittering wheel came to a standstill. The chiefs—Satanta (also known as White Bear), Quanah Parker, Penateka (or Silver Brooch), Ten Bears, and others whose world was entering its great unraveling—dismounted and waited in silence as the vastly outnumbered white men demonstrated their bravery and good faith by walking past them and into a tent to commence negotiations.[2]

As the dust settled, prescient observers detected a hint of pathos in this trademark maneuver of Plains warfare. Within the span of a generation, martial displays that had struck terror in the hearts of their enemies would become a staple of Wild West shows—ceremonies devoid of meaning, meant neither to command respect nor instill fear, but rather, to titillate an audience at the dawn of the age of entertainment.

Entertainment was the last thing on U.S. commissioners' minds as they sat down with tribal representatives to figure out how to bring peace to the southern plains. Although their stated intention was to bargain, they were really there to deliver an ultimatum: surrender and move to reservations or face the full wrath of the U.S. Army. Representing the Kiowas, Satanta expressed his people's revulsion toward U.S. commissioners' insistence that they trade their teepees for houses and take up settled ways. He made his preference clear in the quote that forms the epigraph to this chapter.

The treaty was concluded on October 21, 1867. Chiefs from all the tribes signed the treaty, even though none could read it. The treaty required Kiowas, Comanches, and Apaches to move to a six-thousand-square-mile reservation in the southwestern corner of Indian Territory. In return for ceasing hostilities and making way for Atlantic and Pacific Railroad construction crews that were slicing through Indian Territory, the U.S. government promised to give each Indian a new suit of clothes every year and seeds and implements to undertake farming. The tribes were further promised an annual distribution of twenty-five thousand dollars' worth of goods. A similar agreement was reached with Cheyennes and Arapahos, who had initially refused to attend the council, and whose leaders had already entered into treaties with the U.S. government in October 1865. Their reservation was located north of the Kiowa, Comanche, and Apache Reservation.

Although the treaties did nothing to reform the reservation system, white negotiators were cautiously optimistic that they would hold. Reformers saw reservations as laboratories where Indians could become self-sufficient farmers imbued with Christian morality and democratic values. Turning a blind eye toward cultural differences, they pointed to the Five Tribes' success in developing sophisticated capitalist economies in eastern Indian Territory as a template for economic development on the Great Plains. But all too often, incompetent rascals bent on self-enrichment were put in charge of Indian agencies. In the absence of fundamental reforms, the treaty system would serve only to turn peaceful Indians into hostiles.[3]

After signing the Medicine Lodge Creek Treaty, U.S. and Indian negotiators went their separate ways, the commissioners back to the nation's capital to implement the details of the treaties, and the Indians to their camps and beloved broad vistas.[4]

Of all the soldiers stationed in Indian country, none took a keener interest in the Medicine Lodge Creek council than members of the all-black Ninth and Tenth U.S. Cavalries. Formation of these regiments dated back to August 1866 when General Ulysses S. Grant authorized the formation of black cavalry. To lead them in their new deployments, Grant recommended two officers with sterling Civil War records: Colonel Edward Hatch of Iowa for the Ninth and Colonel Benjamin Grierson of Illinois for the Tenth.

Thirteen dollars a month was meager pay, but it was more than most blacks had reason to expect as civilians in the Gilded Age.[5] The regiments arrived in the southern plains with multiple and sometimes conflicting missions: ensure the safety of westbound caravans; keep Indians on their reservations; respond to intertribal conflicts, particularly those between the Five Tribes and their more bellicose neighbors to the west; and prevent white trespassers from invading Indian country. Uncertain what to make of dark-skinned and kinky-haired warriors, Indians dubbed them "buffalo soldiers." During two decades of service that caused their detractors to reconsider their low opinion of African Americans in uniform, the buffalo soldiers wore their moniker proudly. The most prominent feature of the Tenth Cavalry's regimental crest was a buffalo.[6] Battle-tested and inured to hardship, buffalo soldiers were destined for active campaigning that would take them from the Great Plains and Rocky Mountains to the deserts of New Mexico and Arizona Territories. Toward the end of their service, buffalo soldiers would become a familiar and unwelcome sight to trespassers bent on defying government edicts and putting down stakes in Oklahoma Proper.

─────────────

If anyone doubted the futility of resistance, they were surely dissuaded by the events of November 1868, when Cheyennes and Arapahos learned once again the value (or, more precisely, the lack thereof) of white men's treaties. Major General Philip Sheridan, then commander of the Department of the Missouri (1867–69), entrusted overall command of what came to be known as the winter campaign of 1868–69 to Lieutenant Colonel Alfred B. Sully. Facing record snows, the force marched south from Fort Dodge, Kansas, on November 12 under the leadership of former Kansas governor Colonel Samuel J. Crawford, now in charge of the Nineteenth Kansas Volunteer Cavalry, and Lieutenant Colonel George Armstrong Custer with the Seventh Cavalry.[7] Sheridan's orders were crystal clear: proceed south toward Indian encampments on the Washita River, kill as many warriors and horses as possible, and take women and children into custody.[8]

After marching a hundred miles through bitter cold, Sully recognized the need for a base camp in northwestern Indian Territory and put his soldiers to work building a stockade in present-day Woodward County. Dubbed "Camp Supply," its mission was threefold: launch and sustain military campaigns against Plains tribes; round up non-Indian settlers, illegal traders, whiskey peddlers, and horse thieves; and protect migrants, wagon trains, and herdsmen as they slogged through America's heartland en route to more hospitable environs. It was officially designated as Fort Supply in 1878. As the pace of trade quickened on the Great Plains, the outpost doubled as a headquarters for overland freighters.[9]

From Camp Supply, Custer led a detachment through thickening snow toward Cheyenne and Arapaho winter camps along the Washita River in present-day Roger Mills County. Even though rumors were circulating about the U.S. government's plan to move these groups to smaller reservations and force them to till the soil for a living, they felt secure in their winter camps and settled in for a season of cutting buffalo meat for pemmican, stretching and treating the hides for clothing and moccasins, and honing their weapons for conflicts that were surely coming. None suspected that Custer was heading in their direction. As a blizzard roared in from the north, Osage scouts reported that there were more women and children than warriors. Custer smelled victory. Shivering throughout that frigid night, he and his soldiers waited until daybreak of November 27 to launch their attack on the Cheyenne camp.

Shots rang out in the predawn stillness, and the battle was joined. With no time to raise the white flag of surrender and no place to run, Cheyennes opened fire on the advancing cavalry. Women and children took up arms beside their men, and with their men they died. When the smoke cleared, the Cheyenne body count stood at 150, and as many as 19 soldiers lay dead. Many of the slain Cheyenne women and children were never counted. Fifty-one lodges, along with arrows, ammunition, horse equipment, buffalo hides, and pemmican were torched. Soldiers took fifty-three prisoners and slaughtered nearly a thousand horses and mules.[10] Many of the wounded escaped, vowing to fight another day.

News of the massacre spread quickly across the Great Plains, and Indians who had participated in the Medicine Lodge Creek Treaty were left to ponder the futility of their cause. Further erosion of Indian sovereignty came not on

James E. Taylor, *Battle of the Washita*, November 27, 1868.
Courtesy National Anthropological Archives, Smithsonian Institution, 01604407.

the battlefield, but in Washington, D.C., when Congress passed the Indian Appropriations Act of March 3, 1871. Aimed ostensibly at food allocations for the Sioux Nation but applied to all tribes, the act announced that tribal independence was headed to oblivion and that colonization of the continent was complete.[11]

Thus ended the treaty system that had been in effect for nearly a century. Termination of the treaty system had no effect on making agreements with Indian tribes; it simply made the agreements easier to ratify by requiring a simple majority vote in Congress instead of a two-thirds majority vote in the Senate. Although Congress assumed a legal right to abrogate treaties, it was wary of committing breaches of faith with its dependent nations and exercised this right only as a last resort. Most of the reservations established after 1871 were set aside by executive order, and as the years passed Congress found it convenient to assume that Indian land titles were inferior to other land titles. Henceforth, Indians were presumed to occupy their reservations on sufferance, much as wild animals were kept in a refuge.[12]

To streamline its dealings with Indians, President Ulysses S. Grant (R; 1869–77) directed his administration to establish new policies and simplify its chain of command. Reservations were placed under the supervision of an agent whose job was to prevent Indians from straying off their reservations, to see that they were fed and cared for, and to teach them the rudiments of Anglo-American civilization. Indian agents reported directly to the commissioner of Indian Affairs, who, in turn, reported to the secretary of the Interior.[13]

President Grant's long-range goal was to extend the rights and responsibilities of U.S. citizenship to the land's original occupants.[14] Clearly determined to chart a new course with respect to Native America, he was receptive when the Society of Friends suggested a bold new plan for dealing with Indians as human beings rather than savages. The basis of their plan was to appoint Christian men as Indian agents; they, in turn, would employ Christians to distribute supplies, provide whatever medical treatment they could, and encourage Indians to adopt the ways of their Anglo neighbors. With the support of Vice President Schuyler Colfax (R; 1869–73) and Congress, Grant's peace policy became a cornerstone of U.S.-Indian relations.[15]

In essence, the president's kinder and gentler approach was supposed to make Indians comfortable on their reservations, less so when they left to steal horses and pillage settlements, and amenable to accepting the benefits of Anglo-American beliefs, values, and customs. Among Grant's first appointments was Brinton Darlington, who was tasked with supplying beef on the hoof to Cheyennes and Arapahos at Camp Supply. His son-in-law and agency clerk, Dr. Jesse R. Townsend, watched dumbstruck on a Tuesday evening in March 1870 as warriors unloaded their quivers on five head of cattle. "Oh, how wicked they shoot," wrote Townsend in a letter to incredulous relatives back east. "Those who have seen the Indians on the war path say they would much prefer to be attacked by guns and pistols than by bow and arrow."[16]

Darlington later moved his agency to the intersection of the ninety-eighth meridian and the North Canadian River, about thirty miles west of present-day Oklahoma City. Known affectionately as "Tosimeea" (He Who Takes Out His Teeth) for his unnerving habit of removing his dentures in public, Darlington won the respect and confidence of the Indians under his care—so much so that he made considerable headway in introducing his charges to Anglo ways.[17] But there was not much that he and other Indian agents could do about Anglo hunters whose incessant slaughtering and skinning were putting bison, the mainstay of the Plains economy, on the road to extinction. According to the Indian agent's report for 1879, bison that had blackened the western prairies for eons were all but gone, and the federal government had best prepare to distribute subsidies year-round to keep Indians from starving.[18] By then, Plains Indians were already collecting beef allotments and other provisions at two primary distribution centers: Fort Sill, located in a three-and-a-half-million-acre reservation with a population of fewer than four thousand Kiowas, Comanches, and Apaches; and the Darlington Indian Agency, which served a similar number of Cheyennes and Arapahos on a four-and-a-half-million-acre reservation.[19]

Buy-in to Grant's peace policy from religious groups was expected.[20] Closer to where the action was, there was more than a hint of skepticism. The *Emporia (Kansas) News* questioned the president's wisdom in relying on Christians, no matter how devout and well-meaning, to subdue and pacify the Indians.[21] Philip Sheridan, then officed in Chicago at the headquarters of the Military Division of the Missouri, opined that the reservation system, though far from perfect, offered the only prospect of lasting peace with Indian tribes. But there was a caveat: absent a threat of armed force, Indian agents would be hard pressed to carry on their work, and tribes would be powerless to thwart the relentless push of frontier settlement into Indian country.[22]

Good intentions notwithstanding, Grant's peace policy foundered on corrupt officials, inadequate supplies, and rancid piles of beef. Indians were left with two bad options: stay on the reservation and starve; or leave the reservation to hunt game and plunder settlements, both of which risked military reprisals. Aside from the usual witch's brew of dysfunctions attending U.S.-Indian relations, Grant's peace policy was probably doomed from the start, as neither federal officials nor Quaker agents fully appreciated Indians' attachment to their traditions and willingness to fight to preserve them.[23]

To his credit, Major General John Pope used his leverage as commander of the Department of the Missouri to encourage fair and humane treatment of Indians in his jurisdiction, but with limited success.[24] But they continued to suffer, and none more so than the Kiowas, Comanches, and Apaches, who relied on the Fort Sill Agency for food and supplies and the Cheyennes and Arapahos, who relied on the Darlington Indian Agency for theirs. Once teeming with game animals, the Great Plains were now haunted by the specter of starvation, and Indians learned once again the value of the white man's promises.

Untold gallons of ink have been spilled to chronicle the raids and battles and massacres in the period of wars and reservations that frame our understanding of the western frontier. Following the Battle/Massacre of the Washita in November 1868, one conflict stands out as particularly important to the history of Oklahoma Proper: the Red River War of 1874–75. Among the constellation of factors that led to hostilities, none rankled more than white hunters who butchered their way across the buffalo hunting grounds with impunity, leaving a landscape of rotting carcasses and bleached bones to mark their passage.

A raid on Adobe Walls, a hunters' camp in the Texas Panhandle, in June 1874 was the prelude to hostilities. The hunters repulsed the attack, and when the smoke cleared, three of their own and nine warriors lay dead.[25] Predictions that the Great Spirit would come to the Indians' rescue proved to be overly optimistic, and the war was on. Using guerilla tactics that the army was ill-equipped to handle, warriors fanned across western Indian Territory and the Texas Panhandle, pillaging and murdering at will. The army responded by declaring war on all Indians who had abandoned their reservations.

A few determined warriors soldiered on through the winter and spring of 1874–75 in a last-ditch effort to regain tribal sovereignty. In the end, no single battle determined the outcome of the Red River War. Rather, it was the army's unrelenting pressure that finally brought hostilities to an end. Comanche chief Quanah Parker's surrender at Fort Sill on June 2, 1875, marked not only the end of the Red River War, but also the endgame of Plains Indian resistance.[26] Save for mop-up operations occasioned by more empty promises from the Great Spirit, the U.S. Army had done its job. From the mid-1870s on, the onetime lords of the southern plains were wards of the federal government and depended for their survival on allotments of beef and supplies.

To accommodate soldiers' needs for food and housing and supply them with the wherewithal to protect homesteaders and westbound wagon trains, old forts were strengthened and new ones were built. The most important military outposts in western Indian Territory included Fort Sill in the southwest, Fort Supply in the northwest, and Fort Reno in the middle, just south of the Darlington Indian Agency. The original military camp, enlarged and designated as Fort Reno in July 1875, took its name from General Jesse L. Reno, a casualty of the Battle of South Mountain (better known in the South as the Battle of Boonsboro Gap), Maryland, during the Civil War. Its first permanent commander, Major John K. Mizner of the Fourth U.S. Cavalry, took charge in 1876.[27]

Soldiers assigned to Fort Reno were under orders to protect the Darlington Indian Agency, exert military control over the Cheyenne and Arapaho Reservation, and mitigate conflicts between the Five Tribes and so-called wild Indians along their western borders. When they were not on patrol, soldiers at Fort Reno enjoyed accommodations that were almost plush, at least by frontier standards. As one traveler recorded in the summer of 1878, the buildings combined "beauty and utility in a greater degree than is exhibited at any other military post I have visited." Major Mizner's eye for detail was complemented by his wife's social graces in organizing lavish parties for military couples at Forts Reno, Sill, and Supply. Nearby, Indian Agent John D. Miles was building on Brinton Darlington's success in introducing Cheyennes and Arapahos to the rhythms of settled life. Chopping wood and putting up hay, warriors-turned-farmers were getting their first lessons on traveling the white man's road.[28] Fort Reno and the Darlington Indian Agency fostered the first trappings of urban culture in Oklahoma Proper and shaped Oklahoma City's early development.

Much as Fort Reno and the Darlington Indian Agency influenced central Indian Territory's cultural development during the first few years of settlement, so, too, did overland freighting build its economy. Typically, supplies and weaponry arrived at military outposts at the nearest train depot and were shipped the rest of the way by overland freighters. Their ox- or mule-drawn wagons sometimes stretched a mile or more across the stark landscape, and the view from afar of a wagon train snaking its way across the flatlands prompted one observer to describe them as "poetic, grand, and beautiful."[29] Steeped in biblical lore, an anonymous traveler compared them to caravans that once traversed the deserts of Arabia. Before railroads put them out of business, wagon trains heralded their approach to some village or military outpost with the staccato crackle of a bullwhacker's whip, often likened to the din of battle, but with no enemies.[30]

———

While soldiers stationed at Fort Reno were preserving the peace and overland freighters were sowing the seeds of commerce, lawmakers in Washington, D.C., were deciding how best to govern Indian Territory. Congress's initial efforts to open Indian Territory to homesteading in the 1860s ran afoul of the so-called Indian ring, a cabal of corrupt officials who lined their pockets through control of tribal annuities. Like the railroad ring that siphoned money from railroad contracts, the Indian ring depended on the status quo to keep the cash flowing, and it became a lightning rod for reformers in President Grant's administration.[31] Likewise in the administration's crosshairs was the treaty system that had governed U.S.-Indian relations for almost a century. Few were sorry to see it abolished in 1871. But the problem was that nobody had an alternative with respect to Indian Territory, other than to patch together some sort of territorial governance. In June 1870, the Senate Committee on Territories was considering a bill to organize Indian Territory under the name of "Oklahoma." Although receptive to the idea, the *Emporia News* implored the committee to come up with a better name.[32]

Indian raids notwithstanding, a consensus was building in neighboring Kansas that Indian Territory should be opened to homesteading. Its attractions were obvious, including abundant natural resources and two railroad lines: the Missouri, Kansas and Texas Railway ("the Katy"), whose tracks connected Parsons, Kansas, and Denison, Texas; and the Atlantic and Pacific Railroad, whose line ended at Vinita in the Cherokee Nation.[33] Secretary of the Interior Columbus Delano (1870–75) added the stamp of officialdom in an upbeat report on Indian Territory, whose meager population (60,000) was hard to reconcile with its size (44,154,240 acres) and potential for farming and mining. He was cautiously optimistic that Americans would rise to the challenge of figuring out how to gather Indian tribes scattered across the West into a relatively small area. Secretary Delano's optimism rested on the aforementioned bill introduced in the Forty-First Congress (1869–71) for organizing Indian Territory under the increasingly common moniker of "Oklahoma." He believed that territorial governance would go a long way toward ending tribal feuds and might even induce tribes to give up their two most vexing customs: nomadism and communal ownership of land, both perceived as relics of the past that had no place in the modernizing present.[34]

But not everybody was ready to jump on the bandwagon. Discouraged farmers in western Kansas feared that homesteading down south would siphon off population. What is more, settlement on Indian land represented a breach of faith with tribes that had negotiated treaties with the U.S. government. Besides, everyone knew that railroads, always held in suspicion for their ties to eastern capital, stood to gain the most from opening Indian Territory to homesteading.[35]

While pundits were fueling the debates, Congress was groping toward agreement on what to do with Indian Territory. In December 1874, Congressman
David P. Lowe (R-Kans.; 1871–75) introduced in the House of Representatives
a bill to establish a judicial district in the territory of Oklahoma. At the same
time, Senator John J. Ingalls (R-Kans.; 1873–91) introduced a similar bill in
the Senate.[36] Early in 1875, Colonel Stephen A. Cobb (R-Kans.; 1873–75)
introduced a bill providing for territorial governance that included a path
to citizenship for any Indian man who could prove in open court that he
had resided in the United States for five years, had acclimated to American
culture, and would declare an oath of allegiance to the U.S. Constitution and
renounce all commitments to tribal sovereignty. Back in Kansas, advocates of
settlement were less concerned with Indian citizenship than with the proper
use of God's bounty. Using language that was already entering the common
lexicon, the *Leavenworth Weekly Times* waxed biblical to denounce laws that
banned settlers "from the very Eden of America."[37] To marshal their defense
of Indian Territory, tribal delegates gathered at an intertribal council in
September 1875 to come up with a strategy to head off the movement, still
in its infancy but gaining momentum by the day, to break up the reservations
and allot land to Indians as individuals.[38]

As debates intensified, the pro-settlement camp lined up behind Elias
Cornelius Boudinot, a Cherokee railroad attorney who recognized the futility
of tribal ownership of land and tried to convince Indian leaders to accept
individual title. His ultimate goal was to extend the rights and protections
afforded by the U.S. Constitution to Indians as a prerequisite to establishing
territorial governance in Indian Territory.[39] Boudinot was not the first to
recognize the need to bring order from chaos, but he was well on his way to
becoming the most influential, and he had spent enough time in Washington,
D.C., to know how things worked. As the *New York Sun* put it, "If Col.
Boudinot did not originate the idea he was a wheel-horse in promoting it."[40]

Boudinot's ideas crystallized in a letter published in the *Chicago Times* on
February 17, 1879.[41] His letter was published with a map of central Indian
Territory (Oklahoma Proper), showing what he considered to be part of the
public domain and therefore subject to settlement under public lands laws.
Boudinot's letter became fodder for newspapers across the country, and true
believers accepted it as gospel in what was rapidly morphing from a hotly
debated topic into a bona fide political movement.[42]

As an attorney, Boudinot was the right man for the job. His description of Indian land occupancy began with a delineation of the area in central Indian Territory bordered by the Chickasaw Nation to the south, the Cheyenne and Arapaho Reservation to the west, the Cherokee Outlet to the north, and the Iowa, Kickapoo, Potawatomi, and Shawnee Reservations to the east. He then referred to the Reconstruction Treaties of 1866 to show that the U.S. government had acquired 3,250,560 acres from the Creeks for the sum of $975,168 and 2,169,080 from the Seminoles for the sum of $325,362.[43] Boudinot then turned his attention to Kiowas, Comanches, Apaches, Cheyennes, Arapahos, and others, who had been forced to occupy reservations in ceded land just west of Oklahoma Proper and who were feared as much by the Five Tribes as by whites. Their presence notwithstanding, Boudinot believed that the land they occupied in central and western Indian Territory was part of the public domain, and virtually all of it had been surveyed and sectioned to make way for eventual settlement.

Having laid his groundwork, Boudinot delivered his coup de grâce: a significant portion of Indian Territory acreage had never been appropriated for Indian use, and, in all likelihood, it never would be. Those unappropriated lands were situated west of the ninety-seventh meridian and south of the Cherokee Outlet. "They amount to several millions of acres, and are as valuable as any in the territory," continued Boudinot. "The soil is well adapted for the production of corn, wheat, and other cereals. It is unsurpassed for grazing, and is well watered and timbered."[44]

As Boudinot saw it, the United States' intention to locate Indians and African Americans upon these lands, as stated in the Reconstruction Treaties of 1866, had become irrelevant by 1879. Blacks had long since been granted rights of citizenship by the Thirteenth, Fourteenth, and Fifteenth Amendments to the U.S. Constitution and, at least in theory, were free to move anywhere they pleased. Nor was there any prospect of creating more reservations in Indian Territory, as Congress had enacted laws since 1866 that effectively forbade the removal of more tribes to the area. In the 1878–79 session of Congress, Roger Q. Mills (D-Tex.; 1873–92) introduced an amendment to the Indian Appropriation Bill providing that "no Indian living . . . outside the Indian Territory shall be moved into said Territory." The bill that became law on February 17, 1879—the same day that Boudinot's article was published in the *Chicago Times*—narrowed the restriction to Apaches and other tribes in

New Mexico and Arizona Territories. Even so, the only Indians removed to Indian Territory after the law was passed were stray refugees.[45]

For all intents and purposes, the days of pacifying Indians and relocating them to Indian Territory were coming to a close. Looming on the horizon was the day when Indians would shed their pariah status and engage in the political process as full-fledged citizens. Expressing a common belief, particularly among easterners, whose knowledge of Native America came from magazines and newspapers, that all Indians were basically the same and were equally prepared for assimilation, the *New York Tribune* opined in July 1879, "The Indian, even the sun dancing brave, is just as ready for the polls as were the field-hands of Georgia or the Voodoo worshippers of Louisiana. Give him the ballot; extend the protection of the civil courts over the reservations; do away with all this absurd talk of Great Fathers and presents of useless gimcracks."[46]

While Boudinot was busy managing the firestorm he had ignited, prospective settlers were casting covetous eyes on Indian Territory and wondering how they might partake of its bounty. "Forward to the Indian territory is the order now," ran a typical call to arms in the *Emporia News* on April 25, 1879. "From all over the country come inquiries concerning this wonderful region, and the best way to reach it."[47] Political organization was taking shape in colonies whose aim was to further the cause of settlement. Illegal invasions from neighboring states foretold contentious days to come.

In April 1879, Charles C. Carpenter, a veteran of the successful effort to open the Black Hills to non-Indian settlement, summoned prospective settlers to Coffeyville, Kansas, for a cross-border invasion. Like Buffalo Bill Cody, Carpenter cut a dashing figure with his flowing mane, velvet vest, and beaver hat, and he was a magnet for border ruffians who drifted into his orbit. That stylish outfit was camouflage for a self-serving schemer who was allegedly in league with the railroads. The *Topeka Commonwealth* branded Carpenter as a "scalawag of the worst type, a burly, swaggering, reckless character who would have been lynched by the men he fooled in the Black Hills if they could have caught him." Indian Service inspector John McNeal, who arrived in Coffeyville to assess the situation, agreed. "He is the same bragging, lying nuisance that I knew him to be seventeen years ago," wrote McNeal on May 4.[48] Once gathered in Coffeyville, a wagon train consisting of 112 families crossed the border and proceeded to the North Canadian River, where they set up their camp. Apparently true to form, Carpenter did not join the wagon train. Instead, he became the primary spokesman in absentia for the group, whose invasion made headlines nationwide.[49]

No sooner did the invading force reach its destination than Potawatomi and Sac and Fox Indians showed up to help them build their houses. Relieved to find a welcoming committee rather than armed resistance, the invaders quickly realized that their greeters looked forward to white settlement as a prerequisite to ending abuses at the hands of Indian agents. To a large extent, opposition to non-Indian settlement came from Indian leaders who had grown fat and happy as beneficiaries of federal largesse. As their extravagances came to light, an increasing number of disillusioned tribespeople supported efforts to terminate the agency system and develop more efficient systems of governance.[50]

Back in Washington, D.C., President Hayes was getting an earful from Cherokee and Creek chiefs, who were convinced that railroad corporations and squatters were plotting to steal their land. In a letter to the commissioner of Indian Affairs, Secretary of the Interior Carl Schurz (1877–81) declared most of Indian Territory to be off-limits to homesteaders. Taking exception to Boudinot's pro-settlement letter and invoking section 2147 of the *Revised Statutes*, Secretary Schurz empowered the Indian Department to evict trespassers. As though anyone needed reminding, Schurz acknowledged President Hayes's authority to expel invaders by force of arms.[51] Schurz's warning was a hot topic of discussion at a cabinet meeting on April 25. The next day, the president followed through with a proclamation declaring that homestead and preemption laws did not apply to Indian Territory. In a pattern that came to typify expeditions into Indian Territory, the Coffeyville invaders decided that gunplay was more than they had bargained for, and their invasion fizzled.[52]

The first major invasion of Indian Territory, disorganized though it was, signaled that something big was happening, and none expressed it more forcefully than Charles C. Carpenter, whose settlers' manifesto made it to the *Kansas City Times* and newspapers across Kansas. He threw down the gauntlet to the "*de facto* government at Washington," warning that any attempt to squelch the movement would be futile. "There is no infraction of law in the present migration," insisted Carpenter, "and if the administration attempts to 'stamp out' the invasion by military force, we shall appeal to the God of Battles and the United States Congress to protect us, the invaders, in our constitutional rights."[53]

Carpenter reserved special opprobrium for Major General John Pope, former commander of the Army of Virginia and now commander of the Department of the Missouri, whose braggadocio during the Civil War had won him few friends.[54] Known after his ignominious retreat at the Battle of Second Bull Run (Manassas) as General "Bull Run" Pope, the disgraced officer was assigned to the West in September 1862 and fought with distinction in the Apache Wars. But neither his successful campaigns against Indians nor his attempts to alleviate Indians' suffering after the Red River War ended in 1875 did much to rehabilitate his reputation, particularly when he turned his attention in the late 1870s to keeping hopeful settlers from colonizing Oklahoma Proper. In 1879, a board of inquiry concluded that Pope bore most of the responsibility for the Union loss in the Battle of Second Bull Run. By then, people who spent their days dodging soldiers had had enough of Major General John Pope and his condescending treatment of settlers. "I do not care a fig for General Bull Run Pope," declared Carpenter. "I understand that he has orders from Washington to put me under arrest. He can arrest me and be d——d."[55]

Like so many in the nascent movement, Carpenter claimed to respect the law, and as a former soldier in the Union Army, he was fiercely loyal to his government. But his respect for law and patriotism ended where perceived injustice began. Fortified by Boudinot's air-tight reasoning and imbued with a sense of righteous indignation, Carpenter spoke for all prospective settlers in demanding his right to 160 acres, free of cost, in what he and his ilk believed to be part of the public domain: "Give the white man, as well as the black man, the yellow man and the red man a chance. This is the feeling that inspires the present spontaneous immigration to the Indian Territory. Millions of settlers for defense, if need be, but not one cent per acre for tribute."[56]

The *Kansas City Times*' support for settlement in Indian Territory stood in sharp contrast to the opposition of its cross-state rival, the *St. Louis Globe-Democrat*. Pleased to report that a bill to establish a new territory south of Kansas was sleeping "the sleep of death" in a congressional committee, the paper dismissed the expedition from Coffeyville as a failure and Carpenter as an agitator. "All the stories about the great rush upon the Indian Territory, with which the columns of the *Kansas City Times* were filled for months, were false, through and through," ran one column. "Not fifty white men, in all, have entered the Territory, and they left as soon as they were notified." The *Leavenworth Weekly Times* adopted a similar stance in applauding the Hayes administration for preventing "land piracy" that the *Kansas City Times* was promoting.[57]

As though anyone needed reminding, the *Dodge City Times* opined that railroads—always held in suspicion in the West for their financial clout and price-gouging policies—were the leading advocates of settlement, as they stood to make a pile of money from increased traffic over their rails.[58] Business was already brisk for the region's main economic driver, the Atchison, Topeka, and Santa Fe Railroad ("the Santa Fe," in frontier shorthand), whose line to Wichita had been completed in 1872. An extension to Arkansas City was completed in 1879 and remained as the railroad's southernmost terminus until 1887.[59] The *Dodge City Times* went a step further to brand Indian Territory intruders as speculators who sought contracts to supply troops assigned to guard the Indian frontier. As for the widely feared drain on population, Kansans had nothing to fear. Proof was evident every day as immigrants poured into Kansas to take advantage of the state's fertile soil and abundant resources. Even though Kansas was booming and would likely be unaffected by the goings-on down south, the *Dodge City Times* was convinced that most Kansans were dead set against opening Indian Territory to settlement and establishing a territorial government on their southern border.[60]

Newspaper polemics reflected an escalating battle to sway public opinion, and Oklahoma Proper's fate hung in the balance. Those who stood to gain and lose the most from the outcome included the usual cast of characters whose activities had fueled westward expansion ever since colonists set foot in Jamestown: politicians, whose ambitions did not always square with their guardianship of the public interest; businessmen, whose skills in acquiring, producing, and distributing goods and services were enhanced with each breakthrough in transportation and communication technologies; farmers and stockmen looking for cheap land; and speculators who wanted to grow their capital at minimum risk and for maximum profit. Caught in the crossfire were Indians, whose nomadism and custom of holding land in common put them at a severe disadvantage in the unfettered marketplace favored by Gilded Age businessmen. Bewildered by forces they could neither understand nor control, they preserved what they could of their lifeways and made do with government subsidies, all the while wondering how they and their descendants would fare as modernity came relentlessly on.

About the time Elias C. Boudinot was writing his seminal article for the *Chicago Times* and Carpenter's group was organizing its invasion, a new word was drifting into the frontier lexicon: "boomer." That seems odd, as everyone in close proximity to the frontier knew that booming an area meant quickening the pace of economic development and that boomtowns were the desired outcome. But apparently nobody thought of designating prospective homesteaders as boomers until Dr. Morrison Munford, Carpenter's sponsor in the Coffeyville expedition, coined the word in his pro-settlement articles in the *Kansas City Times*.[61]

Whatever its etymology and date of first usage, the moniker stuck, and it was on everybody's lips when the biggest boomer of them all stepped onto the stage of history: David Lewis Payne. Under his leadership of the newly branded boomer movement, anything could happen. Something certainly did, and it began in a place called Ewing.

CHAPTER THREE

On to Oklahoma!

"On to Oklahoma" were the last words of Capt. Payne, as he
took up his line of march again for the land of promise,
but "Back from Oklahoma" seems his fate.
Wichita City Eagle, *July 22, 1880*

David Lewis Payne was born on December 30, 1836, to a farm family in Grant
County, Indiana.[1] He was known as an "exhorter" for his scholarly acumen,
and some folks wondered if he might become a minister. Hankering for more
adventure than a either a ministerial career or an Indiana farm had to offer,
he and his brother, Jack, headed west in the spring of 1858 to test their mettle
in the Mormon War, a series of intermittent skirmishes between Latter-day
Saints and westerners who felt threatened by their offbeat religion. By the
time Payne and his brother reached Kansas, the hostilities had cooled. And
so, in a pattern that typified western entrepreneurship, Payne set aside his
martial inclinations and opted for less bellicose lines of work, first as a sawmill
operator and, when that went bust, as a hunter. Known in his widening
circle as the "Cimarron Scout," Payne caught a glimpse of his future during
expeditions to Indian Territory.[2]

Then came the Civil War, and Payne was compelled to take up another
career, this time as a soldier. During his service with the Army of the Frontier,
Payne fought at key engagements in Missouri and Arkansas. At the Battle of
Prairie Grove, Arkansas, in December 1862, Payne braved a hail of bullets
to rescue a wounded officer, hoist his inert body onto his shoulders, and carry
him for a half mile to his tent, where surgeons saved his life.[3]

David L. Payne.
Courtesy Oklahoma Historical Society, Oklahoma City, 18792.

When his three-year term of enlistment expired, Payne returned to Kansas, where he tended his farm and served two sessions in the state legislature before returning to military service as a replacement for a poor neighbor who had received a draft notice.[4] His new assignment was with the Eighth Regiment of U.S. Veteran Volunteers. By securing for his regiment a place of honor in advance of General Winfield Scott Hancock's corps during the Civil War's final days, Payne became an eyewitness to Lee's surrender at Appomattox Courthouse.

Following his discharge in March 1866, Payne secured an appointment as sergeant at arms in the Kansas legislature. Bored with sedentary duties, he went to work as postmaster at Fort Leavenworth, where he enjoyed hobnobbing with soldiers and frontiersmen. When Kansas governor Samuel J. Crawford (1865–68) issued an executive order authorizing the formation of volunteer cavalry, Payne jumped at the chance to hunt for Indians in Kansas and to protect wagon trains on the Santa Fe Trail. When his unit was paid off and disbanded in November 1867, Payne, nicknamed "Old Ox Heart" for his courage under fire, drifted back to Fort Leavenworth with no official position, no property to speak of, and no income. His only consolation was his increasing familiarity with Indian Territory—knowledge that would serve him well in days to come.[5]

Pondering his reduced circumstances, Payne answered Governor Crawford's call for volunteers to support Sheridan's winter campaign aimed at putting an end, once and for all, to Indian depredations. He was rewarded with command of Company H of the Nineteenth Regiment of Kansas Volunteer Cavalry and joined a mighty force, a thousand men strong, which marched southwest from Topeka to rendezvous with Custer's Seventh Cavalry in northwestern Indian Territory. After a grueling march that begin with freezing drizzle and ended in a howling blizzard, Payne led an advance party to Camp Supply in time to greet the buckskin-clad and golden-haired Custer when he returned from the Battle of the Washita. Payne's final assignment was to accompany the Seventh Cavalry on a grueling expedition south to the Wichita Mountains and west into the Texas Panhandle. Knowing he could rely on Old Ox Heart, Custer dispatched him to deliver his field report to General Sheridan at Fort Leavenworth. Payne fulfilled his assignment and continued on to Topeka to accept his discharge from the army and a handsome silver and gold watch from his comrades-in-arms, bearing an inscription to commemorate what was, in 1869, just another date in April:

> Presented to Capt. D. L. Payne by Co. H,
> 19th Reg. KVC, April 22, 1869.[6]

In 1870, Payne established a 160-acre stock farm a few miles east of Wichita in Sedgwick County. It was known to locals as "Payne's Ranch," and it served as both a stagecoach way station and a popular stopover for travelers who knew they could count on a hearty meal, a shot of whisky, clothing, and ammunition—in short, whatever they needed to help them along their way, and all offered at no charge.[7] He still had a hankering for politics, but his ambitions were derailed when he was narrowly defeated in a run for the state senate in 1872.[8] But when one door closes, another one often opens, and on July 1, 1877, he accepted an appointment in the Office of Sergeant at Arms as special policeman (often referenced as doorkeeper) of the U.S. House of Representatives.[9] Once settled in the nation's capital, Payne formed a friendship with General Thomas Ewing Jr., the first chief justice of the Kansas Supreme Court and commander of the division in which Payne served during the Civil War. Payne and Ewing supported one another's causes and remained steadfast friends for the rest of their lives.[10]

During his tenure in Washington, D.C., Payne was inexorably drawn into polarizing debates over public lands policies. Given their economic and political clout, it came as no surprise to find railroads at the center of pro-settlement schemes. Two railroad companies already had significant investments in the southern plains: the Santa Fe, whose north-south line to Wichita was completed in 1872 and extended to Arkansas City in 1879; and the Frisco, formerly the Atlantic and Pacific Railroad Company, which started building a line westward across Indian Territory after Congress granted its right-of-way in 1866.[11] More attuned than ever to politics, Payne was receptive to Elias Boudinot's crusade to compel the federal government to open central Indian Territory to homesteaders.

Payne's resignation as doorkeeper and return to Kansas coincided with the first public meeting, held in Wichita in October 1878, to enlist support for the settlement movement. Among Payne's cohorts in the movement's infancy were William R. Colcord, a well-known Kansas cattleman, and his son Charles (better known as "Charley"), who were frequent visitors to a livery stable in Wichita that served as the de facto headquarters of southern Kansas's cattle industry.[12] As the pro-settlement movement attracted more adherents, Payne often dropped in to share his enthusiasm about the Oklahoma country and to popularize Boudinot's argument: the land in question had been purchased with cash; title was vested in the U.S. government; and all Indian title to the land was extinguished. The law seemed to support settlement, as courts had tended to side with settlers when Indian title had clearly been extinguished. All that was needed was a presidential proclamation to open a large swath of the Oklahoma country to settlement.

Neither politicking nor farming had done much to cover Payne's expenses, and rumors that he was in cahoots with the railroads seemed plausible. Specifically, many suspected that the Frisco aimed to take advantage of Payne's experience as a frontiersman and scout and pay him to gather information about Indian Territory. Harry L. Hill, a wealthy Wichita citizen and a member of that city's board of trade, admitted that the booming was done in the interests of the Frisco and other railroads. But he stopped short of branding Payne as a railroad employee, as railroads risked losing their charters if they were known to aid and abet the settlement movement.[13] George B. Jenness, one of Payne's former comrades-in-arms, was ambiguous in describing the relationship between prospective settlers a.id the railroads. Lacking concrete evidence of money changing hands, he concluded that "the railroad companies who were waiting along the borders ready to push their lines into this rich, undeveloped country were giving moral, if not direct financial aid to the boomers."[14] The *New York Sun* might have been close to the truth in suggesting that the Frisco kept illicit payments off the books to avoid litigation.[15]

Although the April 1879 invasion from Coffeyville certainly signaled that something big was afoot, it had less long-term significance than more structured initiatives in Wichita, where business and opinion leaders were expressing their interest in Indian Territory not with slogans and manifestos, but with cold, hard cash. In the winter of 1879–80, they gathered to begin the painstaking task of organizing townsite companies whose aim was to establish commercial centers and, ultimately, a capital city for a new state that would most likely be called Oklahoma. Even though observers back east paid them scant attention, townsite companies were of the utmost importance to the settlement movement. The original townsite company, Payne's Oklahoma Colony, included Payne as president, Dr. R. B. Greenlee as vice president, John Faulkenstein as treasurer, W. B. Hutchison as secretary, W. A. Shuman as corresponding secretary, and T. D. Craddock as general manager. The second organization was the Oklahoma Town Company (later changed to the Southwestern Colonization Society), and it consisted for the most part of Wichita businessmen who took no part in subsequent invasions.[16] Although most investors were from Wichita, others were invited to join the townsite company for twenty-five dollars per share. To attract people of moderate means, shares were often discounted to five dollars. Money received from the sale of shares went to pay for printing certificates and furnishing outfits for cross-border invasions. How much money was collected and whether or not the original shareholders made money remain unclear. Judging from the few documents that survive, two conclusions are beyond dispute: investors had plenty of company in buying shares in townsite companies; and a considerable war chest was raised to further investors' ambitions in the Oklahoma country.[17]

In addition to townsite companies, promoters had another source of revenue: colonies. The first Oklahoma colony was the Southwest Colony Town and Mining Company. With Payne as president and several members of the Oklahoma Town Company as officers, the colony was incorporated under the laws of Kansas in February 1880 with capital stock of $1 million. The company warranted that it would not sell a lot to outsiders for less than twenty-five dollars. Certificates were transferrable, and they entitled their holders to a share in profits and protection in securing 160 acres. Certificate holders were required to join the colony, in person or by proxy, at a designated rendezvous in Indian Territory within five days of receiving notice that an invasion was underway.

Southwest Colony Town and Mining Company certificates blurred the distinction between townsite and colony companies, as certificate holders were entitled to a town lot as well as a share of stock. As noted, the Southwest Colony Town and Mining Company was organized in February 1880, and the Oklahoma Town Company was organized in August of that year. At some point, shares in the Southwest Colony Town and Mining Company were discounted to two dollars. Although the company's books were apparently not open to inspection, it seems clear from the numbering of certificates that hundreds, and perhaps thousands, of certificates were in circulation.

To signal his continuing displeasure with settlement schemes, President Hayes issued a second proclamation, this one in February 1880, declaring that treaties would be honored and invaders would be stopped by armed force. The presidential proclamation failed to impress Payne, whose speeches and affirmations of resolve were enough to convince a small group of men to gather in Wichita to launch an invasion under a full moon on the evening of April 24. In the ensuing weeks, their bold invasion captured the headlines in ways that the Coffeyville expedition never did. With no disrespect intended toward the swashbuckling Charles C. Carpenter and countless others whose exploits have been lost to history, it seems plausible to date the beginning of the boomer movement to the moment Captain Payne and his boomers crossed the Kansas border and entered forbidden land, bound for the North Canadian River. After invoking guidance from the Almighty, the invaders lined up their mounts and wagons and proceeded south toward their rendezvous with history.[18]

As the expedition's official scout, Hill drove a team and wagon loaded with bison skulls some two miles in advance of the main party. His companion, Harry Stafford, threw out skulls at the crest of each ridge to mark their trail. Thereafter, the trail they left for Captain Payne and the others to follow became known as the "Hog's Back Trail," and it was marked as such on maps. When he was not heaving skulls overboard, Stafford helped Hill keep an eye out for soldiers who might put a quick end to their travels.

The boomers' southwestern route took them to the junction of the Chikaskia River and Shoofly Creek, about nine miles south of the Kansas border. They arrived at the banks of the Chikaskia River after midnight and set up camp. The next day, they averted trouble with a small but belligerent band of Nez Percé warriors by handing out tobacco as a peace offering.[19] The ploy worked, and the invaders continued south to find Red Rock Creek swollen with spring rains and sloshing over its banks. Momentarily stymied, the boomers took directions from their surveyor and engineer, C. Goodrich, and set to work building rafts to float their wagons across the torrent while their horses swam. They were now in a hurry, as Hill had spotted a squad of soldiers camped about four miles west of the crossing. The boomers made it unseen to a stand of timber and remained concealed for the rest of the day.

Buoyed by their good fortune in being neither drowned nor arrested, the boomers proceeded to Black Bear Creek. Accustomed by now to playing cat-and-mouse with soldiers, they hunkered down in the woods whenever their scouts spotted soldiers and proceeded westward toward the Arkansas City cutoff from the Chisholm Trail. They forded the Cimarron River just north of present-day Guthrie at a place that came to be known as "Payne's Crossing." Now following one of the most clearly marked thoroughfares on the Great Plains along the future route of the Santa Fe's line through central Indian Territory, the boomers proceeded due south until May 2, when they reached their final destination: the Arbuckle Trail crossing of the North Canadian River near the present-day junction of Interstates 35 and 40 east of downtown Oklahoma City. Their camp on the north bank of the North Canadian River, dubbed "Payne's Springs," was in the vicinity of the present-day University of Oklahoma Health Sciences Complex. Over the next five years, the trail blazed by Payne and his followers became the route of choice for boomer caravans.[20]

For two days, the rain was relentless. Laid up with rheumatism, Payne was in desperate need of shelter. Anxious to alleviate their leader's suffering, the boomers chose a site for a dwelling in what they hoped would one day become the capital of Oklahoma. But Payne, drenched and aching, could not wait for a house to be built. Fortunately, there were several buildings on the south bank of the North Canadian River that had belonged to Cass Wantland, a Texan who started farming near Pauls Valley in 1870 and, three years later, established a ranch along Crutcho Creek between present-day Midwest City and Del City. By the late 1870s, the Crutcho Ranch was swarming with cattle that carried the distinctive Crutch O brand (a crutch and an O). Wantland knew all too well what the boomers were up against, as he had had his share of eviction notices from cavalry based at Fort Reno.[21]

Harry Hill, who had visited the site a year earlier and had used Wantland's abandoned corrals to hold horses, escorted Payne to the ranch headquarters, which amounted to little more than a few dirt-floor huts and pole corrals. The rest of the colonists needed little prompting and followed their leaders across the river to take refuge from the rain. There is no indication that any of the boomers were surprised by the existence of old and dilapidated buildings in the middle of Indian Territory, supposedly off-limits to anyone without an Indian pedigree.

When dawn broke on May 3, Captain Payne felt refreshed. A good night's sleep under a roof, however leaky, was just what he needed, and he set out to find an ideal spot to locate a capital city. He followed Crutcho Creek in a southwesterly direction until he came to a wooded knoll about two miles south of the North Canadian River, a site that would one day succumb to the roar of traffic from Interstate 35.[22] Overcome with emotion, Payne directed his comrades to get to work on building a city.

Now that he had his orders, colony surveyor C. Goodrich gathered his instruments and went to work. Nearby, Harry Hill used a tree stump for a table to sketch a plat for the new city. Before long, the din of chopping and hacking filled the air as the colonists cleared oaks to make room for a public square. Using the plat of Indianapolis, Indiana, as their model, the colonists laid out a long avenue. Streets were oriented according to the points of a compass. In deference to his friend and fellow politician in Washington, D.C., Payne christened the city "Ewing." "There was nothing small about this town," declared the *New York Sun*, "except the length of time it was inhabited, for as surveyed it covered six square miles of land."[23]

The colonists had ample reason to be "in high feather," as the *Sun* put it. Not only had they made it undetected to the heart of Indian Territory, but they were also realizing their dream in creating a city. One of the log houses they built during that feverish spring of 1880 was reserved for Captain Payne, and it survives in the *Sun*'s crude sketch to show what might have become, under more propitious circumstances, the dwelling of Oklahoma City's first mayor, or perhaps Oklahoma's first governor.

Determined to turn their colony into a permanent community, Harry Hill and a few others made a supply run to Arkansas City. To announce their success to folks back home, Payne asked Hill to deliver a letter, subsequently printed in the *Kansas City Times* and *Topeka Commonwealth*, that read in part, "Please say to any that may wish to know that the public lands in the Indian Territory are not only open to settlement, but settled. We are here to stay; are building houses and making homes." Ever the optimist, Payne expected Ewing's population to swell to a thousand within thirty days.[24]

Not for the first time and certainly not the last, Payne's sanguinity proved to be premature when Lieutenant J. H. Pardee led a detachment of soldiers and scouts through the blackjack oaks surrounding Ewing to arrest the colonists. Later that day, Payne received more unwelcome visitors when Lieutenant G. H. G. Gale and a squad of sixteen troopers stumbled into the settlement. Payne saw them coming, and his demeanor in subsequent dealings with Lieutenant Gale suggested that he was more interested in being arrested and having his day in court than putting up armed resistance. Payne went so far as to invite Gale and his men to stay for supper. The pleasantries ended on a sour note when Payne and his men were arrested and escorted to Fort Reno. On the trunk of a tree at the abandoned camp, Payne left a polite note, dated May 15, 1880, for Harry Hill to discover upon his return to Ewing: "We have accepted the invitation of Lieutenant G. H. G. Gale, 4th United States Cavalry, to accompany him to Fort Reno, but will return as soon as convenient for us to do so." He signed the note, "D. L. Payne, President."[25]

As a postscript to the first truly organized boomer invasion, Payne and his followers were taken from Fort Reno to Polecat Creek, where they were held prisoner for two weeks before soldiers set them free near the Kansas border. Payne's suffering was compounded by malarial fever occasioned by exposure to the elements. Harry Hill and the men who had been sent on a supply run to Arkansas City returned to Ewing three days after the arrest to find Payne's note hammered to a tree. "Payne's invasion of the Indian Territory has come to grief, as everybody expected," crowed the anti-boomer *Dodge City Times*. "And there was no fight, notwithstanding Payne's vehement declarations that all the streams of the Indian Territory would run with gore if any attempt was made to interfere with him and his colonists."[26]

Before the spring 1880 invasion, only the most reckless of speculators were willing to risk investing in Oklahoma townsite companies and colonies. All that changed when news of the Ewing arrests hit the streets. True, some Kansas newspapers kept up their anti-boomer rants. In Indian Territory, the opposition found a dependable voice in the *Cherokee Advocate*. Printed in English and Cherokee and distributed nationwide, the *Advocate* fought to prevent the United States from swallowing Indian land. Perhaps naively, the *Advocate* was confident that the American people would demand fair treatment of Indians if they knew the truth about past injustice and were reminded of their govern-ment's treaty obligations.[27] Indian resistance notwithstanding, a new narrative was in the making, and it featured a daring adventurer who was standing up to arbitrary power. Sales of certificates in Payne's Oklahoma Colony surged.[28]

Energized by the shift in public opinion, Payne marshaled his forces for a second invasion. "The Oklahoma boom is booming again and the present boom promises to be a boomer," declared the *Wichita City Eagle* in a vocab-ulary-challenged article on July 1, 1880.[29] Unfazed by presidential orders and unfriendly editors, Payne chose July 6, 1880, to lead a force of three hundred into Indian Territory. In spite of torrential storms and raging rivers that might have put a lethal end to their expedition, the boomers reached the stillborn capital at Ewing and an area to the west dubbed "Council Grove," a three-and-a-half-square-mile area on the North Canadian River south of present-day Wiley Post Airport and east of Lake Overholser. Long since steamrolled by Bethany and Warr Acres, Council Grove's abundant water and timber made it an ideal spot for Plains Indians to hold their councils and bury their dead, and thousands of prairie chickens perched in blackjack and post oak thickets ensured that nobody would go hungry. As commerce steamrolled its way across Indian Territory, Council Grove became a favorite venue for traders to set up their trading posts and for soldiers to negotiate peace treaties with Indians.[30]

Chilled to the bone from downpours and river crossings, Payne became so ill that he was unable to speak, and a bout of inflammatory rheumatism left him hobbling on crutches. Back in Arkansas City, sympathizers were buying machinery and supplies for shipment to Payne's colony and setting up an office to promote immigration.[31] But once again, high hopes turned to disappointment when Payne and more than two dozen followers were arrested and escorted to Polecat Creek, where many of the prisoners had been held after their arrest in May. The *Wichita City Eagle* offered the stab at humor quoted in the epigraph.[32]

When news of Payne's second invasion hit the nation's capital, a frustrated President Hayes called his cabinet together to clarify his administration's position on the irksome Oklahoma Question. His tersely worded proclamation exacerbated the confusion insofar as he failed to mention penalties for unauthorized entries. He then instructed Attorney General Charles Devens (1877–81) to bring the prisoners to trial in the Western District of Arkansas on a charge of conspiracy to violate the Non-Intercourse Act (known variously as the "Indian Intercourse Act" or "Indian Non-Intercourse Act") of 1834, which described a large and ever-shifting region as "Indian country."[33] In dire need of instructions, General John Pope fired off a telegram to the War Department, asking if he should turn the prisoners over to the U.S. Marshal's office in Fort Smith.[34] Secretary of War Alexander Ramsey (1879–81) responded with orders to deliver Payne and his men to civilian authorities. Meanwhile, Devens had his hands full trying to decide what mode of civil proceedings to initiate against the boomers. At some point in the swirl of correspondence between civilian and military authorities, soldiers got word that they were supposed to release all of the prisoners they were holding at Polecat Creek—all of them, that is, except Payne and a few others who had been imprisoned after the first invasion.[35]

Following his imprisonment at Polecat Creek, Payne set out for Fort Smith to answer a federal summons, dated August 13, 1880, commanding the boomer leader to appear in court in Fort Smith by November 1. Failure to appear would be taken as a confession of guilt.[36]

Evidence strongly suggests that railroad companies paid Payne's legal bills and travel expenses to Fort Smith. Captain Thomas B. Robinson, whose cavalry unit was constantly on the prowl for boomers and who participated in Payne's second arrest, informed General Pope that participants in the second raid seemed more respectable than those of the first and were likely the beneficiaries of corporate financing.[37] Railroad support for the nascent boomer movement was apparently an open secret along Kansas's southern border. C. W. Daniels, president of the Baxter Springs Board of Trade, declared it to be beyond dispute.[38] As a board of trade president in a Kansas border town, Daniels had access to insider information, and his testimony corroborates other evidence that the boomer movement was more nuanced than historians have heretofore depicted it. If Robinson's and Daniels' testimonies fall short of irrefutable proof that railroads paid boomers for their services, it certainly illuminates the complex relationships and motivations behind the movement to open Oklahoma Proper to homesteading.

As Payne made his way to Fort Smith for his day in court, the Five Tribes girded for action. Principal Chief D. W. Bushyhead of the Cherokee Nation opined that a "strong combination" had been formed to force court action and encouraged other tribal leaders to collaborate in hiring a lawyer to represent their interests. In Bushyhead's estimation, Payne's forthcoming trial would set a precedent for trials that were surely coming, and railroad corporations would spare no expense to further their pro-settlement schemes.[39]

Payne's journey took him through Emporia, Kansas. Seemingly unfazed by what Judge Isaac Parker, dubbed "Hanging Judge Parker" for his propensity to hang miscreants, might have in store for him, Payne spent the night at the Katy station in Emporia and sat for an interview with J. D. King of the *Emporia News*. Warming up to a familiar tale, Payne told his interviewer about Indian land cessions occasioned by the Reconstruction Treaties of 1866, and how they left unclaimed millions of acres in the geographical center of Indian Territory. He then reminded King that, following the Coffeyville invasion in April 1879, President Hayes had asked Congress to pass legislation pertaining to settlement in Indian Territory, as he doubted the legality of keeping the land off-limits to settlers. Seizing on the president's uncertainty and fired by his own convictions, Payne had assembled a growing cadre of true believers to claim their birthright "in the land of promise, where the green grass waves and the restless pioneer longs to be."

Short-lived though it was, the capital city of Ewing had given boomers a vision of endless possibilities. With financing secured, colonists had framed schoolhouses, hired teachers, and contracted with mills to cut lumber and grind grain, and they stood ready at a moment's notice to move their machinery and prefabricated structures to Indian Territory. All they needed was a presidential proclamation to send them on their way. They eventually got their proclamation, but not the one they wanted. In a disappointing turn of fortune attending Payne's second arrest, President Hayes's proclamation seemed to settle, at least temporarily, the illegality of settlement, even though penalties remained anyone's guess. And now, in August 1880, with two invasions to his credit, Payne was on his way to Judge Parker's court. Undaunted and anxious to answer the government's charges against him, Payne assured King that he would be back in Ewing within two weeks, where he could work "under his own vine and fig tree with no one to molest or make afraid."[40]

Payne's next stop was Muskogee in the Creek Nation, where he responded to critics of the boomer movement in an open letter to the *Indian Journal*.

Launched at Muskogee in May 1876 and relocated to Eufaula in 1877, the *Indian Journal* was subsidized by the Creek government to become a leading advocate of tribal sovereignty.[41] Payne assured his skeptical readers that he had no intention of interfering with tribal politics or treaty obligations, as his sole interest was in land west of the Five Tribes and east of the Cheyenne and Arapaho Reservation that was virtually uninhabited and totally uncultivated. Payne was overly optimistic in envisioning a city of a thousand people within ninety days. But he was clear about what kind of people would populate that city—industrious and sober people who would eschew the sale and consumption of intoxicating liquors, build churches and schools, and maintain good relations with their Indian neighbors. "We do not propose to interfere with anyone's rights," wrote Payne in closing, "but we propose to claim and maintain our own."[42]

Payne was a sick man when he straggled into Fort Smith. Such was his pain from rheumatism that he could hardly walk, and he was compelled to remain in town for a week to recuperate. To add insult to injury, his journey had been in vain, as Judge Parker had decided to postpone the case to November. Payne posted bond thanks to unknown sources, but he lacked sufficient funds to go home. His luck took a turn for the better when a friend financed his return trip to Kansas. During a stop in St. Louis en route to Wichita, Payne announced that five thousand boomers would launch an expedition within sixty days. Some suspected that the invaders were counting on the excitement attending the November elections to divert attention from their illegal enterprise.[43]

The excitement was palpable on October 30 when a raucous crowd, its ranks swelled by two bands, a cavalry troop, and committees from both political parties, met Payne and his entourage at the depot in Wichita and escorted them to the Oklahoma Colony Company headquarters. Ominously, all the excitement was taking its toll on the boomer leader's health. True to form, he insisted that he was just fine, and promised to be "in good trim to lead the Oklahoma hosts to homes in the sunny Southwest."[44]

While Payne was recovering and boomers were celebrating, the Five Tribes were scrambling to prepare for the impending trial. On October 8, Bushyhead wrote Principal Chief Samuel Checote of the Muskogee Creek Nation to propose an international convention where delegates would strategize to defend their interests in court.[45] Bushyhead's proposal hit home among anxious Indians, and on October 20, delegates from the Five Tribes gathered in Eufaula for a two-day meeting. Convinced that the boomer movement threatened to erode Indians' rights and maybe even destroy tribal sovereignty once and for all, the delegates agreed to contribute to a defense fund and authorize a commission to employ outside counsel, all in an effort to keep white settlers out of the Oklahoma country.[46] The Five Tribes were wise to be prepared, as Payne was sure to secure funding from his supposed backers for a vigorous defense.[47]

Although the boomer movement was certainly gaining traction, most Americans remained skeptical, if not downright hostile, to Captain Payne's illegal expeditions. In an open letter to the *Wichita City Eagle*, Judge W. P. Campbell articulated the voice of the opposition. After warning hardworking people to be wary of boomer promises, Campbell proceeded to pick apart the boomer movement with all the erudition one would expect from a judge. First and foremost, boomer leaders were acting with flagrant disregard for the law, mainly because wealthy businessmen—presumably, investors in townsite companies and colonies—were using working men and yeoman farmers as pawns in their moneymaking schemes. At the same time, Campbell accused boomers of a breach of faith in attempting to deprive Indians of what little land they had left. How, wondered the judge, could Indians be expected to honor and respect American laws and ways of life, and ultimately assimilate into an alien culture, when boomers were trampling on their rights and muscling into land that was supposed to be theirs for as long as the grasses grew and waters ran?

Judge Campbell had no objection to commerce. He looked forward to the day when residents of Indian Territory would establish courts and schools, till farms, and launch businesses. In time, they might even build cities on the American model to encourage immigration and promote private enterprise. Linked by rail and telegraph to centers of commerce and industry, whites and Indians alike would benefit from business-building opportunities. "But," the judge cautioned, "whatever is done, let it be done on the principle of rigid justice and good faith to the Indians, they being the judge of what is justice and good faith."[48]

At the time Judge Campbell's article was published in December 1880, Americans were still recovering from the Panic of 1873, a horrific economic contraction precipitated by excessive railroad construction, primarily in the

West, that felled banks and businesses across the land and wreaked havoc among debt-laden cattlemen.[49] Seen in the context of those dark days, Campbell's defenses of working-class interests and the rights of Indians were not the only reasons to oppose the boomers' illegal invasions. The nationwide depression that began 1873 spawned riots that compelled America's most powerful corporations to resort to force of arms to bring their employees to heel. Pitched battles left scores of civilians, soldiers, and policemen dead, leading employers to wonder if Europe's most recent scourge of communism had come home to roost on American shores.

As the years ground on with no relief in sight, vagabonds roamed from town to town, competing for scarce jobs and, if all else failed, looking for handouts. A new stereotype entered America's collective consciousness as the tramp. For most folks, an occasional tramp could be referred to the nearest church for a hot meal and a place to sleep. But when the occasional tramp ballooned into an army of hungry, working-class castoffs, all bets were off. Headlines, short on specifics but promising a riveting read, blared with apocalyptic stories of cities overrun by rabble and crime and mayhem and murder that followed in their wake.

By the late 1870s and just in time for the boomer movement, Americans were obsessed by the tramp scare. Fueled by an ethos of social Darwinism that seemed to justify class and wealth disparities, people fortunate enough to maintain their jobs and the status that went with them perceived tramps not as victims of a dog-eat-dog economy (which, of course, they were), but rather, as the vanguard of a revolution. Social Darwinism originated in England in the writing of Herbert Spencer, whose supposed stroke of genius was to apply Charles Darwin's theory of natural selection to humanity. Popularized in America by William Graham Sumner, social Darwinism was used to defend the modern workplace, where success went to the best and brightest and failure was the outward manifestation of inner dysfunction. Although social Darwinism entered the common vernacular in Europe in 1879, it made its debut in the United States as early as 1877 as a scientific explanation for the tramp menace.

Social Darwinism tended to rear its misguided head in the industrialized East, where mines and factories provided daily evidence that common laborers were not to be trusted. But on the Oklahoma frontier, America's potentially dangerous underclass was on display in squalid boomer camps teeming with scofflaws and down-and-out farmers. The reasoning seemed so simple: just as working-class tramps were looking for free rides in cities, so, too, were boomers bent on snatching free land, never mind the Indians and soldiers who stood in their way.

In an era when social control was tenuous and revolution a very real prospect, it is hardly surprising to find soldiers in Indian Territory dispensing the same brute justice to boomers that their counterparts back east used to quell disturbances and break strikes. Politicos and businessmen with a vested interest in keeping socioeconomic tensions in check encouraged such tactics. But for boomers, military excesses seemed to justify their defiance of laws enacted by a government that was keeping them out of Indian Territory. Seen through the prism of the tramp scare and the flawed sociology that informed it, Judge Campbell's disdain for the boomer movement reflected nothing less than the fear and class consciousness at the heart of Gilded Age inequalities.[50]

On November 16, 1880, Payne chaired a meeting of Payne's Oklahoma Colony to lay plans for an invasion later that month. Under a veil of strict secrecy, colony members thanked their president for his commitment to the boomer movement and expressed gratitude for his return to health. Tearfully, they renewed their support for Payne, who, like "the ancient Samson under the direction of divine providence," would "batten down the Chinese walls of Barbarism which separates us from the Indian Territory and conduct us victoriously to the Land of Promise." Payne responded with an expression of appreciation for his friends' words of encouragement. Following the election of a wagon master for the next expedition, the meeting adjourned.[51] The men dispersed quietly into the night, and we are left to ponder another calendrical coincidence: what are surely among the few surviving, handwritten minutes of a Payne's Oklahoma Colony meeting were dated November 16, 1880, precisely twenty-seven years before the Twin Territories were admitted into the Union as the forty-sixth state of Oklahoma.

As promised, boomers gathered in early December for their third and final major invasion of 1880. In a circular issued from the colony's headquarters in Wichita, colonists were instructed to gather at Caldwell, Arkansas City, and Coffeyville, Kansas; Fort Smith, Arkansas; and Denison, Texas. If, for whatever reason, those locations proved to be unsuitable, colonists were advised to make haste to more convenient spots and prepare for a dash across the border. Financial support came from Dr. Robert Wilson, a wealthy colony member from Texas, who clearly had a soft spot for farmers with an attitude.[52]

When Payne arrived at the colony's rendezvous near Arkansas City, Lieutenant S. A. Mason and forty-eight soldiers assigned to the Fourth Cavalry showed up to halt their journey at the Kansas border. Tensions escalated when Mason learned that more boomers were trickling into Indian Territory from other locations along the Kansas line.[53] To avoid any misunderstanding, General C. H. Smith, second in command of the military department, read his orders from the War Department to the assembled boomers. Smith's warning apparently hit home, as the boomers broke camp and followed the state line toward Hunnewell with yet another military detachment, this one under the command of Colonel J. J. Coppinger, close on their heels. Somewhere along the way, Captain Payne was reportedly relieved of his command because he had signaled retreat when a corporal demanded his surrender.[54]

"We guess the bottom will fall out of that ridiculous movement before many days," asserted the Emporia News. As if boomers did not have enough trouble on their hands, Nez Percé and Ponca warriors were reportedly preparing to wage war against them.[55] Payne's successor during what was clearly a temporary change in leadership was Major Hill M. Maidt of Dallas, an army veteran and former Indian fighter on the Pacific coast who now kept a saloon near the post office in Wichita. To imbue boomers with a sense of righteous duty, Rev. W. Broadhurst drew from Exodus and portrayed President Hayes as Pharaoh, Oklahoma as Canaan, the colonists as the Lord's people, Major Maidt as Moses, and himself as Aaron.[56] From Fort Leavenworth, General Pope sorted through the confusion in a dispatch dated December 12, 1880, in which he assured his superiors that cavalry were apprised of the invasion and were in position to stop it.[57]

Flanked by soldiers, the boomers made it as far as Caldwell, Kansas. Unable to go south and unwilling to go home, they set up camp a few miles south of town to await further developments. Among their number was Harry Hill, an Oklahoma Town Company investor and scout for the April 1880 invasion, who had traded more comfortable accommodations back in Wichita for a tent, cold vittles, and camaraderie with his boomer brethren. In a conversation with Colonel Edward Hatch, Hill promised that boomers would make a run for it, and the military be damned. And then, he threw down the gauntlet.

"You don't dare to shoot us down," said Hill.

"Oh," said Colonel Hatch, "we won't of course shoot you, but we will get off out of range of your weapons, and then shoot your horses."

"Just wait a minute, please," said Hill, his sense of decorum seemingly out of place in a tense situation. He disappeared into another tent and returned with two modern repeating rifles, ammunition belts, and cartridges.

"Do you think you can get out of range of these?" Hill asked the colonel.

Colonel Hatch's answer is lost to history. Perhaps he decided that shooting the boomers' horses would be an unwise course of action. Shivering in the cold and denied their birthright in the Oklahoma country, boomers' patience was wearing thin. Perhaps Colonel Hatch took Hill at his word: shoot our horses, and prepare to reap the whirlwind.[58]

To make their own assessment of the invasion force and Payne's prospects at his upcoming trial, the Five Tribes' international council in Eufaula had authorized a committee to travel to Caldwell. Upon their arrival in mid-December, delegates were immediately driven to what was known as the "Fall Creek camp." Anxious to cultivate good will among their Indian neighbors, boomers extended a warm welcome. G. W. Grayson, a Creek delegate and chairman of the defense commission, reported that boomer numbers were nowhere close to the hundreds that boomer-friendly newspapers had published, but rather, were closer to seventy-five, and their supplies included "thirty-two pretty good lumber wagons with shabby teams." In his formal report to the National Council of the Muskogee Nation in October 1881, Grayson recalled his first up-close-and-personal encounter with what he described as a "worthless horde" of half-clad and hungry backwoodsmen, whose sorry condition was unmatched "in all the balance of Christendom." Grayson quickly perceived that the Five Tribes had far less to fear from rank-and-file boomers than their financial backers, who knew how to bend statutes and treaties to the contours of their own nefarious ends.[59]

Members of the committee were equally unimpressed with the boomers' leadership, which may or may not have included Captain Payne on that cold December day. Likely as not, he was in a saloon somewhere, recruiting boomers in more comfortable lodging than the Fall Creek camp had to offer. Tempers flared when Grayson announced to the motley gathering that the Five Tribes aimed to prevent whites from settling in Oklahoma Proper. "We are doing all we can to prevent the opening of the country," he stormed, "and you had as well go home, for we have bought and can buy your Congressmen like so many sheep and cattle!" Grayson's listeners exercised restraint as he and his committee departed, even as he left behind one parting shot: if the U.S. government permitted boomers to settle in Oklahoma Proper, then the

Five Tribes and their allies would take matters into their own hands, raise an army of five thousand Indians, and drive them out.[60]

Christmas 1880 came and went, and the boomers were still no closer to Oklahoma Proper than Fall Creek camp. Food and supplies donated by sympathizers did little to dispel the gathering gloom. Boomer ranks thinned when a blizzard came howling in from the north and pounded the camp with snow and freezing rain to render smoldering buffalo-chip fires all but useless.

Deposed or not, Captain Payne was receiving letters by the score from sympathizers who were hankering to enlist in the boomer cause. Many of those letters arrived at the boomers' temporary headquarters in a hotel, presumably in Caldwell, where Payne and his top lieutenants took a respite from the December chill to lay their plans for future expeditions. As reported in the *Cherokee Advocate*, their inner sanctum was a hoarder's paradise, where circulars and maps filled the room and stacks of unopened mail languished in piles. The walls were festooned with giant maps whose glaring colors depicted the Oklahoma country's physical features. A map of the future Payne County, divided into townships named after states and prominent people, attracted the visitor's attention, but perhaps not as much as another map, apparently the centerpiece of the cluttered room's decor, illustrating the future capital, its grand avenues radiating from a capitol building where a mule pen, probably erected by Cass Wantland, was one of the few signs of human activity in Ewing. Residential blocks radiated from the imagined state capitol to accommodate a population of thirty thousand.[61]

Some of the unopened mail that lay strewn about the boomer headquarters came from farmers in western Kansas. Claiming destitution and even starvation, they described entire counties that were ready to migrate south. Some were waiting to hear from Dr. Wilson, the Texas millionaire who had cast his lot with the boomers and was now in Washington, D.C., to exert his influence wherever and however he could. Boomer sympathizers throughout Kansas pounced on newcomers and visitors and regaled them with laws, constitutional clauses, Indian treaties, and whatever else they had in their polemical playbooks to sway public opinion in their favor.

Meanwhile, anti-boomer newspapers kept up their invective, branding boomer leaders as railroad hirelings who were lining their pockets at the expense of their gullible and now freezing devotees.[62] Joining the *Cherokee*

Advocate in opposition to the boomer movement was the *Cheyenne Transporter*. Launched on December 5, 1879, at the Darlington Indian Agency, the *Transporter* had a twofold mission: to provide missionaries and Indian rights activists with a platform to keep eastern philanthropists abreast of their progress in bestowing the benefits of Western civilization on Plains tribes; and to support Indians and cattlemen in their efforts to keep Indian Territory off-limits to homesteaders.[63] "A detachment of soldiers is kept in Oklahoma constantly, and the Indians are also aroused against the invaders," ran a cautionary editorial on the eve of the third invasion. "If you want to settle the Territory, just wait until Uncle Sam gives you permission. It is a big thing to undertake to 'buck' the United States Government."[64]

Dire warnings notwithstanding, boomers' optimism soared when the St. Louis law firm Broadhead, Krum, and Phillips opined that parts of Indian Territory were indeed part of the public domain and therefore open to settlement. At a mass meeting at the schoolhouse in Caldwell, boomers and soldiers mixed freely, delivering speeches and discussing what they could do to compel President Hayes to issue the proclamation they had been waiting for. The revelry took a violent turn following one of Payne's rousing speeches when troublemakers threatened to burn in effigy the congressmen who were thwarting their dreams. "The colonists are said to have signs, pass-words and grips, by which they know each other, and there is a secret meeting to-night," reported the *Emporia News* as the final boomer invasion of 1880 stalled and then fizzled out altogether. "They say when they are ready to go, in forty-eight hours they can summon one thousand men to join them. The cry is 'On to Oklahoma.'"[65]

Back in Doniphan County, Payne's former neighbors were apparently unfazed by their favorite son's temporary loss of leadership and boomers' failure to make it past Caldwell. The *Weekly Kansas Chief*, published in Troy, reminded its readers that Doniphan County was home to two extraordinary leaders: J. M. Steele, president of the Oklahoma Town Company of Wichita and the boomer movement's chief agent in Washington, D.C.; and David L. Payne, known to some as the "Cimarron Scout," to others as "Old Ox Heart," and to pretty much everyone after 1880 as "Oklahoma Payne," whose quest to open Oklahoma Proper to homesteading was just getting started.[66]

CHAPTER FOUR

Cattle Kings

The cattle-kings, the land-gobblers, and their followers must go.
A. P. Jackson and E. C. Cole, Oklahoma! *(1885)*

The boomer movement's evolution from sporadic invasions into Indian Territory to a full-blown political movement coincided with what is arguably the most celebrated chapter in the history of westward expansion: the great northern cattle drives.[1] Most of the trails that cowboys followed during the two decades following the Civil War from Texas to the railheads in Missouri and Kansas and, in some cases, on to the northern ranges, took them near and sometimes through Oklahoma Proper. Although their exact routes depended on the weather, Indian activity, and other factors that required quick thinking on the trail, cowboys had no alternative to threading their herds through Indian country. And sooner or later, they were bound to come across boomers, who took a dim view of cattlemen and their marauding herds.

Occasionally, circumstances required cavalry to escort cattle drives through Indian Territory. In addition to ensuring cattlemen safe passage, soldiers were saddled with four additional, and sometimes conflicting, responsibilities: halting boomer caravans, breaking up their camps, and usually arresting their leaders; keeping the peace between the Five Tribes and their bellicose neighbors to the west; encouraging Plains Indians to stay on their reservations and punishing them when they left; and ensuring the safety of civilians. To complicate relationships that were plenty complicated already, many cattlemen took a liking to Indian Territory's vast grasslands. By the 1880s, untold thousands of cattle were blissfully grazing in and around Oklahoma Proper to present the boomer movement with its most vexing challenge: dislodging cattlemen from the Oklahoma range to make way for homesteads.

We therefore take a brief but necessary detour from the politics of settlement to the politics of cattle. Indiana congressman George W. Julian's speech in March 1868 reflected the passions that were swirling in the nation's capital over the proper use of America's dwindling supply of public lands and the corrupting influence of Big Money.[2] But it was in Indian Territory where inequalities spawned by Gilded Age capitalism crystallized, sometimes in debates and often in displays of brute force, over the contentious issue of where cattle could eat. Oklahoma's iconic industry thus had its beginnings in a conflict that put boomers and their scant resources at a disadvantage vis a vis influential cattlemen who were determined to keep the grasslands for themselves. This time, Indians and soldiers had something in common: they were caught between forces that were hard to predict and even harder to control.

Maybe Rogers and Hammerstein got it wrong. In Indian Territory circa 1880, there was not much chance that the farmer and the cowman could be friends.

Oklahoma's range cattle industry had its roots in the seventeenth century, when Spanish settlers brought a sturdy breed of bovines to the New World—lean, long-horned animals whose ancestors had been raised by Moors on the plains of Andalusia. Crossbreeding with northern European breeds produced cattle that were larger and heavier than their Spanish ancestors. Best known as "longhorns," they were well suited to the harsh climate and sparse vegetation of the Mexican North. They were also temperamental—according to their frustrated handlers, they could be as wild as deer and as wary as wolves. They sniffed approaching danger from incredible distances and broke into stampedes at the slightest provocation, prompting one disgusted cowman to deride them as horned jackrabbits.[3]

Ranching on an immense scale dated back to the Spanish land-grant system and, later, the Republic of Texas's effort to encourage colonization by granting huge swaths of land to cattlemen. With the U.S. victory in the Mexican-American War and subsequent Treaty of Guadalupe Hidalgo in 1848, a new international border was created, and Mexican ranchers were compelled to withdraw south of the Rio Grande and leave their sturdy longhorns behind to fend for themselves. When Texas was admitted to the Union in December 1845, the state retained the ownership and control of unoccupied land within its borders. The state also continued the republic's liberal land policy and disposed of vast areas, either by bounty and donation warrants or as homesteads. Land that was not given away was sold at low prices and upon liberal payment terms.[4] Underlying the entire system was the law of the open range. Unlike the herd law back east, which required stockmen to build barriers, the law of the open range was an unwritten rule that allowed herdsmen and their cattle to roam where they pleased across the public domain with unimpeded access to grass and water. Assured of the federal government's tacit approval, cattlemen felt justified in allowing their herds to graze not only in public lands but also on undeveloped, privately owned land.[5]

Texas's land policies and time-honored traditions thus produced farms and ranches that were far larger than those in neighboring states, and they provided plenty of grass for longhorns, whose numbers were growing exponentially. By the time Confederate soldiers returned to Texas after the Civil War, the range was swarming with fat, sleek cattle. Texans were doubly blessed to return to a state that had been relatively unfazed by wartime pillaging and plundering. All an enterprising cattleman had to do was stretch some barbed wire and hire a few cowboys, and he was in business.

Demonized by Indians as "the devil's rope" for the havoc it inflicted on bison migration patterns, barbed wire was in use long before the enterprising Joseph F. Glidden of DeKalb, Illinois, received his patent on November 24, 1874. As ever-more ingenious barbed wire designs flooded the market, a patent war erupted and raged unabated until a court decided in Glidden's favor in December 1880. In what was likely the first public demonstration of barbed wire's effectiveness in restricting longhorns' mobility, salesman John W. "Bet-a-Million" Gates, who went on to join the ranks of the uber-wealthy barbed-wire barons, extolled its virtues to a skeptical crowd in San Antonio's Military Plaza just before a herd of cattle, hooves pounding and slobber flying, was released into a barbed-wire enclosure. "This is the finest fence in the world," declared Gates at the 1876 demonstration. "Light as air. Stronger than whiskey. Cheaper than dirt. All steel, and miles long. The cattle ain't born that can get through it. Bring on your steers, gentlemen!"[6]

Sure enough, Gates's fence held, and sales soared. But there was a problem that even barbed wire could not fix: in the absence of railroads, there was no easy way for Texas ranchers to get their cattle, valued at four to five dollars per head in Texas, to northern and eastern markets, where they fetched up to fifty dollars.[7] Before the Civil War, Texas cattlemen depended on the old Shawnee Trail to solve their marketing problems. Drovers who followed this route to railheads in Kansas and Missouri entered Indian Territory at Colbert's Ferry just south of Fort Washita. They continued through the Choctaw and Cherokee Nations to Fort Gibson, where the trail split into two parallel paths along the Grand Saline River en route to present-day Ottawa County and entered Kansas near Baxter Springs. An alternative route known as the "West Shawnee Trail" diverged from the old Shawnee Trail north of Colbert's Ferry and led due north to Junction City, Kansas.[8]

The Shawnee Trail and its various detours remained in use until the post–Civil War period, when rugged terrain and farms that crept ever-farther westward, sometimes encircled by early and unpatented iterations of the devil's rope, forced cattlemen to rethink their marketing strategies. Their troubles were compounded by the Five Tribes' rising hostility toward cattle, which trampled their land and ruined their crops. The final nail in the Shawnee Trail's coffin was the dreaded Texas (or Spanish) fever, which could wipe out herds that had close encounters with longhorns. Concerns over Texas fever caught the attention of Sidney Clarke, then serving as a U.S. representative from Kansas, who encouraged his fellow congressmen to appoint a committee to investigate the disease's causes and effects. He further asked newspapers to publish information pertaining to Texas fever in hopes of advancing the aims of scientific inquiry.[9] Toss in smoldering resentment from Civil War days among Missourians and Kansans, who knew that nothing good could ever come from Texas, and farmers had all the justification they needed to put an end to cattle drives and their swaths of destruction. The Missouri legislature succumbed to pressure and passed an ordinance against the importation of diseased cattle, leaving cattlemen with no choice but to abandon the eastern trails and seek alternative routes to market.[10]

As the eastern trails fell into disuse, Joseph G. McCoy, an enterprising Illinoisan and the youngest of three brothers, decided not to let Texas fever and stubborn farmers stand in the way of profits. Already in the cattle business and anxious to cash in on the longhorn trade, McCoy chose the remote hamlet of Abilene, Kansas, along the southern branch of the Union Pacific Railway (later, the Kansas Pacific Railway), far from bothersome farmers, regulations, and the challenging topography of Missouri and eastern Kansas, to build an infrastructure to accommodate large numbers of cattle. He then cut a deal with the Kansas Pacific Railway to subsidize a scheme to supply beef to eastern and northern markets. With a site chosen and financing secured, McCoy and his brothers counted on the railroads to expand their marketing reach.[11]

By the fall of 1867, the McCoy brothers had muscled their way into the Kansas cattle business, and Abilene was on its way to becoming the epicenter of a dynamic trade. On September 20, 1867, twenty thousand head of cattle were reportedly in Abilene. A month later, those twenty thousand cattle required twenty railroad cars for shipment from Abilene to slaughterhouses back east. The age of the great northern cattle drives was on.[12]

As predicted, McCoy and his brothers transformed the sleepy village into a well-equipped cattle capital, complete with a shipping yard, barns, offices, and state-of-the-art scales. They also spent thousands of dollars on advertisements in northern newspapers and sent agents into Indian Territory to encourage drovers to bring their herds to their burgeoning cow town.[13] The McCoys persisted, and, over the next two decades, millions of longhorns plodded their way from Texas, through Indian Territory, and on to Abilene and a succession of other cow towns that sprouted along Kansas's fading line of frontier settlement.[14]

When they were not busy counting cattle in that hectic October of 1867, the citizens of Abilene might have turned their attention to the goings-on in Medicine Lodge, some 140 miles as the crow flies to the southwest, where U.S. officials were trying to convince Kiowas, Comanches, Apaches, Cheyennes, and Arapahos to give up their nomadic ways and move to reservations in Indian Territory. At forts and lonely campsites, soldiers wondered who would give them more trouble in the years ahead: cowboys and their immense herds of longhorns; or Plains Indians, who would have to accommodate increasing traffic along cattle trails slicing through their diminishing domain. None had more to worry about than the buffalo soldiers of the recently formed Ninth and Tenth U.S. Cavalries, whose deployment to the West dropped them into the red-hot crucible of Indian uprisings, bison slaughter, pioneer settlement, railroad construction, and a cattle industry set to explode. One thing they knew for certain: their job of policing Indian Territory was not going to be easy.

The trail that became synonymous with the great northern cattle drives was blazed by Jesse Chisholm, a young adventurer of Cherokee and Scottish ancestry from Arkansas who rose to fame as a trader and explorer.[15]

In 1858, he set up a trading post at Council Grove in about the same spot where Captain Payne would establish a boomer camp during the July 1880 expedition. Forced to relocate during the Civil War, Chisholm abandoned Council Grove and joined the Loyal Creeks, Shawnees, and other tribes in their exodus to southern Kansas, where they awaited the end of hostilities and a chance to return to their homes. As the Civil War was reaching its bloody crescendo, Chisholm was busy blazing his trail through Indian Territory. He reopened his trading post in Council Grove in March 1865, just in time to see the first herd of longhorns pass by on the trail he had intended not for cattle, but for trade that would surely quicken after the war.[16] Chisholm died three years later, supposedly from dining on tainted bear grease from a brass pot, and was laid to rest five miles east of present-day Greenfield on the North Canadian River.[17]

Early on, the trail that took Chisholm's name was known alternately as the "Texas Cattle Trail," "McCoy's Trail," the "Abilene Trail," and "Jesse Chisholm's Wagon Road." By the early 1870s, it was drifting into frontier vernacular as the "Chisholm Trail." Its path ran roughly parallel to the ninety-eighth meridian and almost exactly anticipated Oklahoma State Highway 81. The Chisholm Trail entered Indian Territory at the Red River in Jefferson County, proceeded northward past El Reno and Enid, and entered Kansas a few miles south of Caldwell. Towns that developed along or near the Chisholm Trail in Oklahoma Proper include El Reno in Canadian County and Okarche, Kingfisher, Dover, and Hennessey in Kingfisher County.

An alternate route from Texas to the Kansas railheads was known as the "Arbuckle Trail," and it actually predated the Chisholm Trail. It entered Indian Territory south of present-day Ardmore and ran west of Fort Arbuckle, a fort established in 1851 to protect Chickasaws and westbound migrants from Plains Indians and manned largely by buffalo soldiers attached to the Sixth Infantry and Tenth U.S. Cavalry. When the fort was abandoned in 1870, soldiers were reassigned to Fort Sill, which had been established in 1869. The Arbuckle Trail proceeded due north through present-day Oklahoma City before merging with the Chisholm Trail at Red Fork Ranch on the Cimarron River. Typically, herds crossed the Washita River about four miles west of present-day Purcell and proceeded north through present-day Noble and east of the future site of the Oklahoma City oil fields. They then crossed the North Canadian River and continued on to Abilene. It was only later that herdsmen drove their cattle across the Red River and established the Chisholm Trail.[18]

Determining precise routes across Indian Territory is a tricky business. Many of the old-time cowhands liked to reminisce about driving cattle "up the trail to Kansas" and left it to posterity to figure out how they got there. References to the Chisholm Trail might have been more about honoring a frontier culture hero than specifying a route. After it fell into disuse in the late 1880s, the Chisholm Trail survived in the West of our imagination while others, such as the Arbuckle Trail, did not, leaving later generations of scholars and GPS addicts to speculate on trails that cowboys followed from Texas to Kansas.[19] After conducting an exhaustive study in the 1930s aimed at plotting every curve, detour, and river crossing of the Chisholm Trail, H. S. Tennant of the Oklahoma State Highway Department acknowledged that following the North Star and familiar landmarks was not exactly a guarantee of precision.[20]

Jesse Chisholm would have been stunned by the traffic that passed through Indian Territory. The first large-scale cattle drive up the Chisholm Trail was in 1866, just two years before the trailblazer's death; by year's end, some 260,000 cattle had traversed the trail. Except for dips in 1867 and 1868, traffic increased steadily through 1871, when the number of cattle hit an eye-popping 600,000 head. A precipitous drop in 1874 reflected the bank panic in the fall of 1873, which compelled bankers to call in some loans and refuse to renew others. Prices for beef on the hoof plunged and pushed many cattlemen into financial ruin.

As with other nineteenth-century bank panics, the Panic of 1873 eventually faded to a bad memory, and when it passed, cattlemen who had survived the downturn were back in business. Annual estimates from 1876 through 1885 reflect a robust industry, certainly affected but never derailed by the Red River War of 1874–75.[21] With Plains Indians restricted to reservations and bison hunted to the edge of extinction, cattle were free to graze their way through an endless sea of grass from Texas to Dakota Territory, and investors could not get into the act fast enough. Following the McCoy brothers' lead, cattlemen had hit upon a perfect solution to Texas's problem of too many cattle and not enough railroad connections to lucrative markets.

Cattlemen marveled at the luxuriant and largely unspoiled prairie north of the Red River. They also saw dollar signs in those unspoiled vistas. As they and their crews prodded their herds toward Kansas, some skirted the Kiowa, Comanche, and Apache Reservation; brushed up against Fort Reno and the nearby Darlington Indian Agency at the eastern edge of the Cheyenne and Arapaho Reservation; and passed by, and maybe even through, undulating and unpopulated prairie that was apparently assigned to nobody and that contained nary an acre of cultivated land. Those who followed the Arbuckle Trail through present-day Oklahoma City had much the same experience, with a key difference: there was no fort or Indian agency to block their view.

Some of those cattlemen, surely relieved when the Red River War sputtered to its conclusion in 1875, stopped only long enough to enjoy the scenery and allow their cattle to eat and rest before continuing their northward trek. Those who had already passed through Indian Territory might have reflected on the bison that had once swarmed across the plains before hunters got to them and made room for more compliant—and certainly more lucrative—longhorns.

With their cattle fed and watered and rested, trail bosses ordered their cowboys to mount up and resume the drive. Anxious to get their herds safely to market, they fixed their eyes on the northern horizon and never looked back.

But some decided to stay.

One of those cattlemen who stayed was Montford T. Johnson. Born in 1843 near Tishomingo in the Chickasaw Nation, Johnson was the son of Charles B. Johnson, an Englishman, and Rebekah Courtney, a Chickasaw.[22] As he grew to maturity, the younger Johnson formed a friendship with Jesse Chisholm, who recognized the youth's business acumen and persuaded him to establish ranches on the unruly western fringe of the Chickasaw Nation. Shortly before his death in 1868, Chisholm convinced Plains Indian leaders to make room for Johnson's cattle and to trade with him. But there were two important caveats in Chisholm's deals: Johnson had to agree to hire only blacks and Indians; and under no circumstances was he to hire Texans.[23]

Johnson needed no further persuasion. With encouragement from an expanding network of business and opinion leaders in the Chickasaw Nation, Johnson established the Walnut Creek Ranch, whose headquarters were about two miles northeast of present-day Washington in McLain County and some thirty miles from Fort Arbuckle. His manager was Jack Brown, a former Johnson family slave (and, hence, a Chickasaw freedman), who accepted as payment every fourth calf born on the ranch, making him what might have been Oklahoma's first sharecropper.[24] In hiring Brown to run his cattle operation, Johnson set a precedent for entrusting his business ventures to nonwhites. Johnson not only fulfilled the agreements that Chisholm had negotiated on his behalf, but he also spurred economic activity in his native Chickasaw Nation and offered the prospect of steady employment to blacks and Indians, who became the mainstay of Indian Territory's range cattle industry.

Over the next two decades, Johnson expanded his empire westward from his Walnut Creek Ranch to the Chickasaw Nation's western border. Some fifteen to twenty thousand cattle grazed across his Diamond Link Ranch. Communities that later sprouted in that vast domain include Minco, Newcastle, Chickasha, and Tuttle. Johnson diversified his interests by acquiring and operating a store at Silver City, a popular crossing of the South Canadian River whose Main Street was the Chisholm Trail.[25]

Needing another base of operations to accommodate his ever-expanding herd, Johnson followed in Jesse Chisholm's and David Payne's footsteps and established a headquarters in Council Grove. After clearing the area of bothersome panthers and bears, Johnson came across a cache of logs that Chisholm had intended to use for a store. After purchasing the logs from Chisholm's son, Bill, Johnson constructed a ranch house in 1873 about two miles east of Chisholm's trading post at the present-day northwest corner of Tenth Street and MacArthur Boulevard in Oklahoma City. The Chickasaw ranch crew—Vicey Herman (or Harmon), Lon and Lucinda Gray, and Frank Dwyer—were likely Oklahoma City's first permanent residents.[26]

For the next seven years, Montford Johnson's ranch Council Grove was a thriving enterprise at the center of Indian Territory's range cattle business. Such was the pace of activity that the area drifted into the western lexicon as "Johnson Grove."[27] And then, in the spring of 1880, Captain Payne and his colonists changed everything by launching their first invasion to Johnson's range. During one foray through Council Grove, a group of colonists shot and butchered Johnson's hogs and killed some of his calves. Cass Wantland suffered similar marauding at his spread east of Council Grove. Incredulous, ranchers accustomed to being left alone in Oklahoma Proper got a lesson in boomer ideology: convinced that they were in the public domain, boomers assumed that they could do as they pleased with the local fauna and flora and that nature's bounty, like the land itself, belonged to them by right of American citizenship.

Shocked to look at a map and realize that his livestock was in forbidden territory and exposed to further depredations, Johnson abandoned the Council Grove Ranch and drove his livestock back to his home range in the

Chickasaw Nation. Wantland, too, was forced out. For later generations of Oklahomans, a historical marker on the east bank of the North Canadian River on Northwest Tenth Street and a half mile west of the aptly named Council Road, visible most clearly to northbound bikers and pedestrians on Oklahoma City's western trail system, is all that remains of Council Grove's history as a business hub in the heart of the Promised Land.[28]

East of Johnson's and Wantland's ranges was William J. McClure's 7C Ranch, a sprawling enterprise headquartered near Choctaw in present-day eastern Oklahoma County, which comprised much of the Kickapoo and Potawatomi Reservations and was conveniently located between the Chisholm and West Shawnee Trails. McClure, a former soldier in the Forty-Third Missouri Volunteer Infantry, moved to Muskogee in 1867 to find a land ravaged by war. He also found that Indian Territory's vast and mostly unoccupied grasslands offered opportunities in the cattle business. After two years in the Creek Nation, he moved west and bought the 7C Ranch from Bill Chisholm, likely Jesse's son, who had established the outfit in 1865 or 1866.[29]

McClure supplemented his cattle business with a trading post where Potawatomis received their annuity payments and rubbed shoulders with cattlemen when they shopped for tools and supplies. To keep his cowboys on fresh mounts, McClure replenished his remuda with wild horses and kept them in high log corrals on the south side of the North Canadian River in present-day Oklahoma City, not far from the area where Potawatomis held court. In the absence of fencing, 7C cattle—a mix of range cattle and hybrids derived from crossbreeding range cows with white-face bulls that McClure purchased in St. Louis in 1882—grazed where they pleased in the eastern half of Oklahoma Proper. McClure's herd became even larger in 1884 when he bought the Turkey Track Ranch from the Griffenstein family, whose Texas steers had the dubious distinction of introducing Texas fever to central Indian Territory.

The 7C Ranch and trading post were thriving for several years before the Santa Fe completed its north-south line through Oklahoma Proper in 1887. Shortly after railroad crews drove the last spike, McClure became the first rancher to ship his cattle to market from the newly constructed depot at Oklahoma Station. The roundup that year tallied 47,000 head of cattle carrying the 7C brand. To facilitate gathering and loading his cattle, McClure instructed his cowboys to build corrals near the depot—yet more tangible evidence of Oklahoma ranchers' prominence in the range cattle industry.[30]

Roundup on the open range.
Courtesy Oklahoma Historical Society, 19658.50.

Increasing commerce in Indian Territory meant more work for soldiers, who performed double duty as Indian fighters and protectors of northbound cattle herds and westbound migrants. Indians, too, were feeling the heat of an encroaching civilization. Northeast of Oklahoma Proper, Poncas complained that whites were stealing their cattle, cutting down their timber, and plying their young men with contraband whisky. Unable to take much more of the white man's civilizing influence, some wanted to be relocated west of the Kansa (Kaw) Reservation. Far to the southeast, Choctaw governor Coleman Cole was wondering whatever happened to guarantees of tribal sovereignty for as long as the waters ran and grasses grew. "For God's sake," wrote the impassioned governor in an open letter in the *Indian Journal* in February 1878, "when we bought this country, we did not buy white men with it."[31] Chickasaw governor B. F. Overton was similarly vexed with the goings-on in southern Indian Territory. He complained bitterly of ranchers, who allowed their cattle to graze their way across Chickasaw land in direct violation of tribal law. Attempts to extract grazing fees were not entirely successful, as funds did not always make it to the tribe's treasury. Clearly at his wit's end, the governor issued a proclamation on October 4, 1880, ordering all noncitizens to remove their stock from Chickasaw land within sixty days. The December 4 deadline passed, but the cattle remained.[32]

Technically speaking, government beef contractors were the only cattlemen with permits to graze their herds on Indian land. But as traffic on the cattle trails surged after the Red River War, Texas cattlemen felt safe enough from marauding warriors and overworked soldiers to allow their herds to feast on Indian Territory's luxuriant grasslands. Soldiers on patrol were finding it nearly impossible to distinguish between cattle grazing under permit, transient trail herds, and semipermanent grazers that wandered over from Texas and Kansas, known in the cowman's vernacular as "drift cattle." It was even more difficult to kick the trespassers out.[33]

Back in Washington, D.C., officials responsible for feeding Indians were in a tough spot. On the one hand, the Indian Bureau was fueling a red-hot market for beef on the hoof and prodding economic development in the West to new heights. Some of the largest cattle enterprises on the southern plains originated in lucrative contracts to supply Indians with beef.[34] Yet profits for cattlemen were often made at the expense of Indians, whose lands were overrun with Texas cattle and who had reason to doubt the effectiveness of President Grant's peace policy. To make matters worse, unscrupulous cattlemen fulfilled their government contracts by culling unwanted stock from their herds. Some army officers responsible for receiving, inspecting, and issuing stock to Indians gamed the system by allowing substandard cattle to pass muster; others were simply poor judges of beef on the hoof. Periodically, the secretary of the Interior demanded the removal of illegal grazers from Indian Territory and punishment for crooked suppliers, but without the War Department's support, such actions failed to make much headway.[35]

By the late 1870s, ranchers could count on a robust market for their cattle. Customers included not only reservation Indians and consumers back east but also soldiers stationed at western forts, whose army contracts promised them daily beef rations. In addition to the two Indian reservations west and southwest of present-day Oklahoma City, Indian Territory offered three other areas that were ideal for grazing: Oklahoma Proper; Old Greer County between the branches of the Red River and the one hundredth meridian, whose boundary dispute between Texas and Oklahoma Territory would be settled by the U.S. Supreme Court in 1896; and the Cherokee Outlet.[36]

As advances in print technology made newspapers faster and cheaper to publish, headlines throughout the eastern U.S. and Europe blared about fortunes to be made on the open range. True, the price of Texas cattle more than tripled between 1880 and 1883.[37] Yet both fact-checking and accounting principles were still their infancy. More interested in selling newspapers than in reporting accurately, journalists raised exaggeration to an art form and downplayed the disappointing returns on investment that typified the range cattle industry.[38] But no matter: for investors with a yen for adventure, the beef bonanza was in full swing. In Washington, D.C., politicians schmoozed their way into investment schemes and cattle syndicates that were mushrooming in eastern cities. Among them were Senators John J. Ingalls and Preston B. Plumb (R-Kans.; 1877–91), both Republicans from Kansas whose service in the U.S. Senate coincided with the heyday of the range cattle industry and who supported large-scale ranchers at every opportunity.

The U.S. government forbade fencing in public lands and Indian reservations. Yet there was no objection to grazing cattle and cutting hay in the public domain as long as the land was available, at least in theory, to everyone. As many of these enormous spreads were in the public domain, improvements tended to be cheap and temporary. A prominent British writer estimated that sixty to one hundred pounds sterling was sufficient to erect buildings for a run-of-the-mill ranching enterprise.[39]

Given its importance as a conduit for northbound cattle and southbound boomers and its proximity to Oklahoma Proper, the Cherokee Outlet warrants special attention. Although the Outlet remained as Cherokee property long after the Reconstruction Treaties of 1866, it was not easy to access, as the federal government's placement of tribes along the Arkansas River effectively severed it from the Cherokee Nation. By the late 1870s, enterprising Cherokees were cashing in on the burgeoning cattle trade by assessing taxes in the form of grazing fees. Ad hoc arrangements coalesced in March 1883 when taxpaying cattlemen in Caldwell, Kansas, incorporated as the Cherokee Strip Live Stock Association.[40] The association's aims were basically threefold: to protect themselves against fire, thieves, wolves, and other destructive agencies; to assist one another in roundups and branding; and to inspect cattle. United in mutually beneficial grazing leases but plagued by conflicts and corruption, Cherokees and cattlemen relied on the association to resist the federal government's meddling in their business.

Like other livestock associations that were cropping up throughout the Great Plains, the Cherokee Strip Live Stock Association became extraordinarily powerful. Sometimes, that power was exercised by force of arms. Such was the case in the summer of 1884 when the association closed cattle trails between Texas and Kansas with wire fences and dispatched armed cowboys to keep intruders off members' quasi-legal leases. Western cattle dealers' complaints made it all the way to Secretary of the Interior Henry M. Teller (1882–85). The best he could do was order bureaucrats to keep the trails open.[41] Turning from armed standoffs to legislation, some livestock associations compelled legislators to adopt their codes as templates in framing territorial and state laws. As they were governed by cattlemen with vested interests in public lands laws and in opening Indian lands to settlement, livestock associations fostered class consciousness and raised the ire of homesteaders, and none more so than boomers, who considered the public domain as their birthright and who wanted the same access to it as cattlemen.[42]

Organized and mutually profitable grazing leases in the Cherokee Outlet were not replicated farther south. From Oklahoma Proper west to the Texas Panhandle and south to the Red River, ad hoc arrangements between cattle-men and Indians produced nothing short of chaos. Some cattlemen paid Indians a pittance for grazing rights; others simply let their cattle roam where they pleased under the purview of armed cowboys. An agent for the Sac and Fox Tribe described cowboy depredations in his part of Indian Territory: "They come at will, go at will, and do as they please, there being no law to intimidate them, no force for local protection. Armed generally with two 45-caliber revolvers and a Winchester, they are 'Monarchs of all they survey,' and a dispute is studiously avoided by the natives."[43]

While cattlemen who had negotiated grazing leases with individual tribes were clashing over range apportionment, competitors without leasing agree-ments were showing their displeasure by refusing to move their herds. Secretary of the Interior Teller adopted a policy of nonrecognition of Indian leases, even though he favored cattlemen with leases over those who allowed their cattle to graze on Indian land without leases.[44] But there was not much he could do to prevent new herds from grazing their way into Indian Territory and exacerbating an already tense situation. Cheyennes and Arapahos did not know what to fear the most: cattlemen's encroachments on their reservations or starvation.[45]

When government-issued beef was reduced by a third in 1882, soldiers at Forts Sill, Reno, and Supply braced for hostilities. Although they maintained a tenuous peace, experienced soldiers knew that converting Plains Indians into farmers would take years, and denying them their beef allotments only served to exacerbate tensions and delay their inclusion in the national polity.[46] Nor was large-scale ranching much of an option for formerly nomadic tribespeople. In the absence of both capital and the business acumen to deploy it effectively, reservation Indians had little prospect of profiting from the grasslands that had nurtured their people for centuries. Indians often shot and ate the cattle they were supposed to use as breeding stock and oxen intended for overland freighting ventures. As Cheyenne and Arapaho agent D. B. Dyer noted, the Indian method of wintering livestock was tantamount to slow starvation. "The skeleton frames of last winter's dead," declared the agent, "dot the prairies within view of the agency with sickening frequency."[47]

Not all Indians stood by idly as cattlemen despoiled their reservations. Secretary of the Interior Teller reported great progress at various Indian agencies in teaching former nomads to raise and tend their own stock. He estimated that about half of the reservations were better suited to tending stock than farming. Besides, he reasoned, most Indians were more disposed to herding than coaxing crops out of the ground.[48] At the same time, Indians were catching on to the art of entrepreneurship. In August 1884, a delegation of Comanches, Kiowas, and Wichitas called on the Department of the Interior to see about leasing between two and three million acres in Indian Territory to cattlemen.[49] A few Indians became savvy enough in the ways of commerce to elevate themselves to the inner circle of Gilded Age businessmen. When St. Louis hosted the largest gathering of stockmen ever assembled, in November 1884, discussions ranged from cattle quarantines occasioned by Texas fever, to a proposed national cattle trail to replace those that were disappearing beneath the tide of westward migration, and shipping cattle via rail. Among the most frequent contributors to those discussions was Colonel F. B. Severs, known far and wide as the "Jay Gould of the Creek Nation," who complemented his cattle business with stores and a variety of other moneymaking enterprises.[50]

Enterprising individuals notwithstanding, most Indians remained at a distinct disadvantage against the capitalist juggernaut. Major General John Pope, who never stopped making suggestions to improve Indians' lot, injected a dose of reason into debates over the Indian problem. "These Indians cannot be made self-supporting within any calculable time," he explained, "and the sooner that fact is recognized the sooner will the management of them be made to conform to the commonest dictates of humanity."[51]

Major General Pope's pleas for humanitarian treatment of Indians might have fallen on deaf ears in frontier villages and Washington, D.C., but not at the Darlington Indian Agency, where U.S. Indian agent John D. Miles distinguished himself as one of the staunchest defenders of Indian rights. As a Quaker and progeny of English and French parents from Ohio, Miles was a perfect choice to carry out President Grant's peace policy on the Cheyenne and Arapaho Reservation, where he served as Indian agent from 1872 to 1884. During his twelve years at the Darlington Indian Agency, Miles earned the respect of Indians and their advocates for restructuring ration distribution procedures, utilizing Indian workers, and encouraging investments in cattle. In an effort to convert illegal grazing into something positive, Miles offered cattlemen grazing privileges in return for periodic beef deliveries to Indians. For precedent, he looked to the Cherokee Outlet, where Cherokees had tacit approval from the federal government to lease their land to cattlemen. When cattlemen in the Cheyenne and Arapaho Reservation balked, Miles rose to the challenge and called for military support. Weapons were brandished and words were exchanged while officials in Washington, D.C., scrambled to sort out escalating conflicts between reservation Indians, cattlemen, Indian agents, and military commanders. Meanwhile, Miles and his counterpart among the Kiowas and Comanches, P. B. Hunt, did their best to keep Indians from starving by brokering informal agreements to exchange beef for grazing rights.[52]

In August 1882, Agent Miles threw down the gauntlet to cattlemen who were allowing their cattle to graze on the cheap, and sometimes free of charge, on reservation land. Armed with instructions from the Indian Office, he published an ultimatum in the *Cheyenne Transporter*, declaring a one-dollar penalty for each unauthorized animal and warning trespassers whose stock remained on Indian land after August 10 that they would be removed by force of arms.[53] Few were surprised when stockmen refused to budge. As though Miles needed reminding, an army officer offered the opinion that cattlemen would remove their herds only at gunpoint.[54] As cattlemen continued to encroach on Indian land, Agent Miles did what he could to mitigate cattlemen's depredations and alleviate Indian suffering.

The stakes escalated in early 1883 when Secretary Teller ordered all cattlemen without leases to vacate Indian Territory by February 1. "To talk about removing cattle-men and their herds from the Territory in twenty days is the merest nonsense," ran a pro-stockman rant in the *Barbour County (Kansas) Index*. "They have nowhere to go, and if they had the finest location imaginable, their herds are scattered and at this season of the year it would be impossible to move them if they were together, as it would be ruinous in the extreme." The Medicine Lodge, Kansas, newspaper insisted that removal in twenty days would require every soldier in the army to mount up and get to work immediately. In a complaint that rings through the ages, the *Index* reserved special scorn for "kid gloved gentlemen" who sat in their cushioned chairs in the nation's capital, oblivious to the facts on the ground, and imagined that vast herds of cattle could be removed from Indian Territory in less than three weeks in the dead of winter.[55] Then again, most cattlemen were prescient enough to see the handwriting on the wall. As cowman B. H. Campbell admitted in a letter to the secretary of the Interior in January 1883, "Every man with enterprise enough to build a fence has the intelligence to know that we have no permanent rights in the Indian Territory."[56]

By the early 1880s, endless miles of barbed wire were pushing long-distance cattle drives toward obsolescence and compelling cattlemen to abandon the open range in favor of well-defined (that is, fenced) ranches. As farms and ranches consumed increasing acreage across the southern plains, those fences were intended not to keep animals and trespassers *out*, but rather, to keep livestock *in*—a cultural shift with profound implications for the settlement of the West.[57]

In January 1883, a large contingent of cattlemen descended on Washington, D.C., to urge the Department of the Interior to lease them acreage in Indian Territory and, furthermore, to allow them to erect fences and thereby shut out smaller operators. Although Secretary Teller had already refused to comply with cattlemen's requests, he signaled a willingness to allow them to graze their cattle at about fifteen cents per head.[58] Such reports filled the press throughout the 1880s and inflamed already toxic relations between cattlemen, Indians, and prospective settlers. Foreign investment in the West in general and Indian Territory in particular, coupled with the extraordinary latitude that the federal government was granting to ranchers, spawned a new Gilded Age moniker: "cattle barons." Deserved or not, the moniker stuck, and it became ubiquitous in debates about grazing rights.

In August 1884, the *New York Sun* entered the fray with an article asserting that the B.I.T. (i.e., the Beautiful Indian Territory) had been converted into a congressional cow pasture. While easterners were bemoaning Indians' fate and David Payne's boomers were dodging soldiers on their way to Oklahoma Proper, some of the most fertile land on the continent was turning into immense pastureland fenced with barbed wire. The author of the article, who signed his name as "Pioneer," cited three egregious examples of preferential treatment accorded to wealthy and influential stockmen: Cherokees were leasing their six-million-acre Outlet (about the size of New Hampshire) to cattlemen for the grand sum of two cents an acre; Standard Oil Cattle Company was leasing a thirty-by-fifteen-mile tract just south of the Kansas border for about the same price; and the XYZ Ranch was stocked with hundreds of thousands of breeding cows, calves, and expensive shorthorn bulls. Pioneer, clearly a literary sort, closed his broadside with a nod to Shakespeare: "Your readers may as well spare their grief for the 'poor Indian' until some attempt is made to encroach upon his domains, and in the meantime open their eyes and ears and nostrils to the fact that there is 'something rotten' in this beautiful Indian Territory, which contains public lands large enough to make two or three kingdoms like Denmark."[59]

As Pioneer and his ilk railed against predatory cattlemen, congressmen pondered the wisdom of allowing foreigners, and especially British citizens, to acquire some twenty million acres of America's public domain. Branding ranchmen, foreign and domestic, as cattle barons, critics reserved their most passionate tirades for "rich and insolent foreigners who sought to monopolize the public lands and to keep American citizens from securing homes on the public domain."[60] Such criticism seemed justified in 1885 when commissioner of the General Land Office William A. J. Sparks (1885–88) reported to Congress that speculators were to blame for creating land monopolies throughout cow country. Sparks went on to accuse cattlemen west of the one hundredth meridian of enclosing the best forage and water resources, falsifying titles with signatures of cowboys and family members, employing fictitious identities to stake their claims, and faking improvements to appear to be in compliance with public lands laws.[61] In their defense, cattlemen seemed to have history on their side: they had pioneered the southern plains in accordance with the unwritten law of the open range; proposed grazing leases with Indian tribes; and petitioned Congress to uphold rights that they believed were theirs. Perhaps their most compelling argument was that the arid plains were unfit for anything besides grazing, and all they wanted was to protect their considerable investments in keeping things as they were.[62]

Nevertheless, stories of unscrupulous stockmen and politicians on the take became grist not only for journalists and congressmen but also for reformers who sought a balance between the fruits of capitalism and the fairness of democracy. Two of those reformers were A. P. Jackson and Kingman, Kansas, realtor E. C. Cole. Following several excursions into Indian Territory in the 1880s in search of promising townsites, they cowrote a book under the rather ponderous title, *Oklahoma! Politically and Geographically Described—History and Guide to the Indian Territory*. Published in 1885, the book combines biographical sketches of boomer leaders with descriptions of Indian tribes, natural resources, geography, and topography to produce a blistering account of nefarious goings-on in Indian Territory that resonated with the passions that fueled the boomer movement and, four years hence, would produce the Run of 1889. "There never was a more open and glaring swindle upon the face of the American continent," declared the coauthors. As petitions arrived and then died in the Interior Department, home seekers were doomed to failure in their crusade against three of the nation's most powerful adversaries: cattlemen; congressmen; and the U.S. Army.[63]

"The cattle-kings, the land-gobblers, and their followers must go," continued Jackson and Cole. "Oklahoma shall be the home of the free, where, almost at the doors of the capitalist and the poor man, lies a country whose native richness invites, whose fertility will reward the honest farmer with abundant harvest, whose genial climate invigorates and promises long life at small cost to man, and succulent grasses for his cattle, almost the year round."[64]

While Jackson and Cole were trying to change the course of history with a printing press, boomers were using their feet to accomplish the same thing, which was to compel their government to find a balance between the ideals enshrined in the U.S. Constitution and opportunities afforded by free-market capitalism. With a backward glance at the businessmen, politicians, and Indians who jockeyed for advantage in the range cattle industry, we return to a squalid camp on Kansas's southern border in December 1880, where boomers were losing patience with a government that denied them their birthright in Oklahoma Proper, and where the politics of settlement were turning all of Indian Territory into a battleground of Gilded Age politics.

CHAPTER FIVE

Boomers

======

If these people would pay a little attention to newspaper reading
they would know better than to go in there, as the whole country
is closely watched by United States soldiers.

Cheyenne Transporter, *February 10, 1881*

From July 1881 through August 1884, Captain Payne led at least eight intrusions into Indian Territory. Added to his three expeditions in 1880, his attempts to colonize Oklahoma failed nearly a dozen times. Such was the frequency of boomer intrusions that the War Department lost track of them. But not so with cattlemen such as Montford Johnson, Cass Wantland, and Bill McClure, who received regular lessons in boomer tactics in the form of burned ranges and butchered livestock. Cattlemen learned to recognize smoke on the horizon during the fall and winter months as evidence that boomers were passing through their ranges. Montford Johnson's grandson, Neil, declared that boomers sometimes set fires in an effort to weaken cattlemen's resolve and hasten their departure from the Oklahoma country.[1]

Boomers represented an astonishing cross section of American society—professionals, farmers, mechanics, scouts, cowboys, and practically everyone else who populated frontier towns. But the vast majority were down on their luck and desperate for a fresh start. Most lived in tents, wagons, and, if all else failed, holes in the ground. Their food was coarse, and their clothes were often soaked from rain and sleet and perilous river crossings. Worst of all, they lived under constant threat of arrest while cattlemen enjoyed the benefits of their socioeconomic status.[2]

Their ranks thinned by inclement weather, die-hard boomers camped near Caldwell in early 1881 were disappointed to learn that Dr. Robert Wilson, the Dallas millionaire who had volunteered to plead their case in Washington, D.C., had run into a brick wall, as President Hayes refused to change his mind about boomer scofflaws.[3] To alleviate their boredom and earn some cash while they waited for more encouraging news, some boomers at the Fall Creek camp freighted supplies from Wichita to Camp Wood, a military camp just south of the Kansas border. Whatever they thought about working for the same government that was keeping them out of Oklahoma Proper has been lost to history. Meanwhile, the *Wichita City Eagle* chimed in with its own downbeat assessment: unless Congress reversed its policies, pro-settlement activities were nothing more than "time and wind thrown away."[4]

In the days before scientific polling, gauging public sentiment was a tricky proposition. But there were plenty of folks who were determined to sway it. The *Cheyenne Transporter*, eager to discredit the boomer movement at every opportunity, dismissed reports that Caldwell merchants were supportive of boomers camped outside their town. As evidence, the *Transporter* crowed about a fundraising effort that was supposed to supply the boomer camp with a thousand dollars' worth of provisions but that brought in a mere thirty-five dollars. Further evidence of dwindling enthusiasm came from reports that the Fall Creek camp was all but deserted.[5] When six boomers were arrested and detained at Fort Reno in February 1881, the *Transporter* published a warning, quoted as the epigraph to this chapter, to boomers who scoffed the law at their peril.

As winter turned to spring, attention shifted from bedraggled boomers at the Fall Creek camp to Judge Isaac Parker's court in Fort Smith, where Payne had been ordered to answer a federal charge of conspiring to violate the Non-Intercourse Act of 1834. Released on his own recognizance in the fall of 1880, Payne was finally getting his day in court. Yet it was not exactly the day in court that he wanted, as the judge's mandate was to focus on a single issue: did Payne enter Indian Territory twice? If so, he was liable to a penalty of one thousand dollars for the second invasion, as the first one in the spring of 1880 subjected him and his followers only to expulsion. In what amounted to a civil suit arising from a single charge, it was beyond Judge Parker's jurisdiction

Unknown artist, *Capt. Payne Crossing the Line Going to Oklahoma.*
From A. P. Jackson and E. C. Cole, Oklahoma! Politically and Topographically Described; History
and Guide to the Indian Territory; Biographical Sketches of Capt. David L. Payne, W. L. Couch,
Wm. H. Osborn, and Others *(Kansas City, Mo.: Ramsey, Millet, and Hudson, 1885), facing p. 12.*

in the Western District of Arkansas to decide whether or not parts of Indian
Territory were public lands.[6] Payne's attorneys based their argument on the
fact that the federal government had purchased tribal land in central Indian
Territory with the intention of settling Indians and freedmen on it and had
failed to do so, thus leaving approximately fourteen million acres open to
non-Indian settlement under homesteading and preemption laws—or, as the
Cherokee Advocate put it, "squatter sovereignty."[7]

Ever since the international council in Eufaula in October 1880, the Five
Tribes had been anxiously awaiting the court's decision. George W. Stidham of
the Muskogee Creek Nation, a wealthy, self-made merchant who owned several
farms and about forty slaves before the Civil War, spoke for opinion leaders
throughout the nations in denouncing a bill sponsored by Senator George
Graham Vest (D-Mo.; 1879–1903) to organize a territorial government in Indian
Territory. For Stidham, Vest's so-called Oklahoma bill would be nothing less
than "a premeditated and willful" violation of sacred treaties. Two aspects of
Senator Vest's bill were particularly galling to Indians: it compelled them to give
up their common ownership of land and agree to ownership in severalty; and it
forced them to accept U.S. citizenship. As far as Stidham was concerned, Vest's

professed concern for protecting Indian rights from an encroaching civilization was disingenuous at best and, at worst, a blatant attempt to hasten tribal
disintegration and leave hapless Indians at the mercy of a capitalist juggernaut.[8]

In the Five Tribes' estimation, not even the Reconstruction Treaties of
1866, which informed the boomer movement's polemics, could nullify treaties
dating back to the period of Indian removal in the 1830s.[9] They were fortunate
to count on the support of Secretary of the Interior Samuel J. Kirkwood
(1881–82), who assured Principal Chief Samuel Checote that he, too, was
vexed by boomers' repeated incursions into Indian country and hoped that
Judge Parker would rule in the Indians' favor. "I will say individually I am
in full sympathy with the policy heretofore adopted by the Department in
protecting the rights of the Indians," wrote Kirkwood, "and shall use all the
powers of the Government so far as the same can be made available to keep
invaders out of the Territory unless a contrary rule shall be established by the
decision of a competent tribunal."[10]

Boomers had high hopes that their movement would find vindication in
Judge Parker's court. Payne returned to Wichita from Fort Smith to a hero's
welcome, and everyone settled in for what turned into a two-month wait.

Judge Parker rendered his lengthy decision at the beginning of the court's
May 1881 term, and it did not bode well for the boomer movement. After reciting a familiar litany of boomer invasions, arrests, and evictions, Judge Parker
reviewed the treaties that had defined relations between the United States and
various tribes from the removal period of the 1830s through the Reconstruction
Treaties of 1866. Then came his conclusion: the U.S. government purchased
tribal land in Oklahoma Proper for the express purpose of relocating tribes and
freedmen, and any attempt to open the area to homesteading was contrary to
law. As he wound toward his conclusion, Judge Parker hinted at how absurd
it would have been for the federal government to buy land and then allow it
to degenerate into lawlessness.[11]

Boomers were stunned by the court's ruling. Undeterred and lacking a
thousand dollars to pay his fine, Payne heaped praise on the citizens of Wichita
for their untiring support and enjoined the faithful to remain steadfast "until
victory perched upon their banners." Switching from offense to defense,
Payne vehemently denied rumors that railroads were supporting him and
insisted that he stood shoulder to shoulder with hopeful homesteaders, even
as suspicions persisted that the railroads had him in their pockets. Payne's
stirring rhetoric notwithstanding, the *Wichita City Eagle* detected a hint of

despair in a boomer gathering whose enthusiasm seemed to be dissipating to a point where it might never recover.[12]

As boomers pondered their next move, the *Cheyenne Transporter* remained true to form in admonishing its readers not to make fools of themselves by squandering their money on Payne and his fellow schemers.[13] The Five Tribes, meanwhile, were breathing a collective sigh of relief. As G. W. Grayson noted in his report to the National Council of the Muskogee Nation in October 1881, "It is pleasant to know too that in this decision of the United States Court, the Indians have become possessed of one of the strongest levers ever yet placed within their grasp for compelling a just recognition of their rights and the integrity of our whole Indian Territory."[14]

Judge Parker's decision notwithstanding, black leaders envisioned Oklahoma Proper as a potential haven where former slaves could acquire land at little or no cost. As early as April 1882, delegates at an all-black convention in Parsons, Kansas, asked the federal government to reserve every third section of Oklahoma land for southern blacks. Two months later, Senator Henry W. Blair (R-N.H.; 1879–91) introduced a bill that would have given blacks the right to settle on public lands in Oklahoma Proper. Although the bill did not pass, black opinion leaders never gave up in promoting black settlement.

Throughout the 1880s, Kansas's leading black newspaper, the *Topeka American Citizen*, kept a close eye on the boomer movement and political maneuvering in Washington.[15] Across the border in Missouri, the Freedmen's Oklahoma Association looked to the Oklahoma country as its own version of the Promised Land. The St. Louis–based organization, branded in the *Cheyenne Transporter* as "another form of the Payne lunacy," issued a circular promising 160 acres for any African American willing to settle in Oklahoma Proper. Citing public lands laws dating back to the Louisiana Purchase, a frustrated commissioner of the General Land Office countered with a blistering denial that Indian Territory was open to settlement to freedmen or anyone else who lacked Indian ancestry.[16]

———————

In July 1881 Payne switched tactics and made for Texas where a thin strip of (supposedly) public land running south to the Red River afforded an opportunity to reach Oklahoma without crossing the nearly sixty miles of Indian land that had proved so troublesome for invaders from Kansas. To help sway public opinion in his direction, he stopped off in Denison to deliver a lecture.

And then, somewhere near Gainesville, he and a small party crossed the Red River to begin the fourth boomer expedition. When that attempt came to naught, Payne regrouped and invited the Texas faithful to join him on a fifth invasion, tentatively planned for October.[17] "Captain Payne has gone upon the war path again and daubed on the war paint," declared the *Weekly Democratic Statesman* in Austin, Texas.[18] Payne and a reportedly large following crossed the Red River at the mouth of the Little Wichita River in Clay County, Texas, in late November with expectations of reaching Oklahoma Proper in a week.[19]

Reports of a sizeable invasion force turned out to be exaggerated. Certain that more boomers were camped somewhere along the North Canadian River and waiting for the Texas Colony to arrive, Payne called for volunteers to locate their boomer brethren who had invaded the Oklahoma country and to assure them that reinforcements were on the way. Only one person stepped forward—William H. Osburn, an Indiana native, who had recently been elected as secretary of Payne's Oklahoma Colony. Likely fortified by the colony's faith in him, Osburn and his dog, Jack, set out on a solo journey to Oklahoma Proper.[20] Meanwhile, Payne's lectures were failing to gain much traction in Dallas. According to the *Dallas Daily Herald*, boomers were once again trespassing "on the forbidden ground"; and once again, they were sure to come "in contact with the toe of the boot worn by Uncle Sam." The *Weekly Democratic Statesman*'s advice to its readers was unequivocal: leave Oklahoma Payne alone, as people who accompanied him into Indian Territory were "very likely to get themselves into serious trouble."[21]

But trouble was exactly what Payne was looking for. He dismissed reports that a large contingent of boomers had been evicted from Indian Territory in late 1881 and vowed to mount another invasion within days.[22] He kept his word and vowed to mount two invasions in early 1882, the first in January to Payne's Springs in present-day Oklahoma City, and the second in February to Deep Fork near Arcadia in what would become eastern Oklahoma County.[23]

Back in the nation's capital, Secretary of the Interior Kirkwood celebrated the end of his one-year term under President James A. Garfield (R; Mar. 4–Sept. 19, 1881) with yet another report on Indian Territory. His report covered familiar ground and can be summarized in four somewhat redundant points: (1) no lands in Indian Territory were open to settlement, either to freedmen or anyone else, under the provisions of public lands laws; (2) there had never been a time since the Louisiana Purchase of 1803 when land within the limits of Indian Territory was open to settlement; (3) the United States held legal title to Indian Territory and, through various treaty obligations and acts of Congress, reserved it for Indian tribes; and (4) the entire Indian Territory was designated as "Indian country" as defined in the Non-Intercourse Act of 1834, and a later enactment in 1856, which expressly prohibited non-Indian settlement in the area and authorized military force to prevent entry.[24]

The federal government's no-nonsense position on the Oklahoma Question was easier to grasp than the whereabouts of Captain Payne. In April, Kansas newspapers buzzed with reports that Payne and his boomers were camped on the Canadian River. The *Cheyenne Transporter* begged to differ. "Payne is not in Oklahoma," ran a typical rant about Payne's tactics, "and if he has been there since the last time he was bounced he has kept well concealed."[25]

To determine the army's take on events, which were increasingly hard to sort out, the *Leavenworth Weekly Times* secured an interview with General John Pope. Asked if Payne had been arrested recently, the general replied that, frankly, he had no idea. But he might have been, as troops were scouring Indian Territory and were bound to catch up with him sooner or later. General Pope then reminded his listener of the slow pace of communication in those vast environs. It took time to locate boomers, make arrests, travel seventy or eighty miles on horseback from the site of the arrests to Fort Reno, and then telegraph the news to military headquarters. Pope was clearly annoyed by Payne's insistence on having his day in court, particularly as Judge Parker had already levied a thousand-dollar fine against him—which, as noted, he had been too poor to pay, thus rendering the government's courtroom victory rather hollow—so what was there to determine? "He is strangely persistent in his efforts to settle the Oklahoma district," concluded Pope.[26]

To assist soldiers in their hunt for boomers, anti-settlement folks along Kansas's southern border kept an eye out for suspicious activity. One of them was H. C. Hambly of Parsons. In a letter to Secretary of the Interior Henry Teller, Hambly reported on a Payne settlement and called on the War Department to disband it. Hambly estimated the camp's population at 1,500. Upon investigation, Captain Henry Carroll found Hambly's estimate to be on the high side. In three months of intensive scouting, his detachment had discovered only one small party, which was duly arrested and escorted out of Indian Territory.[27] This might have been the same party that passed near the Darlington Indian Agency in early June and that the *Cheyenne Transporter* described gleefully and in depressing detail as "a bedraggled and forlorn looking party."[28]

Payne had more expeditions in the works for 1882. But first he traveled to Washington, D.C., to plead his case before Secretary Teller. To squelch rumors that he had promised to protect Payne, Teller delivered an ultimatum: it would be imprudent and perhaps even disastrous for Payne to lead yet another invasion, and Teller would do everything in his power to enforce federal statutes against homesteading in what the Hayes administration defined as Indian country. Predictably, Payne ignored Teller's warnings and returned to Kansas, where he mustered his followers for two more invasions, the first to Deep Fork in May, and the second to present-day Jones in eastern Oklahoma County in August. Both ended badly, and predictably, for the boomer faithful, with the usual rough treatment at the hands of soldiers and evictions.[29]

The year wound to a close with seemingly clear evidence that Payne had joined forces with none other than railroad mogul Jay Gould—"the latest thing in the way of 'railroad combinations,'" declared the *Wichita City Eagle*.[30] Rumors were flying, and gaining traction, about Payne's relationship with the Frisco, which Gould had controlled since its purchase of the Boston-based Atlantic and Pacific Railroad.[31] Everyone knew that the Frisco wanted to build a line through Indian Territory to Albuquerque. But as of September 1882, it was stalled at Tulsa. Yet even then, a survey corps under Captain H. W. Gleason was surveying a route from the Arkansas River toward the Darlington Indian Agency and Fort Reno that would connect with a survey completed in 1871. Understandably alarmed, Cheyennes and Arapahos met in council on September 16 and agreed to contact the secretary of the Interior to see what he had to say about it. After heated debate, the delegates decided not to interfere with the surveyors with one caveat: they expected railroad officials to confer with them before building a line through their reservation.[32]

Perhaps even more important than promoting settlement, Gould aimed to capture the grandest prize of all in America's rapidly developing midsection: the cattle trade. If Gould could develop a proper railroad infrastructure through the heart of Indian Territory, cattle driven overland from Texas to the railheads in Kansas and shipped to Kansas City and Chicago via the Atchison, Topeka, and Santa Fe Railway could be diverted to St. Louis via the St. Louis–San Francisco Railway. With farms and homes dotting the prairie, lawmakers would be compelled to prohibit cattle drives and leave it to the Frisco to supply eastern markets with western beef at whatever rates it chose to charge. "Thus," concluded the *Eagle*, "the road could be made immensely profitable from the start, even if the local traffic amounts to little or nothing."[33]

Jay Gould was not the only tycoon who aimed to corner the cattle market. If, as the *New York Sun* predicted, Indian Territory were dissolved by the end of 1883, Gould had plenty of competitors ready to participate in the opening of the Promised Land. "And what a race of iron monsters that opening will start!" declared the *Sun* in February 1883. The St. Louis–San Francisco Railway's competitors included the Atchison, Topeka & Santa Fe; the Southern Kansas Railway; the Fort Scott and Gulf; the Missouri Pacific; and the Little Rock and Fort Smith. All of these companies operated terminals near Indian Territory's border, and all had completed their surveys through the area in anticipation of extending their lines. "Powerful forces and gigantic interests are at work," continued the *Sun*, "and Capt. Payne, with his Oklahoma boom, is only a part of a mighty whole." Even though Indian Territory and its storied cattle trails were not quite on the brink of extinction, their days were surely numbered.[34]

If Payne was indeed in cahoots with one of America's richest men, then he had much to ponder in early September 1882 as he and forty others cooled their heels in the guardhouse at Fort Reno following his ninth boomer intrusion and subsequent arrest. The boomer party's arrival at Fort Reno came a couple of weeks after its commandant since 1880, Major George M. Randall, was reassigned to another post. With Agent Miles's cooperation and guidance in the ways of Cheyennes and Arapahos, Major Randall had become adept at adjudicating disputes and ensuring compliance with treaty stipulations.[35] Major Randall was less popular among Payne and his fellow prisoners. The *Cherokee Advocate* wondered if the boomers would be sent once again to Fort Smith for trial or marched to the Kansas border and admonished never to return.[36]

What boomers lacked was a vehicle to counter the bad publicity they were receiving in anti-boomer newspapers, to popularize Oklahoma Proper as the yeoman farmer's birthright, and to earn their cause recognition as a bona fide political movement. All that changed with the publication of the *Oklahoma War Chief*.

The first issue of the twenty-eight-column weekly newspaper, branded on its masthead as the "Official Organ of Payne's Oklahoma Colony" and supported by advertising and sales at ten cents per copy, rolled off the press in Wichita on January 12, 1883. Its editor, A. W. Harris, promised that each issue would be packed with news from Indian Territory and surrounding states as well as from Congress. As was common in the frontier press, the *War Chief* published articles from other boomer-friendly newspapers, most notably the

William L. Couch.
Courtesy of Oklahoma Images Collection, Metropolitan Library System of Oklahoma County.

Wichita Times and the *Kansas City Times*, as well as dispatches from its own correspondents. The *Wichita Times* was effusive in its welcoming message: "The *War Chief* is a big boom for the colonists in helping them in the grand project of opening, for the abodes of men, this now uninhabited region, only used as a hunting ground." The *Times* ended its welcome with a flourish that caught on as the brash new newspaper's call to arms: "All hail to the Chief!"[37]

Harris was clear in identifying boomers' adversaries: officials who lived off the public dole; corporations and individuals bent on controlling public lands; and rival newspapers in league with the alleged land grabbers.[38] The *War Chief* wasted no time in defending Payne in his lawsuit against General John Pope in his capacity as commander of the U.S. Army at Fort Leavenworth.[39] Scheduled for U.S. Circuit Court in Topeka, the trial was expected to settle, once and for all, the question of whether or not Oklahoma Proper was part of Indian country and therefore off-limits to settlement.[40]

While the *Oklahoma War Chief* was girding for action, about twenty-five members of the Ewing Town Company met with Captain Payne, recently freed from jail, in his office on a Tuesday evening in January 1883 to elect officers. Among them was William L. Couch, a native of North Carolina, who had moved with his family to Kansas shortly after the Civil War and purchased a farm near Douglass in Butler County. As railroads crisscrossed the land, Couch took advantage of business opportunities afforded by the quickening pace of transportation to become a fixture in southern Kansas business circles. His ventures included selling grain and operating a grain elevator, dealing in horses and mules, and running a combination hardware and grocery store.

Whatever prospects Couch thought he had in frontier entrepreneurship were derailed in an unforgiving marketplace. With his resources depleted and options dwindling, he was receptive to Captain Payne's proselytizing and, by 1879, was committed to the boomer movement and ready for a fresh start.[41] Praised in the *War Chief* as "an active, wide-awake and zealous member" of the Ewing Town Company, Couch was elected as treasurer and appointed to a five-man committee charged with revising the colony's laws and articles of incorporation.[42] Six years and three months hence, the zeal that Couch exhibited as a Ewing Town Company officer would reveal itself in his election as the first mayor of Oklahoma City.

Throughout its brief but illustrious history as a mouthpiece for boomer news and tirades, the *War Chief* aimed its invective at its two archenemies: railroads and cattlemen. Railroads laid tracks where they pleased and obtained huge chunks of real estate along the way, but howls rent the air when law-abiding citizens tried to claim a few acres. While railroads were slicing their way across the land, stockmen were becoming accustomed to grazing their cattle for a pittance on land that was supposed to belong to the Indians. The *War Chief* unleashed its fury when the secretary of the Interior announced his intention to extend a long-term lease on 2,400,000 acres in Indian Territory to "a company of cattle kings." In the *War Chief*'s reasoning, such leases facilitated the creation of beef monopolies, gave cattlemen free rein to use prime farmland for grazing, and postponed the opening of Oklahoma Proper to homesteading. The *Augusta Republican* likened the barriers erected to protect the cattle kings to "a great Chinese wall, only more forbidding in its character and effects."[43]

As the *Oklahoma War Chief* was muscling its way into debates over public lands policies, Payne was leading yet another incursion (his tenth) into the forbidden land.[44] A circular announcing the invasion, slated to commence on or before February 1, 1883, from Arkansas City, described Oklahoma Proper as the Eden of modern times. The *New York Sun* cautioned its readers to take such hyperbole with a grain of salt, as this particular garden spot was no more open to settlement than Central Park and Boston Common. As Payne and his boomers had been evicted before, the *Sun* predicted that he most likely would be evicted again.[45]

Caution was the furthest thing from Captain Payne's mind as he braved cold and disagreeable conditions and made for the border to rendezvous with his invasion force. Among the onlookers who lined the boomers' route through southern Kansas were Captain Couch's children, who scampered up a tree to get a better view of the caravan as it passed by their house.[46] Payne's first entry in a handwritten diary that he kept for the duration of the invasion practically oozes optimism: "Am sure that we have over one hundred wagons, others coming all the time."[47] By the time they reached Deer Creek to camp, Payne's feet, fingers, and toes were frozen, and his diary entries became less sanguine. "I am not well," he wrote. Still, he managed to record an impression that his fellow boomers were enduring the cold "like heroes."[48]

One of those heroes was C. P. Wickmiller, the expedition's official photographer, whose images of boomers trudging across a frozen landscape took center stage in the boomers' public relations campaign. As the boomer movement faded into history, they became prized possessions among the generation of 1889. Wickmiller (better known as "Wick"), who was something of a pioneer in using photography to shape public opinion, admitted his shortcomings when it came to genuine pioneering in the dead of winter. "Everything was one mass of ice," wrote Wickmiller. "While making the first picture crossing the line into Oklahoma, my hands froze so in a short time I had soft hands. Camping with temperature below zero was no fun for a tenderfoot."[49]

While the boomers were slogging through the winter landscape, the national press was buzzing with news of the invasion and its consequences for Indians. Opinion was divided between Indians who wanted to rely on soldiers to kick the boomers out and others who were spoiling for a fight. Secretary of War Robert Todd Lincoln (1881–85) had furnished the secretary of the Interior with copies of telegrams from General Pope in which he described his preparations to secure Indian Territory from intrusion. Pope did not expect forcible resistance, but he wanted to prepare for any eventuality. Meanwhile, a bill had been introduced into the U.S. House of Representatives providing for two years' imprisonment at hard labor for anyone caught trespassing in Indian Territory. The only exception would be for immigrants on their way to more cordial surroundings.[50]

Blissfully unaware of what might be in store for them if they were caught and convicted of trespassing, boomers watched sullenly as ninety soldiers rode into the campsite they had dubbed "Camp Alice" in honor of Alice McPherson, a boomer's daughter who was about twelve years old and, in W. H. Osburn's recollection, "a very pretty child." The camp was located on the North Canadian River about three miles north and slightly west of present-day Jones in eastern Oklahoma County. Four more companies of soldiers were on their way. The commanding officer sent for Captain Payne to inform him that he was under arrest. "We had some angry words," wrote Payne, "but I consented to the arrest and was allowed the privilege of our camp." Predictably, demoralization set in, and by noon on February 10, half the camp had departed for parts unknown. Payne admitted defeat and advised his followers to pack up and head for home.[51] A correspondent for the *Walnut Valley (Kansas) Times*, almost certainly C. P. Wickmiller, recalled that everyone was disappointed to abandon such a fine country that their government had chosen to reserve for "the great cattle kings and the vagabond Indian."[52]

By the time Payne reached Fort Reno, an old army complaint and a fearful cough were taking a toll on his health, and he was too sick to make entries in his diary for at least two days. He and his fellow captives eventually received word that a military detachment would escort them to the Kansas line and from there to Caldwell, where they would be discharged. This was a "cowardly act," fumed Payne in his diary. "They will not give us any chance in court." Nor would they give their captives a break from their misery. On their three-day slog from Camp Alice to Fort Reno, the five hundred–plus boomers subsisted on beans and biscuits without spoons.[53]

"Safe and sound in Caldwell," declared Wickmiller at journey's end. "Captain Payne was a typical Westerner, a natural leader. You could not help liking him nor say 'no.'"[54] Ill and exhausted, Payne closed his diary by describing the weather in Caldwell as beautiful.[55]

Following the boomers' eviction from Camp Alice, detention at Fort Reno, and a particularly dreary forced march back to Kansas, the war of words went into overdrive. The *Cheyenne Transporter* declared that colonists were beginning to openly curse Captain Payne; some threatened to make "short work of that swindler should he fall into their hands."[56] The *War Chief* fought back, declaring that the government's insistence on denying God-fearing Americans their birthright was nothing less than a subversion of the nation's ideals. "All of this talk and all of this action upon the part of the Government officials is in striking contrast with the boasted genius of this Republic," declared the boomer mouthpiece a couple of weeks after the invaders returned from Camp Alice.

"It is a wretched travesty upon the lauded palladium of American liberty."[57] Editorialist J. S. Wilson's paean to hardy pioneers, published in the *Kansas City Times* and reprinted in the *War Chief* on March 2, 1883, hit on a theme that historian Frederick Jackson Turner would popularize a decade hence as the Progressive Era's most compelling argument for American exceptionalism: the frontier thesis of American history. "The pioneer is a character who travels in advance of civilization, and westward as the star of empire takes its course," wrote Wilson. "He is the conquering hero, who marches with an ax in one hand and a rifle in the other, building up new communities, erecting churches, planting school houses on every frontier. When he moves upon a country it means a repetition of the history of all the States."[58]

Wilson's manifesto railed against the inequalities embedded in Gilded Age capitalism, and it is suffused with passion about the perceived injustice of keeping Oklahoma off-limits to homesteaders.[59] What is more, travelers reported going for miles without catching sight of a single Indian in Indian Territory. One anonymous correspondent reported that he had journeyed sixty miles through the Cherokee Outlet and saw only a few dugouts and ramshackle cabins occupied by cowboys as evidence of human habitation. Farther south, he saw "nothing but earth, air and sky, wild beasts and birds."[60]

As passions swirled across the Great Plains over the definition and disposition of public lands, Payne's latest invasion attained mythic status as the March of the Five Hundred. For weeks after the invasion, the *War Chief* published firsthand accounts of the march, many of them supplied by men destined to participate in the Run of 1889 and the early development of Oklahoma City. The *Walnut Valley Times* correspondent likened the spirit at boomer campsites to the camaraderie among soldiers huddled around campfires during the Civil War. Now facing a whole new set of dangers on the Oklahoma frontier, boomers told ribald jokes as a way of alleviating their trepidation, thus stirring up memories of Stones River, Chickamauga, and the Wilderness. In the evenings, Payne expounded on the prospects for colonization.[61] Aside from the bitter cold, *War Chief* editor A. W. Harris's most poignant memories included the prevalence of buffalo soldiers sent to arrest them and the large U.S. flag that colonists flew to symbolize loyalty to their country. Commenting on the prospects for farming, Harris described Oklahoma as the "Italy of America."[62]

Wagon master Bill Couch was likewise moved to watch the American flag flutter in the breeze at the center of Camp Alice while boomers scrambled to select and improve their claims. Their ranks swelled with the arrival of 6 wagons and 25 men from Arkansas to bring their numbers to about 119 wagons and 600 men. Spirits heightened with news that about 150 men from Texas were camped some forty miles to the southwest on the South Canadian River. A like number of colonists from the Walden and Kansas City colonies were camped to the northeast on the Cimarron River. Altogether, Camp Alice was home to nine hundred souls—a credible force, to be sure, but not enough to turn the tide in the boomers' favor when soldiers showed up for what had become a familiar routine of arrests and evictions.

Before he joined his fellow boomers and their military escorts on their northward trek, the future mayor of Oklahoma City took a last look at the inviting landscape they were leaving behind, which would one day be encompassed in Greater Oklahoma City: "Now, in reference to the country, I will say that in my opinion the reports heretofore given of the richness of the land for agricultural purposes, the fine grasses for hay and grazing purposes, the quantity and quality of timber and water, and the climate, have not been overestimated; in fact, will say, and believe a majority of my comrades will witness, that the country is better, all things considered, than we expected to find."[63]

Scarcely had the boomers unloaded their wagons from their round-trip to Camp Alice than the national press began excoriating Oklahoma Payne. One pundit stretched the bounds of propriety by asking if "someone won't be good enough to shoot Capt. Payne." Incensed, the *War Chief* demanded to know what Payne had done to deserve such calumny, other than exercise his right as an American citizen to settle on public lands? True, he had taunted federal authorities by enlisting Wichita saloon keeper E. N. Ackley to defy laws against trading in intoxicating spirits in Indian country and to drive a wagon laden with whiskey and cigars on the Camp Alice expedition. But rather than bring Ackley to justice, his accusers turned him loose. Why? The reason was simple: to bring him into court for violating laws pertaining to trade and intercourse would bring Oklahoma Proper's legal status into question. Since his spring 1880 expedition, Payne had been trying to force a decision on the Oklahoma Question, but to no avail. All he had gotten was a thousand-dollar fine (a sum that apparently went unpaid, and a decision that he never bothered to appeal) from Judge Parker before he was released on his own recognizance.

Unknown artist, *Capt. Payne's Last Camp in Oklahoma.*
From *Jackson and Cole*, Oklahoma! *facing p. 18.*

The last thing the government wanted was a court case that would strike at the heart of its public lands policies.[64] The *War Chief* caught a pungent whiff of cattle droppings in the government's refusal to budge. It was an open secret that military and civilian officials had interests in the range cattle industry. Those same officials were allied with Indian agents, who were likewise hostile to the boomer cause. As noted in the *War Chief*, "Anything calculated even in the remotest future to stop the flow of 'Government pap' to them is certain to receive their most uncompromising hostility."[65]

As winter turned to spring, Captain Payne applied for an injunction against his two nemeses: Secretary of War Robert Todd Lincoln; and Major General John Pope. Based on his conviction that Oklahoma Proper lay outside Indian country as defined by Congress, he was taking the bold step of forcing the War Department and the local military commander to defend themselves in court. Having spent more than $250,000 to secure Indian Territory from illegal settlement, the government seemed to be on the verge of wearing out.[66] General Sherman went on record to cite the army's two most vexing and costly responsibilities: suppressing Indian outbreaks and keeping boomers out of the Oklahoma country. To make matters worse, arresting officers' hands were tied in dealing with Payne. Whereas Indian killings were all in a day's work, soldiers could not so much as prick a boomer with a bayonet without risking a lawsuit. Nor was there any telling how much the government was paying the railroads to ferry troops around the West.[67]

While Payne was doing his best to tire out the court system, Bill Couch assumed leadership of an invasion (the eleventh) in August 1883, bound for Payne's Crossing.[68] The boomers were duly spotted, and Captain Carroll received orders to retrieve them. He and a detachment of the Ninth Cavalry rounded them up and returned to Fort Reno with about forty wagons and 150 boomers in tow. At some point, a boomer woman died after giving birth to a premature child.[69]

En route to Fort Reno, Couch managed to fire off a memo to Payne, warning him that scouts were on the lookout for more boomers.[70] Five days later, Couch reported from Fort Reno that neither he nor his men were actually under arrest. In what was clearly another hastily written message, he informed the boomer leader that they would somehow ditch their military escort before crossing the Cimarron River and meet Payne's party on the other side. "You will find us scattered all over the country," continued Couch. "Come and bring all the men you can. . . . I will never leave the Oklahoma (country) until tyed [sic] & hawled [sic] out."[71] Couch was unable to keep his word, and in a well-rehearsed choreography, he and his fellow captives were escorted to the Kansas line.[72]

Buoyed by the government's victory in Judge Parker's court in May 1881, the Five Tribes had reason to hope that Kansas courts with jurisdiction over Indian Territory would uphold the prohibition against settlement.[73] They were even more uplifted when, in October 1883, a federal grand jury in Leavenworth found a true bill against Payne for conspiring to enter Indian Territory.[74]

Wondering if his day in court might be at hand, Payne took his message to the people in the Emporia, Kansas, courthouse. After a flattering introduction and rousing applause, he strode to the front of a room packed to overflowing. Sporting a dark blue flannel shirt and nearly new suit of Scottish fabric, Payne used his height to full advantage to tower over his listeners. History is silent on how the destitute David Payne could afford such fashionable attire. Nor do we know whether the ladies, who seemed to be the most attentive, were captivated more by his words or the dashing figure he cut as he warmed up to his favorite topic.

Praising the U.S. government as "the grandest government the sun ever shone on," Payne accused Secretary Teller of practicing fraud and deception with regard to Indian Territory. Teller had allegedly admitted to Senator

Frederic Remington, *The Branding Chute*.
Courtesy of Art Institute of Chicago/Art Resource, New York, ART541622.

Preston Plumb of Kansas that homesteading and preemption laws should be applied to the Oklahoma country and, in a moment of prescience, predicted that it would be opened to settlement sooner rather than later. If enterprising folks wanted to live there, Secretary Teller thought they should make their plans in a hurry, as public lands were being snatched up so quickly that nary an acre would be available within the year.

Payne admitted that he was under indictment in Leavenworth for conspiracy against the U.S. government but had been released (as usual), and he was fairly sure his case would never come to trial. (He was right—his injunction was later denied.) He closed his remarks with an appeal to his followers to stand firm and be ready for the next expedition.[75]

Aside from soldiers charged with keeping Indian Territory free from trespassers, drifters and westbound migrants who were advised not to linger, cowboys who were supposed to keep moving up the trails, and boomers who scurried across

Frederic Remington, *Waiting for the Beef Issue.*
Courtesy of Frederic Remington Art Museum, Ogdensburg, N.Y.

the land and erected their makeshift communities where they pleased, who
lived in or near Oklahoma Proper in the early 1880s, and what do we know
about them? The obvious answer—officially, anyway—is nobody. But along
the western edge of Oklahoma Proper were plenty of Cheyennes and Arapahos,
whose reservation sprawled from the outskirts of present-day Oklahoma City
to the Texas Panhandle, and who traveled to the Darlington Indian Agency
for their allotments. Given the importance of the agency and Fort Reno
in fostering contact between Indians and people of European descent, it
behooves us to consider the multicultural milieu that predated the arrival
of urban pioneers and framed the first stirrings of townsite development in
Oklahoma Proper.

For a glimpse into that period of transition, we turn to Charles F. Colcord.
Long before he made his fortune in Indian Territory (later, eastern Oklahoma)
oil and plowed his profits into Oklahoma City's burgeoning skyline, Colcord
was a cowboy, and one of his jobs was to help distribute beef on the hoof to
Indians at the Darlington Indian Agency. Seemingly little had changed since
1870 when beef was issued at Camp Supply. Typically, Colcord helped to

gather government-issued cattle near the agency, drove them into holding pens, and cut out the Indian agent's prescribed numbers. Nearby, warriors mounted on their finest buffalo horses and swathed in war paint waited for soldiers to open the gates.

As soon as the gates flew open, warriors arrayed in full regalia whipped their horses into a gallop. Wary of granting them too much leeway, the government prohibited guns but allowed more primitive weaponry. Five to twenty warriors maneuvered their horses alongside each steer and let loose a barrage of arrows. "Sometimes," recalled Colcord, "a steer would have so many arrows in him that he would look like a frizzly chicken." When the steers fell writhing in the dust, women descended upon them with razor-sharp knives. Deploying skills they had honed to perfection through generations of following bison across the Great Plains, they skinned the quivering carcasses and sliced off the choicest tidbits to feed their children. "They would eat the liver and heart, blood raw," continued Colcord. Their appetites sated, the women scrambled over the blood-soaked prairie, cut meat into strips, and slung it over their shoulders to carry back to their camps. Men and women went about their business clad only in breechcloth while their children ran stark naked across the killing fields.[76]

During one of his roundups, Colcord might have spotted B. H. Campbell waiting expectantly at the corrals for the show to begin. Campbell, whose two thousand head of cattle grazed on the Cheyenne and Arapaho Reservation with dubious legality, had accepted the beef issue clerk's invitation to drop by for a visit, and he described a Monday morning issue before firearms were banned. The "pip pop of the gun is reverberated on every hand," recalled a spellbound Campbell as the beef issue crackled to life. "To those who have never witnessed this issue it is well worth a visit," continued Campbell, "as neither the pencil nor an encyclopedia could picture out to them the systematical form in which the issue is made."[77]

Indian beef issues provide a fitting metaphor for the clash of civilizations that roared to life when Europeans first set foot in the New World. Jefferson thought it might take a thousand years to populate the continent with yeoman farmers and bestow the blessings of Western civilization on Indians as settlements pushed relentlessly into the wilderness. Instead, it took less than a century to push farms and settlements to the boundaries of Indian Territory and tribal enclaves to the brink of dissolution.

As farms and cities encroached ever farther onto the Great Plains, public lands in the nation's midsection seemed in danger of running out. The passions stirred by U.S. public lands policies took on special urgency in Indian Territory, where Indians tried to preserve what was left of their once mighty empires, cattlemen staked dubious claims to an ocean of cheap grass, railroad moguls chomped at the bit to capture lucrative markets, boomers fomented insurrection against a government that denied them their birthright, and soldiers played referee as best they could, all against a backdrop of Gilded Age politics that favored the few over the many, and the wealthy over the less fortunate.

Clearly, the status quo was unsustainable. U.S. cavalry, remote military outposts, and blustery politicians were no match for the tide of history. The stage was set for a high-stakes showdown. But anyone who expected a quick resolution to the Oklahoma Question was in for disappointment. History was not quite done with the boomer movement. Nor was it done with cattlemen and railroaders who had their own ideas about economic development in Oklahoma Proper.

CHAPTER SIX

Our Sorrow

Resolved, In the death of our worthy leader, Capt. D. L. Payne,
we lost our most forward friend in the Oklahoma cause, and it will
be difficult to replace a leader who will stand up and face the
enemy as did he, in behalf of Oklahoma for many years.
Wichita branch of Payne's Oklahoma Colony, December 4, 1884

Captain Payne was en route from Washington, D.C., to Topeka in April 1884
when a reporter collared him for an interview. Payne expressed confidence
that military confrontations between boomers and soldiers were increasingly
unlikely, as the action was devolving to the courts. Was he planning to
participate in the next expedition, likely to commence within the next week
or two? No, said Payne, he had his hands full dealing with legal matters in
Topeka, most notably the charge of conspiracy that the U.S. government had
filed against him. After hearing what the judge had to say, he would most
likely return to Washington, D.C., to await favorable actions in Congress.
Asked to speculate about prospects for settlement in Oklahoma Proper, Payne
replied, "It is practically open now."[1]

Consumed by legal cases, Payne entrusted leadership of the next boomer
expedition to Payne's Oklahoma Colony vice president Bill Couch, who
had served as wagon master on the trip to Camp Alice in February 1883 and
had commanded the subsequent expedition to Payne's Crossing in August.
Couch set out on his third expedition (and the boomers' twelfth) at the head
of the largest boomer wagon train ever assembled—three thousand strong,
according to Captain George Cooper, treasurer of the Oklahoma colonization
society. By late April 1884, their settlements extended fifteen miles along
the North Canadian River. The main camp was located about a mile west of

present-day Crossroads Mall in Oklahoma City. A few miles north, Couch's father, Meshach, staked his claim to 160 acres on the North Canadian River, known in those days simply as the "North Fork," near the future site of the University of Oklahoma Health Sciences Complex. As the boomers arrived in Oklahoma Proper at the height of the spring planting season, anyone who was not building homes and businesses was planting crops and erecting fences.[2] The elder Couch was too busy to bother with soldiers on patrol and scarcely looked up when Lieutenant M. W. Day and a detachment of seven soldiers showed up for the ritual evictions.

"Stop that plowing!" shouted Lieutenant Day. "You are under arrest!"

Couch eventually looked up and, without stopping his team, replied, "Get off my land!"

That was not what Day wanted to hear. Couch was promptly seized, bound hand and foot, and dumped into a wagon. News of Meshach Couch's rough treatment fanned boomers' resentment toward soldiers, who seemed bent on trampling their constitutional rights. Similar arrests were made all along the North Canadian River as soldiers rounded up colonists, destroyed their structures and improvements, and escorted them back to Kansas.[3] Lieutenant Day's problems were far from over, as boomers were putting up stiff resistance along the Cimarron River, and reinforcements were reportedly on the way.

And where was Captain Payne during all this commotion? According to the *Caldwell Journal*, he and about seventy-five boomers were in Arkansas City, where they held nightly meetings and raised money from prospective settlers. In the welter of court cases that seemed to become more complicated by the day, Payne claimed that he and several others had been released on twenty-five-thousand-dollar bonds and would eventually have to answer two charges: one carried a one-thousand-dollar fine; and the other carried a ten-thousand-dollar fine and two years' imprisonment.[4]

The boomers' most audacious expedition came in May 1884 when Payne took a break from his legal hassles to lead an expedition to the northwestern corner of present-day Kay County. They made camp four miles south of Hunnewell, Kansas, at Rock Falls, Indian Territory, on the Chikaskia River, a tributary of the Arkansas.[5] As its name suggests, Rock Falls was named for waterfalls that were deemed perfectly suited as a power source for the upstart community. Once known as "Rock Ford" for the river's solid-rock bottom, the area had provided a relatively safe, quicksand-free crossing during the heyday of the great northern cattle drives. "Ever since 1866 this glorious country has BEEN A MIGHTY WASTE," seethed the *Oklahoma Chief* (martial moniker gone, for the time being). Judging from the stream of letters and telegrams pouring into its office, the *Chief* estimated that twenty-four hundred settlers representing as many as twelve hundred families would be located in Rock Falls within a month.[6]

A firsthand account of Rock Falls survives in the writings of a printer named Grant Harris. Then only eighteen years old, Harris and two associates, William Cunningham and W. A. Stacey, were working at the *Caldwell Standard* when the word went out that Captain Payne was looking for someone to print his newspaper. Since its inception in January 1883, the *Oklahoma War Chief* had been published in Kansas towns that seemed most conducive to boomer polemics. And now, for the first time, the printing equipment—a Washington handpress and other tools of the trade with a collective value of about four hundred dollars—was set up in the Cherokee Outlet and was waiting for someone to crank it up in the service of the boomer movement. As Harris recalled many years later about operating the first printing press in the Cherokee Outlet, "I have hated the looks of a Washington hand press from that day to this and still have 'corns' on my hands from pulling it, and, what's more, I have never run one since."[7]

Clearly adventurous sorts, Harris and his associates quit their jobs on a Saturday in May and lit out for Rock Falls on rented horses the next morning. They made their way to the makeshift newspaper office and paused to read a proclamation tacked to the door. Signed by Secretary of the Interior Teller, it warned anyone caught red-handed in the act of publishing would be liable to a thousand-dollar fine and imprisonment for one to five years."[8] Surely questioning the wisdom of their career change, the journalists stepped into the building to negotiate a deal with Captain Payne. He offered them a total of twenty-five dollars a week ("big wages in those days," recalled Harris) plus board. They countered with a request for twenty-five dollars each. Without hesitating, Payne pulled a wad of bills from his pocket and hired them on the spot. A week later, the newspaper's first issue printed south of Kansas rolled off the press. From June 4 to August 7, the official organ of Payne's Oklahoma Colony was printed as the *Oklahoma Chief*. The warrior remained, if only in spirit.

Harris's partners soon lost their nerve and hightailed it back to Kansas. Harris, who was allowed to keep the entire salary of twenty-five dollars a week and, as a bonus, pocket the newspaper's ten-cent sales price, was left to summon whatever help he needed to keep the press running. Even though he worked under editors William F. Gordon and J. B. Cooper, Captain Payne dictated content and did most of the writing. Harris sold papers as fast as he could print them until circulation reached two thousand.[9] Such was the pace of printing that his newsprint supplier in Hunnewell came up short, forcing Harris to buy brown wrapping paper from a grocer.

The youthful Harris found camp life to be on the dull side. Between Payne's lectures and an occasional religious service, colonists had little to do but plow a few furrows, knowing their efforts would come to naught as soon as soldiers arrived to escort them out of the territory. The only excitement in camp came when soldiers were rumored to be in the vicinity and Indian attacks were deemed imminent. One night, someone heard voices along the river. Camp leaders posted extra guards and admonished everyone to have their weapons at the ready. When dawn broke, the boomers spotted several Indian men, women, and youngsters who were on their way to Kansas.[10] Clearly, frontier perils were not what they used to be.

As the summer wore on, Harris took on the role of Captain Payne's secretary and helped him sort out his financial records. Harris found the boomer leader to be completely lacking in financial acumen. Although it cost ten dollars to join the colony and another three dollars to help defray surveying expenses, Payne never turned down an applicant for lack of thirteen dollars; he simply took what was offered and tried to remember who had paid and who had not. Typically, Payne wound up with more money than he could account for and forgot where it came from.[11] He made up for his financial shortcomings with generosity and a magnetic personality. Either out of generosity or a poor memory or a combination of the two—and, in all likelihood, sure that he could access more funds from his well-heeled benefactors—Payne never asked anyone to repay their debts.

Back in the nation's capital, President Chester A. Arthur (R; 1881–85) issued a proclamation on July 1, 1884, authorizing the Department of the Interior to use military force to shut down their colony.[12] The proclamation was similar in tone to President Hayes's two proclamations (1879 and 1880) warning invaders to expect speedy and immediate eviction.[13] President Arthur's proclamation had something else in common with its predecessors: it had no effect whatsoever in deterring boomers from their mission. That same month, Payne's top lieutenant, Bill Couch, showed how much he cared about presidential proclamations when he led an expedition to Payne's Crossing. As Couch's expedition coincided with the establishment of Rock Falls, these invasions count as the thirteenth and fourteenth organized attempts to establish permanent settlements in Indian Territory.[14]

While boomers were settling at Rock Falls and President Arthur was issuing his proclamation, a new term was drifting into common usage: the "Oklahoma District." Clearly, the Oklahoma Question had become important enough to warrant an explanation of where exactly the disputed land was located. As noted in the *Evening Star* for baffled Washingtonians, "There are other lands in the Indian Territory under dispute, but the principal ones are the Oklahoma lands, lying in the very heart of the Indian Territory."[15]

While *Evening Star* readers were brushing up on their geography, all eyes were riveted on Rock Falls, where a familiar scene was etching itself into Oklahoma history. On August 6, a detachment of buffalo soldiers rode up to the south bank of the river and glared at the sprawling settlement on the other side.[16] Meanwhile, Major General Hatch, known in boomer circles as the "Border Boss Liar," rode into the colony to read the president's proclamation of July 1. Captain Payne responded by lambasting everyone in the federal government, from the highest level to the lowest, as "a pack of damned thieves." *Oklahoma Chief* editor J. B. Cooper chimed in with his own insults. Failing to provoke a quarrel, Payne offered to pay one thousand dollars to anyone who could assure him of a day in court. In a gesture aimed at forcing an arrest, Payne offered to sell contraband liquor and cigars to the officers. Or perhaps they would prefer to dine with him over cocktails? None took him up on his offers, and as the ranting and raving escalated, a sizeable crowd assembled around the printing office. Officers repeated Hatch's admonition for boomers to pack their wagons and skedaddle. As noted in the *Wichita Daily Eagle*, "The only reply was a torrent of abusive epithets that cannot be published."[17]

Everyone knew that arrests were imminent, but Grant Harris and the colony's officers had something else to worry about. Payne had collected a considerable amount of money from colony subscribers and kept their cash and valuables in a cast-iron safe.[18] If soldiers were to find it, they would undoubtedly confiscate it. Harris waited until the soldiers returned to their camp to stuff the colony's money into a leather grip, lower it into an abandoned water well, and conceal it with brush, hoping that soldiers would be too preoccupied to wonder about a hole in the ground that now housed what might have been the first bank in western Indian Territory.[19]

That evening, boomer leaders gathered in Payne's tent to decide on a course of action. An allegedly drunken Payne squared off with several hot-heads who were spoiling for a fight. The voice of reason prevailed, and the meeting ended with a consensus to break camp the next day. Several wagons left Rock Falls that night, but many boomers elected to stay until the bitter end.[20]

Weeks of governmental inaction came to an end on the morning of August 7, when two companies of the Ninth Cavalry rode into the settlement. Colonists awoke to witness a steady procession of horse-drawn vehicles approaching from the direction of Caldwell and Hunnewell and cattlemen, clearly in a mood to celebrate, appearing from every direction.[21] The higher-ups who arrived in camp included officials from the Union Agency in Muskogee representing the Bureau of Indian Affairs, an official with the General Land Office from Washington, D.C., and representatives of the Cherokee Strip Live Stock Association from Caldwell.[22]

The great unraveling began when soldiers shut down the printing office. Grant Harris managed to print a few copies of the newspaper and tuck them in his pockets before soldiers burst through the door and arrested him and J. B. Cooper. Another detail found Payne outside his tent with a forty-five pistol in each hand and hurling racial insults at any buffalo soldier who dared to arrest him. Payne surrendered to a white officer, who promptly turned him over to a black one. Humiliated beyond words, Payne was force marched around the camp for an hour before he was detained in the newspaper office with several of his top lieutenants, including Cooper, Harris, two of Couch's sons, and the colony's vice president and surveyor.[23]

While soldiers were shackling the ringleaders for eventual delivery to U.S. district court in Fort Smith, John F. Lyons, a Fort Gibson attorney and special agent for the Cherokee Nation, who did double duty as legal counsel for the Cherokee Strip Live Stock Association, was taking in a surreal scene. His observations survive in a report dated November 19, 1884, to Cherokee principal chief D. W. Bushyhead. Lyons watched as soldiers attempted to separate first from repeat offenders, as boomers who had participated in more than one incursion were subject to a thousand-dollar fine. First offenders were to be escorted to the Kansas line and admonished never to return.[24]

With cavalry arrayed on both sides, the caravan of (supposedly) first offenders lurched northward for the four-mile trip to Kansas. Such was the traffic jam that the first wagons reached Kansas while the ones bringing up the rear were still at Rock Falls.[25] Citizens from Hunnewell were on hand (no word on how they got permission to be there) to watch the spectacle; according to the *Wichita Daily Eagle*, they had no trouble with the soldiers' rough treatment of the boomers. Perhaps they would finally get the message and stop trying to force the government's hand.[26]

After loading the printing press and equipment into a wagon, soldiers torched the *Oklahoma Chief* office and anything else that was flammable. As Lyons wrote to a gloating Principal Chief Bushyhead, "The buildings mentioned, comprising the town of Rock Falls were destroyed by fire, and, like unto the famous Cities of Sodom and Gomorrah, Rock Falls was soon in ashes."[27] A bizarre scene endures from a much later edition of a rechristened *Oklahoma War-Chief* of cattlemen, their wives, and soldiers celebrating their achievement with refreshments and intoxicating liquors as flames leapt around them. At one point in the merriment, a drunken cowboy got the bright idea to lasso the stars and stripes and haul it to the ground. As revelers cheered him on, he circled his horse around a group of boomers with the flag dragging behind him. But then, in a display of bravado that galvanized the boomer movement as never before, a thirteen-year-old Lou Brown seized her father's revolver from his holster and leveled it at the cowboy. Bloodshed was averted when Mr. Brown, the colony's treasurer, commanded her to put the gun down. Lou lowered the weapon and burst into tears.

The unnamed cowboy either sobered up fast or simply learned his lesson. Staring down the bore of a loaded revolver, he turned white as a sheet, let loose the flag, coiled his lariat, and rode off to parts unknown. Another cowboy, likewise inebriated and apparently oblivious to the change in mood, was about to sling the flag on his horse to use as a saddle blanket when a commanding officer interceded.[28] Sparks were licking at his heels when an arresting officer mounted up and sped off to Caldwell to telegraph the *New York Times*, the *Washington Critic*, and other eastern newspapers with assurance that spectators approved of efforts to rid Indian Territory of intruders.[29] History is silent as to whether or not the cattlemen's association chastised the cowboys for desecrating the American flag.

In a retrospective of the Rock Falls raid published in April 1886, the *War-Chief* discerned the cowboys' treatment of the American flag and subsequent torching of the camp as the beginning of a new era. Across the land, patriotic Americans were expressing their revulsion at the government's high-handedness by rallying to the boomer movement as never before. Home seekers were becoming more resolute than ever, and cattlemen were left to fight a rearguard battle with little prospect of stemming the tide of settlement that was surely coming. Reflecting on a site that no doubt stood as a boomer shrine until Mother Nature reduced it to dust and time erased it from memory, the *War-Chief* published the boomer movement's answer to Gilded Age politics: "Land for the landless! Homes for the homeless and equality before the law for everybody!"[30]

As the sun set on a smoldering Rock Falls, Grant Harris and the boomer top brass were some ten miles distant, locked in a guardhouse at Hatch's camp. Harris was surprised when a buffalo soldier showed up to escort him to Lieutenant Day's office for questioning. He arrived to find Day in a state of puzzlement. Why, asked the lieutenant, had Harris defied Secretary Teller's proclamation against publishing in Indian Territory? What was it about trespassing and imprisonment that he failed to grasp? "Lieutenant," replied Harris, "I had been working in Caldwell for seven dollars a week and boarded myself. When Captain Payne offered me twenty-five dollars and board the difference in salary looked bigger than the presidential proclamation and I went to work." Harris got the impression that Lieutenant Day had little interest in him. His spirits brightened when Day asked him how long it would take to ride back to Kansas. Harris did a quick calculation and estimated fifteen minutes. "Beat that time a little, if you can," said Day with a laugh. Within minutes, Harris was on his horse and galloping north. Many years later, he liked to tell the story of making it across the Kansas line in less than fifteen minutes.[31]

Captain Payne had a less amusing tale to tell. After flames engulfed Rock Falls, he and his lieutenants were placed under military escort and, under a torrential rain, made ready for a trip to Fort Smith in a cramped and springless wagon. About sixty soldiers guarded them as far as the Cimarron River. As Payne noted in an article published in faraway Sacramento, their heavy escort was put in place to guard against cowboys who might try to kill them.[32]

On August 13, a deputy marshal from Kansas arrived at their camp with a warrant to take the prisoners to Wichita. They would have gone gladly, but their commanding officer was under orders to proceed to Fort Smith. Suffering from rheumatism in his knees and subsisting on a monotonous diet of bacon, bread, and coffee, Payne whiled away the hours enjoying the scenery and fantasizing about farmers tilling the countryside. But the power of positive thinking was not enough to alleviate his failing health. Night brought little relief to the prisoners' travails, as sentinels announced their shift changes by shining lights in their faces to make sure they were all there. About August 19, they made camp some fifteen miles from Muskogee, where Payne watched Creeks and African Americans working side by side in lush fields. When they passed through Tahlequah, the prisoners were paraded past scores of Cherokees who had gathered to catch a glimpse of their nemesis.[33]

The boomers' monthlong journey to Fort Smith ended much as it began, with insults piled on injuries. When, after several days of marching, the party arrived at a creek, the soldiers prevented their prisoners from drinking until the horses had drunk their fill. "If Payne's story is all true, he has been badly used," declared the *Wichita Daily Eagle*. "In fact according to his story one would think that incarceration in British dungeons or transportation to Siberia did not amount to a row if pins compared to what he endured during those terrible weeks in the hands of those tyrannical 'nigger' troops."[34]

By the time the boomer convoy began the final leg of its journey in late August, Payne's attorneys were drafting a petition for a writ of habeas corpus to compel Judge Parker to release the prisoners.[35] But they could not prevent Parker from issuing his summons, dated September 8, 1884, ordering Payne to appear in court in the Western District of Arkansas on the first day of the November term.[36] Like his previous summons in August 1880, this one carried the requisite warning: failure to appear in court would be taken as a confession of guilt to the charges filed against him, which now included introducing and selling whisky in Indian country. As the turf war between U.S. district courts in Fort Smith and Wichita heated up, many predicted that the judge's ruling on Payne's whisky charges would determine, once and for all, which court had jurisdiction in Oklahoma Proper.[37] Charges of peddling intoxicating spirits were particularly vexing to boomers, as cattlemen brought beer and liquor into Indian Territory on a regular basis.[38]

In addition to questions pertaining to trespassing and drinking was the mystery of what became of the printing press that had spurred boomer resistance in the place where both homesteading and publishing stories about it were illegal. The answer comes from a buffalo soldier who, in his later years, worked as a janitor for the *Kansas City Star*. Reminiscing about the Rock Falls raid, he recalled that several soldiers deemed the equipment beyond repair after it was hauled from the *War-Chief* printing office and dumped it in the Cimarron River.[39] Boomers were fortunate to have enough money in their coffers to purchase new printing equipment, and before long, the *War-Chief* was in back in operation in South Haven, Kansas. It remained there until it ceased publication on August 12, 1886—two years and five days after soldiers had dismantled the boomers' Washington handpress and loaded it into a government wagon for a trip to the bottom of the Cimarron River.[40]

The most immediate outcomes of the Rock Falls episode were Payne's surge in popularity and increasing support for the boomer movement. Now perceived as a martyr to his cause, Payne was drawing the attention of progressives bent on ending glaring inequalities spawned by Gilded Age politics. An 1884 promotional poster for Buffalo Bill's Wild West show lists one of the starring attractions as "Oklahoma Payne, The Progressive Pioneer." Although pressing matters forced Payne to renege on his promise to participate in his friend Bill Cody's extravaganza, we can be sure that the moniker resonated among prospective homesteaders who saw Payne as their champion in a fight to the finish.[41]

After friends posted his thousand-dollar bond in Judge Parker's court, Payne beat a hasty retreat from Fort Smith and arrived at the Wichita depot on September 12 to a hero's welcome. One greeter carried the American flag that had been so rudely handled at Rock Falls. Clad in a slouch hat, brown shirt, and blue pants, Payne "looked dirty and seedy," and he clearly suffered from ailments caused by his monthlong captivity. He might also have been suffering from a case of déjà vu. A grand jury appointed by the U.S. district court in Wichita had just handed down an indictment against him and his coconspirators for invading Oklahoma Proper and the Cherokee Outlet. Hoping that the ongoing jurisdictional dispute might accrue to the boomer movement's benefit, Payne and his alleged coconspirators retained J. Wade McDonald of Winfield, Kansas, to represent them. U.S. district attorney J. R. Hallowell would represent the government's case in a trial that Judge C. G. Foster of Topeka had scheduled for November 11, 1884.[42]

Following his tumultuous greeting, Payne joined an exodus from the depot to a nearby skating rink, where an estimated five hundred boomer faithful were waiting to hear from their leaders. Bad press notwithstanding, Payne drew larger crowds than many politicians. Even Ben S. Miller, president of the Cherokee Strip Live Stock Association and now candidate for the U.S. Senate, was unable to match Payne's turnouts.[43] After a rousing rendition of "Give Us a Home" (a patriotic tune dedicated to the boomer cause), attendees at the skating-rink rally passed resolutions denouncing soldiers' cruelties at Rock Falls and harsh treatment of boomer leaders.[44]

Formalities completed, J. G. McCoy, the duly elected president of the rally, strode to center stage. With a map of Indian Territory draped behind him, McCoy set the tone for the evening by comparing the government's treatment of Captain Payne to Russian despotism. He then denounced soldiers for marching Payne and his fellow captives for hundreds of miles at the point of a bayonet before turning them loose like dogs. "If ever there was rottenness in Denmark," declared McCoy with a nod to Shakespeare, "it was in that Indian Territory." McCoy wound toward his conclusion with reference to the Interior Department's de facto policy of leaving cattlemen to do as they pleased in the Oklahoma country. And then, he delivered his coup de grace: "Things were so rotten in the territory that the buzzards had to hold their noses while flying over it."[45]

Applause erupted when McCoy invited Payne to address the crowd. Suffering from chills and fever, his comments were uncharacteristically brief. After accusing Hatch of being "two-thirds drunk on the cattle men's money," Payne reiterated a familiar complaint: marching him across Indian Territory had the dual effect of keeping him away from the courts and keeping the courts away from him. He closed his remarks by announcing yet another expedition and warning cattlemen to stay out of his way. He offered no clues as to the consequences they might suffer if they failed to heed his counsel. The rally ended with a series of resolutions reflecting grievances that had defined the boomer movement since its inception.[46]

And then it was back to business. High on the agenda was retrieving the money that Grant Harris had hidden in the abandoned water well at Rock Falls. After his record-breaking gallop from Rock Falls to the Kansas line, Harris had gone to work for the *Wichita City Eagle*, and he never breathed a word about the boomer stash. Following the skating-rink rally, Payne sought out his former printer and asked about it. Assuming (hoping?) the money was where he had left it, Harris joined Payne and other boomer leaders on an anxious train ride to Hunnewell. From there, they drove to the burned ruins that had once been Rock Falls. Sure enough, when Harris was lowered into the well, he found the leather grip. As Harris wrote many years later, "I have sometimes wondered what would have happened if I had failed to find the money."[47]

While the boomer movement was clawing its way to respectability, railroad companies remained poised at the Kansas border, anxious to extend their lines into what was sure to be a lucrative market. As early as 1884, directors of the Katy, which was part owner of the Southern Kansas Railway, were thinking about extending their line from southern Kansas through Indian Territory and on to Galveston, Texas. President Arthur granted his approval on July 4, but with a caveat: the company had to build at least a hundred miles of road within three years or forfeit its right to continue. Under penalty of forfeiture of all rights and privileges, the railroad was forbidden to do anything aimed at extinguishing Indians' tenure on their land.[48] Texans, too, were hankering for a piece of the action. Tasked with identifying the best route from North Texas to Kansas, Michael L. Lynch, locating engineer for the Gulf, Colorado, and Santa Fe Railway Company, saw enormous potential in shipping Chickasaw cotton and cattle through Oklahoma Proper's open prairie just west of the Indian Meridian.[49]

With so much at stake in Indian Territory and the November elections fast approaching, resolution of the Oklahoma Question could not be postponed much longer. In its ongoing crusade against corporate interests, the *War-Chief* amplified its criticism of politicians with interests in the range cattle industry. Few were more vilified than Senator John Ingalls for introducing a bill in January 1884 to allow cattlemen to occupy as much land as they wanted west of the 100th meridian. Joining Senator Ingalls in the *War-Chief*'s gallery of rogues was Senator Preston Plumb. A quick calculation showed that the 5,419,640 acres of Oklahoma Proper would make 33,872 quarter-section farms, or homes for 74,497 homeless farmers and their families consisting of a husband, wife, and three children. Instead, Senators Ingalls and Plumb were complicit in reserving the land for a hundred cattlemen.[50]

The *War-Chief* was downright giddy about the drubbing that Ben S. Miller was likely to take in the November elections. As president of the Cherokee Strip Live Stock Association, Miller was bent on keeping 6,500,000 acres of the public domain for the association's eighty-two members and off-limits to home seekers. Waxing classical, the newspaper predicted that Miller would be "politically killed so dead that he will be unable to steer his way across the River Styx, and will require a dozen torchlight processions to light him through the dark valley of the shadow of political death." Even though most Kansas boomers belonged to the Republican Party, the *War-Chief* urged them to vote for Democrats, as the Republican Party in power—including President Arthur, Secretary of the Interior Teller, Secretary of War Lincoln, and both Kansas senators—never wavered in its support for cattlemen.[51]

Commissioner of the General Land Office Noah C. McFarland (1881–85) added a sense of urgency to boomer polemics in his annual report on public lands. His statistics indicated that sales, entries, and selections of public lands were more than double those of 1882 and 40 percent above those of 1883. From 1850 to 1880, an astonishing 154,067,553 acres had been granted to railroads, and corporations of various kinds had acquired millions more through evasions of homesteading and preemption laws. Precise figures were difficult to obtain, as public lands appraisals were notoriously inaccurate and probably fraudulent. Nevertheless, McFarland had all the evidence he needed to blame the federal government for putting the nation's treasure at the mercy of monied interests.[52]

National politics and dire statistics notwithstanding, all eyes in Kansas were on the U.S. district court in Topeka, where Judge C. G. Foster had promised a decision by November 11 on the government's case against Captain Payne. He rendered his decision as promised, and it was a bombshell.

"Glory! Hallelujah! Oklahoma at Last Opened!" blared the *War-Chief* on November 20. Using all caps to make sure its readers got the message, the *War-Chief* announced the substance of Judge Foster's decision: "THE TITLE TO THE OKLAHOMA LANDS VESTS EXCLUSIVELY IN THE UNITED STATES; HENCE THE SETTLING THEREON BY CITIZENS OF THE U.S. IS NOT A CRIMINAL OFFENSE." Although Judge Foster failed to render a decision pertaining to the Cherokee Strip, his ruling on Oklahoma Proper was clear: "The long vexed question is at last settled, and the colonists are vindicated in their claim to peaceable possession of Oklahoma."[53]

Judge Foster's momentous decision sent Payne into overdrive. After a hasty detour to share the good news with his sister, he made his way to Wellington, Kansas, to deliver what might have been his most impassioned speech ever. But now that Oklahoma Proper's opening was at hand, Payne needed money even more than inspired oratory. After retrieving the leather grip from Rock Falls, Payne had entrusted the Oklahoma Payne Colony's finances to one of Bill Couch's sons. But finances were no more his strong suit than they were Payne's. Hoping that Grant Harris might once again be of service, Payne summoned him to the Hotel de Barnard in Wellington to help straighten out the boomer books. When Payne returned to the hotel from his rousing speech, he gathered Harris and several boomer insiders to sort out debits and credits.[54] As the night wore on, Payne took a break and wrote an upbeat letter to his sister, promising a visit before his next expedition.[55] Although Payne complained of weariness, he was savoring the sweet taste of victory and slept like a baby.

The boomer accountants showed up bleary-eyed in the hotel dining room for breakfast to find their leader seated at a table and flanked by his longtime companion, Mrs. Rachel Anna Haines—whom he intended to marry once they were happily settled in Oklahoma Proper—and his trusted lieutenant and *Oklahoma War Chief* editor J. B. Cooper. While they waited for breakfast, Payne seemed to nod off, and his companions assumed he was taking a nap. When their food arrived, Cooper placed his hand on Payne's shoulder. "Wake up, Cap," said Cooper, "and eat your breakfast before it gets cold." When Cooper gave his friend a gentle shake, his head lolled to one side, his eyes wide open. He was dead.[56]

Payne's body was taken from the dining room to the back of the Hotel de Barnard, and it stayed there so that mourners could pay their respects. The Reverend S. Price conducted the funeral on Sunday, November 30, at the Methodist Episcopal Church in Wellington. As the church was filled to capacity, the overflow had to wait outside. Like one of Payne's caravans to the Promised Land, thousands lined up in a funeral procession that stretched for a mile. Brushing off rumors of foul play, the *War-Chief*'s epitaph was simple. Under the headline, "Our Sorrow," it reported simply, "the struggle was over and death had done its work."[57]

Scarcely was Payne settled in his grave than Oklahoma colonists announced a fundraising campaign to erect a monument so that future generations would never forget him.[58] The Wichita branch of Payne's Oklahoma Colony published the poignant resolution that appears at the head of this chapter. But of course, not everybody was sorry to see him go. "Thus the career of one whose name has been an eye sore to the public is ended," declared the *Cheyenne Transporter*, "and the result of his labors and publicity will [illegible] into oblivion."[59]

———————————

Payne's Oklahoma Colony recruiter John S. Koller, who often joined Payne on the lecture circuit and had been covering costs for the printing and distribution of boomer literature since late 1883, was at the breakfast table at the Hotel de Barnard when Captain Payne died. "The death of Capt. Payne cast a gloom over the colony," he recalled, "which lingers still in the lives of his devoted followers."[60] But boomers who had given their time and treasure and had even risked their lives for the Oklahoma cause had neither the time nor inclination to let their movement die along with its leader. Judge Foster's decision notwithstanding, nobody expected Oklahoma Proper to be opened to settlement overnight. Victory was within reach, but only if the right person would step into Payne's oversized boots and assume the mantle of leadership.

The right person turned out to be Payne's second-in-command, Bill Couch. A week after Payne died, Couch shook boomers from their sorrow and led Payne's Oklahoma Colony on its fifteenth major expedition. After cutting their way through wire fences enclosing 100,000 head of cattle, they ended their journey of some seventy miles at Stillwater Creek, a tributary of the Cimarron River in present-day Payne County.[61] In a well-rehearsed routine, the colonists laid out a town, built several log houses, and made other improvements as time and weather permitted.

Their act of settlement was going smoothly on Christmas Eve when Lieutenant Day arrived and ordered his detachment of buffalo soldiers to form a line and commence shooting in five minutes. Couch's threat to return fire prompted Day to detail five soldiers to seize him and tie him up. As the detail advanced, colonists made a show of force, and Couch took the opportunity to deliver a speech. Day responded by ordering his soldiers back into line with weapons at the ready. But when the colonists refused to back down, Day retracted his order, said something about his soldiers freezing to death, and asked Couch about a good place to camp. "Camp down the creek," said Couch. "We will be neighborly." Before departing, Day warned Couch that he had until morning to make up his mind.[62]

The next day, Couch dispatched a courier to Arkansas City to send a telegram to President Arthur in which he suggested that, instead of sending more soldiers to Stillwater Creek, he might consider sending a single U.S. marshal with a warrant, with the assurance that everyone would submit to arrest. When Couch's Christmas Day appeal to President Arthur went unanswered and his boomer camp remained in limbo, the *Chicago Tribune* fired a blistering broadside against the military, warning that any loss of life would be tantamount to murder. The *Tribune* then took aim at cattlemen for bribing government officials to usurp public lands.[63]

Back at his military camp, a flustered Lieutenant Day sent a message to his higher-ups at Fort Reno and awaited further instructions. Meanwhile, Major General Hatch, then camped on the Cimarron River, wrote a letter to Couch, expressing dismay that former soldiers who had defended their country in the War between the States were now fomenting insurrection against their government. Insisting that any boomer who killed a soldier would be tried for murder and warning that Indians were bound to cause the colonists even more trouble, Hatch closed with a plea for common sense: "All trouble can easily be avoided by observing the proclamation of the President of the United States and peaceably leaving the Territory as directed."[64]

Responding from "Stillwater, Oklahoma Terr.," Couch reminded Hatch of Judge Foster's pro-settlement ruling and, in an oft-repeated mantra, insisted that boomers were obeying laws pertaining to public lands. Couch denied that he was fomenting insurrection, refused to accept responsibility for bloodshed, and dismissed Indian threats as speculation aimed more at titillating newspaper readers back east than at frightening prospective homesteaders. In Couch's opinion, roving bands of hostile Indians existed solely in Hatch's imagination, and he had brought them up for no other reason than to keep his soldiers on high alert. Couch signed his letter, "Most respectfully yours, W. L. Couch, President Payne's Oklahoma colony."[65]

Hatch's orders to enforce President Arthur's proclamation of July 1, 1884, came through in late January.[66] Adopting a hard-line stance that completely ignored Judge Foster's ruling, Hatch arrived at Stillwater Creek with six hundred soldiers in tow. In the month since Couch's confrontation with Lieutenant Day, the camp had taken on the attributes of a thriving village. Clearly unimpressed, Hatch gave the order to surrender on Sunday, January 25. Couch refused and, as before, threatened to fire if fired upon. Hatch issued another order to surrender that evening. Meeting yet another refusal, Hatch and his soldiers returned to their camp.

They returned Monday morning. After forming a line reinforced with two pieces of artillery, Hatch dispatched a colonel to ask what the colonists wanted to do. Couch responded that he and his fellow boomers were free American citizens, were committing no crimes, and would not submit to military harassment. George Conrad, a former slave from Kentucky, was riding with the Ninth Cavalry when his unit was dispatched to Stillwater Creek. He recalled what happened next: "We were not to fire until ordered; but were told to use our gun butts if the nesters became hostile. As soon as Couch saw us he raised a white flag and agreed to leave within two days if he and his men were not fired on."[67]

Soldiers were not the boomers' only problem. Free American citizens had to eat, and a quick inventory check revealed only five days' rations. When Hatch wisely decided to cut off their supply chain and wait them out, Couch opted to disband. In a final act of defiance, the boomers did not wait two days to vacate their camp, as Hatch had ordered, but left immediately without military escort.

From its new office in Arkansas City, the *Oklahoma Chief* characterized the Stillwater Creek showdown not as a defeat for the boomer movement but as a glorious achievement in the face of Hatch's tyranny. "If this occurrence had happened in Russia under the order of the Czar himself, it would have been in accord with that form of government," declared the newspaper, now edited by S. J. Zerger. Lest anyone doubt the *Chief*'s purpose, the masthead now carried the moniker, "OUR AIM: The Settlement of Oklahoma and the Restoration of the Public Domain to the people."[68]

An immense throng, complete with a brass band, was on hand to welcome the Stillwater Creek party to Arkansas City. Also on hand was an officer of the law to place Couch under arrest. He was promptly released on bond, and his trial date was set for February 10. Nobody was surprised when, like Captain Payne, he was later set free without a word of explanation.[69]

Scarcely had Couch and his fellow boomers unpacked their wagons when 139 delegates from several western states were summoned to the Odd Fellows Hall in Topeka for a two-day boomer convention. Over the din of wild huzzahs and cheers and the howling of dogs who apparently shared the festive mood, Couch was unanimously elected as chairman pro tem of the most important boomer gathering ever assembled. The outrage was palpable as Couch described his run-in with Major General Hatch at Stillwater Creek. Among the cascade of resolutions passed to thunderous applause on February 2 and 3 was an agreement to refer to "Oklahoma Territory" in all proceedings. As though anyone needed reminding, the Indian Territory designation implied Indian sovereignty and ownership of property, neither of which reflected reality in Oklahoma Proper. "The time has come to talk plainly," declared Sidney Clarke, "and the Oklahoma country is as clearly a part of the public domain as any land in the country." Among the convention's most important items of business was to appoint a committee to take the boomers' message to

Samuel Crocker.
Courtesy of Oklahoma Historical Society, Oklahoma City, 1988.

Washington. Members included Clarke, Colonel E. S. Welcome, B. S. Walden, and Colonel Samuel N. Wood, an Ohio-born Quaker and former abolitionist who authored a book about the boomer movement that included the requisite paeans to Captains Payne and Couch as well as a play-by-play report of the goings-on in Topeka. As the convention wound toward its conclusion, Couch invited his listeners to convene in Arkansas City on March 4, 1885—the date of Grover Cleveland's inauguration as president—and prepare to cross the border the following day.[70]

Meanwhile, confusion reigned in the nation's capital over the legality of grazing leases in Indian Territory. Citing contradictory telegrams exchanged by Secretary Lincoln and Secretary Teller in the summer of 1884, Kansas's *Iola Register* questioned B. H. Campbell's authority to allow two thousand cattle to graze in the Cheyenne and Arapaho Reservation. Rising to Campbell's defense, Teller drew a distinction between cattlemen, who were tending to business, and boomers, who routinely flouted the law.[71] Attuned to post–Civil War power structures, the *Oklahoma Chief* perceived more sinister motives in the government's intransigence on the Oklahoma Question. "It has been the policy of the government since its foundation until the Republicans

James B. Weaver.
Courtesy State Historical Society of Iowa, Des Moines, 5000.571.

came to power, to let settlers take any lands not wanted for the occupation of the Indians," declared the *Chief* shortly after the boomer convention in Topeka. "But for twenty years, it has been the policy of the administration to dispose of the public domain to monopolies and to discriminate against the poor settler."[72]

Equally bent on resolving the Oklahoma Question was a new recruit to the boomer cause: Samuel Crocker. Born in 1845 in Devonshire, England, Crocker spent his formative years in Iowa, where he learned at an early age that America did not always live up to its reputation as a beacon of opportunity. To support his crusade against Gilded Age privilege, he turned to his friend and ally in Congress, General James B. Weaver (National Greenback Party–Iowa; 1879–81, 1885–89). Before it dissolved and morphed into the Populist Party in the late 1880s, Weaver's National Greenback Party championed currency reform, labor rights, antimonopoly legislation, and opening Indian Territory to homesteading. As a political freelancer who refused to bow to the dictates of any particular party, Crocker was a regular on the lecture circuit, and his anti-monopoly diatribes became a staple in Progressive newspapers. It was during one of his speaking tours that he became acquainted with the boomer movement, a Progressive cause that suited his temperament and, in the dispiriting days following Payne's death, was in need of a first-class communicator.[73] He entered the fray to find the boomer leadership fending off charges of treason—the same charge levied against Confederate president Jefferson Davis during the Civil War, and a crime that had put fire in the bellies of Union soldiers, who were now standing shoulder to shoulder in their crusade against the government's intransigence.

By June 1885, Crocker was settling into his new job as editor of the *Oklahoma War-Chief*—martial moniker restored, once again hyphenated, and now published in Caldwell. He did the math on acreage that cattlemen were keeping from the plow and, in a famous passage that struck at the heart of perceived injustice, invoked divine inspiration to guide colonists through what was surely the boomer movement's endgame: "Millions of acres fattening countless heads of steers and all rented for two cents an acre! Do not ask why Oklahoma has not been opened to the thousands of home-hungry farmers, but face Jerusalem and pray: 'How long, Oh Lord, how long?'"[74]

Crocker could not have known that another four years would pass before Oklahoma Proper would be opened to homesteading and townsite development. Nor could he have known that Congress, and not the renegade boomers, would fulfill the promise of the Promised Land.

PART II

The Run

CHAPTER SEVEN

A Big Boom

On the settlement of the Oklahoma question
depends the blood of American citizens.

Hon. James Nelson Burnes, March 31, 1885

The election of Stephen Grover Cleveland as president (D; 1885–89) signaled a paradigm shift in presidential politics whose effects were quickly felt in Indian Territory. Branded early in his career in New York politics as a reformer, Cleveland earned distinction as an enemy of entrenched interests and party machines. Democratic Party leaders at the national level took notice and nominated him to take on James G. Blaine of Maine in the presidential election of 1884. Adopting the campaign slogan "A public office is a public trust," Cleveland won the election to become one of only two Democrats (the other was Woodrow Wilson) to rise to the presidency between 1861 and 1933, a period of almost total Republican domination.

President-elect Cleveland had yet to be sworn in when the committee appointed by the two-day boomer convention in Topeka, including Sidney Clarke and Samuel N. Wood, arrived in Washington in the company of Congressman James B. Weaver.[1] Clarke's connections with Washington power brokers enabled him to schedule meetings with Cleveland as well as with members of his cabinet, including Secretary of War William C. Endicott (1885–89), Secretary of the Interior Lucius Quintus Cincinnatus Lamar (1885–88), and Commissioner of Indian Affairs John DeWitt Clinton Atkins (1885–88). His message was clear: cattlemen continued to occupy Indian lands in and around Oklahoma Proper in direct violation of the law. Clarke was certain that Atkins and Lamar were on board and looked forward to U.S. attorney general Augustus H. Garland's (1885–89) ruling on Oklahoma Proper's legal status. "I certainly think now that final action here cannot be many days in the future," concluded Clarke in a letter to Bill Couch. "Be assured I shall do all in my power to reach the right result."[2]

Cleveland's cabinet members were not the only ones who needed to sort out the facts. Less than two weeks after Cleveland's inauguration, Kansas senator John Ingalls, known as an expert in all things western and a member of a Senate investigative committee charged with rooting out land fraud in Indian country, assured his fellow legislators that there were no cattle-men in Oklahoma. "Gentlemen, it has been said that there are cattlemen in Oklahoma," declared the senator, "but I want to state now, and want to be well understood, that such statements are false; that Oklahoma is as free of cattle as was the virgin soil of the Garden of Eden before Adam and Eve were placed therein." Senator Ingalls's Garden of Eden speech shocked even the most jaded boomers and came to epitomize corruption in the nation's highest offices. As one editorialist opined, Ingalls not only desecrated scripture but also demonstrated his willingness to lie in the interests of cattle syndicates.[3] Ingalls's disingenuous claim found its match when Senator George Vest asserted that the Oklahoma country had never been surveyed, sectioned, or subdivided. In fact, all it took was a cursory glance at federal land records to ascertain that Oklahoma had indeed been surveyed, sectioned, and subdivided, and was far better known than the senator from Missouri thought it was.[4] Our final glimpse into senatorial lapses in fact-checking comes from Senator John Tyler Morgan (D-Ala.; 1877–1907), another member of the Senate investigative committee, who declared that the Oklahoma lands were available to neither homesteading nor preemption and, furthermore, that Seminole Indians retained the right to lease their acreage at any time. Apparently, Senator Morgan had yet to peruse the Reconstruction Treaties of 1866 indicating that Seminole land had long since been ceded to the federal government.[5]

Meeting in Arkansas City in mid-March, Payne's Oklahoma Colony members denounced President Cleveland's proclamation of March 13, which ordered cattlemen to vacate the Oklahoma country but retained the ban against homesteading.[6] Shortly after the president issued his proclamation, Couch and Weaver called on Secretary Lamar to vent their frustration. Such were their powers of persuasion that the secretary brushed away tears as he

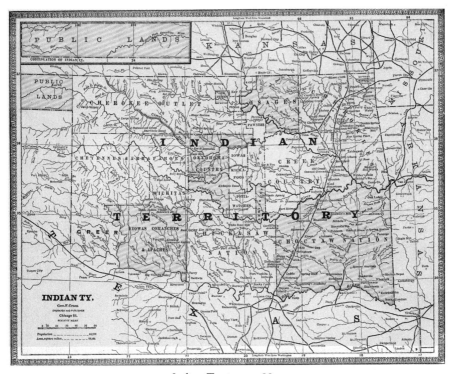

Indian Territory, 1885.
Courtesy Western History Collections, University of Oklahoma Libraries, 2-67-8626.

expressed his sympathy for boomers and exasperation toward cattlemen. Predictably, relocating cattle on such a vast scale ground to a halt when cattlemen resorted to the age-old tactic of procrastination. A common objection was that cattle, already under duress on their overgrazed ranges, would suffer even more on long-distance drives. Oklahoma cattleman Bill Snyder put it this way: "If I can hold on one year more, I'll get out. I'll be d———d if I haven't had my leg pulled enough for those thieves in Washington."[7]

In an attempt to force the president's hand, Payne's Oklahoma Colony members compiled a detailed list of cattle syndicates that routinely flouted the law and, in resolutions telegraphed to Washington, D.C., challenged President Cleveland to explain the legality of designating Oklahoma Proper as Indian country.[8] Meanwhile, Bill Couch was declaring his dismay over devious politicians to anyone who would listen. Referring to Senator Vest's ignorance of surveys, Couch asserted that he could place his hand on a thousand

Unknown artist, *Royal Ranch in Oklahoma*.
From Jackson and Cole, *Oklahoma! facing p. 116*.

cornerstones in Indian Territory. Couch was even more incredulous when
outgoing secretary of war Robert Todd Lincoln claimed that there were no
cattlemen in Indian Territory.[9] Couch supported his assertions with a roster
of about twenty enormous spreads where thousands of cattle were growing fat
on cheap—and, in some cases, free—grass.[10] Meanwhile, stories circulated of
fashionably attired ranchers and their wives greeting their guests, often with
foreign accents, at some rendezvous and whisking them away in handsome
carriages with a liveried driver at the reins. As they approached a ranch's
headquarters, guests marveled to see deer, antelopes, wild turkeys, and other
game hanging from shade trees near the front door. A typical home consisted
of a large hall and dining table heaped with china and silver on the first
floor, a well-furnished kitchen in the rear, and a dugout cellar stocked with
provisions. Upstairs were bedrooms furnished in the latest European decor.
As evening cast its shadow across the prairie, hosts and guests danced the
night away to orchestral music and clinked glasses brimming with contraband
spirits to celebrate their good fortune. A less celebratory mood prevailed at
boomer campfires, where prospective homesteaders filled their bellies with
cold bacon and beans, all the while scanning the horizon for soldiers who
might put a quick end to their repast.[11]

When pressed for proof, Couch brandished copies of treaties and launched into an all-too-familiar explanation of the one with the Seminoles, concluded in 1866, showing conclusively that they had ceded an estimated 2,169,080 acres (ceded to them by the Creek Nation in a prior treaty in 1856) for the sum of $325,362, or about fifteen cents an acre. The U.S. government's stated intention was to give that land to Indians and freedmen. Yet the treaty was concluded just as a bill was winding its way through Congress to incorporate the Atlantic and Pacific Railroad. And then, only eight days after the treaty with the Seminoles was concluded, Congress granted the railroad the odd sections through the Seminole land cession. In so doing, the government clearly nullified its original plan and opened even sections to settlement per the supplementary Homestead Act of 1879, section 2239. As Couch concluded with numbing regularity, it was no mystery why elected officials did not rely on the law to show boomers the error of their ways.[12]

Encouraged by the goings-on in Washington, boomers agreed to give President Cleveland a chance to implement his policies and, for the most part, suspended their invasions.[13] For Couch, suspending intrusions did not mean letting up on his lobbying efforts. In a letter to Henry L. Dawes (R-Mass., 1875–93), chairman of the Senate Committee on Indian Affairs, he offered to help gather testimonies pertaining to cattlemen's illegal grazing leases. Couch aimed to show that the Department of the Interior encouraged bribery in granting grazing leases on Indian land. He also intended to prove that soldiers dispossessed some cattlemen and awarded leases to others, routinely violated liquor laws, and trampled on U.S. citizens' constitutional rights with impunity.

Examples of military outrages were not hard to come by. A Kansas citizen was arrested, imprisoned for ten days, and dragged behind a wagon for several miles while his pregnant wife and children watched. His wife was so trauma-tized that her baby was born prematurely and died. Others were arrested and jailed for weeks without rations. D. J. Odell of Dutchess County, New York, was arrested on the North Canadian River, tied to a wagon under orders from Lieutenant Stevens of the Ninth Cavalry, and dragged a distance of thirteen miles. Boomers detained at Fort Reno were compelled to sleep on the floor with no bedding and were denied mail and telegrams.[14]

Unlike his colleagues in the Senate who turned a blind eye toward illegal grazing, Senator Dawes actually believed allegations of military misconduct.

HARPER'S WEEKLY.

JOURNAL OF CIVILIZATION.

Vol. XXIX.—No. 1475.
Copyright, 1885, by Harper & Brothers.

NEW YORK, SATURDAY, MARCH 28, 1885.

TEN CENTS A COPY.
$4.00 PER YEAR, IN ADVANCE.

EJECTING AN "OKLAHOMA BOOMER."—Drawn by T. de Thulstrup from a Sketch by Frederic Remington.—[See Page 199.]

T. de Thulstrup, after a sketch by Frederic Remington, *Ejecting an
"Oklahoma Boomer."* Front cover of *Harper's Weekly,* March 28, 1885.
Courtesy of Buffalo Bill Center of the West, Cody, Wyo., 12.93.

He also believed that the jurisdictional mishmash that defined Indian Territory had to go. For a glimpse of what lay in store for Plains tribes, Dawes cited the Five Tribes' successful transition to mainstream culture. To replicate their success among the western Plains tribes, Dawes's committee was investigating land fraud as a prerequisite to formulating a plan to bring Indian Territory into the American political system. To mitigate the rigors of frontier travel, the Senate investigative committee toured Indian Territory aboard a special train, complete with sleeping and dining cars. Along their journey, they were admonished to keep an eye out for cattle and evidence of fraudulent land leases. True to form, the *Oklahoma War-Chief* remained skeptical: "The Sub Senate committee is nothing but a notorious, extravagant, dead beat disgrace to the American people and their boasted form of government, and should be exposed through the columns of every journal in the land."[15]

Allegations of fraud and deceit on the part of government officials were pretty much business as usual in the Gilded Age. But it was not business as usual for President Cleveland, whose radar was on high alert for signs of conspicuous corruption. Signaling that a new sheriff was about to assume office, on February 25, 1885, Congress gave the president authority to take whatever means necessary to remove or destroy enclosures in the public domain.[16] Then came President Cleveland's proclamation of March 13 banning both cattle-men and homesteaders from Oklahoma Proper. A bigger and more targeted bombshell dropped on July 23, when the president ordered cattlemen on the Cheyenne and Arapaho Reservation to round up their livestock and vacate the premises within forty days.[17]

The Cleveland administration's long-range goal was to issue 160 acres to each Indian over twenty-one years of age as a surefire way to promote self-sufficiency.[18] The president's plans for Indians were eventually codified in the Dawes Severalty Act (named for Senator Dawes, and alternatively known as the General Allotment Act) of February 8, 1887, a momentous piece of legislation aimed at breaking up the reservations, putting an end to tribal sovereignty, and propelling Indians into a culture that was losing patience with nomadism and communal landownership. The Dawes Severalty Act authorized the president to survey Indian land for eventual allotment to individual Indians. The remaining, and often the most valuable reservation land, would be sold to settlers, and the government would use the income to purchase farming implements for Indian tribes. As full-fledged American citizens, Indians would be protected by the U.S. Constitution and required to pay taxes. In the ensuing years, tribal opinion would be split for the most part between mixed-blood Indians, who accepted American citizenship as the wave of the future, and full-blood Indians, who were bent on maintaining their traditions.[19]

President Cleveland's proclamation of July 1885 banning cattlemen from the Cheyenne and Arapaho Reservation predated the Dawes Severalty Act by a year and a half, and it came at a time of escalating tensions in the Oklahoma country. Responding to threats of imminent Indian attacks, Lieutenant General Philip Sheridan, commander in chief of the army, and General Nelson A. Miles arrived at Fort Reno to oversee what might have been the largest mobilization of troops since the Civil War. During a parley with Cheyenne chief Stone Calf, Sheridan presented a stark choice: stop preparing for war or face extermination. "I won't even leave nits of you," he said.[20] In a less pugnacious message to the president, Sheridan cited quasi-legal grazing leases as the source of the unrest. The president's reply of July 21 was unequivocal: "The cattle leases are void and the Government has an undoubted right to remove the cattlemen and their herds from the reservation and the Indians may be assured of the determination to protect their rights."[21]

Preparations at Fort Reno apparently had their intended effect, and threats of Indian attacks faded. Another thing that seemed to be fading was boomer optimism. "The boomer movement was dying fast in the summer of 1885, like a cucumber withering on a worm-chewed-off vine," wrote one opinion leader. The excitement attending the expedition to Stillwater Creek had faded, and Bill Couch was running out of options.[22] Spirits sank even lower when, on July 15, a U.S. marshal arrested *Oklahoma War-Chief* editor Samuel Crocker at his office in Caldwell. Along the fifty-mile journey to the jail in Cowley County, Crocker was heartened by outpourings of support from merchants and businessmen who offered to pay his bond, no matter the amount, to effect his immediate release. Yet as the *War-Chief*'s most outspoken editor to date, Crocker refused, as he preferred incarceration as a protest against his denial of free speech. To signal the bellicose stance that it would take throughout Crocker's yearlong tenure as editor, the *War-Chief* published an all-inclusive motto on its masthead to reflect the nation's backlash against Gilded Age inequities: "The Settlement of Oklahoma, Restoration of the public domain, Lands for the landless and homes for the homeless, A national currency issued and controlled by the Federal government."[23]

While Crocker managed the newspaper from his cell, his office back in Caldwell was inundated with requests for photos. Especially popular was a shot of the jailed editor seated somewhat incongruously in a parlor. As requests for the parlor picture poured in, the *War-Chief* promised to have the photo lithographed and enlarged. As a bonus, anyone who took out a year's subscription would receive either a lithograph or two of Crocker's books on labor issues.[24]

On September 7, Crocker took a break from mugging for the cameras to interview Couch. Did he have fears of conviction on charges of treason? "None whatever," replied Couch coolly. He was guardedly optimistic about ending illegal grazing on Indian land. Although he expected cattlemen to fight tooth and nail to keep their leases, he doubted that they would make much headway, as pressure was mounting on President Cleveland to make good on his campaign promises. As for resolution of the Oklahoma Question, Couch was practically buoyant. A few weeks after his interview, Couch signaled his tenacity by leading the sixteenth and final major invasion to the site he had previously occupied in present-day Oklahoma City.[25]

Even as the Oklahoma Question was devolving from boomer camps to Congress and the courts, Couch's October 1885 expedition showed that plenty of boomers still preferred action to polemics. Whether voting with their feet or participating in an ever-escalating war of words, few would have disagreed with Congressman James Nelson Burnes (D-Mo.; 1883–89) in his assessment of an issue that had gone from frontier curiosity to the red-hot center of controversies that framed the Gilded Age frontier: relations with Indians; the chasm between the haves and have-nots; the corrupting effects of Big Money in an age of oversized and largely unregulated corporations; and the definition and disposition of public lands. "On the settlement of the Oklahoma question," thundered Congressman Burnes, "depends the blood of American citizens."[26]

President Cleveland's proclamation ignited a firestorm of complaints from Indians, who, accustomed to holding their land in common, had signed leases with cattlemen and come to regret it. Some Indians were dismayed when cattlemen strung fences around their leases, drove off their cattle or simply absorbed them into their own herds, and prevented Indians from setting foot on leased land. One chief told General Sheridan that he had 114 cattle when the fences went up; by the time President Cleveland issued his edict, that number had dwindled to ten. Another chief said that he had a small farm under cultivation on one of the leaseholds. When cattlemen ordered him off his land, cattle swarmed in and devoured his corn. Many confessed that they had been hoodwinked when large sums of money seemed much smaller after tribal members claimed their share. In their defense, cattlemen insisted that their leases had been executed in good faith.[27]

While Indian complaints were drawing attention to grazing leases in the Cheyenne and Arapaho Reservation, trespassing in the Oklahoma country, and drift cattle wandering where they pleased, cattlemen were wondering how they were going to move their immense herds within the allotted time limit of forty days, and where they were supposed to go. Within a week of the presidential proclamation, a delegation of cattlemen was on its way to Washington to lodge a protest. In all likelihood, they were less interested in extending the deadline than in establishing the validity of their leases and securing their right to stay put.[28]

Clearly, the Oklahoma Question could not go unanswered forever. By 1885, a consensus was emerging on the best course of action, and the logic went like this: The Reconstruction Treaties of 1866 forced the Creeks and Seminoles to cede their land in Oklahoma Proper to the U.S. government for far less than it was worth on the assumption that Indians and freedmen would be settled there. But settlement never happened, and in the two decades since the treaties had been ratified, Oklahoma Proper had degenerated into a cauldron of corruption and competing interests. For an increasing number of opinion leaders, the only way out of the morass was for the U.S. government to confirm, once and for all, its title to the land by paying more money to the Creeks and Seminoles. An alternative would have been for the Creeks and Seminoles to buy the land back. But that was impossible for two reasons: neither of the nations could afford it; and the momentum toward settlement, fueled by six years of boomer expeditions and lobbying in Washington, made it absurd to even consider a buyback.[29]

While congressmen were debating the merits of shelling out money to confirm title to Oklahoma Proper, cattlemen had more to fret about than President Cleveland's proclamation, as their industry was on a downhill slide from its peak in 1884. Anticipating a wave of nesters bent on turning the grasslands into farms, many ranchers had borrowed to the hilt at high interest rates to stock ranges that were already overstocked. Predictably, beef prices plummeted, and vast herds were left to fend for themselves on the open prairie.[30] Cattlemen's troubles were compounded when Kansas,

Colorado, Nebraska, and New Mexico Territory bowed to homesteaders' demands and quarantined themselves against Texas cattle and the disease they carried. Hemmed in by barbed wire and strictly enforced quarantines, Texas cattlemen could no longer rely on overland trails to drive their cattle to the northern railheads.[31] As the open range continued to shrink, the future of the cattle industry appeared to lie in cheap beef raised on small farms, mainly in Texas—the only region unaffected by the presidential proclamation, and where former cattle barons would have to be satisfied with smaller herds and restricted ranges.[32]

Indications that the range cattle industry was entering its twilight can be gleaned from the second annual cattlemen's convention in St. Louis in November 1885. Attendance was down from the heavily attended convention in 1884; nearby Kansas sent only a few representatives, and the Cherokee Strip Live Stock Association was barely represented at all. Clearly, stockmen had become their own worst enemies by exaggerating the fortunes to be made in the cattle industry. By the time President Cleveland issued his proclamation, the paradigm shift in raising cattle was well under way. Perhaps cattlemen who shunned the St. Louis convention had the right idea. As the *Barbour County Index* concluded, "The range cattlemen of the Indian Territory and southwestern Kansas were wise in doing no big blowing this year."[33] Mother Nature chimed in on New Year's Eve, 1885, when the first of a series of blizzards came howling across the Great Plains. In what came to be known as "the big die-up," cattle drifted into arroyos and barbed wire fences, where they either froze to death under a blanket of snow or suffocated in bovine heaps. As one ranch foreman recalled, "I never saw such a sight. There are big mounds of cattle, nothing visible but horns, for the snow had drifted over them and you are spared meantime the horrible sight of seeing piles of carcasses." Cowmen estimated their losses during the winter of 1885–86 at 65 to 75 percent.[34]

The year 1885 ended on another downbeat note when reports from Fort Reno warned that Cheyennes and Arapahos, accustomed to quasi-legal lease payments from the cattlemen they loved to hate, were once again poised for attack. Ironically, the same chiefs who had complained bitterly to officialdom in Washington about cattlemen's abuses were becoming the government's most vocal critics. Optimists had hoped that recent deliveries of beef and supplies to the Darlington Indian Agency would pacify disgruntled Cheyennes and Arapahos. But as winter cast its gloom across the land, none doubted that trouble was brewing on the reservation.[35]

Secretary Lamar was none too happy with the boomers' most recent invasion. In a letter to boomer attorney J. Wade McDonald, Lamar expressed
outrage that Couch and his confederates against whom indictments were
pending had broken their promise to stay out of Indian Territory. Then again,
Couch was none too happy with cattlemen's defiance of President Cleveland's
proclamation of July 1885.[36] Even as he continued to defy the law of the land,
Couch agreed with other boomer leaders that Oklahoma's future would be
settled not in Indian Territory, but in Congress. To clarify just where the
Oklahoma Question stood in early 1886, *Oklahoma War-Chief* editor Samuel
Crocker, long since released from jail, fielded questions from his readers. Was
Captain Couch in Caldwell? No, he was in Washington, D.C., "working like a
beaver" with Congress to open Oklahoma Proper to settlement. Even though
the action was shifting from invasions to politics, prospective settlers could
still support the boomer movement by joining Payne's Oklahoma Colony
for the bargain price of two dollars. Members were assured of three things:
colony veterans would familiarize them with the country; they could count
on assistance in securing land as long as nobody else had claimed it; and their
property would be protected against land fraud. Did colonists plan to build a
city in Oklahoma? "The Colony will be very apt to," declared Crocker, "as it
numbers more than thirteen thousand members, at this writing."[37]

Crocker was right about one thing: Couch was indeed working like a beaver.
At the urging of Weaver and William M. Springer (D-Ill.; 1875–95) in the
House of Representatives and Charles H. Van Wyck (R-Neb.; 1881–87)
in the Senate, Couch and his close collaborator and fellow Kansan Sidney
Clarke began in December 1885 to draft a bill providing governance for a
newly designated Oklahoma Territory.[38] Once settled in the National Hotel in
Washington, D.C., the duo spent the next seven months in a fierce lobbying
campaign to push the bill through Congress. They arrived in Washington
to find the House Committee on Territories considering two bills pertaining
to Oklahoma, one offered by Weaver (drafted with Couch's and Clarke's
assistance), and the other by Richard W. Townshend (D-Ill.; 1877–89).[39]
Opposition came from Cherokee chief Bushyhead, who was in Washington
to represent the Five Tribes and his allies in the National Indian Defense
Association. Granted a special hearing before the House Committee on Territories in mid-February, the association pressured the U.S. government to
maintain its treaty obligations. Weaver, who believed that Indian Territory

was nothing less than a foul blot on American civilization, held his temper as he listened to their arguments.[40]

To keep the boomer brethren apprised of his and Clarke's progress (or the lack thereof), Couch kept up a steady stream of correspondence with Payne's Oklahoma Colony secretary A. E. Stinson, and he in turn supplied news to boomer-friendly newspapers. In one anguished letter after another, Couch described stonewalling on the part of congressmen and cattlemen's attorneys.[41] Boomers were encouraged to learn in late March that the House Committee on Territories was looking favorably on a bill for the organization of Oklahoma Territory and the appointment of a commission to negotiate with the Five Tribes to purchase land at $1.25 an acre.[42] After a particularly tough week, Couch expressed hopes that the obstructionists would one day be exposed for all to see. "It is a hand to hand fight," wrote a frustrated Couch on April 8. "Every inch of the ground being contested."[43] Then came the news that the Committee on Territories had voted down both the Weaver and Townshend bills and, in what seems like an abrupt maneuver, entertained yet another Oklahoma bill, this one proposed by committee chairman William D. Hill (D-Ohio; 1879–81, 1883–87), who intended to make sure that legislation pertaining to Indian Territory conformed to recent Supreme Court rulings on tribal rights and privileges.[44]

Near certainty that Congress would entertain the Oklahoma bill in early May turned to disappointment when it was put off until the next session.[45] By June, Couch feared that even die-hard boomers were losing heart: "I have heard from no one out there lately. Hope no one is dead. I judge from the last letters all have the blues, I am still hopeful of success this session.[46] To signal the depths of his despair, Couch reminded Stinson in virtually all of his letters that he was running out of money. Barring an infusion of funds, he and Clarke would have to return to Kansas empty-handed—if, that is, they could scrounge up enough money for train tickets.[47]

As Oklahoma bills waxed and waned, House members enjoyed a moment of levity when Representative Bishop W. Perkins (R-Kans.; 1883–91) asked Weaver, point-blank, if he was the boomers' paid attorney. Weaver replied indignantly that, no, he most certainly was not, although he had contributed money to the boomer movement out of his own pocket and would no doubt continue to do so. And then came the about-face, and Weaver asked Perkins if he was the cattle syndicates' paid attorney. Perkins was likewise indignant at such a bold accusation. Laughter filled the room as the two legislators traded barbs and accusations.[48]

Back in Caldwell, Crocker expressed outrage toward a do-nothing Congress whose refusal to act on the Oklahoma Question was causing prospective homesteaders to rethink their early enthusiasm for the reform-minded Grover Cleveland and the Democratic majority in Congress.[49] Insisting that the Oklahoma bill was one of the most important pieces of legislation to engage Congress—and, hence, the American people—since the Civil War, Crocker ramped up his invective. "No bill of alike importance was ever spurned with such scornful contempt," declared Crocker. Upon his return to Caldwell after seven fruitless months in Washington, a humiliated Couch faced hostile boomers, who shared his disappointment over the way special interests had blocked the Oklahoma bill. Putting on his game face, Couch predicted that at least two-thirds of Congress would pass the bill in its next session.[50]

In late November, rumors circulated that U.S. commissioner of Indian Affairs Atkins had decided to move several tribes, including Comanches, Cheyennes, Arapahos, Kiowas, and Wichitas, east of the ninety-eighth meridian, which included Oklahoma Proper.[51] But a couple of weeks later, Atkins assured friends of the Oklahoma bill that the report had no foundation and, furthermore, that Congress would have the last word.[52]

—————

Couch and Clarke lobbied, Crocker ranted, and boomers boomed in a quickening pace of capital investment, and nowhere was the pace quicker than in railroad construction. An agreement was reached on March 3, 1886, whereby the Boston-based Santa Fe, which owned the securities of the Southern Kansas Railway Company, purchased the entire capital stock of the Galveston-based Gulf, Colorado, and Santa Fe Railway Company (the Gulf and Colorado). The purchase gave the Santa Fe an opportunity to expand into Texas, as the Gulf and Colorado was building a line from Fort Worth northward into Indian Territory to meet the Santa Fe line at Walnut Creek in the Chickasaw Nation. Completion was expected in a year, in plenty of time to move cattle to pasture. As the din of railroad construction moved ever closer to the Oklahoma country, cowboys caught a glimpse of their futures to realize that their freewheeling days were about to change forever.[53]

The quickening pace of railroad construction coincided with the *Oklahoma War-Chief*'s demise. The paper suspended publication on August 12, 1886. Crocker blamed the newspaper's woes on Congress's failure to address the Oklahoma Question and the resulting slump in Caldwell's economy. But neither Crocker nor his hardworking and underpaid colleagues were going down without a fight: "No, friends; we will not abandon so sacred a cause—no, never; but, will buckle on our armor and with renewed vigor and redoubled energy return to the battle with more vehemence and determination than ever before. The suffering, homeless poor shall possess Oklahoma despite the Texas steer and downright cowards of congress. . . . So be it, by the Eternal God!"[54]

Oblivious to Crocker's rants, Santa Fe construction crews continued slicing their way southward. To accommodate the uptick in activity, folks at Fort Reno and the Darlington Indian Agency decided it was time to apply for a post office to serve both outposts. Postal officials mistakenly (but understandably) concluded that the post office would be located at Fort Reno or the Indian agency. On November 15, 1886, officials accepted an application to establish a post office at a place dubbed "Seymour." Postal officials would have been surprised to learn that Seymour was never located in the Cheyenne and Arapaho Reservation. In reality, it was nothing more than a tent village that migrated south with railroad construction crews. Wherever it happened to be on any given day, Seymour was a beehive of activity, complete with hundreds of teams of horses, farm implements of every description, a licensed trading post, and a post office that had been operating for two months before its official designation. The postmaster, William S. Decker, was a licensed trader along the railroad line, and he aimed to expand his mercantile operations from Kansas to the Canadian River. Ironically, the largest noncitizen community in the Oklahoma country never stayed in one place for long, and nobody could find it on a map.[55]

The distance between railroad stations was about ten miles and was determined by the productivity of regions along the way. As construction crews proceeded southward, they established telegraph offices at Ponca (later, White Eagle), Mendota (later, Perry), Deer Creek (later, Guthrie), Seymour (later, in rapid succession, Verbeck, Oklahoma, Oklahoma Station, and Oklahoma City), and Walnut Creek (later, Purcell).[56] Even with modern communication, people still depended on the mail. Jenny Robertson settled with her family near present-day Moore about two years before Oklahoma Proper was opened to non-Indian settlement. While her mother managed a tent full of boarders, Jenny mounted her horse twice a week and carried mail between Moore and the future site of Oklahoma City. In the absence of a bridge, Jenny forded the North Canadian River wherever she could find a safe place to cross.[57]

After the Southern Kansas Railway Company completed a line south from Arkansas City, trains began running on a regular basis to and from Ponca. The first train left Arkansas City on November 29, 1886, just in time for another brutal winter that spelled trouble not only for railroad construction crews but also for cattlemen from Texas to the Dakotas, who were still recovering from the big die-up of 1885–86.[58] Charley Colcord, who had been working as a cowboy in northern Arizona Territory, returned to Kansas to experience the most severe weather in the southern Great Plains since the earliest days of settlement. In a sickening replay of the previous winter, the snows melted to reveal countless thousands of carcasses littering the prairies. And once again, barbed wire fences had proved all too effective in keeping cattle hemmed in.[59]

Braving storms that were extreme even by Great Plains standards, railroad construction workers laboring northward from Texas and southward from Kansas aimed to connect their lines at Walnut Creek by April 20, 1887, the deadline for completion as specified in the Santa Fe's charter.[60] When it appeared that they might miss their deadline, the railway's chief clerk, C. H. Curtis, traveled down the line in a bunk car, picked up the roadmaster and station agents, cut the telegraph line, and made a dash for Walnut Creek, where he and his companions laid low for several days so that the U.S. marshal could not find anyone to serve an injunction. A writ was eventually issued at Muskogee, but it was not served before the railways were linked at Walnut Creek on April 26, six days after the deadline had passed.[61]

Indian outrage over the rapid pace of railroad construction and apparent violation of solemn treaties dating back to 1866 crystallized in two intertribal councils, one at Eufaula in March 1887, and the other at Fort Gibson, with twenty-two tribes represented, in 1888. Their protests fell on mostly deaf ears in Congress.[62] By then, the Dawes Severalty Act providing for individual land allotments and Indian ownership in severalty, passed into law on February 8, 1887, was a hot topic of conversation for Indians, who felt powerless to stem the erosion of tribal sovereignty.

Now that the rails were joined, construction crews headed for what they hoped were more hospitable environs, and Seymour postmaster Decker lost his customers. The Post Office Department approved his request to discontinue service, and Seymour dwindled to two small buildings and drifted out of history. Still convinced that Seymour was located in the Cheyenne and Arapaho Reservation, the department on May 13, 1887, ordered mail delivery to the nearest post office, which was then at Red Rock. By then, a telegraph office had been opened at the rapidly shrinking village of Seymour. When that happened on May 2, 1887, the tiny crossroads was rebranded as "Verbeck," an appellation that stuck for a month.[63]

C. E. Bennington, conductor of a construction train dispatched to build switches for the Gulf, Colorado and Santa Fe Railway, recalled the origins of a railroad siding that flickered into history as the migratory village of Seymour, was dubbed "Verbeck" for a month, and became known as "Oklahoma Station" (abbreviated as "Oklahoma") in June 1887 when the trains started running. When Bennington and his crew arrived at present-day Oklahoma City, an argument broke out as to the best place to build a siding. Some wanted to build it farther north, while others preferred a location close to the North Canadian River. As a compromise, Bennington suggested building a siding east of a big cottonwood tree that, two years hence, became the corner of Broadway and Grand Avenues. "This was agreed to," recalled Bennington, "and Oklahoma City grew from the suggestion."[64]

R. F. Vanderford was living in Strong City, Kansas, when Henry Quinn, foreman of a Santa Fe construction crew, came through town in early May 1887 to recruit carpenters to build depots and section houses at Verbeck and Walnut Creek.[65] Although Vanderford's crew did not build a depot at Norman, they did construct a house, water tank, and extensive corrals to facilitate shipments of cattle from the Chickasaw Nation to the northern ranges. Meanwhile, another crew was dispatched to build depots at Guthrie and Edmond.[66]

By June 12, the entire line, from Arkansas City to Walnut Creek, was in operation. It was not a moment too soon. According to Frank J. Best, Santa Fe clerk and telegraph operator at the time of the opening and freight agent at Oklahoma City after 1895, the completion of the lines in April 1887 came just in time to transport cattle to northern Indian Territory and southern Kansas.[67] A July 1887 timetable shows an express train leaving Arkansas City at 9:40 A.M., reaching the siding that Bennington and his crew had built, known generally as "Oklahoma," at 1:36 P.M., and arriving at Purcell (formerly, Walnut Creek) at 2:55 P.M. The northbound express train left Purcell at 1:00 P.M., reached the North Canadian River at 2:17 P.M., and arrived at ArkansasCity at 6:45 P.M.[68]

"It took from forty to sixty hours to make the trip," recalled George J. Haas, conductor of the freight train's first trip through the Oklahoma country on June 12, whose career with the Santa Fe spanned fifty years (1879–1929). Landmarks were few and far between, and the only place he and his crew could find something to eat was at the Edmond depot. Rest stops were equally scarce. On occasion, he had to pull his train onto a sidetrack to allow others to pass, thus allowing him and his men to catch a few winks until the whistle of a passing train woke them up. For the most part, Haas's cars were loaded with lumber and cattle. Upon arrival at Oklahoma or some other nondescript depot, cargo and livestock were unloaded and transferred to overland freighters for delivery to their final destination. The Oklahoma depot served primarily as a conduit for military equipment bound for Fort Reno and beef and supplies for the Darlington Indian Agency.

Haas was less than two years into his job when demands to open Oklahoma Proper to homesteading were reaching fever pitch, and "interesting things began to happen" aboard his train. He was starting to carry more passengers, and most of them wanted him to slow down along the way so that they could hop safely off the train. Hass told them that he always put on the brakes at the Cimarron River. He was therefore not surprised to find his passenger load lightening as he steered his train southward.[69]

People who preferred to ride in relative comfort depended on Albert R. Glazier, conductor of the first passenger train through Oklahoma Proper. His maiden voyage began in Newton, Kansas, in the predawn stillness of June 13, 1887. At 7:45 A.M., his train crossed the Arkansas River. From that day forward, Glazier never lost his fascination with the wild beauty that surrounded him. "The sky was blue and cloudless, and the freshness and beauty of summer was on the prairies," recalled Glazier. Unless someone flagged him along the way, he stopped only to take on coal and water at Wharton and Edmond. Especially vivid in his memory was the wildlife—so plentiful that hunters blasted away from the train windows to leave trails of dead animals strewn across the prairie.[70]

To improve communications, a post office was established at Oklahoma Station on December 30, 1887. Samuel H. Radebaugh was named as the first postmaster, and he depended on the likes of Jenny Robertson to deliver mail to and from even tinier outposts.[71] A few weeks after Radebaugh set up shop, the Santa Fe appointed A. W. Dunham to manage the depot. Nearby was a house erected under orders from the quartermaster's department to facilitate shipment of military supplies.[72]

When Dunham stepped off the southbound train about 2:00 A.M. on February 20, 1888, Oklahoma Station was the only reporting or agency station between Arkansas City and Purcell, a distance of 154 miles. His first stop was a shack across from the depot that was used to house and feed mule skinners, tenderfeet, and transients who somehow made their way to the middle of Indian Territory. After stepping over several Indians curled on the floor in colorful blankets, Dunham climbed a flight of stairs to find a bed covered by a thin blanket. To ward off the winter chill, he slept in his clothes and used his overcoat for added warmth. Breakfast was served on a long pine table and consisted of sow belly, soggy biscuits, molasses, and black coffee. Oklahoma Station's population swelled when Dunham's mother, two sisters, and a brother came to live with him in a cottage that the company provided for its agent.[73]

The *Oklahoma War-Chief*'s demise in August 1886 did not mean that its irascible editor had quit his proselytizing. His cause had received a major boost in January, when the nation's leading advocate of workmen's rights, the Knights of Labor, added homesteading in the Oklahoma country to its agenda of pro-labor causes. Other issues on the Knights of Labor's agenda included safety and health legislation; the eight-hour work day; nationalization of railroads, telephones, and telegraphs; the abolition of child and convict labor; currency reform; and a postal savings system. Throughout the late 1880s, journalists and speakers of Crocker's ilk roamed the southern plains, and wherever they went, they found people receptive to their tirades against the monied elite and insistence that public lands be opened for homesteading. Farmers were particularly receptive to their message when the historic drought of 1887 reduced Kansas's wheat production by a third and forced half the population of western Kansas off their land.[74] More than ever, Indian Territory beckoned as a land not just of opportunity, but of survival.

Energized by the Knights of Labor's endorsement of the boomer movement, in February 1887 Crocker took to the speaker's podium in Cincinnati, where he shared his indignation over cattle syndicates and railroad corporations with delegates to the National Industrial Convention.[75] While he was delivering his message to convention attendees, Bill Couch was wrapping up another stay at the National Hotel in Washington, D.C. He arrived back in Douglass on March 12 to find the real estate business booming across southern Kansas. "Caldwell is on a big boom," he wrote to Payne's Oklahoma Colony secretary A. E. Stinson on March 27. "Crocker has struck it rich in buying lots. He has made about $2,000.00 so I am informed." To cash in on the bonanza, Couch resolved to get into the real estate business in either Caldwell or Douglass and make some money while Congress dithered on the Oklahoma Question.[76]

While Crocker and Couch were scouting for investment opportunities, Charley Colcord's father convinced his son to quit cowboying in Arizona Territory and return to Wichita, where the real estate boom was reaching epic proportions. Lot values doubled, then tripled, and then quadrupled in a single day. As banks were reluctant to loan money on transactions, landowners and speculators took their profits in cash. "It was the wildest thing you could possibly imagine," recalled the younger Colcord.[77] Oklahoma City's first lawman and, later, one of the city's most renowned real estate moguls could not have known that he was catching a glimpse of his future in Wichita's ever-escalating real estate prices in the spring of 1887.

Colcord learned a lesson in prudence when the boom stalled and then collapsed, leaving his father and thousands of others broke and with no hope of recovery.[78] As the boom-and-bust cycle played out in southern Kansas, boomers, who had always had their own ideas about real estate development, were more determined than ever to plant their stakes in virgin soil. Many of them gathered northwest of Arkansas City and announced their intention to move south on August 16. Several companies of soldiers, including a detachment of the Fifth Cavalry, were camped nearby and were prepared to assist soldiers stationed in Indian Territory in heading off intruders before they could set up their makeshift camps.[79]

Boomer bluster notwithstanding, Bill Couch, who was reeling from the real estate bust in southern Kansas, remained convinced that he and his colleagues could prod the Oklahoma bill through Congress. He and Sidney Clarke were planning another trip to Washington in early December to promote the extension of public lands laws to Oklahoma Proper, the Cherokee Outlet, and the public land strip (later, the Oklahoma Panhandle).[80] But not everyone was prepared to wait for yet another session of Congress to settle the Oklahoma Question. At year's end, reports were coming out of Eldorado, Kansas, that a massive raid, slated for early spring 1888, was in the planning stages. A hundred thousand men were allegedly ready to move, a throng far too large for troops to contain. According to one of the raid's planners, they "mean business from now on."[81] E. C. Cole, a real estate broker from Kingman, Kansas, who had coauthored a book with A. P. Jackson about the Oklahoma country in 1885, aimed to set up an office down south as soon as the country was opened.[82] Upon his return from a four-week trip to Indian Territory to scout potential townsites, he expressed doubts about the new crusade. But he had no doubt that boomers were too stubborn to let up in their efforts to occupy Oklahoma Proper.[83]

Charles F. Colcord.
Courtesy of Oklahoma Historical Society, Oklahoma City, 1111.

Yet even as trains chugged their way across the prairie and boomers kept up their invasions, opening Oklahoma Proper to homesteading and townsite development was not a foregone conclusion. According to Santa Fe agent Frank Best, most people still favored the Indians' answer to the Oklahoma Question and believed that Congress should uphold its promise to leave Indians alone for as long as the grass grew and water flowed. "Neither the Santa Fe nor the public generally expected it to be opened," wrote Best. "To build in a barren country would not be rated a wise move."[84]

The final word in the waning weeks of 1887 goes to Sidney Clarke. While an army of a hundred thousand was planning the mother of all invasions in that bleak winter, Clarke was on his way to Washington to renew his crusade of words in Congress. In his pocket was a recent incarnation of the Oklahoma bill, providing for opening eastern Indian Territory (then occupied by the Five Tribes), the public land strip known as "No Man's Land," and of course Oklahoma Proper to non-Indian settlement.[85]

Clarke had much to think about as he journeyed eastward. As a veteran of Washington politics, he had made the trip many times, and he probably let familiar landmarks whiz by his window with nary a glance. A few passengers no doubt recognized him as a former congressman-at-large from Kansas and current leader of the boomer movement, and he probably shared his mission with anyone who cared to listen. Did he read and reread his Oklahoma bill, scratch notes in the margins, and perhaps rehearse his speeches in silence? Did he review the schedule of appointments that would consume his days in Washington? Or was he content to gaze out the window at a landscape of farms and villages and wonder when the march of Western civilization would one day transform Oklahoma Proper from a prairie wilderness into an agrarian paradise?

There is no way to know. But we can be sure of one thing. Sidney Clarke could not have imagined that sixteen months would pass before officialdom would yield to the tide of history, and another thirteen months before it would pass legislation to provide governance for the Union's newest territory.

CHAPTER EIGHT

Endgame

Oh Joe, here's your mule!
Boomer refrain, late 1880s

Sidney Clarke arrived in Washington to find the reconvened Fiftieth U.S. Congress (1887–89) awash in bills. According to one tally, 902 bills were introduced on a single day in January 1888, including several that aimed to answer the Oklahoma Question.[1] But the bill that was about to capture everybody's attention was introduced on January 6 by the boomers' longtime champion from Illinois and chairman of the House Committee on Territories from 1887 to 1889, William M. Springer, who would settle for nothing less than the creation of a new territory. He went on record to suggest that the Oklahoma Question dwarfed even the discovery of gold in California in its importance and long-term consequences.[2]

Springer's bill to create Oklahoma Territory embraced No Man's Land and all of Indian Territory west of the Five Tribes—about two-thirds of Indian Territory, an area roughly the size of Ohio. It called for the appointment of territorial officers, recognition of townsites that squatters had occupied in No Man's Land, and regulation of the new territory under the purview of public lands laws as soon as Indian claims could be extinguished. The bill declared cattle leases null and void; lessees who refused to cooperate would be removed by presidential order. Railroads were likewise in Springer's crosshairs. Springer not only wanted to ban grants to railroads but also insisted that the new territorial legislature and local governments be prohibited from aiding them.[3]

Sidelined in Kansas by a lack of travel funds, Bill Couch settled for corresponding with Sidney Clarke and, through a continuing stream of letters to
A. E. Stinson, keeping the boomer faithful abreast of developments. Although
he expressed optimism about the prospects for Springer's bill, Clarke singled
out two members of the House Committee on Territories who were bound
to cause trouble: George T. Barnes (D-Ga.; 1885–91) and Charles S. Baker
(R-N.Y.; 1885–91).[4] Wary of the opposition's delaying tactics, Couch fired off
a cryptic telegram to Clarke at the National Hotel in Washington, alerting
him to a delegation of Kansas cattlemen roaming the halls of Congress in
unspecified disguises.[5] As the hearings ground on through January, the bill's
supporters gained confidence that their arguments would win the day, not only
in the House Committee on Territories, but also in both houses of Congress.
Prescient observers expected the committee to schedule a meeting within
days, perhaps as soon as early February.[6]

Clarke was right about one thing: Congressmen Barnes and Baker were
determined to have the last word. In his minority report, cosigned by William
Elliott (D-S.C.; 1887–89, 1891–93, 1895–96, 1897–1903), Barnes made
the case for Congress's obligations toward Indians. In laborious detail, he
reviewed treaties that even tribal allegiances to the Confederacy during the
Civil War and the Reconstruction Treaties of 1866 could not supersede. As
Barnes wound through a legal thicket (including the propriety of grazing
leases, which he believed were consistent with existing treaties) toward his
conclusion, he insisted that creating a territory without the prior consent of
the people who lived there would amount not only to theft but also a derelic-
tion of national honor and abandonment of America's founding principles.
In the minority view, any changes with respect to tribal occupancy of Indian
Territory should be made through the democratic process.[7] In his addendum
to the minority report, Representative Baker implored Congress not to pass
legislation affecting western Indian Territory without the assent of at least
two-thirds of each tribe's male members over twenty-one years of age. With
tribal assent obtained, Baker believed that Congress could create a territory
in conformity with treaties.[8]

Unmoved by pleas on behalf of Indians, a committee appointed by the
Oklahoma Interstate Convention, held on February 8, 1888, in Kansas City to
promote the Springer bill, traveled to Washington to make its case before the
House Committee on Territories. Dr. Morrison Munford of the *Kansas City
Times* was the committee's chief spokesman for the delegation, which included

Sidney Clarke, Samuel Crocker, and Bill Couch, who had somehow mustered the wherewithal to make the trip.[9] The group settled into the National Hotel before bowing to the tyranny of a tight budget and moving to a cheaper hotel closer to the Capitol.

Two days after Crocker's arrival in Washington, Munford secured a get-acquainted session with President Cleveland. Suffering from ill health and too timid to present their case to the president, Munford let Crocker do the talking. After an hour or so of amiable chatting, the president agreed to a meeting the next Tuesday afternoon.[10] Encouraged, Munford and Crocker hastened back to their hotel to share the good news with their colleagues and plan their formal audience with the president. The audience came off on schedule, but inconclusively. Several members returned home shortly thereafter, leaving Crocker, Couch, and Clarke to advance the Oklahoma bill through the House Committee on Territories. In the absence of a presidential proclamation announcing the Oklahoma opening, the trio made do with a pro-settlement speech by Charles H. Mansur (D-Mo.; 1887–93). Couch was so heartened by Mansur's speech that he wrote Stinson, then domiciled at Walnut Creek in the Chickasaw Nation, to predict timely passage of the Oklahoma bill in one form or another.[11]

Congressional hearings and presidential audiences were the last thing on soldiers' minds as they continued to patrol the Oklahoma country. In mid-February 1888, a company of buffalo soldiers rounded up trespassers and escorted them to Fort Reno. Some were released, while others were held for trial. Although boomer leaders were discouraging invasions, not all of the rank and file got the message. Sidney Clarke and his companions were disturbed to read in the Washington press that two companies of regulars had passed through Wichita on their way to the Oklahoma country to make arrests.[12]

Not even cavalry patrols and the inevitability of arrest were enough to dampen the spirits of black leaders in Kansas. Writing in the *Topeka American Citizen*, opinion leaders encouraged their readers to prepare for homesteading in the Oklahoma country before "discontented and oppressed Europeans get there."[13] Black aspirations met stiff resistance among the Five Tribes, whose anti-settlement sentiment remained strong. Yet opinion leaders knew that the status quo was unsustainable, and the best they could hope for was full participation in charting Indian Territory's future. In an open letter to the *Indian Chieftain*, one J. T. C. applauded Congressman Barnes's principled stand against the Springer bill and insistence that Indians be consulted in all negotiations pertaining to settlement and the disposition of Indian lands. But there was a caveat: even though most members of the Five Tribes preferred "civilized and enlightened whites" to unruly Plains tribes as neighbors, Congress needed to know that Indians would not relinquish their land on the cheap.[14]

The politics of settlement were of little concern to A. W. Dunham as he went about his duties at Oklahoma Station. About the time of his appointment as stationmaster in February 1888, a Concord stagecoach, featuring a boot in front and back and drawn by six horses, was making regular runs between the depot and Fort Reno. The cost was three dollars for a one-way ticket and five dollars for a round-trip. Passengers, many of whom were government officials, were allowed forty pounds of baggage at no cost; additional weight was charged at the express rate. In addition to facilitating passenger service, Oklahoma Station served as a distribution center for cargo bound for Indian agencies, including Darlington, and supplies and equipment for soldiers at Fort Reno as well as more distant outposts. It was not unusual for overland freighters to haul supplies 125 miles from Oklahoma Station to far western Indian Territory. Dunham estimated Indian freight alone at a million pounds a month.

In spite of the official ban on grazing in the Oklahoma country, vast herds of cattle were a regular sight at the Santa Fe depot and its environs. During his first year on the job, Dunham oversaw shipment of a thousand cars of cattle, a few cars of buffalo horns, and quite a few cars piled high with bones that enterprising nesters had gathered for sale as fertilizer and other industrial purposes. Dunham spotted those nesters and the buffalo soldiers who chased them with numbing regularity. Whenever soldiers showed up for a raid on boomer camps, the volume of business surged along the Santa Fe.[15]

In the absence of banking facilities, the Santa Fe express company processed money orders and transported money and valuables to Fort Reno and other outposts. Even though most people who passed through the depot were law-abiding citizens and more than likely on official business, Dunham knew to be on the lookout for outlaws. Some used fictitious names to gain access to the depot and proceeded to filch supplies. Then there were the whiskey peddlers from Texas and Kansas City who did a brisk business with Indians. Their business model included camouflaging their contraband and shipping it by express freight. To supply soldiers at Fort Reno with their hard-earned pay, officials sent money to the Santa Fe depot, where it was loaded onto overland freight wagons and shipped the rest of the way under cavalry escort.

But not always. On one harrowing occasion when the escort failed to show up, Dunham stashed some forty thousand dollars in a pair of rubber boots and covered them with trash. "Not even the night operator knew we were taking such a risk," recalled Dunham about his stressful week. "Many bad men were known to be in the country at the time; trains were being held up and robbed at other places, but we were not molested in the least."[16]

In late July 1888, the Oklahoma bill gained the full attention of the House of Representatives. Desperate to keep the bill alive, Springer made a motion that representatives go into a committee of the whole to consider his Oklahoma bill. But during the roll call, only 132 members—31 short of a quorum—responded when their names were called. House members then squared off in a fiery debate over the propriety of allowing so many representatives to be absent from the chamber when momentous issues were up for discussion. As one representative noted in a complaint that rings through the annals of congressional history, "It was unfair to the members who felt it their duty to be in attendance that others should be permitted to go off and look after their political fences at the public expense."[17]

The *Indian Chieftain* concluded that Congress had abandoned the Oklahoma bill, at least in its current session. The pugnacious Springer was certain that his bill would pass before the Fiftieth Congress's adjournment on March 4, 1889. A few weeks later and far from the glare of public scrutiny, the Creek Nation legislature approved the sale of the tribe's remaining interest in the Oklahoma country to the U.S. government, thus signaling the beginning of the end of Indian land claims in central Indian Territory.[18]

The Wichita Board of Trade did its part to hasten the bill's passage by hosting the Interstate Oklahoma Convention on November 20, 1888, at the opera house on Douglas Avenue. Billing the event as a "Monster Oklahoma Convention," Bill Couch, Samuel Crocker, and other members of the organizing committee aimed to create a critical mass of supporters whose collective voice would rattle the halls of Congress. Posters and ads published in the *Wichita Eagle* were nothing less than a call to arms, and they promised that no expense would be spared to make the convention a success.[19] Oklahoma colonies across the land were asked to summon mass meetings to elect delegates. Assured of a rousing welcome in Wichita, Springer overcame his disappointment with Republican victories in the election of 1888 and

promised to attend.[20] Representative Charles H. Mansur informed Sidney
Clarke on November 17 that he planned to attend the convention, only to
reverse course later that day to indicate that he might not make it after all.
But either way, he wished Clarke and his associates all the best and promised
to remain resolute in his support for the Oklahoma bill.[21]

An estimated 500 delegates (9,500 less than the organizing committee
expected) erupted in thunderous applause when Springer stepped onto the
stage. He wasted no time in ripping into cattle syndicates that were leasing
some six million acres in Indian Territory. "The time for their occupancy is
short, and the cattle kings must go," declared Springer. Springer and Mansur,
who did indeed make it to Wichita, together with Weaver and Clarke, delivered daytime speeches and left it to Couch and Crocker to rouse the crowd
during the evening session.[22] Before delegates disbanded, they appointed
Couch, Clarke, and Crocker to take the convention's message to Washington.
As a postscript to the convention, Crocker reported that six hundred dollars
had been raised to defray their travel expenses, and an executive committee
was already raising additional funds.[23]

The Interstate Oklahoma Convention closed with a sense of urgency, and
nobody felt it more keenly than the peripatetic Sidney Clarke. On November
26, convention secretary H. L. Pierce certified Clarke's appointment to travel
to Washington to promote the Oklahoma bill.[24] As he packed his bags, Clarke
probably included his collection of newspaper clippings on what might have
been the most pernicious consequence of congressional foot-dragging: lawlessness in Indian Territory that was intensifying as whites, some legally and some
not, settled on Indian land. Much as Clarke's ownership of Congressman
George W. Julian's speech on the government's squandering of the public
domain reveals his commitment to opening Oklahoma Proper to homesteading and townsite development, so, too, do his clippings on crime signal his
revulsion toward frontier mayhem.[25] While Congress dithered, the West's
most notorious outlaws were branding Indian Territory as a black hole where
heinous crimes were committed with shocking frequency. Boomer rhapsodies
about the Promised Land were hard to keep up when brigands were taking
advantage of lax law enforcement and jurisdictional disputes to wreak havoc.
As contemporary pundits put it, "There is no Sunday west of St. Louis—no
God west of Fort Smith."[26]

Included in Clarke's clippings on murder and bedlam is a thoughtful
editorial penned by one J. H. Gillpatrick about disorder, which increased

exponentially as one traveled west of Fort Smith. During a train ride through Indian Territory, Gillpatrick passed through the smoking car to find prisoners in handcuffs and deputy marshals in authentic border attire—broad hats, cartridge belts, and pistols.

"Is the United States Court in session?" asked Gillpatrick.

"You bet!" replied an unnamed marshal. "She's in full blast."

Gillpatrick soon discovered what that meant. At the time his article was published in November 1888, about 150 prisoners were in Fort Smith awaiting trial or execution, and at least 40 percent of them were under indictment for murder. The U.S. District Court for the Western District of Arkansas, which had jurisdiction over Indian Territory, tried only cases in which people of European ancestry were involved, either as perpetrators or victims, whereas Indians' crimes were remanded to tribal courts. Yet many defendants were of mixed blood, and most had committed their crimes in Indian Territory. To get the lowdown on jurisdictional complexities from an expert, Gillpatrick interviewed U.S. district judge Isaac C. Parker, arguably the best known and most widely respected (or feared, depending on one's perspective) adjudicator in the West. The judge cut directly to the chase: "I think it were better for the suppression of crime and the protection of property there that the courts of the United States had cognizance of all offenses in the Territory."

Gillpatrick closed his interview and left Judge Parker to his deliberations. Back on the street, he was struck by Fort Smith's relatively low crime rate, which he deemed to be on a par with other western communities of similar size. "But over the border diabolism and a saturnalia of wickedness and misrule undeniably prevail. The wolfish and the panther-like propensity of the Indian in his natural state is still in his system after the missionary has practiced all his arts of redemption." For Gillpatrick, the era of accommodation to tribal customs had run its course. The future lay in abolishing tribal sovereignty, ending communal ownership of land, and bringing all tribes and nations under the jurisdiction of the U.S. legal system.[27]

Leafing through Sidney Clarke's clippings, one does not have to wonder what put the fire in his belly to slog through countless meetings in Kansas, travel to Washington for yet more meetings, deliver speeches ad infinitum, and somehow find time to maintain a rapid-fire flurry of correspondence with his boomer colleagues. Settlement of the Oklahoma Question in favor of homesteaders and urban settlers was the only way to stem Indian Territory's descent into anarchy.

On December 18, 1888, the U.S. Post Office shortened Oklahoma Station's designation to "Oklahoma." Samuel H. Radebaugh remained as postmaster, a position that he had held since December 1887.[28] Oklahoma's rebranding came at a time when the boomer movement had gone silent. But ever since the Interstate Oklahoma Convention in late November, business leaders in Wichita had been working behind the scenes to build support in communities as far east as Illinois and as far west as Colorado. Such was their determination to keep the lid on their activities that they convinced the *Wichita Eagle*'s editorial board to keep quiet. But now, in the closing weeks of 1888, the time had come to go public.

The first hint that something big was in the wind came on December 14 when Wild West showman Gordon William Lillie (a.k.a. Pawnee Bill) received a mysterious dispatch from Wichita at his home in Philadelphia: "Colony will start next week. Be sure and come." His arrival in Wichita on December 22 was the signal for business leaders to come clean in their efforts to revitalize the boomer movement by enlisting one of the nation's most illustrious frontiersmen to lead the charge.[29] As noted in (Samuel Crocker's?) handwritten account of the Interstate Oklahoma Convention and the heady days that followed, "Then and there, he established in a few short days his claim to fame as a 'boomer leader' and woke up those fellows in Washington."[30]

None doubted that Lillie was the right man for the job. Like William F. Cody (a.k.a. Buffalo Bill), Lillie had credentials as a bona fide frontiersman. Having befriended Pawnee and other Indian leaders, he expected to lead an expedition southward without interference, particularly as he had no intention of trespassing on Indian land and would confine his colonization activities to Oklahoma Proper.[31] Although he was prepared to fight, Lillie insisted that his intentions were entirely peaceful, and he called on boomers everywhere to help him force the government's hand. He intended to stay in Wichita and, if warranted by continued inaction in Congress, to prepare for an invasion.[32]

As news of Pawnee Bill's impending invasion spread, the showman-turned-activist knew he had a tiger by the tail. As he explained to the *Emporia Weekly News*, he would use his influence to hold boomers in check while Congress debated the Oklahoma bill. And if the measure failed to pass? Then, declared the *News*, "Pawnee Bill will cry havoc! and let slip the dogs of war. Then 'On to Oklahoma' will be the cry of at least 15,000 sturdy pioneers now chafing at delay."[33] There might have been a downside to putting a man

Gordon William Lillie, a.k.a. Pawnee Bill.
Courtesy of Oklahoma Historical Society, Oklahoma City, 7385.

with Lillie's charisma in charge of a boomer invasion. In an interview with the *Washington Post*, Bill Couch, then lobbying in Washington, expressed doubt that anyone with such a "blood-curdling name" as Pawnee Bill stood a chance of compelling Congress to act.[34]

For up-to-date and reliable information, prospective settlers turned to the *Oklahoma City Times*, edited by Hamlin Whitmore Sawyer, printed in Wichita, and distributed every Saturday from the Oklahoma post office. B. R. Harrington was the paper's ace reporter, and he worked tirelessly as well as illegally to publicize the goings-on in Oklahoma Proper. Sawyer and Harrington became so brazen that they moved their printing operation, albeit briefly, to Oklahoma. Circulation boomed, and within thirty days of its inaugural issue, there were subscribers in every American state and territory as well as in Great Britain and Canada.[35] To leave no doubt about his purpose, Sawyer announced on the masthead that the *Oklahoma City Times* was "DEVOTED TO THE SETTLEMENT OF OKLAHOMA."

In its first issue on December 29, 1888, Sawyer published a familiar chronicle of treaties that left millions of acres in central and western Indian

Territory populated by no more than three thousand Cheyennes and Arapahos, who neither owned nor farmed the land. Then there were the cattlemen, whose herds roamed where they pleased and whose owners relied on friends in high places to keep grazing fees low or nonexistent and profits high.[36] To illustrate the futility of keeping farmers out of central Indian Territory and the inevitability of settlement, Harrington cited a farmer named Keith, who, during five years of residence in Oklahoma Proper, had put about two hundred acres under cultivation and shipped some five hundred hogs to distant markets over the Santa Fe. Sawyer and Harrington assured newcomers that an Oklahoma Colony had been organized and would welcome them with open arms.[37]

Times ads and editorials fell on fertile soil. Long before the first issue rolled off the press, the colony secretary and his assistants were busy day and night answering letters from nearly every state in the Union. Typical queries pertained to the natural resources, reliability of transportation, and possibility of communicating with the outside world from Oklahoma Proper. Some were looking for assurance that neither Indians nor soldiers would molest them and that cattlemen, some of whom had refused to obey President Cleveland's order to take their herds elsewhere, would eventually yield to the tide of settlement. To cast as broad a net as possible, Sawyer promised to answer all questions through his columns.[38] Ultimately, Sawyer wanted his readers to know that the Oklahoma country had plenty of room for homesteaders and townsite developers alike—perhaps as many as four or five million people—and that some two dozen townsites had already been laid out along the Santa Fe tracks. All a colonist had to do was select land or a town lot, erect buildings, and, as soon as a land office opened, remit payment at the rate prescribed by law. "Eastern people need not fear to come here," claimed Sawyer, "for all the people here are eastern people, old soldiers, church people and even the honest Quakers."[39] Sawyer might have added that the Santa Fe was ready for them. As noted in the company's stockholder's report on December 31, 1888, "There is every reason to believe that the earnings of the Atchison line will be largely increased by the settlement of this region, as the line passes North and South through its entire length, and is the only railroad by which the country is directly reached."[40]

The Oklahoma City Times afforded Sawyer a handsome income until February 10, 1889, when soldiers arrived in Oklahoma to shut it down. Sawyer promptly moved his operation, first to Purcell and then to Wichita. Although published and distributed at great expense, the newspaper continued in the spring of 1889 to churn out news and editorials to satisfy the nation's craving for the latest from Oklahoma Proper.[41]

While Sawyer and Harrington were pushing the power of the press to new heights and Santa Fe stockholders were salivating over future profits, congressmen convening for the final session of the Fiftieth U.S. Congress returned to work in January 1889 to find Washington swarming with lobbyists. Encouraged by glowing reports in the press and from their allies in Congress, boomers were swelling the populations of Kansas border towns. Merchants enticed them with promises of cheap rent (and more comfortable lodging!) and abundant supplies to facilitate their travels and help them survive their first few weeks in the Promised Land. The directionally challenged were no doubt relieved to find maps showing the Santa Fe route through Oklahoma Proper.[42]

Congressman Springer remained as hopeful as ever that the Oklahoma bill, debated in every session of Congress since U.S. district judge C. G. Foster had ruled in November 1884 that Oklahoma Proper was part of the public domain, would finally make its way into law.[43] He bristled at rumors that he had abandoned his crusade. On the contrary, the bill seemed to be gaining strength, even though a small minority of legislators had resorted to filibustering to prevent a final vote.[44] Leading the opposition in the House was Springer's fellow representative from Illinois, Lewis E. Payson (R-Ill., 1881–91), chairman of the Committee on Public Lands during the Fifty-First Congress (1889–91), who had argued on behalf of the Cherokee Nation against white settlement. Payson's inspiration came from Cherokee governor Joel B. Mayes (1887–91), a staunch defender of his nation's right to enter into grazing leases with cattlemen in the Cherokee Outlet. In an impassioned letter to Secretary of the Interior William F. Vilas (1888–89), Governor Mayes alluded to his people's century-long occupancy of Indian Territory under sacred treaties with the U.S. government. As far as Mayes was concerned, the Cherokees would stay put and continue to benefit from seemingly endless natural resources.[45]

As it turned out, Congressman Springer's optimism was premature. The bill made it out of the House Committee on Territories and passed the House of Representatives on February 1 with a 147 to 102 vote. On February 5, the Senate debated the bill before deferring it to the Senate Committee on Territories, which in turn recommended a favorable vote without amendments.

Even then, the House Indian Affairs Committee was drawing up agreements with the Creek and Seminole nations to finalize the sale of their remaining rights to Oklahoma Proper so that Congress could use it for purposes other than settling other Indians and freedmen as stipulated in the Reconstruction Treaties of 1866.[46]

And then came the bombshell: the Oklahoma bill was derailed following an impassioned speech by Senator Plumb of Kansas, whose allegiance to cattlemen was common knowledge.[47] Incredibly, after four-plus years of writing and rewriting and lobbying and debating, Congress seemed likely to adjourn on March 4 without passing the bill. As they joined the blame game in the Fiftieth Congress's waning days, boomers who had written off Senator Plumb as a paid stooge of wealthy cattlemen might have been surprised, and perhaps even chagrined, to hear his defense of homesteaders. Or maybe they chalked up his comments to yet another rendition of the Washington two-step. At any rate, Senator Plumb's postmortem on the Oklahoma bill serves as a reminder that the Oklahoma Question was far more nuanced than boomer polemicists portrayed it. "The whole trouble about Oklahoma has been got up for ulterior purposes," declared Senator Plumb on the eve of Congress's adjournment. "It had been a contest against the settlers by persons who wanted to speculate in town sites," he continued. "That was the trouble all the time. There were two opposing movements in the matter, one in the interest of the settlers; the other in the interest of town site speculators. It was town site money that secured newspaper articles, that paid traveling expenses, and that kept people in Washington hotels." But that was not all. Like Barnes, Elliott, and Baker, who expressed the views of the minority in the House of Representatives, Plumb believed that negotiations with Indians were the sine qua non of opening Oklahoma Proper to homesteading and townsite development. Whatever his interests in the cattle business, Senator Plumb's comments reveal two commitments: one to prospective settlers; and the other to negotiations that would acknowledge the sanctity of treaty obligations and thereby uphold the nation's honor.[48]

The Senate's rejection of the Oklahoma bill was a few days in the future when news of its passage in the House of Representatives hit the streets of Kansas border towns. Certain that victory was at hand, boomers, who had lined up behind the Wichita Board of Trade's chosen leader, Pawnee Bill, began to have second thoughts about proceeding with their invasion plans. A hundred wagons and scores of boys on horseback had already gathered at the Santa Fe's southern terminal at Hunnewell in late January. By early February, they were camped ten miles south of town on the Chikaskia River, somewhere in the vicinity of the ill-fated Rock Falls settlement. But their enthusiasm was clearly waning, leaving Pawnee Bill and a coleader dubbed "Oklahoma Bill" to watch helplessly as most drifted back to Kansas, leaving only a few blustery diehards to remain in camp and plot their next move.[49]

While Pawnee Bill and Oklahoma Bill's foot soldiers were weighing their options, on February 27 the House of Representatives was considering its annual Indian Appropriation Bill to keep Indians fed and clothed for another year. Representative Samuel W. Peel (D-Ark.; 1883–93), chairman of the House Committee on Indian Affairs, submitted an amendment—section 12—to the appropriation bill, which provided $1,912,952.02 to pay for final rights to the 2,370,414.62 acres of land ceded by the Creeks and Seminoles. No doubt sensing his time was at hand, Springer then added section 13, authorizing the president to open Oklahoma Proper to settlement by proclamation. Representative Thomas Ryan of Kansas (R-Kans.; 1877–89) added yet another clause, authorizing the creation of two land offices in the ceded area. Although the new clauses went down in flames in the Senate, both houses agreed to assemble a joint Senate-House conference. Thanks largely to Kansas senator Bishop W. Perkins's determined stand, the amendments were restored to the Indian Appropriation Bill, and it sailed through the Senate. The only remaining hurdle was to convince the president to issue a proclamation announcing a date and time for the opening.[50]

Crocker and Weaver were at the Capitol when the Senate passed the Indian Appropriation Bill. Drawing on his publishing experience, Crocker offered to get the bill printed. Apprised that the nearest printing office was a mile down Pennsylvania Avenue, Crocker crammed the bill in his pocket and hitched a ride in a horse-drawn streetcar to the printing office and persuaded a startled foreman to gather his type and crank up the press. Back on Pennsylvania Avenue with the printed bill in hand, Crocker feared that he was too broke to afford a return trip to the Capitol. But this time, fate smiled on the Oklahoma cause: searching frantically in his pockets, Crocker came up with the nickel he needed to pay his way back to a cluster of beaming Oklahoma boosters. The bill was duly approved and forwarded to President Cleveland for signing. Oklahoma Proper was one signature away from opening.[51]

In its haste to adjourn, Congress was passing legislation with reckless abandon. At the eleventh hour, Cleveland's assistants pulled the Oklahoma bill from a stack of paper. Loath though he was to open Oklahoma Proper to settlement, the president could either veto the bill and deny funding for Indians or sign it and seal Indian Territory's fate. Cleveland chose the latter and affixed his signature on March 2. The riders attached to the Indian Appropriation Bill said nothing about establishing a territory, and Oklahoma Proper was not even mentioned by name. All they did was define Creek and Seminole land cessions as public lands and open them to settlement.[52]

President Cleveland's reluctant signature authorized the disposition of land under homestead laws and the creation of two land districts. Immediately following the inauguration of his successor, Benjamin Harrison (R; 1889–93), on March 4, the Interior Department was tasked with deciding how to proceed. President Harrison, a Republican from Indiana whose grandfather, William Henry Harrison, had served as the nation's ninth president, thus had plenty on his desk on day one of his administration. At the top of his to-do list was deciding when, exactly, the opening would happen.[53]

"Three cheers for the champions of the Oklahoma bill, three cheers for the *Wichita Eagle* and a tiger for Caldwell!" was how the *Eagle* announced passage of the Indian Appropriation Bill. Celebrations in Caldwell and towns across southern Kansas began in daylight and continued far into the night. Commerce came to a virtual standstill as businessmen poured into the streets to shake hands and indulge in self-congratulations and farmers flocked into towns to join the revelry. Posters and banners quickly festooned the business districts.[54]

Boomer leaders did what they could to keep settlers in check until President Harrison could formulate and issue the long-awaited proclamation.[55] In the meantime, the *Oklahoma City Times* published information about Creek and Seminole land claims that had been extinguished and the amount of money paid into tribal coffers. According to surveys conducted for the Reconstruction Treaties of 1866, the ceded land amounted to 2,159,080 acres; subsequent surveys upped that figure to 2,870,414.62 acres. Homestead laws in effect since 1862 required settlers to secure title in fee simple to their property. Special provisions applied to honorably discharged soldiers who had fought for the Union during the Civil War. To receive patents, homesteaders were required by so-called commutation law to make a minimum payment of $1.25

per acre—in U.S. currency, that is. Scrip from the Revolutionary War or War of 1812—or any other currency, for that matter—would not be accepted as legal tender. Homesteads were to be as close as possible to square in shape, and nobody would be permitted to occupy more than a quarter section (160 acres). Lest there be any doubt, settlers were repeatedly admonished to wait for President Harrison to set a date for the opening and to not venture into Oklahoma Proper a moment too soon. Almost as an afterthought, the *Times* informed its readers that the secretary of the Interior reserved the right to permit entry into Oklahoma Proper for the purpose of developing townsites, which were limited to a half section (320 acres).[56]

Congress careened to the end of the session without providing for territorial governance, meaning that the nation's last generation of pioneers would follow the beaten path of empire and, in the Anglo-Saxon tradition, bring their brand of civilization into a region heretofore reserved for nomads. "This has been the rule from Plymouth Rock to Salt Lake and from Salt Lake to the Golden gate," declared the *Times*. "This is the way the states have all been evolved. When government becomes a necessity the American pioneer is sure to find it."[57]

Subsequent sleuthing revealed why senators had been reluctant to support the Springer bill. It had emerged from the House of Representatives with enormous grants to railroads that would exclude land from settlement. Moreover, shares of stock in prospective townsites were on the market, meaning that speculators were fueling the Oklahoma bill. Even as shares of stock were found scattered across the nation's capital, corporations were making plans to go into the townsite business as soon as the Oklahoma bill became law. As evidence of backroom deals, the *Wichita Eagle* cited the proceedings at a convention in Baxter Springs, Kansas, where one of the most outspoken supporters of the Oklahoma bill was Kansas's former governor, George W. Glick (1883–85). A few days after the convention, a share of stock in the Homestead and Town Site Company of Oklahoma was displayed around Washington. Shares carried a par value of five dollars, and the stock certificates carried two prominent names as principals in the venture: ex-governor of Missouri Thomas T. Crittenden (1881–85) as president; and the aforementioned ex-governor Glick as vice president.[58]

Despite their leaders' best efforts, the boomers kept coming. As noted with a touch of ennui in the *Washington City Post*, "Another invasion of Oklahoma.

Another rout and dispersion of the invaders. The old story over again. The cattle barons still live. The government is silent." Soldiers continued to employ their heavy-handed tactics, which included burning cabins and hunting down men, women, and children at the point of a saber as though they were common criminals. The *Post* bristled at descriptions of the invaders as a mob, as mobs rarely included women and children and farming implements. Nor did mobs plant crops, make improvements to their land, and lay the foundations of peaceful and prosperous communities.[59]

And then, as expected but perhaps not quite believed, President Harrison issued his proclamation on March 23, declaring that Oklahoma Proper would "at and after the hour of twelve o'clock noon on the 22d day of April next, and not before, be open to settlement under the terms and subject to all the conditions, limitations and restrictions contained in the act of Congress approved March 2, 1889."[60] The draft of the original proclamation had designated April 20 as opening day, but someone had the presence of mind to consult a calendar and realized that April 20 fell on a Saturday. The date was duly postponed to Monday, April 22, 1889. The president's revised proclamation contained a warning of dire consequences for early entry.[61]

Celebrations attending President Harrison's proclamation dwarfed anything southern Kansas or Purcell had ever seen, or would ever see again in the waning days of frontier settlement. Businessmen abandoned their offices to hug each other and shake hands, banners were draped on buildings, cannons were fired, and bonfires were lit. More muted celebrations were held in the woods and ravines near Guthrie and Oklahoma, where hundreds of boomers emerged from their hiding places to see for themselves what the excitement was all about.[62]

In all likelihood, a few of those curious onlookers milling around the Oklahoma depot were Chickasaw freedmen from Sandtown, a makeshift community on the North Canadian River about twelve miles north of the Chickasaw Nation and south of present-day Reno Avenue between May and Pennsylvania in Oklahoma City. Ever since the Reconstruction Treaties of 1866, Chickasaw freedmen had lacked constitutional protections and were subjected to cruelties and persecutions that were extreme even by Gilded Age standards.[63] Caught in a Darwinian struggle for survival of the fittest, enterprising freedmen sought opportunity where they could, even if it meant clinging to a riverbank and living off the land—and off the radar—in Oklahoma Proper.

Chickasaw freedmen had been in the area, apparently unmolested and maybe even ignored by sympathetic buffalo soldiers, since 1884 when four families traded unrelenting oppression at the hands of their former owners in the Chickasaw Nation for more promising vistas to the north. Some no doubt worked for and bartered with Montford Johnson, Bill McClure, Cass Wantland, and other cattlemen who were always on the lookout for cheap labor, and who curried favor with their Indian neighbors by keeping white people off their payrolls. Whatever they thought of their prospects, Sandtown residents felt secure enough to establish the Antioch Baptist Church in 1885. The church remained at the heart of Oklahoma City's original black community until urban sprawl and industrial development all but wiped Old Sandtown from the map and its existence from the historical record.[64]

From the Cheyenne and Arapaho Reservation and east into Oklahoma Proper, cattlemen finally got the message. Fearing violence from boomers, they scrambled to round up their herds and drive them somewhere safe, wherever that might be. Acting on orders from Washington, soldiers hastened from Fort Reno to depots along the Santa Fe line to order everyone out of the area and post notices cautioning that anyone who refused to leave would be prevented from filing claims. But there was not much they could do to curtail fights that were breaking out throughout the borderlands of Oklahoma Proper. Those fortunate enough to survive scuffles we will never know about were routinely selling their claims, dubious though they were, for upwards of four hundred dollars.[65]

———————

Now that a date for the opening was set, Harrison's administration sprang into action, first to extend public lands laws to Oklahoma Proper, and then to establish land offices to handle claims. The region was divided into two districts, each of which would need a land office. The eastern land office was originally slated for Oklahoma and was quickly switched to Guthrie. Settlers in the Oklahoma townsite would have to wait a year for their own land office.[66] To service the western district, the administration selected an old stagecoach station on Kingfisher Creek along the Rock Island Railway's surveyed route.[67] Competition for appointments was fierce, as everyone expected an increase in business activity that would accrue to the benefit of land office officials for several years to come. The administration appointed four officers, two registers, and two receivers. There was no time to lose, as President Harrison and Secretary of the Interior John W. Noble (1889–93) wanted the offices to be up and running to accommodate the stampede that was surely coming.[68]

Frank Best, who was transferred from Topeka to Guthrie on April 12 to serve as railroad clerk and telegraph operator, arrived at Guthrie to find the Santa Fe hopelessly unprepared for what was coming. Although maps indicating the city of Guthrie were circulating throughout the West, the outpost's infrastructure was nothing more than a depot, a water tank, a three-room house for the section boss and his family, and a bunkhouse for railroad employees. With Santa Fe agent L. R. Delaney barking orders, Best and his associates put their doubts aside and set to work on their little red-frame depot.

Guthrie was by no means the only place where carpenters were working at fever pitch. Stations were established at Orlando and Seward; sidings were built at Lawrie, Waterloo, Britton, and Moore; Alfred (later Mulhall, named for a rancher by that name), Edmond, Norman, and Noble became agency stations; and sidetracks and depot facilities were expanded at Oklahoma. At the same time, passenger train service was expanded to three daily trains that ran north and south between Purcell and Newton. Freight trains, which ran between Purcell and Arkansas City, experienced a rapid increase in priority shipments. Carload after carload piled up on the tracks, and sidings from Wichita to Gainesville and beyond were snarled with freight cars.[69]

As the Oklahoma Question was entering its endgame, Fred L. Wenner was reporting the news of northwestern Ohio for newspapers in Chicago, Detroit, and Cincinnati. Aiming to capture the land run for newspapers back east, Wenner lined up a three-week sojourn to Indian Territory.[70] By the time he arrived in southern Kansas, the run-up to the opening was in full swing. Prospective homesteaders and townsite settlers were pouring into border towns and emptying merchants' shelves and warehouses as soon as they were replenished. Knowing that livestock would be in short supply, cowboys and horse and mule traders drove their herds to border-town markets. A bewildered Fred Wenner did his best to describe the frantic pace of commerce: "As the opening day approached supplies were soon exhausted and not a horse or mule or any kind of vehicle could be bought anywhere in southern Kansas."[71]

Properly outfitted, folks made for the border in serpentine caravans along cattle trails that were quickly becoming obsolete. Mounted troops did what they could to patrol the main trails leading into Oklahoma Proper, but with more than two hundred miles of border, their effectiveness had its limits. Thousands were camped more or less legally at the borders, polishing their weapons and tending their livestock and, in pensive moments, resting their gaze on the unbroken horizon. On Sunday, April 21, churches in Indian

Territory border towns were filled to capacity. In the absence of churches, boomers enlisted preachers who happened to be in camp to lead them in prayers.[72]

We will never know if Charley Colcord went to church the evening before the opening. What we do know is that the Wichita land bust and collapsing cattle prices left him in dire straits. "I owed a great deal of money," wrote a debt-ridden Charley Colcord, "so about the time of the announcement of the opening of Oklahoma I decided to sell the ranch and everything on it, clean up and make a new start." A friend who was an auctioneer helped him to locate an outfit to make the run into Oklahoma. For $60.25, Colcord bought a team of ponies, a spring wagon, and a camp outfit, complete with a bedroll and a bake oven. He then traveled south from Caldwell on the Chisholm Trail to Bull Foot Station near the northern edge of Oklahoma Proper. Arriving five or six days before the Run, Colcord compared the boomer camp to an army encampment.

Early one morning, Colcord was crawling out of his bedroll, or maybe warming his belly with a steaming cup of coffee, when he heard someone call out, "Oh Joe, here's your mule!" Those unfamiliar with the ways of boomer camps were no doubt happy to know that a mule had been returned to its rightful owner. But veterans knew there was more to it than that. The turn of phrase was not an announcement from the lost-and-found department, but rather, a refrain that echoed across countless campsites to confirm that even stubborn home seekers had a sense of humor. "Oh Joe, here's your mule!" was nothing less than a rallying cry, perhaps even a call to arms, that signified an extraordinary bond among the first wave of homesteaders and townsite developers beyond the ken of subsequent generations of Oklahomans. As Colcord noted, latter-day town criers had heralded daybreak "every morning since the first camps were pitched."[73] They continued to blare their message across his and other campsites as the fateful day approached.

Like Charley Colcord, Frank Best left no record of his attendance at a religious service on that calm Sunday evening in Guthrie. But he did record his astonishment as he watched townsite developers pile off trains Saturday night and Sunday to take possession of the choicest lots in town. Infected with town lot fever and confident that his employment with the Santa Fe did not nullify his right to stake a claim, he took a Sunday afternoon stroll to the townsite, stepped off half a block or so of apparently unclaimed property, drove his stakes in the dirt, and returned to the depot, fully expecting to come back the next day to complete his act of settlement.[74]

That evening, freight train conductor George Haas was traveling north on the Santa Fe when he experienced engine trouble. He pulled over at Guthrie and wound up staying there most of the night to fix it. "There were a few soldiers and deputy marshals around the depot," recalled Haas. "Nobody else in sight, though we were told the black-jacks a half mile east of the depot and the timber along the Cottonwood was [sic] thick with sooners."[75]

At the time Haas recorded his memories in the late 1930s, "sooner" had long since muscled its way into Oklahoma vernacular. And as the generations passed and lived memory of the state's origins faded into myth, the label came to symbolize Oklahomans' pride in a pioneer heritage they loved to celebrate but only dimly understood. Homegrown businesses adopted the term to brand their products and services as a surefire way to bring Oklahomans in the door and onto their rosters of satisfied customers. Most famously, it became identified with one of the state's leading universities and its uber-competitive sports teams. In an increasingly mediated and sports-saturated world, everyone knew that the University of Oklahoma Sooners were, are, and maybe forever will be worthy competitors.

All that was far in the future as farmers and businessmen and women set their sights on the sprawling grasslands and promising townsites of Oklahoma Proper. As the endgame entered its final hours on that Sunday night in April, people who were playing by the rules knew two things: they were the rightful owners of the nation's dwindling supply of public lands; and sooners were getting there first.

CHAPTER NINE

Everybody at Sea

My astonishment was complete—people seemed to
spring up as if by magic as far as the eye could reach.
A. W. Dunham, April 22, 1889

Sooners were not the only ones aiming to get a jump on the competition. Depots along the Santa Fe were the destinations of choice for townsite company officials, who arrived in Indian Territory to find no procedures in place for locating and organizing townsites. Upon discovering the omission, the commissioner of the General Land Office announced on April 5 that lands selected for urban settlement would be reserved from homesteading until such time as Congress could come up with laws pertaining to cities and towns, which were limited to 320 acres.[1]

The absence of clear guidelines was apparently of little concern to the Oklahoma Capital City Townsites and Improvement Company of Topeka. The company was founded under the laws of Kansas as a quasi-municipal body whose purpose was to locate, plat, and develop towns on public lands. Officers offered to post bonds in the amount of fifty thousand dollars or whatever sums the General Land Office might require. On April 2, the company applied to Secretary of the Interior Noble to locate and enter seventeen designated townsites, where its representatives would serve as trustees for future inhabitants under guidelines included in the famed rider to the Indian Appropriation Bill of March 2. But there was a problem: higher-ups in the Department of the Interior did not think they were vested with authority to approve the application. Secretary Noble went on record to say that, even though the president was probably authorized to reserve lands for townsites under section 2380 of the *Revised Statutes*, he could not do so for the benefit of townsite corporations.[2] As one official noted, homestead and townsite laws were totally incompatible, and any attempt to build a town according to homestead law would "result in confusion and disorder of most perplexing character."[3]

On April 20, President Harrison set aside a quarter section just east of the Oklahoma depot to provide the army with a base of operations. The 160-acre reserve was known during its brief existence as the "Military Reservation." A century later, revelers and baseball fans knew it as Bricktown, one of the most popular entertainment venues in Oklahoma. The army's presence at the Oklahoma depot dated back to 1887 when the quartermaster's department erected a building to facilitate shipments of military supplies. As Secretary of War Redfield Proctor (1889–91) noted at the time, the army would maintain a presence near the depot until somebody could come up with a more efficient and cost-effective way to ship supplies to and from Fort Reno.[4]

Competition for townsite development ramped up a notch when John Holzapfel of the Kansas Oklahoma Colony, whose advance party had visited Oklahoma Proper in November 1888, chartered two freight cars and a passenger coach for a trip from Arkansas City to Purcell, where the colonists planned to detrain and spend the weekend getting set for the opening. As the train chugged through the Cherokee Outlet, Holzapfel witnessed thousands of prospective settlers trekking across the prairie—some on foot, others on horseback, and still others with babies bouncing on their laps in wagons piled high with the accoutrements of settlement. "All had high hopes and anticipations," recalled Holzapfel. "It was a jolly good natured caravan of red-blooded Americans, the salt of the earth, and they were going to a new land, 'a land that floweth with milk and honey.'" Wonder turned to astonishment when he saw a throng of people, presumably sooners, brazenly parading around the Guthrie depot. In their defense, President Harrison's proclamation of March 23 had warned people that "entering upon and occupying said lands" before noon on April 22 would disqualify them from staking claims. That rather ambiguous turn of phrase encouraged settlers to linger in what was increasingly known as the "Unassigned Lands" without occupying a particular tract of land and wait for the signal to stake their claims. For precedent, settlers looked to pioneers, who, since the dawn of New World settlement, had ventured into the wilderness and claimed squatter's rights with the assurance of legal protection when the time came to organize a territory. They had no reason to suspect that settlement in Oklahoma Proper would be different.[5]

Holzapfel found Oklahoma, unlike Guthrie, to be nearly deserted, save for a few soldiers. He stepped off the train and barely had time to glance at the cluster of buildings before a lieutenant tapped him on the shoulder and ordered him back on board. Holzapfel complied and stayed seated until the train screeched to a halt at Purcell on Friday evening. He and his party left under horse power the next morning and drove north until they reached the South Canadian River. They camped for the night and continued on Sunday to Barrows Crossing some thirteen miles southwest of the Oklahoma depot. Some members of his party traveled to Jenkins Ford, leaving Holzapfel and a few companions at Barrows Crossing to witness a rising tide of anxiety. Tensions escalated as some people cast caution to the wind and forded the river to begin their quests for homesteads. An old Irishman named Greeley circulated a petition demanding that soldiers seize the miscreants and bring them to justice. After enough law-abiding people had signed the petition, Greeley entrusted it to his son, who promptly mounted his horse, forded the river, and set off at a gallop for Oklahoma to deliver it to the commanding officer. Holzapfel saw Greeley's son several days after the opening to discover that he and his friends had secured claims. But on that Sunday evening before the opening, Holzapfel's main concern was with the South Canadian River—churning and frothing from recent rains, and sure to bring somebody's dreams to a watery end the following afternoon.[6]

What was arguably the most consequential townsite company filing came on Friday, April 19, when five businessmen received their charter from the Kansas secretary of state in Topeka for the Seminole Town and Improvement Company. The term of the new corporation was set at twenty years, and its roster of directors reads like a Who's Who of the boomer movement: J. W. Wilson and L. H. Crandall of Topeka; J. A. Hudson of Lincoln, Illinois; Sidney Clarke of Lawrence, Kansas; and W. L. Couch of Douglass, Kansas. The Seminole Town and Improvement Company's purpose was to purchase, locate, and lay out townsites; sell and convey property in lots and subdivisions; construct and operate street railways, electric and gas light, water works, irrigation canals, toll bridges, and ice manufactories; and facilitate the sale of negotiable securities in the interest of the corporation.

Congress insisted that townsites be developed for the benefit of their inhabitants and that homesteads be granted to actual settlers. Presumably, Congress intended to give occupants possessory rights that could either grow into title or be sold. Looming over the Seminole Town and Improvement Company's business model—and, indeed, all business models in those hastily organized townsite companies—were conflicting definitions of "occupant" as envisioned in Congress's act of March 2, 1889. Did it refer only to people who lived on the lots they claimed? Was it restricted to claimants who improved their lots or leased them to tenants? If an occupant had the right to sell his or her possessory rights, was it similarly legal for a townsite company to occupy a townsite and then sell its possessory rights to the lots it had surveyed and staked?[7] As opening hour approached, these and other questions pertaining to townsite development in Oklahoma Proper, increasingly identified as the Unassigned Lands, remained unanswered.

———

Certain that the Oklahoma land run would be the scoop of their lives, journalists flocked to the borders of Indian Territory. One of them, Fred L. Wenner, managed to climb into a baggage car on the first train to pull out of the station on April 22. He shared his cramped quarters with some of the best-known opinion leaders of his day, including Frank H. Greer, publisher of the *Daily State Capital* (heretofore published in Winfield, Kansas; later in Guthrie); Dennis T. Flynn, a native of Pennsylvania and son of Irish immigrants, who served as Guthrie's postmaster before his election in 1892 as Oklahoma Territory's delegate to Congress; Victor Murdock, who represented his father Marsh's newspaper, the *Wichita Eagle*; and William Allen White, a Kansas-born newspaperman who rose to national prominence as a champion of progressive causes. Only three people on that train beat Wenner to Guthrie: two trainmen in the locomotive cab and a female schoolteacher from Kentucky who rode on the cowcatcher.[8]

Somewhere in the procession of southbound trains was Hamilton S. Wicks of *Cosmopolitan Magazine*. Upon catching a case of Oklahoma fever, he threw a few flannel shirts in a suitcase, stuffed it with maps of "the new Eldorado," and boarded the Penn Limited, determined to get as close to the action as he could. The hours crawled as the train clattered past the lush farms of Pennsylvania, beneath the towering peaks of Appalachia, through the prairies of Illinois and Iowa, and onto the Kansas plains, where pioneers were about to drop the curtain on three centuries of America's continental expansion. "From the peace and reserve of a mere traveler I was at once hurled into the conflict for personal supremacy with a seething mass of 'boomers,'" wrote Wicks. "It was as though I had suddenly been interjected into a confused Fourth-of-July celebration, where the procession had resolved itself into a mob."[9]

Oklahoma before the opening, April 1889.
Courtesy of Oklahoma Images Collection, Metropolitan Library System of Oklahoma County.

Finding every car loaded beyond capacity, Wicks bribed a brakeman to secure a seat in a caboose. Like Fred Wenner, Wicks found himself in the company of power brokers: Colonel D. B. Dyer, a future mayor of Guthrie; Judge John Guthrie ("large, pompous, and genial"), for whom Guthrie was named; C. R. McLain, who, later that day, cofounded with J. M. Ragsdale the Commercial National Bank of Guthrie; and Jim Geary, "an old scout and plainsman, as cool-headed a *rustler* as ever drew bead on a redskin." As Wicks wrote about his encounter with history in the making, "Civilization and barbarism seem here to come into immediate contact; industry and shiftlessness here stand face to face; order and lawlessness seem to glare at each other across the border."[10]

As the train chugged into the Cherokee Outlet, Wicks witnessed caravans snaking their way southward. A typical party consisted of a prairie schooner jammed with farming tools, dogs, and chicken coops and drawn by scrawny horses or mules. At the reins was a man sporting a shaggy beard; next to him was a "slatternly-looking woman" surrounded by equally ragged children. Traveling alongside those rickety outfits were flashy real estate men seated in carriages drawn by sleek, high-stepping horses. Some rigs were drawn by one horse, others by two, and they jockeyed for space with people of all descriptions on horseback. Those who trudged across the prairie on foot kept pace with the throng as best they could, smiling and waving their hands like revelers

T. M. Richardson.
Courtesy of Oklahoma Historical Society, Oklahoma City, 12696.

on parade. "Everyone imagined that Eldorado was just ahead," wrote Wicks, "and I dare say the possibility of failure or disappointment did not enter into the consideration of a single individual on that cool and delightful April day."

Traffic slowed to crawl at stream crossings and halted altogether at the southern edge of the Cherokee Outlet, where boomer camps and livestock stretched to the horizon and soldiers struggled to keep the horde in check. The gaiety that Wicks had observed en route to the border was gone, replaced by steely determination: "All was excitement and expectation. Every nerve was on tension and every muscle strained. The great event for which these brawny noblemen of the West have been waiting for years was on the point of transpiring."[11]

Far to the south, T. M. Richardson, a banker and lumberman from Texas, was more prepared than most to succeed in the Promised Land. For ten days before the Run, he and his two sons had been doing business in Purcell, where he had opened a lumberyard in preparation for the opening. He had also obtained a safe, heavy oak desks, stationery, checks, passbooks, and other tools of the banking business in Dallas. He then loaded his supplies and enough lumber to build a temporary bank into a chartered boxcar and routed it to the Oklahoma depot, where it rested on a siding for several days before the Run. Meanwhile, the Richardsons shared everyone else's hardships, which in their case included sleeping on the floor of their lumber office as opening day approached. Like Hamilton Wicks, the Richardsons were fortunate on the morning of April 22 to secure seats on a northbound train. Less fortunate travelers were packed in the aisles and piled high on the coaches, on the back of the tender, and even on the engine.[12]

Among those who traveled in less plush accommodations from Purcell to Oklahoma was Andrew Jackson Burton, a coal miner from Georgia who teamed up with a German miner named Walters and clambered on one of twenty-six coaches. "A lot of the people on the train were drunk," said Burton, "and you could hear guns shooting everywhere. All the windows on the train were shot out." Walters hunkered down between seats, but Burton stayed where he was, perfectly willing to face a hail of bullets rather than cower in fear. As the train crossed into the Unassigned Lands, people began diving from the coaches and running for claims. If they got their stakes planted, they fired their weapons and shouted in victory. As near as Burton could tell, everyone aboard his coach, mostly but not exclusively male, was packing heat, and the air was so thick with gunpowder and tobacco smoke that he could hardly see.[13]

Among those who bailed off the train early was Joseph Bouse, a Pennsylvania native who was spending the winter in Florida when he caught Oklahoma fever. Instead of returning to Philadelphia, he teamed up with a Floridian nicknamed "Friday," in a nod to Daniel Defoe's imaginary helpmate, and bought tickets to Purcell. Upon their arrival, Bouse surmised that cowboys would be the ones to outrun, as they knew the country better than anyone. As people swarmed onto the trains, the duo managed to squeeze into a coach. About twenty miles into the Unassigned Lands, a steep grade forced the train to slow down, and Bouse knew it was time to make their move. Bouse managed to slide off the train gracefully, but Friday went tumbling head over heels, spilling the contents of his knapsack. Apparently unhurt, Bouse and Friday brushed themselves off and set off in search of a claim as their train, oblivious to their departure, continued over the horizon and disappeared from sight.[14]

Santa Fe agent A. W. Dunham did not have to travel to see the drama unfold. All he had to do was climb on a stationary boxcar at the depot and fix his gaze northward, before providing the description of what he saw that appears at the head of this chapter. Nearby, Irving Geffs, a soldier stationed at the Oklahoma depot who chronicled the townsite's origins under the rather odd pseudonym, Bunky, claimed that white tents "dotted the country as far as the eye could see at twenty minutes past twelve."[15]

Like Dunham, Bill Couch and Samuel Crocker did not have to go far to see history in the making. As the boomer movement faded into history and Congress finally stepped up to the plate to answer the Oklahoma Question, both men went to work on a Santa Fe grading team. With Couch assigned as a leader and Crocker as his bookkeeper, their team laid three-quarters of a mile of siding in preparation for the opening. Like Frank Best in Guthrie, the former boomers assumed that a position with the railroad was sure to give them a leg up in the red-hot competition for homesteads and town lots. When they spied eighty-niners coming hard over the horizon, they dropped their tools and sauntered in a westerly direction. When Couch reached the Oklahoma townsite's western limit, he staked a claim on 160 acres bounded by present-day Fourth Street on the north, Walker Avenue on the east, Reno Avenue on the south, and Western Avenue on the west. Nearby, Crocker was planting a stake on his own eighty acres.[16]

Satisfied that the law would be on his side, Couch returned to the tracks to fetch his tools and resume work on the siding. As he passed by the depot, he might have bidden a good-day to station agent Dunham and wished him good luck in what was sure to be an eventful afternoon. Couch might have caught a glimpse of Bill McClure, recently arrived from the Kickapoo and Potawatomi country. Knowing the lay of the land better than most—and, better yet, knowing where U.S. engineers had placed cornerstones during their surveys in 1873 and 1874—McClure had ridden west from his 7C Ranch headquarters for five or six miles before obtaining a fresh mount from one of his cowboys, who was waiting for him at a prearranged rendezvous. McClure made the rest of the trip so quickly that he drew rein about thirty minutes ahead of slower paced eighty-niners. He thus had plenty of time to stake a claim to 160 acres in what later became the Maywood Addition in the vicinity of the present-day Oklahoma City National Memorial and Museum. He also secured two town lots at the intersection of First and Harvey Avenue. Citing the Supreme Court's ruling that the 7C cowboys had been in the Unassigned Lands legally when they delivered a fresh horse to their boss, McClure's grandson, William J. McClure, confirmed to posterity his grandfather's standing as Oklahoma City's first legal resident.[17]

As a director of the Seminole Town and Improvement Company, Couch was pleased to see his associates detrain a few minutes past noon. Hoping to

Unidentified engraver, *The Rush for the Promised Land:*
Over the Border to Oklahoma, U.S.A.
From Graphic, May 11, 1889. Copyright © Dickinson Research Center,
National Cowboy & Western Heritage Museum, Oklahoma City, 1996.027.1461.290.

get a jump on the competition, members of the company had spent Sunday
night on the railroad right-of-way.[18] At a few minutes past noon on Monday,
Charles Chamberlain, a civil engineer and the Santa Fe's townsite location
engineer, was in position to begin his survey. His main base of operations
was designated as Main Street, and in short order the best lots were taken.
Before he and his crew could make much headway, the swarm of humanity
that Dunham witnessed from atop the boxcar, together with trainloads of
pioneers from Purcell and Arkansas City, arrived at Oklahoma to plunge the
townsite into a welter of confusion.

What the Seminole Town and Improvement Company had hoped would
be an orderly survey was quickly morphing into bedlam.[19] As people raced for
lots and sober men danced like lunatics, Bunky spotted an old lady driving
her stake in the center of the Santa Fe tracks. With her act of settlement
complete, she sat down and refused to budge when soldiers tried to persuade
her to move. At about three o'clock, a southbound train arrived and disgorged

its passengers into what had become, in Bunky's charged prose, "a surging, crowding, running, yelling mass of humanity."[20]

To make matters worse, more townsite companies were barging in, including the Gainesville Town Company of Texas, the Oklahoma Capital City Townsites and Improvement Company, and John Holzapfel's Kansas Oklahoma Colony. Holzapfel's group made the fifteen-mile trip from Barrows Crossing and arrived at Oklahoma in the company of James H. Harrison, a surveyor and engineer from LaCygne, Kansas, and a cousin of President Benjamin Harrison. Other prominent members of the Kansas Oklahoma Colony included Rev. James Murray as president and C. P. Walker, who was credited with surveying the street that marked the townsite's western boundary and that bore his name, as secretary.[21]

Harrison wasted no time in lugging his equipment to the Military Reservation. No sooner did he set to work than soldiers showed up with the unwelcome news that he was trespassing on military property. As Holzapfel recalled, "We, being out of reach of railroads and telegraph, had not heard of it." Apparently unfazed, Harrison crossed the tracks and began surveying west of the depot along present-day Reno Avenue. At the same time, members of the Kansas Oklahoma Colony were establishing their headquarters in a tent about where the Oklahoma Gazette was later located and, later still, the site of the American National Bank. The Kansas Oklahoma Colony's first order of business was to call for the election of a mayor and city clerk. After some four hundred ballots were tallied, what was coming to be known as "the Colony crowd" elected James Murray as mayor and C. P. Walker as city clerk.[22]

A stone's throw from the Colony crowd's improvised election booth, representatives of the Seminole Town and Improvement Company, known increasingly as "Seminoles" (hereafter for clarity the "Seminole faction"), were selling lots as fast as they could mark them off along the rapidly developing Main Street. Town founder, journalist, and civic leader Angelo C. Scott was astounded at the audacity of people whose scheme was, in his estimation, fraudulent and unlawful.[23] Such was the acrimony between the rival townsite companies that Colony crowd supporters earned the moniker "Kickers," later modified to "Kickapoos" (hereafter for clarity the "Kickapoo faction"), for their inclination to kick every idea that originated with the Seminole faction.[24] In typical frontier fashion, neither the Seminole nor the Kickapoo faction had any qualms about misappropriating tribal names and symbols to promote their agendas.

Angelo C. Scott.
Courtesy of Oklahoma Historical Society, Oklahoma City, 1840.

Sidney Clarke and General Weaver certainly saw nothing fraudulent or unlawful about selling town lots. As a director of the Seminole Town and Improvement Company, Clarke watched with alarm as voters streamed out of the Colony crowd's tent. To signal his displeasure, he and Weaver climbed on a farm wagon and did what they could to attract attention. Struggling to make themselves heard above the fray, they called for a mass meeting the following evening at the corner of what was already becoming the intersection of Main and Broadway. Years later, one observer likened Oklahoma on the afternoon of April 22 to a carnival with more politicians and orators per acre than had ever been assembled on a half section of land.[25]

Clarke might have been one of the few orators with actual experience as a public speaker, as he had listened to President Lincoln deliver speeches and had delivered plenty of his own. And now, perched on a wagon west of the Santa Fe depot, he put that experience into the service of the Seminole faction, adding a few homegrown theatrics that included bending over like a jackknife and unbending with a jerk until he stood on his toes. At one point, he jerked up so quickly that his straw hat flew off his head and sailed into the crowd.[26]

The Colony crowd's election came to nothing. But Clarke's and Weaver's call for a mass meeting the next day came to fruition and became a standard means of doing business. As colonists drifted from the Kansas Oklahoma Colony's headquarters to Clarke's and Weaver's impromptu soapbox, people kept pouring into the townsite and driving stakes wherever they could find an unclaimed place, with no regard for streets or lots or, in at least one instance but possibly more, the railroad tracks.[27] Busy settlers looked up from their labors to see the sun setting and realized with alarm that they had nowhere to bed down for the night. "Oh, where are we to sleep tonight?" asked a well-dressed woman to a friend. A rough-looking eavesdropper volunteered an answer that neither wanted to hear: "You'll sleep out under the sky like the rest of us, and, be d——— glad to get the chance, lady!"[28]

Far to the northwest, the Wichita Board of Trade's designated leader, Pawnee Bill, stood in the vanguard of four thousand hopeful settlers. His involvement in opening the Unassigned Lands was destined to catapult him ever further into the national spotlight as a Wild West showman and a founding father of Oklahoma.[29] Nearby, Charley Colcord was preparing to ride into history on what he considered to be one of the fittest horses along the Unassigned Lands' western boundary. Then came the signal, and the starting line disappeared in a kaleidoscope of motion and dust and horses and oxen and wagons of every description. Colcord reflected with a touch of whimsy that some oxen must have been pretty fast, as he spotted two families with ox teams plowing and planting their gardens. Unlike his competitors who whipped their horses to a frenzy only to drop by the wayside, Colcord rode at a steady pace. "After that it was easy for the good riders to pick their claims," wrote Colcord. The future real estate mogul managed to stake a claim southwest of Hennessey and promptly sold it, presumably for a profit, before returning to his base camp to retrieve his camping outfit and striking out for Oklahoma.[30]

Somewhere along the Santa Fe line, freight engineer George Haas had fixed his engine and was back in business. But there was not much he could do to prevent delays in shipments due to the explosion in railroad traffic. As the sun rose ever higher, he had to wait on a sidetrack while eighteen passenger trains streamed by. "These trains were a mile or two apart running slow and loaded as I never saw trains before," said Hass. "There were people on the steps, on top of the coal tenders, on the cowcatchers and on top of the coaches." He returned to Guthrie that evening to witness a city in the making.[31]

One of those busy railroad employees was Frank J. Best. He awoke on Monday morning with every intention of completing the act of settlement that he had begun the previous evening. Instead, he was stuck at the Guthrie depot, where the onslaught of humanity left him no time to eat, let alone see to his claim. About midnight, he looked up bleary-eyed from his post at the Santa Fe ticket office to confront a six-foot, bearded Texan with an attitude.

"Are you the fellow, Best, that has a line around a bunch of lots several blocks south of the land office?" he demanded.

Wary of trouble, Best replied in the affirmative.

"Well, you're a damn sooner and you know it," announced the Texan for all within earshot to hear, "and what's more I can prove it. Now I want to be fair, so I will tell you what I'll do. I'll give you $150 for the lots or I'll go take 'em anyhow. Take your choice and be damn quick about it." And with that, the Texan dropped his money on the counter and glared at the befuddled agent.

Best decided not to press the matter. He scooped up the money and, a couple of days later, deposited it in the Commercial National Bank of Guthrie—recently founded by McLain and Ragsdale—blissfully unaware that the bank would go belly-up a few months later when the nefarious bankers lit out for parts unknown with the people's money stashed in flour barrels. As Best remarked many years later about his effort to get ahead of the competition, "So much for even trying to be a sooner."[32]

Frank Best's banking woes were far in the future when the Richardsons stepped off the train at Oklahoma and watched in disbelief as settlers scrambled for lots. Within minutes, angry shouts—"This is mine!"; "You get out of here!"—filled the air. Everyone bolted for cover when a man unwrapped his bedding to reveal a Winchester rifle. "I staked this lot," growled the man, "and the rest of you get out of here!" Suddenly, a woman broke through the crowd and ran up to him as she hollered, "Oh, my dear, please don't kill anyone else!" Bluff or not, the man and, presumably, his wife got their point across. Whether they got their lot is anyone's guess.[33]

Threats notwithstanding, the Richardsons plunged into the mayhem. After collecting the supplies and equipment that he had shipped to the depot, T. M. Richardson claimed a lot on the northeast corner of the intersection of Clarke Street (later, Grand Avenue; eventually, Sheridan Avenue) and Harvey Avenue.[34] Within minutes, he was trading lumber for gold coins, silver dollars, greenbacks, demand notes, due-bills, two-cent pieces, and even wooden nickels.[35] Unhappy with his location, Richardson paid three hundred dollars for a lot just east of Broadway on Main Street, which was a block north and two blocks east of his original claim and, more to the point, closer to what was beginning to look like the heart of the business district. He then erected a tent and posted a sign bearing the inscription "Oklahoma Bank."[36]

As the afternoon wore on, E. E. Elterman from Bloomer, Wisconsin, spotted Richardson's sign and, after sizing up the banker and his crude establishment, decided that the Texan was trustworthy. "I understand you folks are going to start a bank," said Elterman. "I am going to start a dry goods store here and I want to be your first depositor." Richardson made his own judgment and decided that the fellow was trustworthy as well. Moments later, Richardson had his first deposit in what would one day blossom into the First National Bank and Trust Company of Oklahoma City. A few days later, Elterman opened up shop as J. H. Wedemeyer & Company, later rebranded as Wedemeyer, Clay and Company, which grew into one of Oklahoma City's most prosperous businesses.

T. M. Richardson's son joined the business boom by opening a lemonade stand. Such was the pace of business that he emptied his bucket before the sugar had time to dissolve. With a few coins jingling in his pocket, he started scouting for diversions, with limited success. "There was no amusement of any kind conducted when we were first here," he recalled in a teenage lament that rings through the ages. "I never saw any dogs in town after the first night and there were only a few women, but they came in later."

The Richardsons' first night in town was spent under the watchful gaze of two or three hundred troops charged with maintaining law and order. Part of their routine was to lower the American flag each evening as the bugler sounded out "Taps." Before he fell asleep in the tent next to his father and brother on that extraordinary Monday night, the younger Richardson became aware of someone wandering through the campsite and inquiring about a mule that had broken loose from his wagon. Someone shouted, "Joe, here's your mule!" On that night and for many nights thereafter, settlers ended their days with "Taps" and the pioneer's jingle echoing across their campsites—a last hurrah from the Oklahoma frontier that was about to give up the ghost. As pioneer journalist Frank McMaster wrote some two decades after the opening about concern for Joe's mule, "In all the after days it was one incident that us better remembered today than all the other blended incidents of the first day of Oklahoma's virgin settlement."[37]

"Taps" and good-natured queries about Joe's mule notwithstanding, disorder reigned as an estimated six thousand people made their beds wherever they could find space.[38] Adding to the confusion was a sprinkling of the frontier's most pernicious characters: moonshiners. Dr. Virgil Andrew Wood, a Georgia native who had been practicing medicine in Wallaceburg, Arkansas, for several years before the opening, rode into Oklahoma on April 22 to find law and order in short supply. "Moonshiners popped up from almost every strip of timber and almost every ravine," wrote Wood in a letter to his hometown newspaper. It was altogether too much for the Arkansas physician. He concluded his letter of April 22 with a common sentiment that undercuts mythic representations of the first wave of settlers: "As for myself, I have taken the hardest race of my life today but without avail. There is talk of a town election tonight. We are not candidates. I will close and get away before the shooting starts. I never came here to fight. I could have done that nearer home."[39]

Then again, Wood's only boomtown experience was at the Oklahoma townsite. What he apparently failed to perceive were the hundreds of people, including U.S. marshals and soldiers, who had been staking lots, erecting tents, and performing other odd jobs to make the opening as orderly as possible. Thanks to their efforts, the wild rush at Guthrie was not replicated at Oklahoma. As the *Oklahoma City Times* noted with a dash of condescension toward the townsite's northern neighbor, "There was not the same suffering as at Guthrie and in fact there is a lack of dirt and dust." Nor was there much fodder for eastern newspapers, whose readers could not get enough of frontier mayhem. In the *Times'* decidedly partisan view, stories of violence and murder existed in fevered imaginations and not the rapidly developing streets of Oklahoma.[40]

The other good news was that nearly every townsite and homestead claim was occupied by nightfall. A *Los Angeles Times* correspondent who took the train from Guthrie to Purcell captured the post-Run panorama: "All over the level lands approaching the Canadian River bottom the lights of campfires burning in the open air or the lights of lamps glimmering through canvas tents give the entire country a weird but pleasing look. There was no timber line to obstruct the view for miles of distance. It was a fine spectacular scene."[41]

———————

"Everybody at sea," was how the *Oklahoma Times* described the scene as thousands of eighty-niners awoke on Tuesday morning to the unsettling realization that nobody was in charge. Soldiers, of course, were on constant patrol, but their surfeit of responsibilities did not include establishing civilian governments. As the morning wore on, citizens tried to compel townsite company surveyors to reconcile their plats and reach a consensus. But as tempers flared and conflicts escalated, there was a groundswell of support for the mass meeting that Clarke and Weaver had suggested (demanded?) the previous day. To make sure everyone got the message, half a dozen boys were rounded up and mounted on ponies. Equipped with bells, they dashed through the townsite to summon people to a three o'clock meeting at the northwest corner of Main and Broadway. They did not have far to ride, as the townsite then consisted of 320 acres bounded by present-day Reno Avenue on the south, Seventh Street on the north, Walker Avenue on the west, and the Santa Fe tracks on the east.[42]

No sooner had people gathered at the appointed hour than Angelo Scott and another Kansan, M. H. Woods, were elected as chairman and secretary, respectively. After heated discussion, attendees resolved to commission a new survey. They also agreed to elect a committee of fourteen citizens to conduct the survey and adjust lots. As everyone was a stranger and nobody knew the nominees, a cry went through the throng, "Let's see him!" Nominees were duly hustled through the crowd and made to stand on boxes next to the chairman and secretary. "If the crowd liked his looks they voted him up; if not, they voted him down," recalled Scott. Within minutes, the eighty-niners had their committee of fourteen. Arguably, the citizens' committee of fourteen was as pure a form of self-government as one is likely to find in the history of westward expansion.[43]

Angelo Scott and his brother, W. W. Scott, were former publishers of the *Iola Register*, and they arrived at Oklahoma on April 22 with the hearty support and encouragement of their newspaper brethren back in Kansas.[44] They resumed their partnership immediately after the Run of '89, when they launched the *Oklahoma Times*. In a pattern that typified frontier entrepreneurship, Angelo Scott opened a law office and, in his spare time, operated a hotel. As a writer and publisher, he was a natural to chronicle his adopted city's beginnings, and his position on what came to be known as the "citizens' committee of fourteen" gave him an insider's perspective of mass meetings and high-stakes deliberations. As the tent shuddered and flapped and lanterns flickered in the April breeze, committee members spent a sleepless night hunched over maps and puzzling through the best way to plat streets and lots. Many years later, Scott was still vexed over the committee's failure to provide for a downtown park. But he thought he could explain it: "I suppose the reason we did not have that vision is that practically every one of us was a small town man, with little idea of parks or beauty."[45]

When dawn broke on April 24, the citizens' committee of fourteen had the makings of a plan. They employed a surveyor and instructed him and his crew to begin surveying and measuring off lots. In the hours and days to come, the results of their labors came to be known as the "citizens' survey." None doubted they were courting trouble, as hundreds of people who had staked lots were bound to be disappointed if their claims turned out to be in the middle of a street or alley. City builders saw trouble coming as the Seminole and Kickapoo factions faced off in what was destined to become a bitter rivalry. Railroad company officials were there too, trying to figure out how to secure a right-of-way through the congested townsite. As noted in the *Times*' detailed history of the Oklahoma townsite's first two weeks, surveyors laboring under the auspices of the citizens' committee of fourteen made repeated efforts to reconcile their survey with the Seminole townsite company's survey, but to no avail. The committee of fourteen's progress report was well received at a mass meeting on Wednesday evening. After giving its stamp of approval to the citizens' survey, the crowd joined in singing the doxology before dispersing to tents and campfires.[46]

Charley Colcord was one of the lucky ones. During a conversation with George Patrick, Colcord mentioned that he was willing to part with his team for the right price. Patrick offered to take it in exchange for a town lot that was already sprouting a modest structure. Satisfied that he was getting the better end of the deal, Colcord shook hands with Patrick to become the owner of lot one, block one—the first lot surveyed. Having spent his childhood in Kentucky before his family migrated west, Colcord was doubly pleased to do business with Patrick, a fellow Kentuckian. After grabbing a bite to eat at the Blue Front Restaurant and purchasing a few supplies, he took a quick inventory and found that his liquid assets consisted of ten dollars and forty-five cents. "That was everything I had," recalled Colcord. "Everybody else was in the same fix. There was very little money in this new country."[47]

While Colcord was counting his pocket change, the citizens' committee of fourteen was dispatching a subcommittee of five to follow the survey team and determine, as best they could, what to do about rival claims. In many cases, as many as half a dozen claimants were attempting to settle on the same lot. Predictably, as the surveyors and subcommittee members wound their way through the streets, a crowd began to gather, and voices were raised in frustration. To enable officials to do their work, someone nailed three long boards together to form a triangle. The tribunal, perhaps resembling a giant wedge of cheese, thus had a barrier and proceeded, more or less unimpeded, through the milling throng. Conflicts between rival townsite companies left visible scars in the form of irregular street angles, referred to at the time as "jogs," at the intersections of Grand Avenue and Broadway, Robinson, Harvey, and Hudson Avenues.[48]

South of Reno Avenue, another organization was platting an area destined to thrive, however briefly, as an independent community dubbed "South Oklahoma." As Holzapfel explained, the nascent townsite's population was growing so rapidly that it was already in dire need of an area to siphon off the overflow.[49] To establish governance for South Oklahoma, citizens held an election on April 27. George W. Patrick, who had recently traded his lot and flimsy dwelling near the depot for Charley Colcord's team, was elected as mayor. So brief was South Oklahoma's duration that Patrick and his fellow officers never had an opportunity to hold office.[50] Patrick did, however, have an opportunity to help measure lots along Reno Avenue and unwittingly participate in creating the famed jogs in the business district.

Patrick's story survives in the memory of Joseph Bouse, recently arrived from Purcell to find the entire townsite in a hopeless state of confusion. After a series of adventures that were replicated in countless ways across the Unassigned Lands during the week of April 22, Bouse and his sidekick Friday arrived at the depot to witness men measuring lots on the south side of Reno Avenue. Lacking proper instrumentation, the men were using a lariat, perhaps borrowed from a compliant cowboy, with a knot tied thirty feet from its end. When Bouse spotted them, they were about a half block west of the depot, working their way in a westerly direction and marking thirty-foot lots along Reno Avenue. Bouse later learned that the man in charge of the survey crew was none other than George W. Patrick, who was pocketing dollar bills and issuing receipts as evidence of title to the lots he was measuring.[51]

Patrick's crew eventually wound its way to the corner of Reno and Walker Avenues. As his flagman was planting a marker at the intersection, Patrick looked up to realize that another survey crew on the north side of Reno Avenue had been marking twenty-five-foot lots. Vexed to see his survey unraveling, Patrick announced his intention to start over. His new survey, presumably based on twenty-five-foot street frontage, was going about as smoothly as could be expected until he encountered a woman who had staked two lots

Oklahoma (townsite), April 27, 1889.
Courtesy of Oklahoma Historical Society, Oklahoma City, 5172.

totaling sixty feet in length, apparently by using another cowboy's lariat. "She told Patrick whose hog ate the cabbage," said Bouse about an encounter that might have spun out of control. The woman then pointed to a bulldog tied to a trunk, glared at the future mayor of the stillborn South Oklahoma, and said, "I staked and got title to 60 feet right here. There is not power enough this side of hell to take me off, much less give me 50 feet nothing doing." History is silent on Patrick's response to the belligerent claimant. Nor do we know if she had to call in her bulldog for backup.[52]

━━━━━━━━

Tensions throughout the Oklahoma townsite were reaching fever pitch on Friday, April 26, as the rival survey crews came ever closer to what would surely be a confrontation at Main Street. To forestall disaster, opinion leaders called for a mass meeting at six-thirty the following evening at the corner of Main and Broadway to nominate a temporary mayor and city recorder with the authority to appoint police and maintain order. All attendees would be entitled to vote by voice, and their chosen leaders would remain in office for five days to give them time to organize a more structured election.[53]

When dawn broke on Saturday, April 27, it seemed unlikely that a mass meeting would be enough to keep tempers in check. If anything, one might expect a gathering of thousands of disgruntled settlers to spiral into violence. At two o'clock, two thousand citizens who had situated themselves between the converging survey crews at Main Street anticipated the mass meeting by holding an impromptu election. With Angelo Scott presiding, a motion was made and duly carried to appoint a committee of ten citizens—five from each side of Main Street—to adjust and harmonize the conflicting surveys. Representatives from the north side included James B. Weaver, William L. Couch, Angelo C. Scott, Moses Neal, and M. M. Beatty. Their counterparts south of Main Street included Judge John T. Voss, John Wallace, C. P. Walker, M. V. Barney, and C. T. Scott. Determined to settle their differences peacefully, the committee of ten spent the rest of the afternoon figuring out how to adjust the strip between the two surveys.

As citizens gathered for the mass meeting at six-thirty, the ad hoc committee elected earlier that afternoon appointed General Weaver to give a report. Anxious to put their differences aside and get on with the business of building a city, his listeners were receptive. Cheers erupted when Bill Couch and W. P. Shaw were elected as temporary mayor and recorder, respectively. Hastily written articles of confederation were adopted with a promise to publish them so that citizens could remain informed. As noted in the *Oklahoma Times*, "The day which opened ominously, closed with everybody happy in the assurance of an ultimate settlement of all difficulties."[54]

It was thus in a spirit of buoyant optimism that the mass meeting adjourned, but not before settlers joined in a thundering rendition of "Praise God from whom all Blessings Flow." But beneath the celebratory mood, trouble was brewing, and none saw it with more prescience than *Oklahoma Times* publisher Angelo C. Scott. He had been on high alert since arriving at the evening meeting expecting to preside, only to find that his position had been usurped by an attorney with the Seminole Town and Improvement Company. He subsequently learned that a cabal of Seminole townsite supporters had assembled at the afternoon meeting to plot a takeover of the agenda at the mass meeting that evening. Their primary objective was to promote an election five days hence on Wednesday, May 1, leaving little time for an opposition to muster its defenses. "These men were the most coherent group on the townsite, and they knew their politics," wrote Scott. "They wanted the election over at once, for they knew that the longer their projected steal of the townsite was scrutinized, the less chance they would have of controlling the election."[55]

Cabals and shady politics remained beneath the radar as Oklahomans basked in the glow of their mass meeting sing-along. But as they returned to their dwellings, they glanced skyward to see thick, black clouds swirling overhead. The mood quickly morphed into fear, and everyone scurried home to protect their merchandise and household goods. Construction was put on hold as settlers throughout the Unassigned Lands ran for what little cover they had and braced for the storm as it roared its way across the prairie.

Apparently, the storm damage was minimal, and homesteaders and town lot owners awoke on Sunday morning with much to be grateful for. In a land imbued with Christian meaning since the earliest days of the boomer movement, it was only fitting for people to flock to religious services. In Oklahoma, Rev. Charles C. Hembree, formerly of Kansas City, conducted divine services at the corner of Main and Broadway in accordance with the forms of the Presbyterian Church. On higher ground to the north, Rev. James Murray presided at an equally well-attended service under the auspices of the Methodist Episcopal Church, and W. P. Shaw conducted a Sunday school.

At seven feet tall, W. P. Shaw towered above his congregation to deliver a rousing lesson at lots that he and Rev. Murray had staked with the intention of building a church. To signal their resolve, they erected poles on each lot and festooned them with white flags. Within weeks, construction of Oklahoma's first Methodist Episcopal Church was completed—a fitting tribute to people who built a community in six days and left the seventh to rest and relax and give thanks for safe passage to the Promised Land.[56]

PART III

City Building

CHAPTER TEN

Born Grown

In fact the men who came to Oklahoma as office holders
each gave birth to an evil and paternity to a strife.
Frank McMaster, April 1909

To enforce compliance with President Harrison's proclamation of March 23, soldiers in the Unassigned Lands spent the last few weeks before the opening on the lookout for prospective homesteaders who could no longer be restrained. As the clock ticked closer to noon on April 22, soldiers were equipped not only with weaponry but also with pencils and paper to record the names of suspected sooners. Their lists include some of the boomer movement's most illustrious leaders, including Crocker, Couch and several of his relations, and H. Stafford—surely Harry Stafford, a member of Payne's expedition to Ewing in the spring of 1880.[1]

While soldiers were figuring out what to do with their gallery of rogues, settlers were beginning their second week much as they had ended their first, dividing and platting town lots and keeping the lid on conflicts. One of their first acts was to elect yet another committee, this one composed of Couch and five other men, to adjust property boundaries between the Seminole faction's and citizens' surveys. On Monday, April 29, Couch issued an official proclamation calling for an election of permanent officers on May 1. His proclamation laid out the ground rules for the election and divided the townsite into two voting precincts representing two wards. One voting booth was set up north of Clarke Street at the junction of Main and Broadway, and another south of Clarke Street at the junction of California and Broadway.[2] As the best organized of Oklahoma's emerging factions, the Seminoles had the upper hand in orchestrating a campaign blitz to elevate their candidates to the city council. According to Angelo Scott, nobody had an inkling that a Seminole coup d'etat was in the making.[3]

As Election Day approached, many of the men who had signaled an early interest in politics blended into the citizenry, their names largely lost to Oklahoma history. As the Colony crowd's John Holzapfel explained, most members of his colony admitted that the whole land run experience had been a lark, and when the dust settled, they went home.[4] Kansas Oklahoma Colony members who stayed put to become leading citizens included James B. Wheeler, who later donated land for a park that bore his name; Robert Kincaid, a banker and railroad builder; and John and Eugene Wallace. These four men organized the Bank of Oklahoma City and arranged for construction of the Farmers National Bank building at the corner of Robinson and Grand Avenues. Others who chose to stay in their adopted city were Dr. Delos Walker, who practiced medicine for twenty years, helped to organize the first public school, became the first president of the school board, and served for several years as president of the local board of health; Delos's brother, C. P. Walker, who surveyed Walker Avenue; D. M. Phillips, who established the O.K. Bus and Baggage Company and, later, operated the Phillips O.K. Cab Company; Robert A. Davis, who cofounded Overholser & Avey Insurance; and James H. McCartney, a one-term city councilman and President Grover Cleveland's appointee to the board of trustees charged with finishing the deeding of city lots in Oklahoma County. McCartney and John Holzapfel built one of Oklahoma City's first brick buildings on Grand Avenue.[5]

As dawn broke on Wednesday, May 1, the excitement was palpable. Blissfully unaware that the Seminole faction aimed to hijack their election, eligible voters (white men, that is) flocked to hastily erected booths to cast their ballots. Troops remained on alert, ready to march at a moment's notice to quell disturbances. If they had had access to metropolitan newspapers, Oklahomans would have been shocked to learn of crime and riot in their rapidly forming streets. Yet news from the outside world was hard to come by, as the townsite's connectivity was restricted to a single telegraph wire that was reserved almost exclusively for railroad business, making it well nigh impossible for residents to send or receive telegraphic messages. A second wire reached Oklahoma on or about May 10, but by then the election had faded into history with neither crime nor riot to report.[6] Bill Couch was elected as mayor with 766 of the 1,360 votes cast for the city's top position. Also-rans included Ben S. Miller and James Murray with 266 and 328 votes, respectively. Rounding out the Seminole-dominated slate were John A. Blackburn, recorder; O. H. Violet, police judge; Ledru Guthrie, city attorney; M. C. Quinton, city treasurer; and Charles Chamberlin, city engineer. First ward councilmen included Sidney Clarke, F. G. Hudson, John Wallace, W. T. Richardson, C. T. Scott, W. C. Wells, and J. E. Jones. Their counterparts in the second ward were C. T. Scott (inexplicably included as a winner in the first ward), W. C. Wells, J. E. Jones, C. P. Walker, and J. F. Woodford. As Angelo Scott later explained, "It was a clean-cut victory for the Seminole Town Company."[7]

A week and three days after the Run of '89, Oklahoma had a municipal administration beyond the purview of any outside influence, including the U.S. Congress, whose ranks were dominated by the Seminole faction and suspected sooners. In weeks to come, the townsite would be torn by increasingly belligerent factions: Seminoles, who not only controlled the levers of power but also profited from their ongoing sale of town lot certificates and did their best to protect sooner claims; and Kickapoos, whose adherence to the rules of settlement provided scant protection from rules and regulations handed down by their elected officials. The stage was set for a showdown. The Oklahoma townsite's fate hung in the balance.

—————————

As Oklahomans were enjoying their first few days of settlement, the Scott brothers' rival newspaper, the *Oklahoma Chief* (published erroneously as the *Oklahoma Pioneer* in early editions, and unrelated to the defunct *Oklahoma War-Chief*), was publishing rhapsodies about the "Beautiful Land": "He who sees Oklahoma clothed in the fresh green hues of spring, on every hand suggesting the peace, plenty, and happiness that will bless her favored people, cannot fail to understand the spirit that moved Captain Payne, Couch, Crocker, and hundreds of others to the persistent efforts that at last opened the legislative barriers." Natural resources included abundant timber along creeks and streams and good, clean water at shallow depths. If the Choctaw Coal and Railway Company would hurry up in extending its line from the Indian Territory coalfields to Oklahoma, manufacturers would soon have access to cheap coal to fuel their industries, and homeowners would be able to heat their homes when cold weather set in.[8]

Paeans to the Beautiful Land were muted when the winds of spring came thundering across the Unassigned Lands. The big blow from the northwest began on Saturday, May 4, and did not let up for a week. As most people had yet to build houses, there was little they could do to mitigate the damage as gale-force winds blew down their tents and dust threatened them with suf-focation. The rain came on the second Sunday after the opening, and it fell in torrents rarely seen since settlers first put down roots in the Southwest. And then, in a pattern that Oklahomans would come to recognize as typical, the clouds parted and winds subsided and dust settled to reveal spring in all its glory.

Bad weather seemed to have little effect in stemming the flow of immi-grants. Real estate agents, reportedly as ubiquitous as lemonade stands, did a brisk business in the rapid-fire exchange of town lots. Although most sales were initiated when eighty-niners decided to take their profits and leave, there were still more buyers than sellers. As carpenters swarmed into the townsite to build homes and businesses, real estate prices obeyed the inexorable law of supply and demand and kept right on rising.[9] "The record of these days is best told by the hammer and the saw," declared the Scott brothers in their inaugural issue of the *Oklahoma Times* on May 9, "with the streets taking on shape and business enterprises of every kind throwing open their doors. No pen can adequately describe the novel scene." Waxing classical, the Scotts acknowledged that Rome took far more than a day to build, whereas Oklahoma City was springing up in a fortnight.[10] Later generations of Oklahomans would adopt the description "born grown" for their upstart metropolis.

The Scotts' competitor at the *Oklahoma Chief*, editor R. W. McAdam, was equally upbeat about the pace of urban development. Laboring in a squalid, twelve-by-sixteen-foot tent, McAdam, who had learned his trade in New York, Washington, and western Kansas, apologized for any mistakes he might make (such as his masthead, misprinted early on as the *Oklahoma Pioneer*), as he was publishing the best newspaper he could in a sea of distractions. He congratulated his fellow pioneers on their "magnificent record" since the opening: a thousand frame buildings were standing; capital was pouring in from all parts of the country; and strangers were arriving at the depot at a breakneck pace to build businesses and participate in city planning.[11] The *Chief* reserved special praise for G. A. Beidler, Samuel H. Radebaugh's successor as postmaster after the opening, who had overseen the post office's move from its original sheet-iron shanty to a two-story building on Main Street. Beidler was known for treating his patrons with patience and courtesy in the most trying of circumstances. The post office's relocation to more fitting accommodations on Main Street was matched by commercial development along Reno, California, Grand, and Broadway to put those avenues at the heart of the business district. Given the number of Texans who were moving into the townsite, some wondered why nobody had thought to name a thoroughfare after the Lone Star State.[12]

To satisfy an insatiable demand for building materials, trainloads of lumber were piling up at the Santa Fe depot. Competition came from sawmills, which were popping up around the townsite. At the risk of discouraging investment in the lumber business, the *Chief* cautioned against cutting down too much timber, a practice that threatened agricultural growth and marred the landscape. Fortunately, water was in ample supply at depths of only twenty feet and was relatively free of shale, alkali, and other impurities that could threaten a town's growth. Visionaries imagined the North Canadian River as a vital source not only to supply drinking water but also to power mills and industries not yet imagined. Activity at the depot included lumber shipments and shipments of Texas cattle bound for the Cherokee Outlet and beyond.[13]

Other news during the first eighteen days of settlement came at a rapid clip: construction of City Hall on Grand Avenue was nearing completion; plans were afoot to break ground for a fifty-thousand-dollar hotel; businessmen were organizing a board of trade; a log corral on California Avenue (presumably, the one that Bill McClure had used to pen his wild horses) was slated for demolition to make way for brick-and-mortar buildings; and a Chinese laundry was up and running on Broadway under the management of Sam Quong, an "Americanized Mongolian." Workloads at the depot were sure to increase when two railroad companies that were laying tracks through Indian Territory reached the depot. Every now and then, folks looked up from their feverish city building to glimpse Cheyennes and Arapahos—"hard looking specimens," according to the *Chief*—who were in town to purchase supplies before hastening back to their reservation west of town. Another common sight was overland freighters lined up at the depot to load merchandise. Although advances in transportation were pushing ox-and-mule-drawn wagon trains into extinction, they remained in 1889 the only viable option to provide Fort Reno, the Darlington Indian Agency, and other remote outposts with food and supplies.[14]

To supply settlers' most basic needs, L. L. Land chartered a railroad car to deliver general merchandise to the store he was opening. He and his business partner, R. T. Wright, secured a hundred feet of street frontage for a rock building and rented twenty-five feet of their frontage to J. P. Sheppard, whose meat market enticed customers with deer and other game hanging across his storefront. To supply distant markets, Sheppard shipped carloads of deer and quail from the Santa Fe depot.[15]

To finance their businesses and safeguard their money, entrepreneurs turned to the town's two banks: the Oklahoma Bank, founded by T. M. Richardson; and Citizens' Bank, whose president was James Geary. As noted in the *Oklahoma Chief*, "Both houses have abundant working capital, and are managed by safe and competent financiers."[16] To expand on business-building articles in the local press, the Oklahoma Bank's advertisements assured potential depositors and lenders that it was "not a wild-cat bank, but [has] come to stay."[17]

━━━━━━━━

The *Oklahoma Times* and *Oklahoma Chief* were up and running when Frank McMaster arrived in town to launch yet another newspaper. As opening day approached, he was living in Chicago and reporting for the *Chicago Times*. Like so many adventurers of his generation, he succumbed to Oklahoma fever and shipped his printing equipment to Oklahoma and, on May 21, published the first issue of the *Oklahoma Gazette*. Rechristened with little fanfare on July 24 as the *Evening Gazette*, McMaster's newspaper became an invaluable source of local news and earned him a seat at the table with the town's most influential opinion leaders.[18]

Like R. W. McAdam, Frank McMaster had a tale to tell about acquiring a town lot. When survey crews reached Grand Avenue on April 27, McMaster learned that the two lots he had claimed were located in the street. Infuriated by his forced relocation, McMaster quickly realized that, thanks to the Seminole company's survey crew, Main Street and all the streets to the north ran perpendicular to the railroad tracks but not truly in an east-west orientation. When adjustments were made between the citizens' and Seminole company surveys, so-called wedge lots were created to fill in the cracks in the middle of the block. From then on, McMaster was a staunch supporter of the Kickapoo faction in its escalating vendetta against the Seminoles and their allies in the municipal government. He famously dubbed Grand Avenue "Stolen Avenue" because its relocation deprived so many settlers of their lots without compensation.[19]

Operating from his cramped quarters, McMaster did his part to keep his fellow Oklahomans informed about the urban transformation. At Needham

& McDonald's photograph tent at the corner of Broadway and California, photos of Cheyenne and Arapaho chiefs were on sale for ninety-five cents a pop.[20] Businessmen who set up shop on California Avenue included realtors, attorneys, a barber, a baker, and a purveyor of dry goods. Delmonico Restaurant, housed in a twenty-four-by-forty-foot building, offered prompt and courteous service that compensated for its lack of seating. One of Delmonico's owners, Captain Victor Sherman from Texas, ran a real estate business next door, where he lived with his family. Farther down the street was the Chop House ("a fine lunch counter"), the Palace Clothing House, and a branch of the Purcell-based Oklahoma Dry Goods Company. At the corner of California and Broadway was Gilpin & Frick, a twenty-five-by-sixty-foot hardware store that opened for business on the day of the Run. T. J. Starr, Oklahoma's pioneer tinner, occupied a twenty-five-by-thirty-five-foot shop and was earning a reputation for galvanized ironwork and roofing.[21]

Among the townsite's earliest and most successful businesses was McNabb's Oklahoma Flour and Feed Depot. With several years of experience under his belt, Ohio native C. A. McNabb launched his business on the day of the Run as a purveyor of flour, feed, and other frontier necessities. Like T. M. Richardson at the Oklahoma Bank, McNabb prepared for frontier commerce by importing two carloads of flour and feed, which had been resting on a railroad siding awaiting his arrival. His first location was on the old Reno Trail, the main route linking the Santa Fe depot and Fort Reno and situated between present-day California and Reno Avenues. McNabb remained there until May 1889, when he relocated his business to more spacious digs on Broadway between Main Street and Grand Avenue. He quickly became known as one of the city's most generous, energetic, and successful businessmen.[22]

Another energetic business leader was Henry Overholser. Like Richardson in banking and McNabb in farming supplies, Overholser did not leave his fate in the new country to chance. Prior to his arrival, he arranged for several carloads of prefabricated wood-frame buildings that he had purchased in Michigan to be hauled to a railroad siding. In the weeks following the opening, he erected six two-story buildings on lots he had purchased on Grand Avenue. Within a month of arriving at the Oklahoma townsite, Overholser was elected as president of the Board of Trade, precursor to the Oklahoma City Chamber of Commerce.[23] "Mr. Overholser was not a grafter as many thought," recalled E. E. Brown, a former journalist from No Man's Land. "He was a good shrewd businessman, and he chose Oklahoma City because it was a good commercial center." Rather than go to the trouble of staking a claim, Overholser let eighty-niners do the hard work and then, once the dust had settled, bought the lots he wanted along Grand and Robinson Avenues. Over the next few months, Overholser rose to the pinnacle of his adopted city's business elite.[24]

L. L. Land, R. T. Wright, J. P. Sheppard, T. M. Richardson, James Geary, C. A. McNabb, and Henry Overholser represented the first wave of businessmen, whose entrepreneurial spirit spawned an infusion of capital into the townsite. They also typified the frontier businessman on several levels: most had engaged in another enterprise before migrating to Oklahoma Proper; regardless of their places of birth, most were in their twenties or thirties and came from an adjoining state; and their shifts from one line of business to another reveal more interest in profit than a particular career path. Instant partnerships—that is, the pooling of capital and expertise by individuals who, hours or perhaps days earlier, had been complete strangers—were common and usually sealed with a handshake, fortified by the knowledge that pioneers were destined to sink or swim together.[25]

R. W. McAdam was probably still in his filthy tent when he learned that businessmen had invested upwards of twenty thousand dollars in the Oklahoma townsite in only three days. He was downright giddy to learn where the investors came from: Guthrie. As the *Oklahoma Chief* reported with undisguised relish, they "were disgusted with the situation in the windy wonder of Cottonwood Creek" and had decided to put their money where it was most likely to grow. "Every day brings fresh arrivals of solid business men from Kingfisher and Guthrie, anxious to cast their lot in this city of destiny," declared the *Chief*. In language reflecting a rivalry destined to grow more intense with each passing day, the *Chief* suggested that residents of the Oklahoma townsite could display their competitive edge by trouncing Guthrie's baseball team. In case readers were slow to get the point, the *Chief* went beyond sporting competition: "Everybody who visits Oklahoma City has a good word to say of the coming metropolis. Not so Guthrie."[26]

———————

Less than two weeks after the election of May 1, city recorder John A. Blackburn assured Oklahomans that municipal books and stationery were expected any day and, furthermore, that certificates would be issued to lot holders right away. Fees were set at $2.00 for issuing and $2.50 for recording certificates of ownership. But before certificates could be properly issued and recorded,

Henry Overholser.
Courtesy of Oklahoma Historical Society, Oklahoma City, 5945.

Oklahoma (townsite), 1889, viewed from atop the Santa Fe depot.
Oklahoma Images Collection, Metropolitan Library System of Oklahoma County.

claimants would have to swear that there was no evidence of prior occupancy when they settled on their lots.[27]

The absence of record-keeping paraphernalia did not delay the municipal government in posting city ordinances. Ordinance number one, approved by Mayor Couch and attested by city recorder Blackburn on May 4, announced penalties for anyone who squatted on lots and obstructed streets and alleys. Entering, improving, digging, and driving stakes on another person's lot would be treated as a misdemeanor. If convicted, miscreants could expect police judge O. H. Violet to levy a fine not to exceed one hundred dollars, plus court costs. Anyone unable to pay the fine would be required to work on the streets (the frontier's version of community service) as a means of restitution.[28] Ordinance number two, likewise approved and attested on May 4, provided a framework for publishing the municipal government's ordinances and edicts and, over the objections of R. W. McAdam at the *Oklahoma Chief*, designated the Scott brothers' *Oklahoma Times* as the city's official newspaper for a period of one year. Borrowing from similar ordinances in Kansas, the city council provided the Scotts with a rate and schedule of remuneration for doing the people's work.[29] Although pleased to land a city contract, the Scotts worried that readers would confuse their newspaper, the *Oklahoma Times*, with its soon-to-be rival, the *Oklahoma City Times*, set to open up shop under the editorship of H. W. Sawyer and his gutsy reporter, B. R. Harrington. To eliminate the confusion, the Scotts renamed their paper the *Oklahoma Journal* in its second issue on May 16. They began publishing on a daily rather than weekly basis on June 3.[30]

Frank McMaster was apparently less vexed by his competition than by the municipal government's de facto monopoly on selling lot certificates. City ordinance number three guaranteed owners of lot certificates that their property rights were secure, assuming they had been duly filed with the city recorder. In a May 24 rant, McMaster reminded his readers that lot certificates issued by city officials owed their supposed legitimacy to the Seminole Town and Improvement Company, and no matter how closely lot occupants adhered to U.S. statutes, they risked incurring fines for failure to comply with the peculiarities of Seminole regulations. And then, McMaster threw down the gauntlet: "The secret lies in the fact that the entry of that town company into the territory, was in violation of the law, yet the ordinance is really framed to protect their illegal acts."[31]

Drawing on his legal training, McMaster explained how public lands were transferred to private ownership. In essence, townsite companies were organized to buy town lots from the federal government and then sell them to individuals. According to U.S. statutes, townsite company managers were obliged to serve as trustees for property-holding citizens. Citizens' meetings were in essence stockholder meetings, whose purpose was to regulate municipal affairs in accordance with general U.S. and townsite laws. Although U.S. laws did not regulate the number of town lots that an individual could purchase, buyers could be granted preference in ownership only by occupying their property or properties. Details pertaining to preference and occupancy were left entirely to local regulations. The bottom line was that a town lot owner had to comply with local regulations and give evidence of ownership by making improvements. Only then could an individual exercise exclusive dominion over his property. Entirely different regulations pertained to homesteads, as individuals acquired rural property directly from the U.S. government, and abandoned land reverted to federal ownership.[32]

Rules governing lot ownership were not enough to dissuade some urban pioneers, derided in the local press as town lot hogs, from grabbing as many lots as they could.[33] Nor were the rules enough to prevent armed and organized bands of claim jumpers from acquiring other people's property. To cite a single example, Dr. Childs of Cincinnati filed a claim on a quarter section between Oklahoma and Fort Reno and erected a cabin. After a brief absence, he returned to his claim to find a notice tacked to his door threatening violence if he refused to vacate.[34]

The task of keeping such conflicts from escalating fell to Captain Daniel F. Stiles. A native of Massachusetts and soldier since August 1861, Stiles had served at Fort Leavenworth, Kansas, and Forts Crawford and Lyon in Colorado prior to his assignment as provost marshal at Oklahoma. He arrived at his new post in April 1889 with a battalion of the Tenth and Eighteenth Regiments of U.S. Infantry. Known as a strict disciplinarian and delicately poised between civic and military authorities, Stiles was praised in the *Kansas City Times* for exercising "the most prudent action" in the discharge of his duties. Yet supporters of the Kickapoo faction perceived Stiles, whose quick temper sometimes got the best of him, as a Seminole lackey and berated him at every opportunity for what they perceived as military overreach.[35]

Stiles's diplomacy was tested when a businessman named Saunders erected a tent on the west side of Broadway over the objections of a government employee, who had claimed several lots and insisted that the Seminole Town and Improvement Company had reserved this particular lot for him. Assuming that the municipal government would face up to a town lot hog, Saunders

opened a fruit and cigar stand on the contested property. To his dismay, Captain
Stiles showed up at daybreak with a squad of soldiers and force marched him to
the guardhouse, where he remained confined for twenty-four hours. Saunders
was released without any charges and with no explanation. "If an American
citizen has not the right to protest against military interference with rights that
are heaven-born, the word 'republic' is a mockery," declared Saunders. As a
postscript, the *Oklahoma Chief* offered a challenge to the citizenry: "Let the
fair-play loving citizens of Oklahoma City say whether it was an outrage or no."[36]

Conflicts did not end with isolated threats of intimidation and brazen lot
grabbing. In a scandal that reached all the way to the U.S. attorney general's
office, seven hundred lawmen were implicated in a plot to use their official
positions to gain early access to the Unassigned Lands and claim choice properties. To speed them along their journeys, the lawmen purchased sixty-five
ponies from an Indian chief and gathered food and supplies to facilitate their
illegal entry. They avoided detection by taking disparate routes to preassigned
positions. The word on the street was that the miscreants had agreed to transfer
their claims to a syndicate of businessmen from Topeka and Kansas City. A
member of Congress, unnamed in an *Oklahoma Chief* exposé, was said to be
"badly involved in this wholesale grab."

Among those who had inside knowledge of the scam was George W. Cole.
After arriving at Oklahoma on April 22, he apparently gathered sufficient
intelligence to inform U.S. attorney general William Henry Harrison Miller
(1889–93) about the lawmen's plot. Attorney General Miller thanked Cole
for his information and promised a thorough investigation. But then, in a
bizarre twist that cannot be made up, Cole came under fire for somehow
seizing the townsite's meager water supplies on April 22 and 23 and selling
the precious liquid to thirsty eighty-niners. When a commanding officer,
Colonel Wade, heard about Cole's perfidy, he dispatched a sergeant to drive
him from the well. Disgusted with what he considered military interference
in his entrepreneurial endeavors, Cole skipped town for parts unknown. In
spite of Cole's alleged misconduct at the water well, the *Oklahoma Chief*
supported his allegations that "tricksters and monopolists" were thwarting
orderly settlement.[37]

Tricksters and monopolists, and probably the officers who arrested them,
slaked their thirst in an entertainment district known throughout the sunny
Southwest as "Hell's Half Acre." As the pace of construction hit warp speed,
tents gave way to more spacious accommodations for gamblers, saloon keepers,

Daniel F. Stiles.
Courtesy of Oklahoma Historical Society, Oklahoma City, 6113.

and entrepreneurs of dubious distinction to ply their trades. Mrs. Edith Barrows, an immigrant from Nebraska, whose father had staked a lot on the corner of Broadway and Grand, recalled what it was like to live a stone's throw from Hell's Half Acre. "There were a good many saloons in Oklahoma City in the early days," recalled Mrs. Barrows. "One time someone called my mother and asked her how many saloons there were in Oklahoma City and she replied that she did not know as she did not frequent them very much, but that there were so many between Fourth and Broadway and Grand Avenue, a woman never walked that part of town."[38]

Joining soldiers in what must have seemed like a losing battle was Charley Colcord, who had parlayed his connections to become Oklahoma City's first chief of police. As a former cowboy, he knew better than most the main source of his adopted hometown's troubles: cowboys. "They had never done anything but ride the range," he wrote about his former hard-riding comrades, and "could not find anything to do when the range went out and nearly every one of those gangs that infested the country during the early years were made up of former cowpunchers. A lot of good men who could not stand the strain of changed conditions went this route."[39]

Upon their arrival at Oklahoma, usually announced with pistol shots and lots of whooping and hollering, those cowpunchers probably made a beeline for "Battle Row," a notorious stretch of real estate between Main Street and Grand Avenue that must have seemed like heaven on earth for entertainment-starved troublemakers. Establishments that branded Oklahoma as a haven for outlaws included the Vendome, known as the plushiest bawdy house on the street; Two Johns Saloon next to City Hall; and a house of ill repute operated by Mrs. "Big Anne" Wynn, who came to Oklahoma from the mining camps of Colorado, pitched a tent on Front Street (later, Santa Fe Avenue) on the day of the Run, and stocked it with women willing to provide female companionship for the overwhelmingly male population. As onetime city manager Albert McRill noted, "Satan reigned unmolested for many years."[40]

Charley Colcord was apparently one of the few cowboys to stay on the right side of the law. He got his job when city recorder Blackburn, who served as acting mayor during Couch's many absences, asked him to head up Oklahoma's tiny, low-budget police department, which operated with no legal authority and whose sole source of revenue were fines levied from lawbreakers. Lacking permanent headquarters, city authorities held court in a tent, first on California Avenue, and later on Grand Avenue. Once convicted of a crime, prisoners had no place to go. So, with a can-do spirit that typified communities throughout the Unassigned Lands, somebody acquired two-by-eight timbers from a sawmill southwest of the townsite and built a wooden, fourteen-by-sixteen-foot jail. Merchants donated the hardware, and residents took time from their work to pitch in and install it.

The most common crime was public intoxication. Relieved of their firearms, lawbreakers were packed into the jail until they sobered up. Colcord returned their guns and, on their way out, slapped them with fines ranging from one to five dollars. But if they were broke, Colcord had no choice but to release them. He had little time to fret about his unpredictable income, as he stayed busy arresting fifteen to twenty men on a daily basis. Winding through streets that were usually teeming with horses, cattle, and wagon trains, Colcord was a familiar sight in Hell's Half Acre. As he wrote about his career as a lawman, "At that time the gamblers had houses all over Oklahoma City—tents were everywhere along the west side of the Santa Fe. For a long time there were more gambling outfits and dives than anything else."

One of Colcord's most harrowing experiences as a lawman started when cowboys rode into town from Bickford Springs, which was about six miles

Main Street, Oklahoma (City), June 1, 1889.
Courtesy of Oklahoma Historical Society, Oklahoma City, 20699.69.36.9R.

west of the townsite, and wound up on the losing end of a fight with a group of gamblers. Tensions escalated when bloodied and bruised cowboys made their way back to their ranch headquarters to enlist help in putting things right. Colcord's radar was on high alert when he visited Cook's Saloon at Grand and Broadway to see who had dished out the beatings. One of the gamblers, clearly drunk, drew his weapon and took aim at Colcord. With a little help from law-abiding friends, Colcord managed to disarm the gambler, confiscated his and others' weapons, and admonished them to clear out. When he got word that cowboys with a score to settle were heading back to town, he walked west on Grand Avenue to meet them. Employing negotiating skills that would later make him one of Oklahoma City's most successful businessmen, Colcord compelled the cowboys to surrender their guns and go home. "If these fellows had gotten together," recalled Colcord, "we probably would have had a general killing."

Aside from gamblers and cowboys and drunks in Hell's Half Acre, Colcord described his fellow urbanites as "the most cosmopolitan bunch anyone ever met." Many of the adventurers who arrived in town with the first wave of eighty-niners did not stay for long and left the painstaking work of city building to "the real settlers."[41]

C. S. "Bud" Peniston was an Arkansan by birth who went to work in 1887 at the Suggs Ranch—an enormous swath of real estate that stretched from south of Lawton to the Red River and east to the railroad—for fifteen dollars (later raised to forty-five dollars) per month. Peniston left the ranch to make the Run of '89 and was rewarded with a 160-acre homestead. Unfortunately, the land was not of the best quality, as soldiers had already staked their claims, some by proxy, to the best parcels. To make matters worse, a drought set in, making marginal land even less desirable. Forced once again to ponder his career options, Peniston drifted up to the Oklahoma townsite to work in a hardware store. He arrived just in time for a typhoid epidemic that carried off settlers by the score. "We all lived in dugouts," continued Peniston about his days as an urban pioneer. "In the early days men worth seventy-five thousand dollars lived in them and thought nothing of it." Peniston later went to Gainesville, Texas, and faded from the historical record.[42]

Indiana native S. L. Dunham (relation, if any, to Santa Fe stationmaster A. W. Dunham unknown) moved with his family to Kansas, where his father farmed for several years before making his way to the Beautiful Land and spending all the money he had ($2.50) as a down payment on a homestead. When he learned that his homestead had been designated as school land, the elder Dunham traded a one-eyed horse and an old buggy for a lot behind the Citizens' Bank at the corner of Main and Hudson. It was presumably from this location near the present-day Hightower Building and its across-the-street neighbor, the Devon Tower, that S. L.'s father and oldest brother operated the Star Restaurant, Oklahoma's first full-service eatery. Seven decades later, entrepreneur and philanthropist Frank J. Hightower opened the Cellar Restaurant in the basement of the Hightower Building to feature classic French cooking and give Oklahoma City its first taste of haute cuisine.[43]

Haute cuisine was far in the future as the Dunhams and their customers side-stepped mosquito-infested mud puddles that dotted the urban landscape. As S. L. recalled, "There was an awful lot of Malaria, and so severe was this epidemic, that people died by the dozens."[44] Thomas H. Jordan, a native of New York State who constructed the first stores along Broadway for $2.75 a day, described Oklahoma as a damp and swampy place where a stroll across town could turn deadly. Navigating past tents and swamps at night with nothing but torches to light his way, Jordan bought water for ten cents a bucket, perhaps from the duplicitous George W. Cole.[45]

But still the people came, lured by the promise of a fresh start and encouraged to learn that circumstances were not nearly as dire as the eastern press would have them believe. Receiver Admire of Kingfisher was incensed by slanderous reports in the nation's newspapers. "The stories circulated in the eastern press in regard to the disorder, confusion, danger and outlawry that exist in Oklahoma are absolutely false, and in many cases maliciously so," he wrote in a letter to the *Kansas City Times*. "Better order has existed in this town from the very outstart than would have existed under similar circumstances in any town in Kansas." Waxing hyperbolic, he insisted that the "good humor and decency" on display every day in the Oklahoma country could not be found "in the history of the world." In Admire's opinion, Americans were better off without laws than with them. Perhaps more enlightened than its peers, the *New York Sun* agreed with Admire to suggest that "it is hard to govern the American people when they govern themselves."[46]

Frank Best of the Santa Fe Railroad agreed. In a description that is difficult to reconcile with eighty-niners' accounts of raucous gambling dens, murder on a daily basis, and police chief Charley Colcord's encounters with drunks and trigger-happy cowboys, Best had nothing but praise for his law-abiding and churchgoing neighbors. Perhaps his position at the Guthrie depot afforded him few opportunities to witness the drinking and shooting that captured other peoples' attention. "They were the most peaceful accumulation of men you could imagine," wrote Best. "By common consent local rules were formed, not backed by any law, yet crime was at the minimum." In his estimation, Oklahoma Proper was wild primarily in the imaginations of writers and journalists, whose lurid stories created lasting and misleading impressions of life on the rapidly vanishing frontier.[47] Scarcely had the dust settled from the Run of '89 than urban pioneers began to organize chapters of the Masons, Odd Fellows, Knights of Pythias, and other associations whose activities would surely hasten the city's cultural development.[48]

The longer Oklahomans waited for Congress to provide for territorial governance, the more they realized that they might be better off as they were. A consensus was emerging that isolated homesteaders were the only ones who might benefit from political organization as a defense against bandits and claim jumpers.[49] The *Oklahoma Chief* relied on tried-and-true biblical imagery to dismiss complaints from people who had failed to get a foothold in the Oklahoma country, accusing them of harboring sour grapes, much as Adam had probably resented his expulsion from Eden. "We imagine old Adam sat down on a stump, after his expulsion, and cursed Eden, saying he'd be dad blasted if he'd live in such a dog gone country, anyhow," railed one editorial. The *Chief* urged its readers to treat such misguided individuals gently and to consider the true source of their disappointment.[50]

Meanwhile, back at the Santa Fe depot, newcomers with an intention to stay were learning what frontier hospitality was all about. Mrs. E. G. Remmers, whose father made the Run of '89 on horseback and staked a claim in an area dubbed "Nine Mile Flats," only to relinquish it when eleven others claimed the same property, arrived from Texas at the Oklahoma depot with her mother on June 10, 1889. By then, her father had secured two lots at Second and Harvey Avenue for twenty-five dollars each, including the expense of buying the rights of rival claimants. "When we arrived at the station, there was such a large crowd of men there, we thought there was a circus in town, especially since we saw so many tents," recalled Mrs. Remmers. "Several men carried mother off the platform and held her up in the crowd. Mother was a southern woman, and it embarrassed her to be carried through the crowd but she laughed with the rest." The day after their arrival, two ladies from Kansas called on the Remmerses to see if they needed anything and to offer their assistance in any way they could. Assistance of a different kind was available back at the depot, where an African American with a team of oxen met trains and offered to take people up town for twenty-five cents. He had a saddle on one of the oxen, and he alternated between riding and walking.

Some of Mrs. Remmers's earliest memories of living in the two-story home that her father built at Second and Robinson Avenues (apparently, the first two-story home in town) were of persistent flooding. "I used to ride in a row boat after a rain over to Robinson where the First National Bank building now stands," she recalled. Sidewalks and many of the houses along Robinson and Broadway were built on stilts.[51]

Neither floods nor the diseases they spawned were enough to dissuade Oklahomans from fulfilling their sacred mission to build houses of worship. The first religious services were conducted in tents, with benches fashioned from boards and beer kegs and floors sprinkled with sawdust. Ad hoc services gave way to more formal doings two blocks north of the Remmers home, where Rev. N. F. Scallan, who had arrived in Oklahoma on May 7 after performing missionary work at Purcell and among the Ponca Indians, set about building the town's first church. Prior to construction, Catholics gathered on May 19 at Indiana House on Main Street between Robinson and Harvey Avenues.

Santa Fe depot, Oklahoma (City), Independence Day, 1889.
Courtesy of Oklahoma Historical Society, Oklahoma City, 6505.

Doubling as a man of the cloth and an architect, Father Scallan might have shoveled the first dirt at Northwest Fourth and Harvey to begin construction of Saint Joseph's Church—Catholic in denomination, but open to all worshippers. The first service was held on July 1, the cross was raised on the spire on July 31, the bell was placed in the tower on August 2, and the first Angelus rang at 6 o'clock that evening.[52]

An entirely different kind of celebration was in the works for the Fourth of July. Oklahoma City (as it was increasingly, if not officially, known) was only a few weeks old when town founders announced their intention to commemorate America's birthday with a parade through the fledgling business district, exhibitions of boomer life and enterprises, feats of horsemanship, sack racing, infantry drills, a baseball game, a gun tournament, and, best of all, Indian dancers in full regalia. In the spirit of community, Bill McClure and his family invited organizers to build a grandstand on their property, which later became the Maywood Addition. As the holiday weekend approached, promoters fanned out across the country to festoon railroad depots with lavish posters printed in bright, bold colors that were sure to draw not only tourists but also businessmen looking for a place to grow their capital. Committees were appointed to secure special rates from the Santa Fe and solicit money to defray expenses.[53]

Promoters were disappointed when the crowd fell short of the twenty thousand revelers they were expecting. But the show went on, and it included a horse race in which Bill McClure's son and hometown favorite, Dave, finished first. Riders were in position for a second race when the unthinkable happened: the grandstand, hastily built and unable to withstand the foot stomping of excited horse racing fans, came crashing to the ground.

Etta Dale, a young immigrant whose family had just arrived in Oklahoma City from No Man's Land, and her friends had just stepped away from the grandstand and were sipping cold drinks when the entire edifice collapsed. At least one person died on the spot, and three others died the next day from their injuries. As Dale recalled about Oklahoma's unlucky coming-out party, "It was a tragic experience."[54]

While revelers were recovering from Oklahoma City's Fourth of July tragedy, business leaders in Guthrie formed a Territorial Executive Committee and summoned delegates to a convention on July 17 to organize and establish a government. Several proposals were on the table, including one pitch to divide the region into four counties and corresponding county seats: Weaver (county seat at Guthrie); Couch (county seat at Oklahoma City); Springer (county seat at Cooper); and Perkins (county seat at Sells). Organizers further proposed that convention attendees appoint a county judge and three commissioners for each county and, under the auspices of a newly created provisional government, assume the authority to elect a delegate to Congress. This structure was to remain in place until Congress could get its act together and pass legislation to establish a new territory.[55]

As opinion leaders throughout Oklahoma Proper were mulling the wisdom of taking matters into their own hands in such a brazen and probably extra-legal fashion, Frank McMaster at the *Oklahoma Gazette* was conducting a census of his adopted hometown. Published in mid-June 1889, McMaster counted, "in round numbers," 6,000 residents and 1,603 dwellings and places of business, including 5 newspapers, 4 banks, 44 lawyers, 53 doctors, 21 drug stores, "and every business to catch a victim or inflate a metropolis." As far as the upcoming convention in Guthrie was concerned, McMaster voiced the opinion of most Oklahomans in questioning its organizers' motives. Come what may, McMaster urged caution: "So long as a government was absent there was neither a spoken wish for its coming nor a valid reason shown for giving it a life. In fact the men who came to Oklahoma as office holders each gave birth to an evil and paternity to a strife."[56]

CHAPTER ELEVEN

Status Quo

When will there be a governor in Oklahoma[?]
(Oklahoma City) Evening Gazette, *December 28, 1889*

The grandstand collapse on July 4, 1889, obscured what promoters had been billing as the main attraction of the entire extravaganza: Indian dancing, a guaranteed crowd pleaser sure to lure visitors to Indian Territory. Oklahoma City's overwhelmingly white pioneers (as immigrant Jim Simpson observed in the 1890s, "Oklahoma City belonged to the white man"[1]) were likewise captivated by aboriginal cultures, and they relished opportunities to interact with honest-to-goodness Indians, who often camped on the outskirts of the business district for days at a time to trade and shop. Their natural suspicion of white people soared when white men came in contact with Indian women. If a white man came calling at an Indian camp, the chief might emerge from his teepee and ask what he wanted. But if a white man arrived with a woman, his host might assume that he wanted to be sociable and sometimes invited the couple into his tent, where a fire often hissed and popped in the center and beds were arrayed around the perimeter. If an Indian began to eat, his visitors would be invited to partake, as long as they ladled their food from the communal pot. Alfred Smith, a former slave who had been auctioned off at age nine in Chattanooga, Tennessee, arrived in Oklahoma City by way of Tulsa to discover what Indian hospitality was all about. "If you did not eat with him," recalled Smith, "you were called a high hat and no good."[2] As long as their ways were respected, most Indians gave no signs of hostility toward their new neighbors.[3]

Edith Barrows's trepidation about strolling through Hell's Half Acre did not extend to Indian camps. She occasionally accompanied her father on horse-trading ventures to present-day Bricktown and watched him pay as much as fifteen dollars for the finest Indian ponies.[4] Clearly a domestic sort, Barrows paid special attention to Indians' culinary customs. She watched in fascination as Indian women mixed water and flour and other ingredients in a rock bowl. They proceeded to wave their dough in the air, fashion it into balls, and drop them in a skillet over a fire. Next, they cut meat into small pieces and dropped it into the skillet. Apparently, vegetables never made it to the menu. When it came time to dine, Indians sat on the ground and took turns doling out meat and flour balls and flavoring them with cupfuls of soup from their concoction.[5]

None were more attuned to Indian tastes than butchers. Jeff Randolph, a native Kentuckian of Cherokee, Creek, and African American descent, watched Indians snatch up body parts that butchers discarded and eat them on the spot.[6] In a later age, nutritionists would come to recognize what Indians knew instinctively: to compensate for the lack of vitamins in their meat-centered diet, they ate raw organs and entrails that would lose their dietary value through cooking.[7] To entice customers of European descent, the Blue Front Butcher Shop on Main Street always had three or four deer carcasses and quail by the hundreds hanging from hooks. To broaden the Blue Front's offerings, the proprietor bought catfish—one the length of a wagon, and then some!—that fishermen caught at Dead Man's Crossing near Council Grove, hoisted them next to the game animals, and sliced off chunks for their customers.[8] Competition came from J. P. Sheppard's meat market on California Avenue, where deer, quail, and other game were similarly arrayed in front of the building.[9]

Even though Indians were gradually acclimating to an alien economy, they retained their Native customs. They were particularly enthralled with horse races, where, slathered in paint and clad in shirts and blankets, they bet everything they had. Sac and Fox Indians shaved their heads on either side, leaving long braids extending from their foreheads to the backs of their necks adorned with trinkets purchased from the post trader. Festooned with brass jewelry and glass ornaments, they were an extraordinary sight for visitors not yet accustomed to frontier ways.[10]

L. L. Land, a native of Kentucky who, along with R. T. Wright, operated a general merchandise store between Broadway and California Avenues, had daily opportunities to witness how his Kiowa, Comanche, and Kickapoo customers handled money. "The Indians spent most generously," recalled Land. After receiving their government payments, the men traveled to Oklahoma City in the company of their women, with dogs in tow, and—providing the weather was warm—pitched their camps at Walnut Grove a mile and a half southeast of the Santa Fe depot. Upon entering Land and Wright's store, they requested change for their ten and twenty dollar bills, purchased merchandise one item at a time, and motioned to their women to carry it outside. Purchases often dragged on for hours, leaving the proprietors hard pressed to tend to customers used to a brisker pace of commerce. Indians celebrated the end of a shopping spree with an evening of dancing and accepted the coins that the audience tossed into their circle. The ever-popular fire dance required barefoot performers to cavort across a three-inch bed of hot wooden coals. Every few steps, they hopped into a tub of water laced with an undisclosed herbal mixture to prevent their feet from blistering.[11]

Even more alluring than Indian dancing were the beef issues at the Darlington Indian Agency. Flora Ragon (née Gilpin) often visited Fort Reno at the invitation of Major Woodson, who, from time to time, invited young people to observe the famed slaughter. Perched near a corral where dozens of fat beeves awaited their fate, Ragon watched as warriors jumped on their ponies bareback and waited for a government agent to release one steer at a time. With a customary flourish, the Indians gave chase until their prey dropped from exhaustion. Its pursuers quickly slid off their mounts, slit the animal's throat, caught its steaming blood in containers, and drank their fill. Next on the scene were women and children, who deftly skinned the carcass in preparation for a barbecue.

It was all too much for Margaret Robberts from Kingfisher, who joined Ella Brownlee Leach and her father on a surrey ride to the agency. As the butchery wound toward its conclusion, she leaned her head on her friend's shoulder and fainted. The ladies from Kingfisher must have missed out on nighttime celebrations that featured dancing around a bonfire. "We always looked forward to these events," said a more intrepid Flora Ragon, "hoping for an invitation from Major Woodson. We were always friendly with the Indians and never experienced any trouble."[12]

Following her near-death experience at what was supposed to be a festive Fourth of July celebration, Etta Dale was similarly captivated by displays of Indian prowess. With projectiles flying and horses galloping at full tilt, beef issues were not without their risks, and she was always relieved to return to El Reno. In 1891, Miss Dale took on less adventurous pursuits when she signed on as a teacher in Banner. Four and a half decades later, the El Reno Board of Education honored her lifetime of teaching in Canadian County by christening its newest building on Choctaw Avenue in El Reno as Etta Dale Junior High School.[13]

Oklahomans were still recovering from the grandstand collapse when mayors representing several provisional town governments called for a meeting to formulate a response to Guthrie's territorial convention on July 17. The meeting was to be held on July 15 in Frisco, a tiny outpost about fifteen miles west of the Oklahoma townsite ("just a wide place in the road," according to Angelo Scott) on the north side of the Canadian River. To elect delegates, citizens of the Oklahoma and South Oklahoma townsites assembled on July 12 in two mass meetings, one in front of South Oklahoma mayor T. J. Fagan's office, and the other in front of the Overholser block. Everyone knew what was afoot: Guthrie was making a brazen attempt to seize power so that Congress would see the wisdom of bestowing permanent capital status on that city.[14] In addition to Oklahoma and South Oklahoma, towns represented at what came to be known as the "Frisco Convention" included Frisco, Lisbon, Reno City, Norman, El Reno, Noble, Kingfisher, and Alfred. Angelo Scott, who was elected as the Frisco Convention secretary, characterized his town's forty or so representatives as "a queer mix-up" of Seminoles and Kickapoos, whose battle for control of Oklahoma's provisional government was reaching full fury. "Every 89er will see at once that this was a delegation that wouldn't bear shaking; it would explode," wrote Scott. But for once, the rivals put their differences aside and came together in an effort to squelch what was widely perceived as Guthrie's usurpation of congressional authority.[15]

As the Frisco Convention wound toward closure, Sidney Clarke read its resolutions to some two hundred delegates. Those resolutions ended with a stirring testament to frontier democracy and a rebuke of Guthrie's ploy to elevate its interests above all others: "Believing, therefore, that the attempt to establish a so-called provisional government would be detrimental to the best interests of the people of Oklahoma, we not only declare our hostility to it, but we also give notice that we refuse to recognize any such government by every honorable means in our power."[16]

Guthrie's convention on July 17 came off as planned, but attendance was sparse and the atmosphere decidedly downbeat. Organizers held perfunctory sessions, but in the end they did not even bother to submit their resolutions and documents to the public. The best they could do was agree to reconvene in late August for a last-ditch effort to convince community leaders that a provisional government—based, of course, in Guthrie—was in everybody's best interest. When delegates gathered in late August, the *Oklahoma News*, published every Friday at Lisbon, was on hand to chronicle the convention proceedings. Wary of generalizations, the *News* was careful to avoid branding everyone in Guthrie as unsavory. But it had no doubt that a minority of "schemers" was behind the convention.[17]

On September 10, a self-proclaimed territorial central committee assembled at Frisco to encourage participation in an election that Guthrie business-men had scheduled on October 22 and to vote against the adoption of their so-called constitution. Attendees were unanimous in adopting resolutions denouncing Guthrie's attempted power grab. They were likewise unanimous in entrusting their fate to Congress. The meeting adjourned on a high note, as a congressional delegation was expected to arrive a few days later to assess settlers' needs. Settlers expected the delegates to gather the intelligence they needed to persuade their fellow legislators that it was high time to establish governance in the Unassigned Lands.[18]

While opinion leaders were arguing the merits of a provisional govern-ment, women were filling their traditional roles as guardians of culture. Many put their talents to work in churches, where they helped to pay off debts by organizing box suppers and dinners, tacking comforters, and sponsoring Christmas bazaars.[19] Among those with a bent toward education was Mrs. L. H. North of Massachusetts, whose résumé included a five-year stint as a Methodist missionary with Zulu and Kaffir people in South Africa. She later taught school in Alabama and, somewhere along the way, married fellow New Englander Lyman Hoyt North. As a Mount Holyoke graduate and former missionary and teacher, she put her home to use as Oklahoma City's first school. Monthly tuition was a dollar per pupil and seventy-five cents for multiple children from the same family. But apparently, cash flow was not her primary concern, as she waived tuition for families that were too poor to pay. As other private schools cropped up around town and cracks began to show in her business model, Mrs. North closed her school after the first year.[20] Nevertheless, cultural pursuits remained high on her agenda. In early

September, the local press reminded readers that North was launching a chautauqua in October as a vehicle for literary discussions.[21]

Alice Beitman (later, Mrs. A. S. Heaney) had a similar story to tell. She and her family in El Dorado Springs, Missouri, had been captivated by stories of Oklahoma Proper's impending opening to homesteaders. Her brother Charles made the Run of '89, staked a claim near Britton, and promptly fired off a letter to his sister insisting that she drop everything and join him. She quickly resigned from her job, made the trip to Britton, and filed a claim close to Charles and another brother, William, and a sister, all of whom were proud to own land patents signed by President Grover Cleveland.

Realizing that she was not cut out to be a full-time homesteader and equipped with a lifetime teaching certificate from Illinois, Beitman decided that her fellow pioneers could use some refinement. Toward that end, she made the twelve-mile trek to the Oklahoma townsite, where she opened the Young Ladies Seminary in an empty store building at the corner of First and Robinson. Early on, Beitman borrowed chairs from the Methodist Church, whose services were then conducted in a tent, and returned them every Saturday. When she was not enjoying the beef issue at the Darlington Indian Agency, Flora Ragon attended classes at Beitman's converted store, where backless benches were fashioned from boxes and slates and pencils sufficed for writing assignments. Sponges were attached by strings to students' slates so they could clear their work and begin anew. About fifty children ranging from primary to tenth grade were packed into the classroom.[22] Beitman's teaching ended on Fridays. On weekends, she was busy proving up her claim.

Credit for establishing a graded school system goes to Mrs. Fred Sutton and Professor F. H. Umholtz. For twenty-five dollars, the duo acquired enough furniture to launch a subscription school in a spare room on First Street between Broadway and Robinson where the First National Bank Building later stood. The front room of the makeshift schoolhouse was used to store machinery. Parents were charged one to two dollars per month, depending on which grade their children were entering. Laboring in dim lighting and assailed by the cacophony of construction, Sutton and Umholtz's students showed the characteristics one might expect from pioneer progeny; as Mrs. Sutton recalled some two decades later, they "were all imbued with that energetic, restless spirit which permeates the veins of the Oklahoman." As Oklahoma morphed from village to metropolis, Mrs. Sutton pointed with pride to her former students and said to anyone within earshot, "He or she was a pupil of mine in '89."[23]

Aside from territorial governance—or, to be precise, the lack thereof—nothing was more worrisome to Oklahomans than uncertainty over the Choctaw Coal and Railway Company's route. Better known as the "Choctaw Road," the railroad company had long served as a conduit to supply eastern markets with Indian Territory coal. As opening day in the Unassigned Lands approached, company officials turned their attention westward to what would surely be a surge in demand for coal to heat homes and fuel industries. Accordingly, the railroad began to lay tracks from McAlester in the Choctaw Nation toward townsites along the Santa Fe line that were expected to mushroom into cities. But even as construction crews sliced their way westward, nobody knew exactly where their tracks would intersect the Santa Fe. Nor was anyone confident that that the lucky town could guarantee a right-of-way through increasingly organized business districts. As everyone knew, capital hates uncertainty, and people with capital were not likely to invest in Oklahoma if they might have to forfeit their property for a railroad right-of-way. Contrary to images of pioneers coming together for the common good, many property owners squared off to defend their claims. Tensions mounted with rumors that soldiers would be summoned to clear a right-of-way. A *Times* editorial on September 9 ended with a desperate plea for cooperation: "We must have the Choctaw road. It is to the interest of every property owner and business man in the city and all should contribute liberally to buy the right of way."

Always ready to believe the worst about their northern rival, residents of the Oklahoma townsite fanned rumors that Guthrie officials had bribed the Choctaw Road to bypass the townsite. Meanwhile, suspicions swirled that Seminole faction supporters and their sooner sympathizers—"lawbreaking political hacks," in the *Times'* estimation—were in league with railroad interests to lay out a town four miles north of Oklahoma. Few doubted that the Seminole faction was involved, but there was no truth to allegations of railroad cooperation in the scheme. In a pattern that had become routine, citizens gathered for a mass meeting in early September at the corner of California and Broadway to discuss the Choctaw Road.[24]

A few days later, Mayor Couch called another mass meeting to order. Major W. W. Monroe then spoke on behalf of the Board of Trade to report what everyone surely knew: if a right-of-way could not be guaranteed, then the Choctaw Road would bypass the Oklahoma townsite altogether. Monroe confirmed rumors that the city council would resort to armed force to clear the right-of-way. To preclude such drastic measures, Monroe recommended buying property along the right-of-way for thirty to forty thousand dollars. But that sum could be reduced by a third if people could be induced to accept fair prices for their property. After other speakers had had their say, a resolution was adopted that the city council would offer no more certificates for lots along the Choctaw Road's proposed route.[25]

None doubted what would happen if push came to shove: the city council would call on Captain Daniel Stiles and his soldiers to clear the right-of-way. Yet Stiles's ability to execute his orders was increasingly compromised by his alleged abuse of authority. In a September 9 rant under the headline "Czar Stiles," the *Times* accused the provost marshal of violating laws that he was sworn to defend: "His actions have been those of a despot rather than that of a man, whose only business is to keep the peace. It is high time that he should confine himself strictly to his line of duty."[26] The toxic relationship between Stiles and *Times* editor Hamlin Sawyer was on full display one day when the two nearly came to blows during a chance encounter. "I would hash you if you didn't have that uniform on!" declared Sawyer. In a flash, the fiery captain ripped off his coat, threw it on the ground, and growled menacingly, "Don't worry about the uniform!" Although they stopped short of an unseemly brawl, Sawyer continued to enrage his nemesis by misspelling his name as "Styles." When the captain stormed into the *Times* office to demand that his name be spelled correctly, Sawyer answered by referring to him as "Stiles, not Styles" in his near daily diatribes.[27]

In the summer of 1889, citizens signaled their dwindling trust in Captain Stiles and the city council to which he was tethered by scheduling a vote on a Kickapoo-inspired city charter. Ominously, Captain Stiles suggested that a charter election represented as much of an insurrection as Confederate states' withdrawal from the Union in 1861.[28] Carefully laid plans burst into the headlines when a committee of fifteen representatives from the Kickapoo faction announced September 21 as the date for a referendum on a charter aimed at curbing the administration's allegedly corrupt policies. As Election Day approached, the buzz was all about three propositions that would be on the ballot: (1) the adoption or rejection of what came to be known as the "citizens' charter"; (2) the adoption or rejection of the school system as provided in the charter; and (3) whether or not city officials should remain in office. In reference to the third proposition, the citizens' charter declared that a council member who vacated the ward of his residence would be kicked off the city council. To settle once and for all the city's name, article 1, section 1 of the citizens' charter declared that the "name of this body politic shall be 'Oklahoma City.'"

Critics of the Seminole-dominated administration blamed fiscal misman-agement for its increasingly tenuous grip on authority. Specifically, the city was in debt to the tune of $1,800. Worse, city improvements and necessities of governance—including paraphernalia as basic as record books—had not been paid for. A bit of sleuthing in municipal records revealed that the city had collected nearly five thousand dollars and paid for nothing but a jail, dubbed the "cottonwood bastile [sic]" in the Times, at an expense of only two hundred dollars. Some demanded the city councilors' ouster; more forgiving citizens favored retaining them, claiming that the citizens' charter would curtail misconduct and ensure an honest government. Unconvinced, the Times expressed what appeared to be the will of the people: "The present government has no longer any powers." And then, the Times drew its line in the sand: "One with power must be set up. A vote on the citizens' charter will be had."[29]

The consequence of Congress's foot dragging was to leave seventy-five thou-sand people without a federally sanctioned government. The best anyone could hope for was that Congress would get its act together in the spring of 1890. In light of his own apparent dillydallying, one could only assume that President Harrison had been kept in the dark regarding the goings-on in Indian Territory, and particularly Guthrie's provisional government scheme.[30] All the more reason, then, for Oklahoma (henceforth) City to roll out the red carpet for congressmen whose arrival was expected on the morning of Tuesday, September 17. On the eve of their arrival, the Times encouraged its readers to greet them with the enthusiasm they so richly deserved. Dipping into their mythological repertoire, the editors likened them to Aladdin and his magic lamp in their ability to raise cities from the desolate plains and lighten the hearts of grateful citizens.[31]

When the train from Guthrie arrived at 9:30 A.M., citizens took a break from their labors and flocked to the Santa Fe depot to catch a glimpse of the dignitaries. Included in the delegation were William M. Springer of Illinois, Charles H. Mansur of Missouri, Samuel R. Peters (R-Kans., 1883–91) and Bishop W. Perkins of Kansas, Charles S. Baker of New York, and John M. Allen (D-Miss.; 1885–1901). Upon their arrival on a picture-perfect day, they were whisked away for a three-hour carriage ride through the Beautiful Land. But of course, no visit with such high-profile visitors could go without discussing the prospects for territorial governance. In a portent of things to come, members of the Kickapoo committee of fifteen found a moment to alert their visitors to Captain Stiles's alleged outrages against the people. Of particular concern were rumors that the city council would call on Stiles to thwart the upcoming election. The congressmen suggested that the committee collect the petitions that were then in circulation and forward them to one of their number. They further promised that Captain Stiles would be reprimanded for any attempt to interfere with the election.[32]

In typical frontier fashion, a barbecue was ready when the congressmen returned from their tour at Round Grove northeast of town. Likewise in frontier fashion, the congressmen came with speeches in hand. Their appetites sated, people settled into their seats for the duration. Mayor Couch called the assembly to order at 2:00 P.M. and asked the Reverend James Murray to invoke "the divine blessing on the multitude." Next at the podium was Sidney Clarke, who delivered the official welcome and "tendered the freedom of the city to the visitors." The most notable speakers on that self-congratulatory day included Mansur and Springer, author of the bill that had opened Oklahoma Proper to settlement. When Springer stood to deliver his speech, the crowd erupted in raucous cheers and waving of hats and handkerchiefs. Perkins, Peters, Baker, and Allen (the funny orator of the day who apparently strained a muscle on a swing around the circle) followed with praise for what settlers had accomplished in less than five months and promises that their interests would soon rise to the top of Congress's agenda.[33]

But Oklahoma City was not done yet. Evening was coming on fast, and everyone agreed that the time had come to set politics aside and get ready to party. As daylight faded and stars filled the sky, Oklahoma City left its hardscrabble beginnings behind and dug in for an unforgettable night of dancing and dining in the Bone McKinnon Building. Irving Geffs pushed the limits of his lexicon with a description of revelers who might just as well have been dancing the night away beneath a New York or San Francisco skyline: "The most brilliant display of beauty and fashion ever witnessed in the great southwest was that of last night at the banquet and ball tendered the congressional visitors." An estimated one hundred gentlemen and an equal number of ladies, joined by officers in their neat-fitting uniforms, swayed to an orchestra that offered everything from the lazy waltz and vivacious gallop to

Men striking a deal near the Santa Fe depot in Oklahoma (townsite), 1889.
Courtesy of Oklahoma Historical Society, Oklahoma City, 18008.

the stately quadrille. The *Times*, less hyperbolic than the star-stricken Geffs but no less enthusiastic, reported that the guests laughed and joked through the evening and enjoyed "the wit and sociability of our intelligent, highly cultivated gentlemen and ladies." Before bidding their hosts farewell and heading south the following morning, the congressmen made more promises to hasten legislation to establish a territory. But perhaps they left Oklahoma City convinced that these pioneers were doing just fine on their own.[34]

The congressmen's train disappeared over the southern horizon, and Oklahoma City turned its attention to the city charter election. There was a consensus that the Kickapoo committee of fifteen had done its homework in drafting a charter in accord with the will of the people. It had been published verbatim in the local press, and copies were on display all over town. But nobody could afford to be complacent, as city councilors were already signaling their intention to delay the election. To forestall a postponement, the Kickapoo committee of fifteen dispatched several of its members to visit the city council to obtain assurance that the election would be held as scheduled. The Kickapoo faction took heart from other communities, including Guthrie, East Guthrie, West Guthrie, South Oklahoma, Reno, and Kingfisher, that had adopted charters by popular vote.[35]

Councilmen John E. "Jack" Love and J. B. George, the only Kickapoo sympathizers on the city council, argued vociferously that the people, and not the city council, should be the final arbiters of how their city was governed. In their opinion, four months of agitation on the subject was enough, and to delay the election at this late date was nothing short of unmanly. George struck at the heart of the matter in asking what city councilors planned to do about the public debt of approximately two thousand dollars. When no satisfactory answer was forthcoming, George drove home his message: the city council had forfeited its claim to legitimacy.

The *Times* agreed. Two days before the election, it published a clarion call for citizens to unite in the face of tyranny: "No true, liberty loving citizen would for a moment refuse the public the right to exercise the free use of the ballot, unless for mercenary motives, he preferred to shamelessly saddle upon himself the righteous indignation of all honest, good citizens. The names of these men will go down in history noted for their infamy."[36] Then came the bombshell. On the evening of Thursday, September 19, apparently before or immediately after the Kickapoo delegates pled their case and city councilors Love and George expressed their minority views, Mayor Couch issued a proclamation forbidding the election altogether, branding it "unlawful and seditious."[37]

News of the city council's perfidy spread like wildfire, and none doubted that a showdown was coming. The *Times* warned city councilors that they would be courting disaster if they called on Captain Stiles to squelch the election. Moreover, if anyone was injured, or worse, the city council would be held responsible. "The people have decided that they have the right to hold an election and they are going to hold it," concluded the *Times*. "It is for the courts to decide as to its legality and it will be for the courts to overthrow the present city government and they will surely do it."[38]

<hr>

Dawn broke on Saturday, September 21, to reveal a glorious fall day. Standing at the corner of Main and Broadway, Angelo Scott breathed deeply on that "cloudless, serene, and cool" Oklahoma morning—a perfect day for the people to make their voices heard at the polls.[39]

And then, as feared, Captain Stiles and his soldiers turned out in force to shut down the election. As the *Times* reported in grammatically challenged and hastily written prose, "They stuck with bayonets and clubbed muskets the retreating citizens in a merciless manner, inflicting in many cases, serious wounds." Under direct orders from Mayor Couch, managing editor Hamlin Sawyer and associate editor Mort L. Bixler were arrested and carted off to jail for obstructing soldiers in the discharge of their duty.[40] Bedlam reigned as the tranquil fall morning descended into a nightmare of clubbing and stabbing. Heroes on that bleak day included Roscoe Bell's father, an Oklahoma City resident who had emigrated from Winfield, Kansas, participated in the Run of '89, and secured a lot at the corner of Main and Harvey. The elder Bell, a former soldier in the Union Army, arrived at the north side of what later became the Herskowitz Building on Grand Avenue (and, later still, the Cox Convention Center) to find that Captain Stiles, in accordance with *Casey's Infantry Tactics* (1862), had ordered his soldiers to fix bayonets and charge. Bell raised his hand and, in a commanding military voice, ordered the soldiers to stand down. He then solicited the help of former Confederate soldiers who had settled in Oklahoma City to defuse the crisis.

Among the soldiers who rose to Bell's aid was Major Allen of Mississippi. Firmly convinced that his former Civil War foe was in the right, Allen later spearheaded a fundraising campaign to defray legal expenses that Bell was sure to incur when news of his interference became known to civilian and military authorities. But perhaps Major Allen's concern was unfounded. Advised of the military's intervention in what was strictly a civilian matter, President Harrison shot off a terse telegram to Captain Stiles: "Repair to the Military Reservation and cease your interference with the municipal affairs of Oklahoma City."[41]

Bell's legal worries and President Harrison's cease-and-desist order were in the future as soldiers systematically shut down the election. Stymied at the original polling place, stubborn citizens opened another one on Broadway just north of Main Street and quickly dispersed when soldiers descended on that one too. Convinced that the election was a lost cause, Kickapoo opinion leaders did what they could to convince people to clear the streets. Meanwhile, guards were posted at the polling places, and alleged ringleaders were rounded up and jailed for conspiring to overthrow the municipal government.[42]

Support for Oklahoma City's charter election and outrage over its repression poured in from other communities, including South Oklahoma, whose boundary with its northern neighbor was vanishing in the juggernaut of urban development.[43] *Evening Gazette* publisher Frank McMaster was already fretting about his adopted city's image problem, particularly with regard to its competitive neighbor to the north. As he wrote on September 24, "Guthrie is in spasms of joy over what it terms Oklahoma's riots."[44]

As life returned to something akin to normal, angry charter supporters demanded that Captain Stiles be court-martialed. The provost marshal's superiors at Fort Reno responded by launching a cursory investigation. Few were surprised when they refused to bring charges against him.[45] Meanwhile, the local press kept pouring on the invective, branding Captain Stiles as a brazen criminal and excoriating him for giving no indication of the firestorm he was about to unleash on unsuspecting citizens. Ongoing fury toward the city council was fueled by revelations that Mayor Couch had sent a written requisition for troops prior to Election Day. Even though they expected agitation to subside and the legality of the citizens' charter to devolve to the courts, the *Times* wondered if citizens would signal their loss of confidence in the city council by refusing to pay their taxes.

The suppressed election of September 21 marked the beginning of the end of Oklahoma City's provisional government. But there was no end in sight to the war of words waged in the local press. At the end of the month, the city council announced its intention to levy additional taxes, branded in the *Times* as an occupation tax. This tax, combined with previous reports that the city's books were hopelessly out of balance, seemed to confirm charges of corruption. In a brazen call for civil disobedience, the *Times* admonished its readers to resist the occupation tax.[46]

And then came reports that Captain Stiles had been exonerated of all wrongdoing on September 21. "Of course, this will only make the brute more obnoxious and despotic," railed the *Times*. "However, we will say to the people, bear patiently, for it will not always continue." Apparently, at least five U.S. senators and several members of the House of Representatives were trying to get to the bottom of the matter and put a stop to the city council's alleged whitewashing.[47] City councilors and Captain Stiles were well advised to watch their backs after a notice was found posted at the post office. Authored anonymously by someone representing Las Gorras Blancas, or White Caps, a group active in New Mexico Territory and elsewhere in the Southwest aimed at resisting Anglo-American settlement, its message was unambiguous: Mayor Couch, Captain Stiles, and City Attorney Ledru Guthrie had to die. At the bottom of the placard was a cartoon of a body dangling from a scaffold. Lest anyone assume that such posters were little more than scare tactics, the *St. Louis Republic* reported that the White Caps had agreed shortly after the stymied election to purchase two hundred Winchester rifles. Armed to the teeth, they would be in a position to force the adoption of the citizens' charter.

On September 27, the *Times* added a word of warning: "The revolutionists have a deadly hatred for Mayor Couch and Captain Stiles, and it needs but a spark to kindle the fires of civil strife."[48]

September ended on another downbeat note when a city council meeting turned violent. The fracas began when Councilman Love suggested holding a vote on the citizens' charter the following Saturday in a last-ditch effort to regain the people's trust in their government. Predictably, Love's suggestion fell on deaf ears. Insults flew, and *Robert's Rules of Order* went out the window. Things went from bad to worse when Abe Couch, a member of the mayor's family (most likely his brother), appeared at the door and called Love a liar. Even though Abe was packing heat, Love went on the offensive and knocked him across the room before he had time to draw his weapon. As Mayor Couch was reaching for a chair to clobber Abe's attacker, Love's Kickapoo ally, Councilman George, caught the mayor from behind by both arms and forced him to his knees. Love, meanwhile, had Abe pinned to the floor and begging for mercy. But then, an unknown assailant emerged from the darkness and whacked Love on the head with a revolver, leaving two or three painful but not life-threatening wounds to his scalp. A reporter who covered the brawl had no doubt that Abe Couch had provoked it by barging into the room with every intention of shooting Love.

Recuperating in George's office with his head swathed in bandages, Love said he was sorry that his passions had gotten the best of him. "We must have our differences settled at once and stop this infernal trouble that is killing our city," insisted the *Times* the next day. "If the people don't rule in Oklahoma, it is the only place in the country where the stars and stripes are emblematic of our blood bought liberties, that the people do not rule." Sawyer feared that if councilmen and their collaborator, Captain Stiles, were allowed to remain in positions of authority, "we can never expect to make anything out of Oklahoma City."[49]

———

We will never know exactly when Mayor Couch decided to resign from a job that seemed to bring him nothing but trouble. One moment he was fending off renewed demands for a vote on the citizens' charter; the next he was trying to defuse the people's anger over his administration's alleged fiscal misman agement; and the next he was fretting over clearing a right-of-way for the Choctaw Road. The *Times*'s vendetta flared into an unseemly confrontation one Saturday evening in mid-October. As Sawyer spun the story (for all his authority as mayor, Couch had no claim to the power of the press), he and Bixler were making their rounds and visiting with subscribers along California Avenue when they bumped into the mayor. What began as a civil encounter took a turn for the worse when the editors asked Couch to confirm rumors that he would request military assistance to collect the so-called occupation tax. Incensed, the mayor demanded to know why the *Times* persisted in referring to city officials as thieves and thugs. When Sawyer accused the mayor of corruption, Couch became unhinged and went at him with his fists. For reasons that remain unclear, Couch then backed across a twelve-foot sidewalk and crashed through a merchant's window. The proprietor, R. L. Overstreet, and a man named Mitchell did what they could "to preserve the peace and dignity of the city." But Couch could not be placated and turned his ire toward Mitchell, threatening to beat him up as well. It was only after "coming into uncomfortable contact with Mitchell's fist" that Couch came to his senses. With his coattail flapping in the breeze, Couch beat a hasty retreat to conclude what Sawyer and Bixler counted as the fourth or fifth altercation in which the mayor finished second.[50]

Mayor Couch's problems were compounded by lot jumpers, who continued to confound economic and community development. A typical squabble comes to us from Clarence Trosper, whose father, Hugh, had set up housekeeping on Fifth Street. Clarence might have been fetching firewood for his family's brand-new cookstove, when he was distracted by the goings-on across the street, where a man had tacked shingles to his dwelling, stacked some blocks nearby, and departed. He returned to confront another man who had torn down his shingles and thrown his blocks into the street. As cursing escalated into fisticuffs, somebody had the presence of mind to call on Captain Stiles to settle the matter. The provost marshal showed up with a detachment of soldiers to arrest the combatants and escort them to the Military Reservation. As Trosper recalled, "Scenes like that were everyday occurrences and we soon got accustomed to them."[51]

Rivalries and the fights they spawned cropped up not only in the streets but also in sports, where friendly games had a way of turning ugly. One steamy summer day, a fistfight broke out at a baseball game between Oklahoma City (the home team) and Guthrie. Officers and soldiers managed to quell the disturbance on the field. But after the game, players and fans decided to resolve their differences on a railroad coach attached to a freight train chartered for the return trip to Guthrie. Santa Fe agent Frank Best, who had the ill fortune to ride in that particular coach, recalled what happened: "In a flash, there were eight or ten revolvers in action, being used as clubs. Men shouting, women screaming, the aisles blocked, and the guns barely missing me as they were swung." Hunkered down behind a seat, Best found himself in the company of a friend—a hunchback, as it turned out—who happened to be on the same coach.

Unhurt but sorely shaken, Best ran into him the next day.

"Things looked mighty scary on that train last night," said Best.

His friend drew himself up to his full four feet, put on his game face, and declared, "I was not scared a bit, been in closer places many a time."[52]

Frontier bluster did not extend to another of Couch's problems, and that was sanitation—less problematic in the winter months, but potentially lethal under the sweltering Oklahoma sun. In a typical rant about the sorry state of infrastructure, the *Times* castigated citizens for throwing their refuse on the ground and digging shallow pits for their privies that saturated the ground with toxins that were sure "to breed pestilence and death" in warm weather.[53] To make matters worse, buffalo wallows had become breeding grounds for mosquitoes. Although infill projects were making the city more habitable, residents remained at risk for malaria and other mosquito-borne illnesses. Fortunately, city planners were coming to the realization that the business district lay at a higher elevation than previously thought. "Thanks to a slight elevation, drainage projects posed no great problem," ran a hopeful editorial in the *Oklahoma Chief*. "No town could have a prettier location than Oklahoma City."[54]

Like anyone who arrives at a crossroads, Mayor Couch needed a push from untenable circumstances and a pull into something more alluring. In his case, the push came from the seeming impossibility of governing a fractious and hastily built city. The pull came from his family's disputed claim at the western edge of town. Unless Couch and his family could prove up their claim in accordance with laws pertaining to homesteading and preemption, they risked losing it to rival claimants John C. Adams, Sarah A. Waynick, John M. Dawson, and Dr. Robert W. Higgins.[55] And so, in a letter dated November 11 to city council president Sidney Clarke, Couch tendered his resignation, citing his "interests and rights as a homesteader" as his main reason for stepping down. In conclusion, he showed a willingness to accept blame for whatever mistakes he had made in guiding his adopted city through its first seven months of existence: "I have endeavored at all times to discharge my duties, and if in anything I have failed it has been an error of judgment."[56]

Sidney Clarke stepped in as temporary mayor, but everyone knew that he was not in the running for a permanent job. Among the likely front-runners was Henry Overholser. Even though he had never belonged to the Seminole Town and Improvement Company, he had always marched to the tune of the city councilors and might be expected to continue their policies. Another possible candidate was Dr. Andrew Jackson Beale, a former member of the Kentucky legislature who had served the Confederacy as a surgeon in the Ninth Regiment of Kentucky Mounted Infantry, during which time he had been grievously wounded at the Battle of Murfreesboro, taken prisoner at Fort Delaware, and eventually exchanged before retiring with the rank of captain.[57] Stunned by the busted election of September 21, he joined other opinion leaders at an evening meeting on October 14 to form the Kickapoo Council, whose officers included a sachem, chief, scribe, and wampum leader. The Kickapoo Council's constitution codified several bold objectives, including placing limits on the city council's authority, putting an end to lot jumping, and compelling Congress to provide for governance. The council's guiding principle seems ripped from the *Federalist Papers*: powers not delegated to the federal government by the Constitution or prohibited by it to the states "are reserved to the states respectively or to the people."[58] As the duly elected sachem of the Kickapoo Council, Beale was at the red-hot center of Oklahoma City's contentious politics when Couch announced his resignation.

No matter their qualifications, neither candidate had a moment to lose in mounting his campaign, as the election was slated for November 27. In a community where everyone was an immigrant, settlers tended to form associations and friendships with people from their native states and with those who shared characteristics that facilitated social bonding. As Beale was born and bred in Kentucky, he knew he could count on others from the Blue Grass State, including Charley Colcord, to support his candidacy.[59] Another benefit to having Colcord on his side was his influence with cowboys, who continued to exert a powerful influence in municipal affairs, even as the open range they cherished was vanishing under streets and buildings and crisscrossed by fences. Overholser's support came largely from the Seminole faction, whose devotees were not about to relinquish their control of City Hall without a fight. Concerned that partisanship might once again flare

Andrew J. Beale.
Courtesy of Oklahoma Images Collection, Metropolitan Library System of Oklahoma County.

into violence, the *Evening Gazette* admonished the Kickapoos to tone down their rhetoric and stop their endless criticism of the place they had chosen to call home: "Oklahoma is not a paradise but there is no valid reason why the Kickapoos should represent it as a hell."[60]

Two weeks of feverish politicking ended on November 27. At the first city council meeting after the election, voters crowded into the council chamber to see history in the making. City council president and acting mayor Sidney Clarke called for order and, after a cursory reading of minutes from the previous meeting, asked city recorder John Blackburn to announce the election results. The suspense was palpable as he unsealed the ballot boxes to find 369 votes for Beale and 355 votes for Overholser.

With a scant fourteen-vote majority, Dr. Beale became Oklahoma City's second mayor. Kickapoos celebrated their victory with a display of fireworks and, as Irving Geffs reported, "great and prolonged rejoicing." In an early signal of deference to federal authority, Beale requested that a U.S. commissioner administer the oath of office at the next city council meeting on Monday evening, December 2.[61] One of his first acts as mayor was to appoint Charley Colcord as Oklahoma City's first official chief of police. As a grateful and, for the time being, underpaid Charley Colcord later explained, he kept his job as the city's lone policeman with as much authority and essentially the same pay as he had enjoyed before the watershed election of November 1889.[62]

On the day he was sworn into office, Mayor Beale published an open letter in the local press under the heading "Beale's Manifesto," and it included proposals that constituted fundamental responsibilities of any municipal government: strict economy; security of property; street improvements; a fire engine; a water system; and graded schools. But Oklahoma City was not just any city. It was an upstart metropolis wracked by dissension over property rights—far from unusual in western towns, but rarely, and perhaps never, as contentious as in Oklahoma City. Such was the extent of lot jumping in late 1889 that Frank McMaster declared in the *Evening Gazette* that offenders should be punished by death.[63] Writ small, conflicts over town lots in Oklahoma City were a microcosm of disagreements over U.S. public lands policies that had fueled the boomer movement and framed socioeconomic inequalities in Gilded Age America.

Perhaps exhibiting a penchant for wishful thinking, Beale suggested that the worst was behind them. With a laser-like focus on the entire city's welfare, he encouraged the Kickapoos and Seminoles to put their differences aside and work together for the common good. "Our interests here are mutual," wrote Beale, "and I trust and believe that in the condition that confronts us, I shall meet your cooperation in all matters calculated to promote the interests of our city." To signal his resolve to run a lean and mean administration, the new mayor suggested that he and the city council serve without pay. The only exception would be the city recorder, whose salary he aimed to cap at twenty-five dollars per month. His reasoning must have seemed like manna from Heaven to former boomers who had arrived in the Promised Land with little but the clothes on their backs and fire in their bellies to create a better life: most Oklahoma City residents were poor, and any money extracted from them through taxes should be spent on public works. As Beale declared in his manifesto, "I have every reason to believe that the people of Oklahoma City would cheerfully pay a reasonable tax to meet all necessary and legitimate expenses of our city government, provided it is applied as I have suggested."[64]

As if on cue, one of Oklahoma City's most visionary entrepreneurs stepped onto the stage of history: Charles Gasham Jones. Born in Greenup, Illinois, Jones arrived in the Oklahoma country on the prowl for business opportunities. He found them in the waters of the North Canadian River—ideally suited to fuel a flour mill, light plant, and other enterprises that were on Mayor Beale's

Charles G. "Gristmill" Jones.
Courtesy of Oklahoma Historical Society, Oklahoma City, 23139.G22.

agenda. There was only one problem: the river was too far south to be of much use. Jones's solution was to recruit business leaders to fund construction of a six-mile canal from the North Canadian River toward the Santa Fe depot.[65]

Enthusiasm for the canal was running high when former mayor Couch threw the first dirt on December 9 for what was to be Oklahoma City's first public works project, aptly dubbed "the big ditch" in the local press. But at the outset, not everyone was on board, as many suspected Jones of orchestrating yet another scheme to deprive people of their property and divert attention from the sorry state of municipal finances.[66] Naysayers notwithstanding, both the canal and Jones's flour mill were completed by Christmas Eve, and five thousand people turned out to watch spigots release a torrent of water into the business district. "But it proved a failure," wrote pioneer journalist Fred Wenner, with "the water disappearing in quick sands underlying its course and into gopher and ground hog holes in the banks as fast as it flowed in from the river."[67] For Scott, memories of the unsuccessful canal project remained poignant forty years later. "Every patriotic man in town had subscribed to it. The men who sought so earnestly to put this 'gigantic undertaking' across and sank thousands of dollars in it—'sank' is the word—deserve all honor."[68]

Jones, nicknamed "Gristmill" for his later success in the milling business, had engineered a costly failure. The good news was that hundreds of men were given employment at a time when Oklahoma City's feverish construction projects were slowing down. Jones's subsequent successes in luring railroads to Oklahoma City eclipsed his ill-fated canal and earned him a place in his adopted city's pantheon of city builders.

———————

The big ditch was nearing completion when, just before Christmas, Major Chaddick of the Choctaw Road wrote a reassuring letter to Mayor Beale, indicating that his company would likely build a line through Oklahoma City. Most greeted the news like an early Christmas present while others, wary of more disappointment, knew that financial sacrifices would be required to clinch the deal. "Oklahoma will have to present the road with a clear and good right-of-way through the city," declared the *Oklahoma Chief*, "and it is going to cost her a great many thousands of dollars. Can she do it? Will she do it?"[69]

Rumors about the Choctaw Road's intentions were partly to blame for the epidemic of lot jumping in December, and they set the stage for a showdown between Mayor Beale and Seminole sympathizers, who still dominated the city council. Disagreements intensified when Beale sought to depose Councilmen J. E. Jones and W. C. Wells on the grounds that they had moved from the second ward and thereby relinquished their right to serve as the district's representatives. The mayor's support came from 154 voters who had signed a petition declaring that Jones and Wells were part of a conspiracy aimed at obstructing the will of the majority as expressed in the recent mayoral election, albeit by a razor-thin margin of fourteen votes.[70]

Beale's call for an election on December 30 to replace the two councilmen unleashed a firestorm of protest. City officials characterized the mayor's action as nothing less than an act of revolution that would plunge the city into anarchy. The signatories went on to castigate Mayor Beale for his membership in "a secret clan" (i.e., the Kickapoo Council), whose avowed purpose was to destroy the city government. "The emergency is great," concluded the signatories. "It must and will be met."[71]

With the city council in open rebellion, Mayor Beale fired off a dispatch to Secretary of the Interior Noble in which he accused his detractors of capturing the city government before the dust had even settled from the Run of '89 and proceeding to pass ordinances in violation of U.S. laws, grant franchises to favorites, issue lot certificates with no legal standing, evict people from their lots and houses at bayonet point, and generally stir up trouble at every opportunity. Convinced that the Seminole group's ultimate goal was to convince Congress to uphold and ratify "the certificate system of occupancy," Beale made his case for federal intervention.

Secretary Noble's reply arrived in a telegram on Christmas Eve, and it was not the present Mayor Beale was looking for. In a strongly worded statement that came straight from President Harrison, Noble warned Beale that his proposed election would provoke a breach of the peace and would not be tolerated. "He directs me to say you should allow the present status of affairs to remain undisturbed, until Congress has provided a lawful government," wrote Secretary Noble. "The general good conduct that has characterized the people of Oklahoma should not be put in jeopardy by any factional proceedings. Peace and good order must be preserved."[72] What President Harrison and Secretary Noble perceived from Washington was becoming increasingly clear in the Unassigned Lands: Oklahoma City had neither the legal nor physical power to subdue the rebellious spirit of lot jumping. Military authorities agreed, and shortly after the exchange of telegrams, General Wesley Merritt ordered two cavalry troops to proceed to Oklahoma City to protect property owners and quell any disturbances that might arise.

Between Christmas and New Year's Day, Secretary Noble's status quo order effectively suspended the provisional government's attempts to regulate property ownership. It would remain in effect until May 2, 1890, when Congress passed legislation to bring territorial governance to the Unassigned Lands. During the intervening four months, it was U.S. marshals, and not the provisional government, who called the shots in Oklahoma City. Frank McMaster spoke for many when he wrote on December 28, "Most of the Oklahoma newspapers are much concerned over the question of 'who will be the next governor of Oklahoma? The *Gazette* is more concerned over the greater conundrum, 'When will there be a governor in Oklahoma!'"[73]

CHAPTER TWELVE

1890

With all our hardships I prefer those times to our present times.
Many of us fought against the progress of modern times.
Mamie Page, January 12, 1938

The new year dawned, and the prospect of curbing lawlessness continued to brand Oklahoma City, and especially Hell's Half Acre, as a haven for outlaws. More than likely, Bill Couch's decision to resign as mayor was due to the seeming impossibility of bringing law and order to his adopted hometown. At the same time, he had at least two other compelling reasons to retire from political office: he had to prove up his claim southwest of town or risk losing it to rival claimants; and his fellow Oklahomans needed a strong voice in Washington to lobby for territorial governance. He was surely tempted to stay home, as he and his wife, Cynthia, had just finished construction of a four-bedroom house at the present-day intersection of Walker and Reno Avenues to accommodate their three sons and two daughters. On the same quarter section, seven other claimants were making their own plans for permanent residence and waiting for the General Land Office to determine who could stay and who would have to go.

Even though they lacked a well and had to carry water from a neighbor, the Couches recalled homesteading as a happy time of berry picking and fishing in nearby streams. But duty called, and, putting aside his qualms about leaving his claim, Couch boarded a train for Washington to resume his role as a gadfly in Congress. Except for a few days spent with his family over Christmas, he stayed in Washington until early April 1890.[1] Reasonably sure that congressional action was imminent, Couch returned to Oklahoma City to continue proving up his claim.

Couch and his sons were hard at work one day erecting fences when they realized that a rival claimant, John C. Adams, was chopping down posts as fast as they could put them up. "My father wished to avoid trouble," recalled his son Eugene. "The next day we went out to put up new posts." Only this time, Eugene's father was packing heat, and when Adams emerged from his dwelling brandishing a pistol, the former mayor coolly raised his forty-five and told him to drop it. Adams complied and scurried back to his house. Having been tipped off that Adams kept a Winchester within easy reach, Couch knew that his troubles were far from over. He told his other son, Ira, to retrieve Adam's pistol where he had dropped it and prodded his boys toward home.[2]

Couch was right: Adams was not done with him. He rushed back to his house, grabbed his Winchester, and hollered for Couch to halt. Couch turned to see his neighbor take aim and fire. Under a hail of bullets, the elder Couch defended himself and his sons as best he could, turning and kneeling and returning salvos in what had become a running duel to the death. When they reached the present-day intersection of Shartel and Reno Avenues, a bullet struck the elder Couch squarely in the knee. His daughter, Mrs. Tom Bird, was three years old when her father was gunned down. As she explained many years later, he might as well have been struck in the heart, as gangrene was inevitable and almost certainly fatal.[3]

Cynthia and her children helped Bill into the house. Before long, a neighbor came to fetch the children, and the Couch family settled in for a grim vigil whose outcome was all too predictable.[4] "How vividly I remember the scene," recalled Couch's friend, Angelo C. Scott, who attended the former mayor's final hours, "the dying man propped on pillows, the sad-faced wife, the meager surroundings. And this to be the pitiful and untimely end of one who had fought so valiantly and long for the opening of the 'beautiful land.'"[5]

Bill Couch languished in agony for several days before he died. His funeral service was held on April 22, 1890—a year to the day after the Run of '89. His granddaughter and most zealous guardian of his legacy, Edna Mae Couch, spent a forty-year career as a dietician at the University of Oklahoma. In her spare time, she maintained her family's archives with an aim of writing her grandfather's biography. Sadly, she never quite pulled it off. Edna Mae did, however, offer a pithy postmortem for a man who had been at the center of Oklahoma politics since boomer days and, for better or worse, steered

Oklahoma City through its infancy: "His errors were of the head and not of the heart. He was afraid of no man or any set of men."[6]

Adams was arrested and held over for trial in federal court in Wichita for Bill Couch's murder. He arrived at a preliminary hearing in the custody of Police Chief Charley Colcord, flanked by four soldiers with loaded rifles. Adams was convicted of murder and sentenced to life in prison. He was later granted a new trial based on a legal technicality. His term was reduced to seven years, but he walked after serving only five.[7]

As the decades passed and Oklahoma City's most famous shoot-out faded from collective memory, the 89ers Association recommended naming the north and south drives around the Civic Center and between the present-day Hightower Building and the Oklahoma City Art Museum after Bill Couch and Charley Colcord, whose names had been chosen from a list of twenty-five candidates. The association further recommended naming the circle driveway at the east end of City Hall "'89ers Circle." Mayor John Frank Martin (1935–39) agreed and presented its recommendations to the city council for ratification.[8]

As of this writing in 2018, street signs commemorating two of Oklahoma City's founding fathers are among the few tangible reminders of the life-and-death issues that defined the generation of 1889.

═══════════

Less than two weeks after Bill Couch was laid to rest, President Harrison brought Oklahoma Territory into existence by signing the Organic Act of May 2, 1890. The process of attaining territorial status as a prerequisite to statehood followed the model of state formation articulated in legislation passed by the Confederation Congress in 1784 and 1785 and especially in the Northwest Ordinance of 1787. Its provisions thus predated the U.S. Constitution, and they guaranteed that the federal government's expansion into the Unassigned Lands would be democratic in character.[9] That might have piqued the interest of historians, but as far as homesteaders and urban pioneers were concerned, only one thing mattered: Oklahoma was now a territory! Within its borders were six counties formerly designated as the Unassigned Lands and No Man's Land (later, Beaver, Texas, and Cimarron Counties), and its residents could finally enjoy the rights, privileges, and responsibilities afforded by U.S. laws. Oklahoma Proper's dalliance with frontier democracy and its corollary in ad hoc governments was coming to an end.

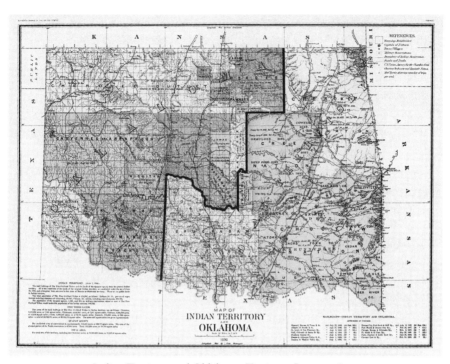

Indian Territory and Oklahoma Territory, June 1, 1890.
Courtesy of Oklahoma Historical Society, Oklahoma City, ITMAP.0023.

News that the president and Congress had done their duty reached Guthrie about seven o'clock in the evening of May 2. Within an hour, the town was ablaze with bonfires. Pistol shots rang out across the flatlands as revelers paraded through town, discharging their weapons and cheering their hearts out. As noted the *Evening Star*, "Dispatches from other points in the new territory state that the news was received with great rejoicing."[10]

Under the auspices of the Organic Act, President Harrison announced his slate of territorial officials: George W. Steele of Indiana as governor; Robert Martin of El Reno as secretary; Warren Lurty of West Virginia as U.S. marshal; Edward B. Green of Illinois as chief justice of the Supreme Court; and Abraham J. Seay of Missouri and John F. Clark of Wisconsin as associate justices. The three judges did double duty as district judges. Finally, Horace Speed of Guthrie was named U.S. district attorney.[11] In mid-May, the Senate confirmed Steele and Martin as governor and secretary, respectively. After receiving their commissions from the Department of the Interior and reciting their oaths of office before a U.S. Supreme Court justice, they packed their bags for OklahomaTerritory.[12] Like so many presidential appointees and government officials, most men appointed to offices in Oklahoma Territory had served in the Union Army. Military experience was not exactly a requirement, but it was certainly a résumé booster, as every president but one, from Grant to McKinley, had been a soldier. The only exception was Grover Cleveland, who had hired a substitute to do the fighting for him during the Civil War. Steele, Martin, and all three members of Oklahoma Territory's Supreme Court shared a common lineage as Union soldiers.[13]

To accommodate territorial growth, the Organic Act provided that all reservations in western Indian Territory would automatically come into Oklahoma Territory when they were opened to settlement. Indian Territory to the east remained as an amalgam of federal and tribal authority until 1907, when it joined Oklahoma Territory to become the state of Oklahoma. Old Greer County was technically included within Oklahoma Territory's boundaries but was specifically exempted from the application of homestead law or further settlement until the Red River boundary dispute with Texas could be settled. Future controversy was assured when the capital was located temporarily in Guthrie. Seven county seats in counties designated by number were established at Guthrie (County 1), Oklahoma City (County 2), Norman (County 3), El Reno (County 4), Kingfisher (County 5), Stillwater (County 6), and Beaver (County 7).[14]

The same act of Congress that opened the Unassigned Lands to non-Indian settlers authorized the president to appoint commissioners to negotiate with western tribes to open their surplus lands for settlement. Designated as the Jerome Commission for its chairman, former Michigan governor David H. Jerome, the group included Warren G. Sayre of Indiana and Alfred M. Wilson of Arkansas. Over a period of five years, they negotiated with tribal leaders to assign allotments to each man, woman, and child on official tribal rolls. The federal government did its part by purchasing surplus land and opening it to homesteading through land runs and lotteries. In the ensuing years, tribal land in central and western Indian Territory dwindled and, in some cases, disappeared altogether under a relentless tide of homesteading and urbanization.[15]

Governor Steele arrived in Guthrie aboard a special train from Arkansas City, Kansas, at four o'clock in the morning of May 23 and eventually made his way to Guthrie, where he and other presidential appointees took part in a grand procession led by the Guthrie Silver Cornet Band through a throng of ten thousand joyous Oklahomans. After the requisite speeches, organizers put on a reception under the glow of electric lights. More revelry was slated for Oklahoma City, where the governor and his entourage were shown every courtesy in spite of the simmering rivalry with Guthrie. When the festivities sputtered to a close, Governor Steele made his county appointments. Many hoped for a decline in partisanship, as none of Governor Steele's appointees had been affiliated with the Seminole faction, which had dominated the provisional government. With a few exceptions, Steele's appointees were former soldiers in the Union Army.[16]

Among Governor Steele's first official acts was to ask Congress to appropriate money to help farmers through a drought that belied the territory's designation as the Beautiful Land. Congress responded with a forty-seven-thousand-dollar appropriation, and Oklahoma City became County 2's distribution center for flour, potatoes, beans, sugar, and pork destined for remote homesteads and villages.[17] On July 8, the governor turned his attention to politics and, in keeping with the Organic Act, called for an election on August 5 to select twenty-six representatives to a lower chamber (the House) and thirteen representatives to an executive council (the Senate). On the basis of its population (18,794 per the 1890 census), County 2 was eligible to send five representatives to the House and three to the Senate. The laws of Nebraska were to remain in force until the legislature could draw up legal and banking codes. Until county and township governments could be organized, the governor retained the authority to fill posts by appointment. As the legislature was slated to meet for the first time on August 12, candidates had less than a month to organize their campaigns.[18]

In the absence of other forms of entertainment, nothing could draw a crowd like politics. As voters throughout Oklahoma Territory prepared for Election Day, parties and factions came out in force. Some flocked to the Democratic and Republicans Parties; others, desperate for drought relief and perhaps aggrieved by socioeconomic inequities that the traditional parties seemed ill-equipped to rectify, sided with the Farmers Alliance, commonly known as the "People's Party," which later morphed into the Socialist Party. Although the Seminole faction had more or less vanished as a political organization, its influence in Oklahoma City politics remained a force to be reckoned with.[19] Oklahoma City newspapers admonished voters to cast their ballots wisely, as the results would determine the territory's future for generations. Choose only the cream of the crop, advised the *Oklahoma Journal*: "There is plenty of good timber in Oklahoma, and from the reputations made even in their short residence in this territory they can be picked out and put forward. Pick them out."[20] As resentment still rankled over Guthrie's ill-fated power grab in the summer of 1889, the *Journal* could not resist a plea for legislators to locate the permanent capital in Oklahoma City: "As in ancient times all roads led to Rome, so in these times in Oklahoma all roads should lead to Oklahoma City."[21]

Election Day on August 5 arrived during a week of historic rainfall.[22] Accustomed to hardships, voters slogged through the mud to cast their ballots for Oklahoma Territory's first legislature. When the votes were counted, Oklahoma City's representatives included C. M. Burke, C. "Gristmill" Jones, Sam D. Pack, Dan W. Peery, and Hugh Trosper in the twenty-six-member assembly (House of Representatives) and James L. Brown, L. G. Pittman, and Dr. J. W. Howard in the thirteen-member council (Senate). Technically, Republicans held a majority in both houses. The council consisted of six Republicans, five Democrats, one People's Party representative, and one Independent, who generally voted with the GOP. The assembly consisted of fourteen Republicans, eight Democrats, and four Populists. But from day one, regional loyalties trumped party considerations to produce some unlikely alliances.[23] Voters also had an opportunity to dispense with their counties' numerical designations and choose more lyrical names for the territory's seven original counties: Payne, Logan, Kingfisher, Oklahoma, Canadian, and Cleveland Counties, all located in the former Unassigned Lands of central Indian Territory; and Beaver County in No Man's Land.

Shortly after his appointment, Governor Steele signaled the end of the U.S. marshals' regime in Oklahoma City by appointing a commission to divide the 320-acre village into wards, designate election officials, and set a date for the city's first legally sanctioned election since the Run of '89. One of the commissioners, D. W. Gibbs, served as de facto mayor from Oklahoma City's incorporation on July 15 to Election Day on August 9, when William J. Gault was elected as the city's first lawful mayor. He served in that position from August 12, 1890, to April 12, 1892. Rounding out the slate of municipal officers were W. W. Witten as police judge, H. B. Mitchell as city attorney, M. S. Miller as treasurer, T. M. Upshaw as city clerk, and Charley Colcord, who retained his position as city marshal. The city council included Dr. C. A.

Peyton, J. A. Borrows, J. W. Boles, J. A. Regan, John C. Romick, and M. N. Miller. As Angelo Scott noted, "This election was a clear victory for the Democrats from the head to the tail of the ticket."[24] But the big news, and a topic that was sure to capture legislators' attention, was the location of a permanent capital. The Organic Act famously left that thorny issue to the governor and legislature.

All eyes were on Guthrie as the territory's governor and legislators gathered for the first time at two o'clock in the afternoon of Wednesday, August 27, 1890. After dispensing with more preliminaries, both houses of the legislature got down to business at the appointed hour on Friday, August 29. Oklahoma Territory was now up and running.[25]

Well, almost. Significant legislation had to wait until after the weekend. On September 2, Governor Steele called for an election on November 4 to elect a territorial delegate to Congress.[26] That same day, Councilman Brown of Oklahoma County threw down the gauntlet by introducing Council Bill No. 7 to relocate the capital and Supreme Court from Guthrie to Oklahoma City. Brown's bill further specified that the legislature would convene in Oklahoma City during the first two weeks of February 1891. Governor Steele was tasked with issuing a proclamation within five days of January 5, 1891, giving notice of the legislature's and Supreme Court's change of venue.[27]

Before anyone had a chance to respond in a meaningful way to Brown's bold initiative, it was time once again to party. In Oklahoma City, celebrations attending the first legislative session took the form of a ball on September 10 at the opera house on the southeast corner of Grand and Robinson Avenues. The gala began with orchestral music and a grand march led by Governor and Mrs. Steele. A lavish banquet ensued in the Grand Avenue Hotel dining room. Toasts and cheers filled the room as opinion leaders decked out in their most dashing attire congratulated one another on their success at the ballot boxes. Assemblyman Dan W. Peery recalled the evening as Oklahoma City's grandest occasion to date—grander, perhaps, than the reception of the congressmen a year earlier.[28]

Sadly, the festive mood was short lived. Upon their return to Guthrie and the resumption of the first legislative session in the McKennon Opera House, legislators lined up on either side of Council Bill No. 7.[29] After heated debate and Logan County legislators' attempts at postponement, the bill passed the council by a slender seven to six majority and landed on the assembly's calendar. If the assembly were to vote in favor of the bill, then Governor Steele's signature would pass it into law and mark the beginning of the end of Guthrie's aspirations as a permanent capital of the territory and, eventually, the state of Oklahoma.[30]

Until Council Bill No. 7 eked its way out of the council, the citizens of Guthrie were confident that the capital would remain where Congress put it. Complacency turned to outrage when news of the council vote hit the streets and ramped higher after it sailed through the assembly. No sooner did the House adjourn and begin to empty into the streets on October 2 than a mob besieged Speaker of the House Arthur N. Daniels in front of Guthrie's Palace Hotel. With a rising sense of panic, Daniels protested that Dan Peery had the bill for delivery to Governor Steele. Whether he had possession of the bill or not, Peery knew he had to act fast. With a mob of Guthrie partisans in hot pursuit of several legislators, who might or might not have Council Bill No. 7 tucked in their pockets, Peery made a mad dash from the opera house to a nearby butcher shop, where he hid behind a refrigerator and waited for the crowd to rush by in search of him and other legislators.

As the cacophony subsided, Peery heard a black man call to another, "What is the matter, Rastus?"

The unseen Rastus replied, "Matter enough I reckon, that fellow Peery done stole the capital and gone to Oklahoma City with it."

Languishing in the butcher shop, Peery surely experienced a rise in blood pressure as he heard passersby speculate on his fate at the end of a noose. He remained in hiding until dark before daring to return to the opera house, where his colleagues wondered where he had been all afternoon. All agreed that the streets were not safe, so "Gristmill" Jones accompanied Peery to the Noble Hotel and, for insurance, handed him a Colt .45. Meanwhile, Oklahoma City attorney H. B. Mitchell, apparently then in Guthrie, fired off a telegram to Mayor Gault requesting aid for Oklahoma County's beleaguered legislators. In response, a group of fifteen to twenty people, including Charley Colcord, arrived from Oklahoma City to lend their assistance.[31] At some point, Sidney Clarke showed up to deploy his oratorical skills in the service of crowd control. With assistance from Marshall William Grimes, Clarke was to some degree successful, as tempers cooled and the streets of Guthrie returned to something akin to normal. As the *Oklahoma Daily Journal* noted about the end of a tense day in Guthrie, "The danger now was with the ignorant and drunken."[32]

News that Oklahoma City was just a signature away from becoming a capital city inspired a much different reaction to the south, where people signaled their joy by pouring into the streets with firecrackers popping and horns blowing.

Somebody detonated a hundred pounds of dynamite a few miles from town to announce the joyous news to the whole territory.[33] The party continued when Oklahoma County's delegation returned home to a hero's welcome. More explosions thundered across the prairie. But beneath all the hoopla were suspicions that Governor Steele would veto the capital removal bill. To shore up their defenses, Oklahoma City delegates agreed with a group from Kingfisher that, if worse came to worse, they would vote to move the capital to their town at the territory's western border. Apparently, Oklahoma Cityans thought any town was preferable to Guthrie as a territorial capital. Amid all the excitement, Oklahoma City businessmen coolly insisted that capital status was not vital for their city to prosper. There was even a concern that becoming the capital might derail the city's ambition to become a center of commerce. The strongest supporters of Council Bill No. 7 were real estate speculators; as the *Guthrie Democrat* put it, "They think this will bring a boom in their line."[34]

Back in Guthrie, the maneuvering continued, with Logan County representatives doing their best to squelch the bill and their counterparts from Oklahoma County trying to push it through to the governor.[35] Governor Steele received Council Bill No. 7 on Thursday, October 8. He was slow to act on it, and when he did, he sent it back to the legislature. Nobody was surprised to learn that his signature was conspicuously missing.[36]

Governor Steele's refusal to sign Council Bill No. 7 did not end Oklahoma City's bid to become the capital. If anything, it intensified the cross-territory rivalry. It certainly sent editorial invective into overdrive. The *Oklahoma Daily Journal* described Guthrie citizens as "a set of raving maniacs" at the height of the crisis, and they stood in stark contrast to the calm and collected citizenry of Oklahoma City, who never deviated from their business-building activities. "That is the difference between the towns," opined an editorial on October 16. "Guthrie is built altogether on wind, and when it was believed that fact was to be made apparent to the world she went all to pieces." As tempers cooled and Oklahoma City legislators accepted the futility of their cause, the legislature took up a bill to locate the capital in Kingfisher no later than February 15, 1891. The multitasking Angelo Scott took charge of construction planning for Kingfisher's capitol complex. Most people expected Governor Steele, now branded as "the czar of Oklahoma and the governor of Guthrie," to veto the bill, even though doing so would serve only to exacerbate the bad blood between Guthrie and

Oklahoma City. By mid-October 1890, Oklahoma City opinion leaders were in open revolt against the Steele administration and the Santa Fe Railroad for showing such favoritism to Guthrie. Given a fair chance and another year of economic development, none doubted that Oklahoma City would be so far ahead of its rival "that nobody will remember that Guthrie ever existed."[37]

The legislative sparring continued through December, with no end in sight. A low point was reached when the sergeant at arms was summoned to break up a fracas that nearly degenerated into violence.[38] Decades later, Angelo Scott, whose plans to build a capitol in Kingfisher were among his few unfinished projects, reflected on Steele's short and contentious term as territorial governor. "I never felt that he enjoyed his position among us," wrote Scott, "and while no breath of scandal touched his administration, I fancy he was glad to get back to Indiana and back to Congress, where he had been before. He did not stay with us long."[39]

Toxic relations in Guthrie notwithstanding, the news was not all bad. The Choctaw Road, which at one time was in dire financial straits, was on track to complete its line from McAlester to El Reno by early 1891. Its passage through Oklahoma City would be a boon to business on two levels: it would create direct rail links to every town in Oklahoma and Indian Territories (increasingly abbreviated as the "Twin Territories"); and it would provide access to cheap coal to stimulate industry. The prospect of railroad connections, together with increasing circulation of money and nonstop construction, were putting Oklahoma City in position to become a railroad hub.[40]

Good news (for some, anyway) on the political front came when Republicans gathered in Guthrie and nominated Judge David A. Harvey and Dennis T. Flynn to run for territorial delegate to the U.S. House of Representatives. Harvey (R–Okla. Terr.; 1890–93) went on to win his party's nomination by a vote of thirty-six to sixteen. Support came from Governor Steele, who forced Republicans to nominate Harvey of Oklahoma City over Flynn from Guthrie. If Guthrie were to keep the capital, reasoned the governor, then it was only fair (and perhaps wise) to let Oklahoma City have the delegate. At their convention, Republicans affirmed their support for the Harrison administration, demanded equal rights for all (black or white, rich or poor), and favored opening Indian reservations to non-Indian settlement. Although Guthrie Republicans were disappointed over Flynn's loss to Harvey in the November 4 election, they pledged their full support for Oklahoma Territory's first official delegate to Congress.[41]

More good news came as a result of President Harrison's status quo order in December 1889. His more or less successful intervention in Oklahoma City politics had put a stop to the army's role in keeping the peace, and educators began to cast covetous eyes on the 160-acre Military Reservation east of the Santa Fe depot. Even though a public school system was up and running in February 1891 under the leadership of Dr. Delos Walker as president of the school board, teachers still had to scramble for whatever accommodations they could find. That began to change when the city council persuaded Sidney Clarke to lobby Congress to turn the Military Reservation over to school use.

With assistance from Captain Stiles, Clarke settled into his familiar role as Oklahoma's lobbyist in chief to promote what became known as the "School Reservation Bill." Clarke and his team, which included David A. Harvey's successor, Dennis T. Flynn (R–Okla. Terr.; 1893–97, 1899–1903) from Guthrie, persevered. As the clock ticked toward the end of the congressional session, teachers back at home did their part by canvassing the entire town and informing every woman they could find that their children's future depended on their support of an upcoming vote on issuing school bonds set to mature in twenty years. As part of the get-out-the-vote campaign, women made arrangements to take care of other women's children so they could go to the polls and cast their ballots.

On the last day of the session and with approval from the House Committee on Public Lands, Congress authorized the transfer. Clarke surely had a sense of déjà vu, as the eleventh-hour legislation took the form of a rider attached to an appropriation bill. Perhaps inevitably, suspicions circulated that Flynn's allegiance to Guthrie had tempered his enthusiasm and caused unnecessary delays in the bill's passage. Funding was assured when the Oklahoma City electorate voted in favor of the school bond issue. As Mrs. A. S. Heaney (formerly, Alice Beitman), who became principal in the third ward, noted with justifiable pride, the bond issue would never have passed without women's votes, which predated passage of the Nineteenth Amendment to the U.S. Constitution by nearly three decades.[42]

━━━━━━━━━━

While Sidney Clarke and his team were orchestrating the transfer of the Military Reservation to school use, men with less noble aspirations were busy transferring land to themselves. For a glimpse into the post-Run frenzy of land theft and real estate speculation, we turn to John H. Burford, a registrar with the U.S. Land Office in Oklahoma City. On November 22, 1890, he fired off an impassioned plea for assistance to Secretary of the Interior Noble. Perhaps more attuned than most to the law of unintended consequences, Burford was highly critical of President Harrison's ambiguous proclamation opening Oklahoma Proper to homesteading and townsite development. As noted with mounting alarm at the time of the Run, many eighty-niners believed that the prohibition against early entry did not preclude them from roaming as they pleased between March 23 (the day of the presidential proclamation) and the fateful hour on April 22 as long as they did not occupy a particular tract.

Because soonerism was loaded with contested meaning, thousands of prospective settlers felt justified in scouring the countryside in search of choice town lots and homesteads and claiming them after the stroke of noon on the day of the Run. Predictably, people who held a strict interpretation of what it meant to be a sooner (that is, a person who jumped the gun and/or staked a claim to a homestead or town lot before noon on April 22, 1889) were not inclined to relinquish their properties without a fight. As Burford noted in his letter to Noble, "The unfortunate law under which the lands of this Territory were opened to settlement has created a state of affairs which is simply appalling, deplorable, and makes an honorable man shrink from its consequences."

Burford estimated that a third of homestead entries were illegal and accused the men who held them of maintaining their status "by the deplorable crime of perjury." As evidence of pandemonium, Burford cited his office's contest docket, which groaned under the weight of two thousand cases pending for trial with more flooding in daily. In just one week, no fewer than fifty people had committed willful perjury, and many of them arrived at the land office with lawyers in tow who were complicit in their deceit. It was not unusual for an alleged sooner to threaten violence against anyone who might testify against him. Recognizing safety in numbers, some were forming associations to keep their properties through intimidation and murder. And who, exactly, were these reprobates? Burford cast a wide net to implicate former boomers, cowboys, ranchmen, railroad employees, and even U.S. marshals. Clearly at his wit's end, Burford asked (begged?) Secretary Noble to dispatch detectives and maybe secret service agents to the Oklahoma City branch of the U.S. Land Office.[43]

Challenges notwithstanding, jobs with the Department of the Interior were coveted positions. Three days after the Run, Senator John Sherman (R-Ohio; 1861–77, 1881–97) wrote a glowing recommendation to Secretary Noble on behalf of William F. Harn, a fellow Ohioan and editor of the *Mansfield Herald*, whose dream job was to work in an Indian Territory land office.[44] Harn's big break came in December 1890 when the Oklahoma City office, surely at the registrar's urging, agreed to take him on. He went to work in January after a thorough reading of the Department of the Interior's instructions to employees of the General Land Office (GLO). Inspectors, special agents, and others who worked for the GLO were expected to prepare weekly reports on their activities and exercise strict economy in their spending. Word counts were to be submitted with telegram charges, and travel expenses in excess of one dollar required sub-vouchers for livery hires and the feed for and stabling of horses.[45]

During his tenure with the GLO, Harn succeeded in putting a number of sooners behind bars. His career came to an end when Grover Cleveland was elected as president for the second time in 1892 and, as was customary at the outset of new administrations, put his own appointees in office. Harn stayed in Oklahoma City and, after an unsuccessful bid to become U.S. marshal for Oklahoma Territory, opened a law practice and speculated in real estate. In 1897, he bought a 160-acre farm northeast of Oklahoma City for $450. When Governor Charles N. Haskell (1908–11) relocated the state capital from Guthrie and thereby put a contentious end to the capital fight, a site-selection committee chose the northern part of Harn's farm for the capitol building. Harn and his real estate partner, J. J. Culbertson, subsequently platted most of the remaining property into town lots for Oklahoma's wealthiest and most politically connected families.

Harn died of heart disease on December 15, 1944. Nearly three decades later, his home at 313 Northeast Sixteenth Street was placed on the National Register of Historic Places. Later still, what was left of his property was preserved as a ten-acre historic site known as the "Harn Homestead." In the ensuing years, volunteers refurbished dilapidated structures to accommodate special events, relocated territorial-era buildings to the property, opened a gift shop, planted a garden that would have made a pioneer proud, and raised funds for a full-time staff. Well into the twenty-first century, the Harn Homestead remained the state's most popular venue for children to stake their claims in annual reenactments of the Run of '89.[46]

———————

Although immigrant experiences were unique in their particulars, they can be generalized to a broader population whose roots in Oklahoma remained shallow through the first full year of settlement. Prairie fires, floods, windstorms, predators—these and other hazards, coupled with Gilded Age inequalities, were all in a day's work, and they united townspeople and homesteaders in a common cause to put the frontier behind them and join the rest of the nation in its expanding networks of trade and commerce. As early-day immigrant George Turner noted in a comment that resonates from his time to ours, "In our little cabins and rude sod shanties, we dreamed and hoped for better times."[47]

One of those dreamers was Mary Ellen Carver, whose home near present-day Spencer necessitated regular grocery runs through Oklahoma City's all but impassable thoroughfares. During the winter months, she and her family traveled in a light cart or on horseback, "as mud would be hub deep on the Main Street of Oklahoma City." Her mother often rode into town sidesaddle, clad in a long black dress or riding skirt to cover her best dress.[48] A much more enjoyable outing came on July 4, 1890, when patriots held a giant picnic seven miles north of town. A platform (more sturdy, perhaps, than the grandstand built a year earlier) was constructed for a day of speeches and patriotic singalongs.[49] Those who preferred more lively entertainment flocked to an undisclosed location to gawk at an itinerant Assyrian, who traveled in the company of a big red bear with a knack for performing. People always threw a few coins to the Assyrian (ten to twenty-five cents was the going rate), but after his bear nearly mauled him to death in a wrestling match, Oklahoma City mysteriously dropped off his itinerary.[50]

In the Assyrian's and his bear's absence, entertainment-starved Oklahomans made do with medicine and tent shows, spelling bees, square dances, debates, and, as modernity came relentlessly on, nickelodeons and silent moving pictures. And, of course, nobody was ever very far from a saloon. In one pioneer's estimation, there were two saloons for every other business establishment. But for members of the generation of 1889 accustomed to entertaining themselves, nothing could beat old-fashioned sociability. As pioneer Mamie Page recalled with a dose of nostalgia, "People were more sociable and neighborly in the earlier days. If people were sick we visited them, sat up with them, washed and cooked for them. We felt this was our duty. But now things are changed. We scarcely know our neighbor. With all our hardships I prefer those times to our present times. Many of us fought against the progress of modern times."[51]

Impromptu entertainment was always in the offing when cowboys came to town. As pioneer L. L. Land explained, cowboys delighted in riding their horses on the sidewalks and blasting away at windows. Even lawmen tended to give cowboys a wide berth. Land concluded his remarks about the West of

Oklahoma City, 1890.
Courtesy of Oklahoma Images Collection, Metropolitan Library System of Oklahoma County.

his youth with a rather low-key accolade for America's favorite culture hero: "The cowboys did a lot of damage but never killed anyone."[52]

While new forms of entertainment were on their way in, others were on their way out, including beef issues at the Darlington Indian Agency. Ohio native Henry J. Stevenson spent several years working his way across the West before arriving in Oklahoma City, where he opened a photograph gallery on Broadway between Grand Avenue and Main Street. He operated as the Stevenson Art Gallery for about a year before moving to El Reno in 1896 to be closer to honest-to-goodness Indians and their famed bovine slaughters—relics of the Wild West that he aimed to capture on film. He apparently had a change of heart about photographing the beef issues when he caught wind that Indians would be permitted to use bows and arrows to kill their cattle. Clearly ahead of their time in terms of animal rights, Stevenson and a Rev. Grainger lodged a protest with El Reno mayor T. F. Hensley and argued against the use of primitive weaponry on two grounds: it was brutal, and flying projectiles posed a danger to onlookers.

Whether or not their protest was effective is unknown. What is certain is that expert riflemen were henceforth assigned to kill government-issued cattle, and displays of Indian prowess on horseback became one more casualty as modernity steamrolled its way across Oklahoma Territory.[53]

One morning, the Clark family from Chicago was gathered in the lean-to kitchen of their homestead about two miles southwest of Tecumseh, when one of the children, Winifred, noticed "a queer movement" in the woods. The movement grew more visible until she recognized what was happening: "A long line of negroes, about three or four hundred people," were marching close together, "trailing along like Indians." The procession came to a halt about fifty yards from the Clarks' home. While some of them sat down to rest, a tall woman stepped forward to explain that floodwaters had driven her people from their homes in Memphis. As nobody had offered to help them, they decided to make their way to Oklahoma Territory, long publicized as African Americans' last, best hope for a fresh start.[54]

The Clarks felt sorry for them and handed out what little food they had before bidding them Godspeed. A few of them, perhaps enticed by the Clark family's kindness, decided to remain in the Tecumseh area. After the territorial governor issued an appeal for help, many of them kept heading west until they reached Kingfisher at the western edge of Oklahoma Territory, where they were allowed to establish a settlement.

Winifred became fascinated with her new neighbors, and the stories she told about them open a portal into black culture at the dawn of Oklahoma history. One night, she attended a dance deep in the woods and watched in awe as the girls, their hair platted in short braids and festooned with white strings, swayed to a cadence whose meaning she could not fathom. She was also on hand for a baptizing in the Little River. As Winifred explained, "They lashed the water and made a great fuss but finally walked out meekly." Young boys were asked to join the choir, but according to Winifred, there was a problem: the songs they had learned were more suitable to saloons than religious services.

Winifred learned at an early age that many African Americans depended on white people for help and often stole rather than beg. She and her sister once caught a black man named Arthur red-handed as he helped himself to her family's corncrib. Winifred told him to keep enough to feed his horse and to ask her if he needed more. He responded, "I never will do it again if you'll not tell de Boss." Arthur often came to the Clarks' home before supper and lingered in the shadows, always eager to share stories of slavery days "befo de wa.'" When supper was served, he accepted what was offered and took it home to his wife.[55]

While Tecumseh's African Americans were enjoying their camp meetings and baptisms and the occasional theft, a Paiute shaman in Nevada named Wovoka (The Cutter) was igniting a firestorm with his claim that God had promised to cleanse the earth of white men in a mighty flood of mud and water. Once the white men were gone, the overgrazed prairies would blossom with lush grasses; elk, deer, and antelope would once again frolic across the prairies; and the bison would return in vast numbers to provide God's chosen people with the sustenance they needed to return to the ways of their ancestors.[56]

From Christian neighbors, Wovoka learned all about the Son of God's miracles among the Jews of ancient Israel. As Indians flocked to Nevada to hear his message, Wovoka upped the ante to declare that he was the risen Lord, the Wanekia, which translates from Lakota Sioux as "makes live savior."[57] The new Messiah chose as his sacrament the ghost dance, a ceremony rooted in Indian traditions that would herald fulfillment of the Word of God.

Emboldened by the Indian Christ's message, his New World apostles fanned across the West to tutor their Indian brothers and sisters in ghost dance doctrine and ritual. To spread the word among southern tribes, Sitting Bull—not, as was widely reported, the famed Hunkpapa Sioux leader from Standing Rock Reservation in South Dakota, but rather, an Arapaho chief from Wind River Reservation in Wyoming—traveled to the Darlington Indian Agency with an alarming nuance to the Wanekia's prophesy. In Sitting Bull's cosmology, the Indian renaissance would be heralded by a wall of fire that would send white people scurrying back to their European homelands. Indians, divinely chosen to survive the inferno, would need only to wait for a twelve-day deluge to extinguish the flames. Purged of all impurities, Mother Earth would then give birth to a new age of Indian sovereignty.[58]

But not everyone was patient enough to wait for prophesies to be fulfilled. In preparation for the race war that was surely coming, Indians stockpiled weapons and ammunition. For protection against the white man's superior firepower, warriors were advised to don ghost shirts sewn from unbleached muslin or sheeting and emblazoned with sacred symbols. As Minneconjou Sioux band chief Kicking Bear declared to skeptics, "I tell you, my cousins, *that holy shirt has the power to turn away bullets!*"[59]

Soldiers stationed near Indian reservations from Montana and the Dakotas to Oklahoma Territory responded to rising tensions by stepping up their patrols and doing what they could to discourage the ghost dance, known to journalists nationwide as the "Dance of Death to Come."[60] Reports from

Fort Sully, South Dakota, published in late November in the Oklahoma City *Evening Gazette* left no doubt about what Northern Plains Indians had in store for their white neighbors: "They were all well armed with Winchester rifles, had plenty of ammunition and were well equipped with ponies. They were uniformly insolent and reticent." Some vowed to cut off the ears of any soldier who dared to interfere with their sacred ceremonies.[61] With characteristic aplomb, President Harrison directed Indian agents to limit their activities to separating friendly Indians from ghost dancers and to "avoid action which might cause irritation." But by mid-November, he sensed dark days ahead and directed the secretary of war to prepare for armed intervention.[62]

Although the disturbance became front-page news nationwide, few correspondents knew enough about Indian ways to perceive the ghost dance as more than a prelude to battle. This was no ordinary war dance. At its core, the ghost dance was a pan-Indian expression of deep spirituality and a last line of defense against a marauding civilization.

Settlers in Oklahoma Territory who had dismissed the movement as a fleeting craze changed their tune in September 1890 when some three thousand Cheyennes, Arapahos, Caddos, Wichitas, and Kiowas followed Sitting Bull's instructions and held a ghost dance about two miles south of the Darlington Indian Agency. When they were not dancing, they poached cattle that had drifted within range of their weaponry. Some of them belonged to Montford Johnson, whose cattle offered far better eating than the mangy longhorns issued at the Indian agency.[63]

As calls for protection poured into Fort Reno from settlers along Oklahoma Territory's western flank, Captain Jack Hayes put the Fifth Cavalry on high alert. *Evening Gazette* readers were alarmed to learn that the agitation "had reached a point far above his expectation." There was danger, too, from northern Indian Territory, where Osages were falling in behind the Wanekia and "indulging in the ghost dance with a great deal of religious and war-like fervor."[64] To ascertain what Oklahoma City might be in for, Captain Stiles sent a detachment of cavalry on an intelligence-gathering mission to Fort Reno.[65] Meanwhile, far to the north, Lakota Sioux gathered near the tiny village of Wounded Knee were about to discover the deficiencies of the ghost dance ritual, and to realize how little protection their magic shirts offered from the bluecoats' bullets.

A ruckus west of Oklahoma City on a cold December night confirmed everybody's worst fears and sent people running for cover. Men who knew how to handle firearms mustered in the center of town where hardware merchants W. J. Pettee and Gilpin & Frick were distributing rifles and ammunition. Tensions mounted when a man rode in from Yukon shouting, "The Indians are coming!" Citizen-soldiers responded by taking up posts at the city's main entrances and kept their gazes fixed on the western horizon as a stream of wagons laden with farm implements and household goods poured into the city. Convinced that Armageddon was at hand, some farmers had their cows and pigs in tow.

Homesteader, educator, and civic leader Alice Beitman was attending a Sorosis Club meeting of the local literati when she heard the electrifying news that Indians from the Cheyenne and Arapaho Reservation, inspired and energized by days of frenzied dancing and convinced that the Great Spirit would deliver them from the white man's road, were massing for attack. As the staccato *pop-pop-pop* of warning shots filled the air, she took refuge and braced for battle. On her way to shelter, Miss Beitman might have run into Myrtle Hill Allen, then a child, who admitted decades later that she was paralyzed with fright at the imagined horrors to come, and who had been advised to hunker down in a judge's two-story brick dwelling across the street from her house. Businessmen who girded for action included T. M. Richardson from the First National Bank. He and his fellow defenders locked and loaded their weapons and watched the minutes crawl by, each lost in his own thoughts as they waited for the signal to commence firing. "Everybody was on tiptoe, awaiting the arrival of the Indian advance guard," wrote flour and feed dealer C. A. McNabb. "It was thunderous, hair-raising, gore-inspiring to those who were called upon to defend the city and its precious populace."

And then, in a twist that juxtaposed relief and disappointment in equal measure, Oklahoma City's gallant defenders realized that Indians had nothing to do with the advancing hubbub. It turned out that a band of hell-raising youngsters was bearing down on the city in celebration of a wedding with a time-honored charivari. McNabb, apparently more disappointed than relieved at the battle that never happened, concluded his account of the Indian scare of 1890 with a dose of frontier bravado: "There has never existed in my mind the least doubt of the successful termination of that battle. Had it been fought as anticipated, the Cheyenne Indian tribe would today have been extinct."[66]

Oklahoma City's first full calendar year of settlement thus closed not to the crackle of gunfire, but rather, to the banging of pots and pans by young folks bent on having a good time.

Postscript

This city, in fact, has more to offer to induce all manner of manufacturing
and industrial enterprises to locate here than all the western cities combined.

Oklahoma Journal, *December 26, 1890*

Although towns in Oklahoma Proper were unique in their particulars, their
patterns of growth typified urban development across the Great Plains from the
early 1870s to century's end, the last and most frenzied era of town building in
American history. The most successful towns owed their geneses to railroads'
policy of building switches at ten-mile intervals. As agents of colonization,
railroads promoted townsite settlement to ensure a steady stream of customers
in need of transportation services. Development that began at the depots
quickly devolved into private enterprise to chart the direction and character
of urban growth.

Typically, private enterprise took the form of townsite companies, whose
platting began at the depots and continued in an orderly and usually geo-
metrical pattern on either side of the railroad tracks. Towns coalesced when
bankers, merchants, physicians, attorneys, and others who formed the basis
of urban life moved in to build what they hoped would be permanent communities. Three features of townsite development distinguished towns in the
Great Plains from eastern cities: wide thoroughfares designed to accommodate
wagon trains, cattle drives, and other mainstays of western commerce; grid-like
streets and alleys that made sense in a landscape that offered few impediments
to urban sprawl; and a woeful lack of public space to accommodate everything
from courthouses, jails, and schools to parks and public services.

Bent on turning a fast buck, pioneer businessmen in the Great Plains were fueled by the Gilded Age gospel of free enterprise, and they paid scant attention to land that could not be sold for profit. But sooner or later, those same pioneers and their successors recognized their conundrum: without merchants, townsites could never become viable; and without social institutions and public spaces, townsites could not mature enough to endure.[1] Visitors to Myriad Gardens in downtown Oklahoma City might be surprised by Angelo Scott's regret that the citizens' committee of fourteen was too busy surveying business lots during the first week of settlement to bother with public spaces.[2] Visitors to Oklahoma City's favorite entertainment venue, Bricktown, might be similarly surprised to know they are watching a ballgame, or perhaps enjoying a cruise along the Bricktown Canal before an evening of drinking and dining, in an area that was once used to house soldiers and stable horses, and that it was converted to school use by settlers who were tired of educating their children in stores and warehouses.

Although communities in Oklahoma Proper and, after May 2, 1890, Oklahoma Territory fit the pattern of Great Plains urbanization, they were unique in their astonishing pace of urban growth. A rather maladroit turn of phrase—"born grown"—drifted into Oklahoma vernacular to describe a process that has few, if any, parallels in American history. But "born grown" is really just a slogan, and it does nothing to reveal the personalities and historical forces that shaped Oklahoma Proper from 1866 through 1890. Nor does it do much to illuminate the lasting significance of the Run of '89, not only as the Big Bang of Oklahoma history, but also as a defining moment in America's unrelenting territorial expansion. That defining moment was recorded in the U.S. Census of 1890, when bureaucrats announced, with little fanfare, the closing of the frontier: "Up to and including 1890 the country had a frontier of settlement, but at present the unsettled area has been so broken into by isolated bodies of settlement that there can hardly be said to be a frontier line. In the discussion of its extent, its westward movement, etc., it cannot, therefore, any longer have a place in the census reports."[3]

─────────────

Ironically, Indians were the first casualties of Oklahoma City's born grown narrative. In a land once known as Indian Territory and rebranded by Choctaw chief Allen Wright in his native Muskogean language as "the land of the red people," Indian voices were hard to hear. Even though tribal destinies in America's rapidly developing midsection hinged on resolution of the

Oklahoma Question, we hear far more *about* Indians than *from* them. To understand why, we turn to the clash of civilizations that played out on the southern plains between 1866 and 1890. Much as victors get to tell the story of the battle, so, too, did people of European descent assume control of the levers of communication—chiefly through newspapers, written correspondence, and eventually oral history interviews—to exert a lopsided influence in framing the early history of central Oklahoma.

During the period of wars and reservations following the Civil War, journalists and frontiersmen alike tended to describe Indians as foes of progress with a stark choice: trade hunting for farming and assimilate into the dominant civilization, or face extermination. As the Indian wars of the 1870s sputtered to a close and tribal sovereignty entered its twilight, advocates of assimilation ramped up their rhetoric, and Indians were perceived increasingly as curiosities—"the mysterious other" who offered entertainment in ceremonial dances and beef issues and had odd eating habits, and whose future lay in leaving their ancient customs behind and accepting the white man's road. But as we have seen, to reduce Indians—primarily Cheyennes and Arapahos in the west, Kickapoos, Shawnees, and Potawatomis in the east, and the Five Tribes in present-day eastern Oklahoma—to curiosities is to belittle their role in shaping the early history of central Oklahoma. If ever there was a clear-cut case of historical malpractice, writing Indians out of their own story is it.

Unfortunately, Indians lacked the advantages afforded by written communication, and they had no way to record for posterity what it was like to watch an alien culture steamroll its way across their former hunting grounds. A new paradigm was in the making, and it rested on the Gilded Age ethos of social Darwinism that justified socioeconomic inequalities. As they pitched their teepees near the Santa Fe depot and settled in for a few days of trading with their busy new neighbors, those Indians could do little but reflect silently on the economic tsunami that leveled everything in its path, and on a future they could neither fathom nor resist.

Indians were not the only ones whose voices were muted. Ever since the earliest days of the boomer movement, blacks from the Old Confederacy and freedmen from the Five Tribes had perceived Oklahoma Proper as a place where the color of one's skin mattered less than hard work and perseverance. Encouragement came from freedmen's associations and even the Republican Party, whose interest in extending its influence in Oklahoma Territory dovetailed with blacks' interest in seizing opportunities, wherever and whatever they might be. Although we will never know how many blacks participated in the Run of '89 and, more importantly, how many stayed, we know enough to realize that black migration was a significant factor through the first full calendar year of settlement. We can also surmise that Oklahoma City's original settlers in Sandtown were likely among the first ones to welcome them. But as the optimism of 1889 faded and Oklahoma City became just another outpost of Gilded Age bigotry, blacks found themselves in their familiar role as second-class citizens. Increasingly marginalized in all-black neighborhoods and towns, blacks in Oklahoma Territory struggled to find the promise in the Promised Land.

Indian and black experiences on the Oklahoma frontier take us straight to one of the Gilded Age's most contentious issues and this book's central theme: the definition and disposition of public lands. Since the dawn of the Republic, Americans were faced with the unique challenge of figuring out what to do with a seemingly endless supply of land. As the frontier pushed westward, a familiar dichotomy developed between wealthy individuals and corporations determined to expand their holdings and people of lesser means who took seriously the nation's promise as a land of opportunity. The dichotomy deepened as the federal government assumed the role of referee. Some politicians, all too often with their hands in the till, favored vast land grants to railroads, timber companies, and other corporations. Others, animated by Jefferson's vision of yeoman farmers tilling the land from sea to shining sea, did what they could to promote homesteading as a means of populating the continent and ensuring the formation of family farms and small businesses. Inevitably, control over such vast riches opened the door to corruption and left the land's original inhabitants caught in the crossfire, with dire consequences for the orderly advance of American civilization.

In Indian Territory, disagreements over the Public Lands Question (often capitalized, as most major issues were, for emphasis) spawned the boomer movement in the 1880s and culminated in the Run of '89. For once, Lady Fortune seemed to look kindly on small "d" democrats who traced their lineage to bedrock American ideology. On that picture-perfect Monday afternoon, history seemed to offer a decisive moment when everything changed.[4] The iconic imagery still resonates, maybe even sends shivers up and down our spines. But did everything really change?

Far from the homesteads that frame our understanding of Great Plains settlement, urban pioneers scrambled to build businesses, buy and sell real estate, and establish industries with a laser-like focus on turning a profit. Some arrived at Oklahoma Station after noon on April 22, 1889—or perhaps a bit earlier—and stayed only long enough to sell their hastily acquired lots for multiples of their original values. Others, supplied with the wherewithal to launch their enterprises and perhaps connected with friends in high places, stuck around for the long haul in a place that had lost none of its appeal since boomers had unfurled their *On to Oklahoma!* banners a decade earlier. But countless thousands arrived destitute, searched in vain for the opportunities they had been promised, and drifted from the pages of history, their dreams derailed by entrenched privilege and an unforgiving economy that belied America's hallowed reputation as "a city on a hill."

And all of them—rich and poor, white and black, northerners and southerners and even a few foreigners—were quickly embroiled in squabbles over municipal and territorial governance that nearly upended the entire enterprise. Military intervention in Oklahoma City's election in September 1889 stands out as a shocking example of imperial overreach. A year later, disagreements over who should be calling the shots in Oklahoma Territory came to a head when Guthrie and Oklahoma City legislators faced off in a fight to the finish. "The fight continued for 38 days," recalled the level-headed Angelo Scott. "For days and weeks we talked of nothing else and thought of nothing else but the capital fight."[5] What Scott left unsaid was what the territory's first legislature might have accomplished in a less bellicose atmosphere, and how legislators might have steered the new territory toward more productive pursuits.

Turmoil in Guthrie did little to slow down the Unassigned Lands' transformation from a raw frontier into a powerful link in the nation's expanding commercial network. Oklahoma City boosters, of course, wanted everyone to know that their city was special and that they were uniquely endowed to put land that was so recently public to good (that is, private) use. The *Oklahoma Journal* in December 1890 offered the heavy dose of frontier boosterism seen in this chapter's epigraph. The *Journal* expanded its tribute with accolades for urban planners whose business acumen was (no surprise here!) second to none.[6]

The generation of 1889 had ample reason to be proud of its accomplishments and optimistic about Oklahoma City's future. In the absence of regulations aimed at creating a level playing field, Gilded Age entrepreneurs had free rein to grow their businesses, plow their profits into further expansion, and invest in the red-hot real estate market. Lured by the prospect (inevitability?) of making money fast, successive waves of settlers descended on Oklahoma City to participate in its post-frontier expansion. But, as in the rest of America, not everyone was on board with the capitalist juggernaut. Those who felt most victimized by the unregulated marketplace and least represented by either of the major political parties flocked to the People's, or Populist, Party. Grounded in the Jeffersonian tradition as refined and synthesized by Jackson and Lincoln, populists in the 1890s railed against eastern capital and rejected an economic system that favored the few against the many. The roster of Oklahoma populists reads like a Who's Who of boomer leadership, most notably Sidney Clarke, James B. Weaver, and Samuel Crocker. Supported by a sizeable contingent of municipal officers and territorial legislators, they stood in the vanguard of a growing legion of small farmers and laborers who felt shut out of a rigged political system. None imagined that, some two decades hence, the Populist Party would form the basis of the state's Socialist Party to render Oklahoma, along with North Dakota, as one of only two states where a third party nearly toppled the two-party system.

Debates over the Public Lands Question did not end with the Run of '89. In ways that few anticipated and nobody was prepared for, they degenerated into a free-for-all destined to mire Oklahoma Territory's court system in a hopeless tangle for decades to come. At issue was a twofold question: who was the first to claim a homestead or town lot; and how could he or she prove it in a court of law? Answering those deceptively simple questions countless thousands of times, sometimes truthfully but often not, embroiled Oklahoma Territory in a nightmare of litigation that falls under the rubric of the sooner cases.

"Soonerism" (an inelegant moniker if ever there was one, but descriptive nonetheless) had its roots in the boomer movement, came under intense scrutiny after President Harrison issued his famously ambiguous proclamation of March 23, popped into the legal lexicon at the time of the Run, and continued unabated through the 1890s. Although a thorough treatment of the sooner imbroglio lies beyond the scope of this book, tantalizing glimpses can be seen in land registrar John H. Burford's impassioned plea for help from Secretary Noble and William F. Harn's efforts to weed out the impostors. For another perspective of the litigious swath of destruction that resonated throughout the 1890s, we turn to James L. Brown, the lawyer and territorial representative from Oklahoma City who set the legislature on fire (figuratively speaking) with Council Bill No. 7. He arrived in Oklahoma City on April 23, 1889, to find steady employment in his chosen profession. "There was much contention over the possession of, and the right to make homestead entries upon, public lands and town lots, as there were so many more claimants for the land than there were quarter sections and lots opened to settlement," wrote Brown in a 1909 retrospective. To register a dispute, a claimant had to initiate a law suit, commonly known as a contest, in the local land office. Disputes that failed to reach resolution in the land office could then be appealed to the commissioner of the General Land Office in Washington, D.C. Contests that remained unresolved were referred to the secretary of the Interior. Claims of ownership were devilishly hard to ascertain, and the legal wrangling they spawned captured the public's attention through the first full calendar year of settlement and for many years thereafter. Thousands who entered Oklahoma Proper at the appointed hour knew nothing about the land they were about to claim, other than it had suddenly become theirs under public lands laws. Others—including, but by no means limited to, cattlemen, lawmen, well-heeled entrepreneurs, and railroad employees—knew plenty about the land and townsites, had no doubt about where they were going, and had contrived a way to get there first.[7]

———————

The years passed. Voices raised in righteous anger or in defense of duplicity have long since been stilled and, for the most part, forgotten altogether. But, as visitors to the Century Chest exhibit at the Oklahoma History Center can attest, one voice has literally survived—that of Dr. Angelo C. Scott, whose contribution to the chest buried in April 1913 and resurrected a century later (on, of course, April 22) was a wax-cylinder recording of his greeting to the people of 2013.[8] Everyone who has listened to Dr. Scott's communiqué from the generation of 1889 to Oklahomans of the twenty-first century felt a shudder up and down their spines, maybe even felt tears welling in their eyes and words stalling in their throats. I know I did.

Which leads to the question: what happened to the people who lived, fought, and in some cases died for the Oklahoma cause? A woefully short but necessarily selective cast of characters begins, of course, with David Payne, who died at the breakfast table four and a half years before his vision came to fruition in the Run of '89. For all the controversy that swirled around him, he has a legitimate claim as a founding father of Oklahoma.

Payne's successor, Bill Couch, lived long enough to see the federal government fulfill the boomers' dream and served as Oklahoma City's first mayor,

only to get shot by a rival claimant and perish of gangrene. Sidney Clarke
went on to serve in the territorial legislature, chaired the statehood committee,
and continued to shuttle between his adopted city and the nation's capital to
lobby on behalf of Oklahoma. He died in Oklahoma City in 1909.[9]

Although he suffered from blood poisoning, Samuel Crocker canvassed the
territory as a Populist candidate for Congress in 1890. He was disappointed
to receive only 17 percent of the vote. During his recuperation from both
illness and disappointment, he penned his last book, *That Island* (1892), a
utopian novel describing the transition of an island nation from oppressive
capitalism to populism. His lifelong commitment to Populist causes did not
mean he was averse to turning a buck in Oklahoma City's booming real estate
market. In his later years, he often reminisced about clearing seven thousand
dollars in a single year. He never married and died of natural causes in 1921.[10]

Crocker's friend and fellow crusader James B. Weaver ran for president on
the third-party Populist ticket in 1892. He collected a respectable 8.5 percent
of the popular vote and gathered twenty-two electoral votes, mainly in the
populist heartland, by winning in Kansas, Colorado, Idaho, Nevada, and one
elector each from North Dakota and Oregon. Weaver would no doubt have
added to his tally if citizens of the Twin Territories had been eligible to vote in
the presidential election.[11] When Populists merged with the Democratic Party at
century's end, Weaver went with them and campaigned vigorously for William
Jennings Bryan in his presidential runs in 1896, 1900, and 1908. After serving
as mayor of his hometown of Colfax, Iowa, Weaver retired from public service.
He died in 1912 knowing that many of his political goals remained unfulfilled.
But over the course of the new century, the populist flame burned ever brighter
to influence public policy in ways Weaver could never have imagined.

Gordon William Lillie leveraged his notoriety as a boomer leader to electrify
his career as a showman. In 1908, he joined forces with Buffalo Bill Cody to
create the greatest Wild West show of all time, and he was in the catbird seat
when motion pictures made their debut. But his most lasting contribution to
preserving the frontier of his youth was to promote conservation of the West's
iconic species: the American bison, hunted to the brink of extinction before
making a comeback at his ranch near Pawnee and the Wichita Mountains
National Wildlife Refuge north of Lawton. Like so many of his generation,
Lillie played a part in closing the frontier that he loved and then spent the
rest of his life preserving it as America's fifty-first state of mind. He died in
his sleep in 1942.[12]

With territorial status achieved and boundless opportunities ahead, former boomers and pioneer businessmen spawned the born grown narrative, and a new paradigm came into focus. Former cowboy and lawman Charley Colcord took part in the Cherokee Outlet opening in 1893 and staked a claim near Perry. Following a brief stint as a U.S. marshal, he returned to Oklahoma City in 1898 to become one of his adopted city's most successful real estate developers and civic leaders. Using wealth derived from investments in Indian Territory's burgeoning oil industry, he added a jewel to Oklahoma City's skyline: the twelve-story Colcord Building. Completed in 1910 at a cost of $750,000, the Colcord Building is one of the few turn-of-the-twentieth-century buildings to survive (and thrive) well into the twenty-first century. After he died at his Delaware County ranch in 1934, his body, flanked by a police honor guard, lay in state at the Oklahoma Historical Society building.[13]

T. M. Richardson's First National Bank survived various changes of ownership to merge in 1927 with its across-the-street competitor, Frank P. Johnson's American National Bank, to become the First National Bank and Trust Company of Oklahoma City. The "First" (as it was known by the state's banking cognoscenti) reigned as one of the largest and most successful banks in the Southwest before succumbing to the oil-patch depression of the 1980s. At the time of his death in 1915, Richardson was president of the Western Lumber Company and the Baltimore Investment Company.[14]

Henry Overholser's building spree continued in 1890 with the Overholser Opera House and Overholser Theater, both on Grand Avenue. His elegant, twenty-room Victorian mansion at the corner of Northwest Fifteenth Street and Hudson, completed in the spring of 1904 and placed on the National Register of Historic Places in 1970, became a favorite venue for festive galas and sumptuous feasts under the watchful eye of Henry's wife, Anna, the grand dame of Oklahoma City's social elite. Henry Overholser suffered a stroke during a European tour in 1911, lingered as an invalid, and died in 1915.[15] A half century later, the front lawn of Overholser's mansion became a passable soccer field for a youngster from the other end of the block who would one day have the good fortune to research and write about his hometown's beginnings.[16]

Following his brief tenure as mayor of Oklahoma City (November 27–December 30, 1889), Dr. Andrew Jackson Beale stayed put for about ten years before returning to his native Kentucky. He died at his sister's home in Cynthiana on January 4, 1909, at the age of seventy-three. In resolutions drawn up shortly after he died, Dr. Beale was praised as a man who, in his

multiple roles as a citizen, soldier, statesman, and physician, remained true
to the trust that people had placed in him. Those resolutions concluded, "As
a comrade, while we mourn his loss, we know that he has 'passed over the
river and is resting under the shade of the trees.'"[17]

Undeterred by his failed canal project, Gristmill Jones remained active in
both business and Republican Party politics. He was elected to several terms
in the Oklahoma Territory and, later, Oklahoma legislature, served two terms
as mayor of Oklahoma City (1896–97; 1901–3), and ran unsuccessfully for
Congress in 1908 and governor of Oklahoma in 1910. In collaboration with
his friend and business partner, Henry Overholser, Jones did yeoman's work
to develop railroad infrastructure to accommodate the territory's and, after
1907, the state's quickening pace of business. Ninety years after his death
in 1911, his farmstead near Jones in eastern Oklahoma County joined the
Overholser Mansion on the National Register of Historic Places.[18]

Captain Daniel F. Stiles's military career ended on a cheerless note. He was
nearing retirement when the army called for the abandonment of its military
camp on July 23, 1892. To liquidate its property, the federal government
announced an auction of government buildings on July 29 and sale of surplus
firewood on August 20. The next year, Stiles was blindsided by charges that
he had participated in a plot to rig the bidding. Before a tribunal headed by
Colonel John C. Bates of the Second Infantry and thirteen other officers,
Captain Stiles spent twelve days in a court battle to defend his honor and
preserve his legacy as a career army officer with an unwavering sense of duty.
In his closing arguments, lead defense attorney Selwyn Douglas excoriated
Stiles's accusers for bringing baseless charges against a man who had served as
a bastion of law and order during the first three years of settlement. "No man,"
declared Douglas as he pointed to the graying officer, "is to be convicted upon
such a charge whose head has been whitened by the snow of 30 winters in the
service of his government." Stiles was acquitted of all charges and devoted
the rest of his life to community projects. One of his last public appearances
was at the laying of the Carnegie Library cornerstone on August 16, 1900.
A month later, he died at his residence at 325 Northeast Fourth Street. He
was fifty-nine years old.[19]

On the educational front, none of the eighty-niners made a more lasting
impression in higher education than lawyer and journalist Angelo C. Scott,
whose 1913 recording practically oozes with erudition. After serving a stint
in the territorial legislature and rising to become president pro tempore of the

Senate from 1895 to 1897, he accepted an invitation to teach English and literature at Oklahoma A&M College (later, Oklahoma State University). No sooner was he named president of the college in 1899 than he began to assemble some of the most acclaimed scholars of any land-grant college. He also coached oratory teams, established an informal music department, encouraged the development of athletics, and wrote the college's first fight song. He later returned to Oklahoma City to practice law and teach English at Epworth University (later, Oklahoma City University). The author of numerous articles and books, including *The Story of Oklahoma City* (1939), Scott was named Oklahoma City's Most Useful Citizen in 1937. He died in 1949 and was returned to his homeland for burial in Iola, Kansas.[20]

Stories from the generation of 1889 survive in books, newspaper and journal articles, correspondence, oral history interviews, historic markers, and at least one wax-cylinder recording. But how about Old Oklahoma itself? What happened to the places that framed the eighty-niner story? Other than first-class museums and historic sites, where can we go to catch a glimpse of what the pioneers of 1889 saw or get a sense of what they felt?

For starters, no matter where you are in the six counties of central Oklahoma, you are smack dab in the middle of what was once home to free-range cattle, and you might be following in the footsteps of cowboys who worked for Montford Johnson, Cass Wantland, Bill McClure, or some other cattleman who reigned like a feudal monarch over vast grasslands. To drive along State Highway 81 is to follow a main route of the Chisholm Trail. Except for some signage, you would never know it unless you meander down one of the dirt roads that branch off the highway. The prairie swells are unmistakable signs of untold thousands of cattle that pounded a new landscape en route to the Kansas railheads. But keep in mind that the Chisholm Trail was not a straight and narrow path. Exact routes depended on a host of factors, including weather, the prospect of encountering Indians with a taste for longhorn beef, or maybe just a trail boss's best guess of how to get to Kansas fast and with a minimum loss of livestock.

When you pass through El Reno, take a detour to historic Fort Reno and find a quiet place to survey the countryside. Imagine soldiers assembling their supplies and saddling their horses as they prepared to round up intruders who had no respect for presidential proclamations banning them from land that,

Oklahoma City, Indian Territory, February 22, 1890.
Map drawn and published by T. M. Fowler, Morrisville, Pa.
Courtesy of Oklahoma Historical Society, Oklahoma City, CTPMAP PKC.0005.

in their estimation, was theirs by right of American citizenship. Visualize, too, Fort Reno as a place where Oklahoma Proper saw its first glimmer of urban culture. Then rest your gaze on the northern horizon. Just a couple of miles distant, agents assigned to the Darlington Indian Agency handed out supplies and seed and manufactured goods to the former sovereigns of the western plains and then watched them shoot their meat, often with tourists at their side, to witness the death spiral of Indian hegemony.

If your travels take you near Jones in eastern Oklahoma County, try to imagine the tension that rippled through Camp Alice when soldiers showed up for their all-too-familiar roundup of settlers with an attitude. As you check out the antique shops and trendy eateries in Guthrie, picture tents stretching to the horizon and a frazzled Santa Fe agent casting his lot with the lot grabbers, only to lose his nerve when a six-foot Texan threatened him with violence. And when you whiz past Purcell on I-35, think of trains packed to overflowing with trigger-happy adventurers waiting for their chance to bail out and make a run for a slice of the Promised Land.

But if you are looking for trails and campsites and river crossings, you are out of luck. Even though historians have mined the historical record to map routes and resting places across Indian Territory, the landmarks familiar to boomers are mostly forgotten and buried beneath subdivisions and highways and plowed under by farmers more interested in crops than in preserving Oklahoma Proper for posterity. Council Grove, a cross-cultural watering hole where Jesse Chisholm traded, boomers camped, and cattle grazed, became Bethany and Warr Acres. Oklahoma City's original settlement of Chickasaw freedmen at Sandtown has vanished to the point that some historians question its very existence. Even David Payne's future capital of Ewing is lost forever. The next time you navigate your way through the intersection of Interstates 35 and 40 south of downtown Oklahoma City, divert your attention from boaters on the Oklahoma River and imagine a group of Kansans, tired and wet and thankful that they had escaped arrest, straggling into dilapidated huts a short distance downriver to bed down for the night.[21]

And the Oklahoma townsite? Simply put, history has not been kind to ramshackle architecture. There is no sign of the clapboard depot where passengers on the Santa Fe line detrained, gathered their belongings, and set out on the adventure of a lifetime. Visitors to Bricktown know that they are in for a good time, but they will look in vain for signs of its original use as a military camp and, later, a jail for gamblers and cowboys who stubbornly resisted the imposition of law and order. Nor are there any signs of the saloons and gambling dens clustered near the Santa Fe depot that earned the moniker "Hell's Half Acre." What we have instead is a delightful mural at the entrance to Bricktown depicting scenes derived more from the Oklahoma of our imagination than the rough-and-tumble frontier that was so unyielding to settlers' dreams.

Overlay the downtown area with a map of the 320-acre townsite, toss in pioneer stories and sepia-tinted photographs, and you come up with some jarring juxtapositions: newcomers and dignitaries arriving at the Santa Fe depot to a tumultuous welcome near the entrance to Bricktown; citizens gathering in mass meetings to frame their own laws under the townsite's precious few shade trees near the Skirvin Hotel; surveyors encased in a two-by-four wooden triangle plowing through crowded streets and marking off town lots with lariats in Myriad Gardens; horse racing fans at a Fourth of July celebration rising to their feet as Dave McClure crossed the finish line and, moments later, feeling a sickening lurch as the grandstand buckled, likely near the Chickasw Bricktown Ballpark; soldiers fixing bayonets and breaking up a citizens' election north of Cox Convention Center and west of Chesapeake

Arena, home of the Oklahoma City Thunder; hungry customers lining up for a square meal at the Star Restaurant in the shadow of the Devon Tower; Indians pitching their tents and trading horses for money and supplies along the railroad tracks before lighting up the night with ceremonial dances in the Boathouse District; stagecoaches and overland freight trains setting out for Fort Reno and the Darlington Indian Agency along the Oklahoma–Fort Reno Road, known in the first hours of settlement as Reno Avenue; John C. Adams and Bill Couch trading shots, one of them fatal, west of the Civic Center; butchers hanging deer and quail carcasses outside their shops and tossing scraps to vitamin-deficient Indians along California Avenue, known in a later age as the Bricktown Canal; drunks and lot jumpers force marched at gunpoint through Hell's Half Acre to an army jail in Bricktown; and townspeople running for cover as cowboys rode wherever they pleased, hell-for-leather and guns a-blazin', and with lawman Charley Colcord in hot pursuit. Whether you are a born-and-bred Okie, a transplant, or a first-time visitor, slow down, do what you can to shut out the urban racket, and imagine a world that will forever be beyond our reach. In most ways that count, it is beyond our understanding.

Then take a ride on the Bricktown Canal and hop off the boat at the statuary near Bass Pro Shop. Maybe it will be a sunny spring day, and maybe there will be a lull in the traffic on I-40 so you can breathe deeply and let your imagination drift to another spring, when everything was new and nothing was impossible. As you look at those pioneers' faces, you might wonder where they came from and where they were headed in their pell-mell dash across the prairie. Were they aiming for a homestead, as seems likely, or a town lot? Were they there legally, or were they destined for a day in court?

You decide.

Notes

PREFACE

Epigraph. "Story of Oklahoma," *New York Sun*, February 17, 1889.

1. For a thorough treatment of the populist movement in Oklahoma, see Worth Robert Miller, *Oklahoma Populism: A History of the People's Party in the Oklahoma Territory* (Norman: University of Oklahoma Press, 1987).

CHAPTER ONE

Epigraph. "Our Land Policy—Its Evils and Their Remedy," Speech of Hon. George W. Julian of Indiana in the House of Representatives, March 6, 1868 (Washington, D.C.: Office of the Great Republic, 1868), folder 51, box 7, Sidney Clarke Collection, Research Division, Oklahoma Historical Society, Oklahoma City (cited hereafter as Clarke Collection).

1. David La Vere, *Contrary Neighbors: Southern Plains and Removed Indians in Indian Territory* (Norman: University of Oklahoma Press, 2000), 3–29, 54.

2. Robert V. Remini, *The Life of Andrew Jackson* (New York: HarperCollins, 2009), 212–19; "Story of Oklahoma."

3. Jack Larkin, *The Reshaping of Everyday Life, 1790–1840* (New York: HarperCollins, 1989), 5. For a similar estimate of Indian emigration, see Grant Foreman, ed., *A Traveler in Indian Territory: The Journal of Ethan Allen Hitchcock* (Norman: University of Oklahoma Press, 1996), 11.

4. As cited in Foreman, *Traveler in Indian Territory*, 144, 156–57; and La Vere, *Contrary Neighbors*, 74, 94–95.

5. Roger L. Nichols, *American Indians in U.S. History* (Norman: University of Oklahoma Press, 2003), 130.

6. For an overview of overland freighting on the Great Plains, see Henry Pickering Walker, *The Wagonmasters: High Plains Freighting from the Earliest Days of the Santa Fe Trail to 1880* (Norman: University of Oklahoma Press, 1966).

7. Angie Debo, *A History of the Indians of the United States* (Norman: University of Oklahoma Press, 1970), 10, 125.

8. Andrew K. Frank, "Seminole (tribe)," in *Encyclopedia of Oklahoma History and Culture*, accessed September 16, 2015, http://www.okhistory.org/publications/enc/entry.php?entry=SE011. See also Grant Foreman, *The Five Civilized*

Tribes: Cherokee, Chickasaw, Choctaw, Creek, Seminole (Norman: University of Oklahoma Press, 1934).

9. Debo, *History of the Indians of the United States*, 180–83.

10. Mary Jane Warde, *When the Wolf Came: The Civil War and the Indian Territory* (Fayetteville: University of Arkansas Press, 2013), 256–57.

11. Ibid., 257; Edwin C. McReynolds, *Oklahoma: A History of the Sooner State* (Norman: University of Oklahoma Press, 1954), 229–34.

12. Julian speech, "Our Land Policy."

13. Ibid., 3; H. W. Brands, *American Colossus: The Triumph of Capitalism, 1865–1900* (New York: Anchor Books, 2010), 238–42; Homestead Act, May 20, 1862, Avalon Project, Documents in Law, History and Diplomacy, Lillian Goldman Law Library, Yale Law School, http://avalon.law.yale.edu/19th_century/homestead_act.asp (hereafter cited as Avalon Project).

14. "Story of Oklahoma"; Arrell M. Gibson, "The Homesteader's Last Frontier," *American Scene* 4 (1962): 30.

15. McReynolds, *Oklahoma: A History*, 234; Gibson, "Homesteader's Last Frontier," 27.

16. Treaty between the United States of America and the Seminole Nation of Indians, concluded March 21, 1866, art. 3, p. 4, folder 20, box 4, T. H. Barrett Collection, Research Division, Oklahoma Historical Society, Oklahoma City (hereafter cited as Barrett Collection).

17. Ibid., art. 3, p. 5.

18. Ibid., art. 3, p. 4. See also "Story of Oklahoma." A succinct account of the Reconstruction Treaties of 1866 can be found in McReynolds, *Oklahoma: A History*, 229–34.

19. The congressional act incorporating the Atlantic and Pacific Railroad Company and section 2257 of the *Revised Statutes of the United States* are excerpted in S. N. Wood, *The Boomer: The True Story of Oklahoma, or the Beautiful Land* (Topeka: Bond and Neill, 1885), 31–34.

20. "Story of Oklahoma."

21. Ibid.

22. Patrick W. Riddleberger, "George W. Julian: Abolitionist Land Reformer," *Agricultural History* 29, no. 3 (July 1955), 108–10. Julian was elected as the Free Soil (FS) Party candidate to the U.S. House of Representatives in the election of 1848. Active in the elections of 1848 and 1852, the short-lived Free Soil Party opposed the expansion of slavery into the western territories, arguing that free men on free soil comprised a morally and economically superior system to slavery. Julian was one of the party's founders.

23. Julian speech, "Our Land Policy."

24. Larry O'Dell, "Clarke, Sidney," in *Encyclopedia of Oklahoma History and Culture*, accessed August 21, 2015, http://www.okhistory.org/publications/enc/entry.php?entry=CL005. Congressmen-at-large were elected to the U.S. House of Representatives by voters of an entire state rather than by those of a single congressional district.

25. Simon Winchester, *The Men Who United the States: America's Explorers, Inventors, Eccentrics, and Mavericks and the Creation of One Nation, Indivisible* (New York: HarperCollins, 2013), 6–17. See also Joseph J. Ellis, "The Domain," chap. 3 in *The Quartet: Orchestrating the Second American Revolution, 1783–1789* (New York: Knopf, 2015).

26. Julian speech, "Our Land Policy," 5.

27. Ibid., 7.

28. Ibid., 7–9.

29. Ibid., 9–15.

30. Ibid., 15–16.

CHAPTER TWO

Epigraph. Satanta quoted in Dee Brown, *The American West* (New York: Simon and Schuster, 1995), 112. For a more complete version of Satanta's speech, see Debo, *History of the Indians of the United States*, 219–20.

1. Henry D. and Frances T. McCallum, *The Wire That Fenced the West* (Norman: University of Oklahoma Press, 1965), 11.

2. Brown, *American West*, 110; S. C. Gwynne, *Empire of the Summer Moon: Quanah Parker and the Rise and Fall of the Comanches, the Most Powerful Indian Tribe in American History* (New York: Scribner, 2010), 225–26; Warde, *When the Wolf Came*, 284–86.

3. "The Indian Treaty," *New York Tribune*, November 2, 1867. For an intriguing account of reformers' efforts to inculcate Plains Indian tribes with Christian, middle-class values of labor and thrift, see Murray R. Wickett, *Contested Territory: Whites, Native Americans, and African Americans in Oklahoma, 1865–1907* (Baton Rouge: Louisiana State University Press, 2000), 15–28, 94–116.

4. Treaty with the Cheyenne and Arapaho, October 14, 1865, Avalon Project, http://avalon.law.yale.edu/19th_century/char65.asp; Treaty with the Apache, Cheyenne, and Arapaho, October 17, 1865, Avalon Project, http://avalon.law. yale.edu/19th_century/apchar65.asp; Treaty with the Kiowa, Comanche, and Apache; October 21, 1867, Avalon Project, http://avalon.law.yale.edu/19th_century/kicoap67.asp (all accessed January 12, 2016). For a summary of the various treaties between the U.S. government and Plains tribes that agreed to move to reservations in Indian Territory between 1865 and 1867, see La Vere, *Contrary Neighbors*, 183–84.

5. William H. Leckie, *The Buffalo Soldiers: A Narrative of the Negro Cavalry in the West* (Norman: University of Oklahoma Press, 1967), 3–18; Wickett, *Contested Territory*, 133–34.

6. Leckie, *Buffalo Soldiers*, 26–27.

7. John B. Carmichael, "Fort Supply, Indian Territory," *Oklahoma Magazine* 2, no. 1 (Spring–Summer 1997): 17–19; Susan Peterson, "Fort Supply: Isolated Outpost," in *Early Military Forts and Posts in Oklahoma*, ed. Odie B. Faulk, Kenny A. Franks, and Paul F. Lambert (Oklahoma City: Oklahoma Historical Society, 1978): 78–81.

8. McReynolds, *Oklahoma: A History*, 244–46; Brown, *American West*, 103.

9. Carmichael, "Fort Supply, Indian Territory," 20; Peterson, "Fort Supply," 78–80.

10. McReynolds, *Oklahoma: A History*, 245–46; Brown, *American West*, 106–9; "Important Indian News," *Emporia (Kans.) News*, December 4, 1868; "The Right Kind of a Peace Commission," *White Cloud (Kans.) Chief*, December 3, 1868.

11. Appropriations Act of March 3, 1871, 25 U.S. Code § 71, Legal Information Institute, Cornell University Law School, https://www.law.cornell.edu/uscode/text/25/71. See also Molly K. Varley, *Americans Recaptured: Progressive Era Memory of Frontier Captivity* (Norman: University of Oklahoma Press, 2014), 102–3; Roxanne Dunbar Ortiz, "Land Reform and Indian Survival in the United States," in *Land Reform, American Style*, ed. Charles C. Geisler and Frank J. Popper (Totowa, N.J.: Rowman and Allanheld, 1984), 152–53, 162.

12. Debo, *History of the Indians of the United States*, 294.

13. For an overview of the reform movement during Grant's administration, see Ari Hoogenboom, "Spoilsmen and Reformers: Civil Service Reform and Public Morality," in *The Gilded Age: A Reappraisal*, ed. H. Wayne Morgan (Syracuse: Syracuse University Press, 1963), 69–90.

14. Ulysses S. Grant, first inaugural address of Ulysses S. Grant, March 4, 1869, Avalon Project, http://avalon.law.yale.edu/19th_century/grant1.asp (accessed December 28, 2015).

15. "Civilization of the Indians," *(Washington, D.C.) Daily National Republican*, March 16, 1870; Jesse R. Townsend, "Grant's Peace Policy," *Sturm's Oklahoma Magazine* 11, no. 5 and 6 (January–February 1911): 5; "Civilization of the Indians"; Wickett, *Contested Territory*, 43.

16. Jesse R. Townsend, "Camp Supply 40 Years Ago," *Sturm's Oklahoma Magazine* 12, no. 1 (March 1911): 10.

17. "Canadian County in Making Long before Opening," *El Reno Daily Tribune*, April 22, 1934; Sandra W. LeVan, "The Quaker Agents at Darlington," *Chronicles of Oklahoma* 51, no. 1 (Spring 1973): 93–94.

18. Edward Everett Dale, *Cow Country* (Norman: University of Oklahoma Press, 1945), 11–13; idem, *The Range Cattle Industry: Ranching on the Great Plains from 1865 to 1925* (Norman: University of Oklahoma Press, 1960), 24; "Pioneers Earned Livelihood by Selling Bones of Buffalo," and "Fort Reno Established for Protection of Indian Agency," *El Reno (Okla.) Daily Tribune*, April 22, 1934; "Fort Offered Protection to Agency at Darlington," *El Reno Daily Tribune*, May 2, 1937.

19. Dale, *Range Cattle Industry*, 123.

20. For an example of discussions occasioned by President Grant's peace policy, see "The Presbyterian (Northern) General Assembly—Discussions on the Indian Question," *(Washington, D.C.) Evening Star*, May 30, 1870.

21. Untitled article, *Emporia News*, November 11, 1870.

22. Sheridan's letter was published in an untitled article, *Evening Star*, May 9, 1870.

23. For a thorough analysis of Grant's peace policy/Quaker peace policy, see Wayne A. White, "'This Faithfulness Destroyed Them': The Failure of Grant's Peace Policy among the Kiowas and Comanches," *Chronicles of Oklahoma* 93, no. 2 (Summer 2015): 182–99. See also Nichols, *American Indians in U.S. History*, 147–48.

24. Richard N. Ellis, "General John Pope and the Southern Plains Indians, 1875–1883," *Southwestern Historical Quarterly* 72, no. 2 (October 1968): 154.

25. "Murder of Buffalo Hunters in Indian Territory," and "Aggressive Indians to be Punished," *New York Tribune*, June 30, 1874; Leckie, *Buffalo Soldiers*, 113–40.

26. Michael D. Pierce, "Red River War (1874–1875)," in *Encyclopedia of Oklahoma History and Culture*, accessed August 24, 2015, http://www.okhistory.org/publications/enc/entry.php?entry=RE010; La Vere, *Contrary Neighbors*, 198.

27. "Fort Reno Was Launched as Important Post for Indians in 1874," *El Reno (Okla.) American*, May 4, 1939; Carolyn Barker, *Fort Reno: The Military Post* (El Reno, Okla.: privately printed, 1993), 1; "Fort Reno Established for Protection of Indian Agency," and "Fort Reno Indian Campaigns Helped in Settling Territory," *El Reno Daily Tribune*, June 16, 1975; "Fort Offered Protection to Agency at Darlington."

28. Stan Hoig, "Fort Reno," in *Encyclopedia of Oklahoma History and Culture*, accessed August 24, 2015, http://www.okhistory.org/publications/enc/entry.php?entry=FO037; "The Ride from Fort Sill to Leavenworth," *Leavenworth (Kans.) Weekly Times*, July 4, 1878.

29. Walker, *Wagonmasters*, 129.

30. "Stories of Freighters: Life on the Santa Fe Trail in Early Days," unsourced and undated newspaper article, Scrapbook, May 6–November 10, 1897, box 36, vol. 1, 21, Frederick Samuel Barde Collection, 1890–1916, Research Division, Oklahoma Historical Society, Oklahoma City (hereafter cited as Barde Collection).

31. Kathlyn Baldwin, *The 89ers: Oklahoma Land Rush of 1889* (Oklahoma City: Western Heritage Books, 1981), 8. See also "The Bull-Dog of the Treasury," *(Washington, D.C.) National Republican*, January 1, 1869.

32. Untitled article, *Emporia News*, June 3, 1870.

33. Austin B. Griggs, unpublished paper presented to the Guthrie Rotary Club, February 20, 1939, folder 1, box 1, Santa Fe Railroad Collection, Research Division, Oklahoma Historical Society, Oklahoma City (hereafter cited as Santa Fe Railroad Collection). Griggs was valuation engineer for the Atchison, Topeka and Santa Fe Railway and a student of railroad history.

34. Delano's report and excerpts are cited in "The Indian Policy," *Emporia News*, December 15, 1871.

35. "Oklahoma, Wichita," *Wichita City Eagle*, March 26, 1874.

36. "Oklahoma," *Leavenworth Weekly Times*, January 21, 1875; "Oklahoma," *Wichita City Eagle*, December 24, 1874.

37. "Oklahoma," *Leavenworth Weekly Times*, January 21, 1875.

38. La Vere, *Contrary Neighbors*, 91–126, 202–3.

39. Thomas Burnell Colbert, "Boudinot, Elias Cornelius (1835–1890)," in *Encyclopedia of Oklahoma History and Culture*, accessed August 24, 2015, http://digital.library. okstate.edu/encyclopedia/entries/B/BO026.html; Debo, *History of the Indians of the United States*, 128, 296–97; Gibson, "Homesteader's Last Frontier," 28.

40. "Story of Oklahoma."

41. Augustus Albert to E. C. Boudinot, March 25, 1879, folder 1, box 2, Boomer Literature Collection, Western History Collections, University of Oklahoma Libraries, Norman (hereafter cited as WHC Boomer Literature Collection).

42. "Story of Oklahoma." The map was printed at government expense as Senate Executive Document No. 20 and was authorized by the first session of the Forty-Sixth Congress (1879–81).

43. E. C. Boudinot to Augustus Albert, March 31, 1879, folder 1, box 2, WHC Boomer Literature Collection. Boudinot's letter is reproduced in "Oklahoma," *Emporia News*, April 25, 1879.

44. Boudinot to Albert, March 31, 1879. See also Treaty between the United States of America and the Seminole Nation of Indians, concluded March 21, 1866, art. 3, p. 4, Barrett Collection. The terms of Indian treaties as they pertained to central Indian Territory remained a hot topic of debate throughout the 1880s as the boomer movement gained traction, and newspapers routinely published synopses of them. See "Payne's Pretexts," *(Vinita, Cherokee Nation, I.T.) Indian Chieftain*, May 22, 1884; "Intruders on Indian Lands," *Evening Star*, August 6, 1884.

45. Debo, *History of the Indians of the United States*, 266.

46. *New York Tribune* article excerpted in "The Indian and the Ballot," *(Tahlequah, Cherokee Nation, I.T.) Cherokee Advocate*, July 30, 1879.

47. "Oklahoma," *Emporia News*, April 25, 1879.

48. *Topeka Commonwealth* and McNeal quoted in Carl Coke Rister, *Land Hunger: David L. Payne and the Oklahoma Boomers* (New York: Arno Press, 1975), 45. See also Gibson, "Homesteader's Last Frontier," 28. McNeal's and others' letters are quoted at length in the *New York Sun's* detailed history of the boomer movement under the headline, "Story of Oklahoma," cited liberally in this work.

49. "Oklahoma," *Emporia News*, April 25, 1879; Stan Hoig, "The Boomer Movement," in *Encyclopedia of Oklahoma History and Culture*, accessed August 7, 2015, http://www.okhistory.org/publications/enc/entry.php?entryname=BOOMER%20MOVEMENT.

50. "Oklahoma," *Emporia News*, April 25, 1879.

51. "The Cabinet Meeting Yesterday," *National Republican*, April 26, 1879. Schurz's letter to the commissioner of Indian Affairs is reproduced herein in its entirety. The only exception to Secretary Schurz's ban was Old Greer County in present-day southwestern Oklahoma, then claimed by Texas. For a brief history of Old Greer County, see Michael J. Hightower, "The Businessman's Frontier: C. C. Hightower, Commerce, and Old Greer County, 1891–1903," *Chronicles of Oklahoma* 86, no. 1 (Spring 2008): 20.

52. Untitled articles, *Evening Star*, April 26, 28, 1879; Rister, *Land Hunger*, 47.

53. "A Loud Call for the Fool-Killer," *Leavenworth Weekly Times*, May 8, 1879.

54. James M. McPherson, *Battle Cry of Freedom: The Civil War Era* (New York: Ballantine, 1988), 525.

55. "A Loud Call for the Fool-Killer."

56. Ibid.

57. "Still-Born," and "What Policy Should Be Pursued," *Leavenworth Weekly Times*, June 12, 1879.

58. Untitled article, *Dodge City (Kans.) Times*, December 27, 1879.

59. Griggs, unpublished paper presented to the Guthrie Rotary Club, February 20, 1939. See also Berlin B. Chapman, "Oklahoma City, from Public Land to Private Property: Surveying the Townsite," pt. 1, *Chronicles of Oklahoma* 37, no. 2 (Summer 1959): 212.

60. Untitled article, *Dodge City Times*, December 27, 1879.

61. Hoig, "Boomer Movement."

CHAPTER THREE

Epigraph. "On to Oklahoma!" *Wichita City Eagle*, July 22, 1880.

1. Rister, *Land Hunger*, 5. For a complete biography of one of the West's most colorful and least known characters, see Stan Hoig, *David L. Payne: The Oklahoma Boomer* (Oklahoma City: Western Heritage Books, 1980).

2. Rister, *Land Hunger*, 1–10; A. P. Jackson and E. C. Cole, *Oklahoma! Politically and Topographically Described—History and Guide to the Indian Territory* (Kansas City, Mo.: Ramsey, Millett and Hudson, 1885), 7–18. Jackson and Cole's book, published just a year after Payne's death in November 1884, is excerpted in Dan W. Peery, "Captain David L. Payne," *Chronicles of Oklahoma* 13, no. 4 (December 1935): 438–56. See also "Story of Oklahoma."

3. Jackson and Cole, *Oklahoma!* 10–11; Rister, *Land Hunger*, 11–12.

4. Jackson and Cole, *Oklahoma!* 9.

5. Rister, *Land Hunger*, 11–23; Hoig, *David L. Payne*, 10–20.

6. For Payne's campaign with Custer and the Seventh Cavalry, see Hoig, *David L. Payne*, 21–31.

7. "Oklahoma Payne," *Oklahoma War Chief*, January 19, 1883; untitled article, *Emporia News*, July 29, 1870; Rister, *Land Hunger*, 24–27.

8. Rister, *Land Hunger*, 28–32; Sidney Clarke, "At the Grave of Capt. D. L. Payne: An Address Delivered on Decoration Day, 1885," in 89ers Association, *Oklahoma: The Beautiful Land* (Oklahoma City: Times-Journal Publishing, 1943), 29–30.

9. D. L. Payne appointment as employé in the Office of Sergeant at Arms as Spl. Policeman of the House of Representatives of the United States, dated and signed July 1, 1877, item 2, folder 5, box 1, David Payne Papers, 1877–1884, Research Division, Oklahoma Historical Society, Oklahoma City (hereafter cited as Payne Papers).

10. Jackson and Cole, *Oklahoma!* 9–10; Fred E. Sutton, a Payne Boomer, "April 22, 1889–April 22, 1929," in 89ers Association, *Oklahoma: The Beautiful Land*, 17;

"Story of Oklahoma"; Stan Hoig, "The Old Payne Trail and the Boomer Colony Sites," *Chronicles of Oklahoma* 58, no. 2 (Summer 1980): 159n9.

11. "Story of Oklahoma"; Chapman, "Oklahoma City, from Public Land to Private Property," pt. 1, 212.

12. Charles Francis Colcord, *Autobiography of Charles Francis Colcord, 1859–1934* (Tulsa: privately printed, 1970), 98–99.

13. "Story of Oklahoma."

14. Captain George B. Jenness, "Fight of Payne and the Boomers," *Sturm's Oklahoma Magazine* 8, no. 2 (April 1909): 25; Hoig, *David L. Payne: The Oklahoma Boomer*, 13–14.

15. "Story of Oklahoma."

16. Rister, *Land Hunger*, 51–52.

17. "Story of Oklahoma." Rumors circulated in the 1880s that the original shareholders in the Oklahoma Town Company lost money from their investments. Samples of Payne's Oklahoma Colony certificates are found in items 1, 5, and 6, folder 18, box 2, Payne Papers.

18. Hoig, *David L. Payne*, 67–70. For President Hayes's proclamation in February 1880 warning settlers and squatters to stay out of Indian Territory, see untitled article, *Evening Star*, February 12, 1880.

19. "Story of Oklahoma"; Hoig, *David L. Payne*, 70–71.

20. Hoig, *David L. Payne*, x, 72–73; Hoig, "Old Payne Trail," 151–52, 158n2; Eugene Couch, interview by Harry M. Dreyer, April 29, 1937, vol. 21, 106–10, Indian-Pioneer Papers, Western History Collections, University of Oklahoma, Norman (http://digital.libraries.ou.edu/whc/pioneer/, hereafter cited as IPP online). The Indian-Pioneer Papers are also available on microfilm. See Indian-Pioneer Papers, Research Division, Oklahoma Historical Society, Oklahoma City (hereafter cited as IPP microfilm). Hoig's chronology of boomer intrusions is on display at the Oklahoma Territorial Museum in Guthrie. See Chronology of Boomer Intrusions, Oklahoma Territorial Museum, Guthrie, Oklahoma.

21. Neil R. Johnson, *The Chickasaw Rancher*, rev. ed., ed. C. Neil Kingsley (Boulder: University Press of Colorado, 2001), 190; Hoig, "Old Payne Trail," 153–54, 159n8; Lewis Cass Wantland, interview by Mildred B. McFarland, March 1, 1938, vol. 95, 99–105, IPP online.

22. Hoig, "Old Payne Trail," 153–54.

23. "Story of Oklahoma."

24. Payne's letter excerpted in Rister, *Land Hunger*, 59.

25. Ibid., 60–64; Hoig, *David L. Payne*, 78.

26. "Story of Oklahoma"; untitled article, *Dodge City Times*, May 22, 1880.

27. L. Edward Carter, *The Story of Oklahoma Newspapers* (Oklahoma City: Western Heritage Books, 1984), 3–14.

28. Rister, *Land Hunger*, 65–66; Warde, *When the Wolf Came*, 301–2; "Story of Oklahoma."

29. "City and County News," *Wichita City Eagle*, July 1, 1880.

30. Ray Asplin, "A History of Council Grove in Oklahoma," *Chronicles of Oklahoma* 45, no. 4 (Winter 1967–68): 434–40; William H. Osburn, "A Tribute to Captain D. L. Payne by his Private Secretary, W. H. Osburn, also Colony Secretary during the Fourth Raid," pt. 1, *Chronicles of Oklahoma* 7, no. 3 (September 1929): 275.

31. Hoig, *David L. Payne*, x; Rister, *Land Hunger*, 67–68; "On to Oklahoma," *Emporia News*, July 16, 1880.

32. "On to Oklahoma!"; "Payne Captured and at Ft. Reno," *Cherokee Advocate*, May 26, 1880; Rister, *Land Hunger*, 72–73.

33. "The Indian Territory Trials," *Cherokee Advocate*, September 8, 1880.

34. "On to Oklahoma!"; "What Shall Be Done with Payne?" *Emporia News*, July 23, 1880.

35. "On to Oklahoma!"

36. The President of the United States of America to the Marshal of the Western District of Arkansas, Court Summons for D. L. Payne, August 13, 1880, item 1, folder 13, box 2, Payne Papers.

37. Rister, *Land Hunger*, 71–73.

38. "Story of Oklahoma."

39. D. W. Bushyhead to Samuel Checote, September 10, 1880, doc # 30765, box 23, Creek Nation Foreign Relations Collection (D. L. Payne, 1880–1881), Research Division, Oklahoma Historical Society, Oklahoma City (hereafter cited as Creek Nation Foreign Relations Collection). See also microfilm roll CRN 37–2.

40. "Payne's Project," *Emporia News*, August 13, 1880.

41. Carter, *Story of Oklahoma Newspapers*, 14.

42. D. L. Payne to the editor of the *Indian Journal*, August 20, 1880, item 4, folder 8, box 1, Payne Papers.

43. Rister, *Land Hunger*, 74; untitled article, *Iola (Kans.) Register*, September 10, 1880; untitled article, *Dodge City Times*, September 25, 1880; "Oklahoma," *Wichita City Eagle*, November 4, 1880.

44. "Is That So?" *Wichita City Eagle*, November 11, 1880; Rister, *Land Hunger*, 74–75; untitled article, *Wichita City Eagle*, November 18, 1880.

45. D. W. Bushyhead to Samuel Checote, October 5, 1880, doc. no. 30767, box 23, Creek Nation Foreign Relations Collection. See also microfilm roll CRN 37–2.

46. Actions of the International Convention held at Eufaula, Creek Nation, I.T., October 20, 1880, doc. no. 30768, box 23, Creek Nation Foreign Relations Collection. See also microfilm roll CRN 37–2.

47. Untitled article, *Cherokee Advocate*, October 27, 1880.

48. "The Oklahoma Question," *Wichita City Eagle*, December 2, 1880. See also "The Oklahoma Question," *Cherokee Advocate*, December 22, 1880.

49. Walter Prescott Webb, *The Great Plains* (Boston: Ginn, 1931), 273–80.

50. For a fascinating look into the tramp scare and rise of social Darwinism in the 1870s and early 1880s, see Michael A. Bellesiles, "The Terror of Poverty," chap. 4 in *1877: America's Year of Living Violently* (New York: New Press, 2010).

51. Meeting of the Payne's Oklahoma Colony, Wichita, Kansas, November 16, 1880, item 5, folder 12, box 2, Payne Papers.
52. "Oklahoma," (*Darlington Indian Agency, I.T.*) *Cheyenne Transporter*, November 26, 1880; Hoig, *David L. Payne*, 99–100.
53. "Miscellaneous," *Iola Register*, December 17, 1880.
54. "The Oklahoma Scheme," *Wichita City Eagle*, December 16, 1880.
55. Untitled article, "On to Oklahoma," *Emporia News*, December 17, 1880.
56. Rister, *Land Hunger*, 80–83.
57. "Oklahoma Scheme."
58. "Story of Oklahoma."
59. G. W. Grayson to the National Council of the Muskogee Nation, in General Convention Assembled, October 1881, doc # 30780, box 23, Creek Nation Foreign Relations Collection. See also microfilm roll CRN 37–2; Rister, *Land Hunger*, 91.
60. Rister, *Land Hunger*, 91–92.
61. "The Oklahoma Boomers," *Cherokee Advocate*, December 22, 1880.
62. "The Oklahoma Boom," *Emporia News*, December 24, 1880; Rister, *Land Hunger*, 85–88.
63. Carter, *Story of Oklahoma Newspapers*, 16.
64. "Boomers," *Cheyenne Transporter*, November 26, 1880.
65. "Oklahoma Boom"; Rister, *Land Hunger*, 85–88.
66. Untitled article, *Weekly (Troy) Kansas Chief*, December 30, 1880.

CHAPTER FOUR

Epigraph. Jackson and Cole, *Oklahoma!* 54.
1. Two notable memoirs survive as riveting accounts of the cowboy era: E. C. "Teddy Blue" Abbott and Helena Huntington Smith, *We Pointed Them North: Reminiscences of a Cow Puncher* (New York: Farrar and Rinehart, 1939); and Andy Adams, *The Log of a Cowboy: A Narrative of the Old Trail Days*, illustrated by E. Boyd Smith (Boston: Houghton, Mifflin, 1903).
2. Julian speech, "Our Land Policy."
3. Johnson, *Chickasaw Rancher*, 134.
4. McReynolds, *Oklahoma: A History*, 252; Dale, *Range Cattle Industry*, 4–5; Dale, *Cow Country*, 24–25; Webb, *Great Plains*, 207–15.
5. Joanne S. Liu, *Barbed Wire: The Fence That Changed the West* (Missoula, Mont.: Mountain Press, 2009), 6–7, 23–25; McCallum, *Wire That Fenced the West*, 12, 205.
6. McCallum, *Wire That Fenced the West*, 41, 81, 98–111 (Gates quoted on 71). See also Liu, *Barbed Wire*, 44–51, 62–71; Webb, *Great Plains*, 295–318.
7. Edward Everett Dale, "The Cherokee Strip Live Stock Association," *Chronicles of Oklahoma* 5, no. 1 (March 1927): 61; Webb, *Great Plains*, 216–17.
8. Dale, *Range Cattle Industry*, 47–49.
9. "Important to Stock Raisers," *Emporia News*, June 21, 1867.

10. Jimmy M. Skaggs, "Cattle Trails in Oklahoma," in *Ranch and Range in Oklahoma*, ed. Jimmy M. Skaggs (Oklahoma City: Oklahoma Historical Society, 1978), 7–9; Gary Kraisinger and Margaret Kraisinger, "The Early Chisholm Trail to Abilene, Kansas, 1867–71," *Chronicles of Oklahoma* 93, no. 2 (Summer 2015): 150–52; "Spanish Fever," *Emporia News*, January 19, 1867.

11. Dale, *Range Cattle Industry*, 38; Dale, *Cow Country*, 31–32.

12. Untitled article, *Emporia News*, September 20, 1867; Byron Price, "Prairie Policemen: The United States Army's Relationship to the Cattle Industry in Indian Territory, 1866–1893," in Skaggs, *Ranch and Range*, 46.

13. Daniel J. Boorstin, *The Americans: The Democratic Experience* (New York: Random House, 1974), 14–17; Dale, *Range Cattle Industry*, 41; Webb, *Great Plains*, 216–27.

14. Brands, *American Colossus*, 207–8; Skaggs, "Cattle Trails in Oklahoma," 7; Price, "Prairie Policemen," 46; Webb, *Great Plains*, 222–23. Estimates vary widely on the number of cattle that made the trek from Texas to the Kansas cowtowns. Skaggs puts the total at 15 million, and Price uses a more conservative estimate of 10 million. Webb cites the U.S. census of 1880 to provide a much lower—and far more precise—number of 4,223,497 cattle driven north from Texas between 1866 and 1880.

15. Stan Hoig, "Jesse Chisholm: Peace-Maker, Trader, Forgotten Frontiersman," *Chronicles of Oklahoma* 66, no. 4 (Winter 1988): 352–57. For an overview of Jesse Chisholm's role in blazing Oklahoma's trail of economic development, see Michael J. Hightower, *Banking in Oklahoma Before Statehood* (Norman: University of Oklahoma Press, 2013), 91–95.

16. Stan Hoig, "Chisholm, Jesse (ca. 1805–1868)," in *Encyclopedia of Oklahoma History and Culture*, accessed August 21, 2015, http://www.okhistory.org/publications/enc/entry.php?entry=CH067; Asplin, "History of Council Grove," 434–40.

17. Hoig, "Jesse Chisholm," 351, 370; Asplin, "History of Council Grove," 442.

18. H. S. Tennant, "Two Cattle Trails," *Chronicles of Oklahoma* 14, no. 1 (March 1936): 113. For the establishment of Fort Arbuckle, see Johnson, *Chickasaw Rancher*, 16.

19. Skaggs, "Cattle Trails in Oklahoma," 9. See also Skaggs, *Ranch and Range*, foldout map. For a thorough study of the lesser-known Arbuckle Trail and its relationship to the Chisholm Trail, see Kraisinger and Kraisinger, "Early Chisholm Trail," 150–81.

20. Tennant, "Two Cattle Trails," 121. Webb likened cattle trails through Oklahoma to "a short section of rope with both ends badly frayed." See Webb, *Great Plains*, 262.

21. Dale, *Range Cattle Industry*, 43. Dale's grand total for the entire era, 1866–85, is 5,421,132, far fewer than estimates supplied by Skaggs (15 million) and Price (10 million), and closer to precise figures supplied by Webb (4,223,497).

22. C. Neil Kingsley, "Johnson, Montford T.," in *Encyclopedia of Oklahoma History and Culture*, accessed May 2, 2016, http://www.okhistory.org/publications/enc/entry.php?entry=JO012.

23. Johnson, *Chickasaw Rancher*, 38.

24. Ibid., 57–58.

25. For a sketch of Silver City and a firsthand account of its brief history, see J. C. Malcolm, "Notes on Silver City by J. C. Malcolm," *Chronicles of Oklahoma* 36, no. 2 (Summer 1958): 210–13.

26. Johnson, *Chickasaw Rancher*, 83; Asplin, "History of Council Grove," 443.

27. Osburn, "Tribute to Captain D. L. Payne," pt. 1, 275.

28. Johnson, *Chickasaw Rancher*, 144, 190; Asplin, "History of Council Grove," 450. The Daughters of the American Revolution erected the Council Grove historical marker in 1941.

29. Patricia Lester, "William J. McClure and the McClure Ranch," *Chronicles of Oklahoma* 58, no. 3 (Fall 1980): 296–98.

30. William J. McClure, "The First Legal Settler in Oklahoma City," in 89ers Association, *Oklahoma: The Beautiful Land*, 72–77.

31. Untitled news brief; "Protest of the Choctaw Chief," *Indian Journal*, February 6, 1878.

32. "Gov. Overton and the Cattle Men," *Indian Journal*, January 18, 1881.

33. Price, "Prairie Policemen," 51–54.

34. Dale, *Cow Country*, 13–14.

35. Price, "Prairie Policemen," 51–54.

36. Dale, *Range Cattle Industry*, 123.

37. Donald J. Berthrong, "Cattlemen on the Cheyenne and Arapaho Reservation, 1883–1885," *Arizona and the West* 13, no. 1 (Spring 1971): 6.

38. For an exhaustive analysis of one ranch's disappointing returns on investment as it transitioned from the chaos of the 1880s to increasingly accurate reporting, improved management, and financial stability at the turn of the twentieth century, see Mary Jo Billiot, Randy McFerrin, and Douglas Wills, "Returns in the Western Range Cattle Industry: Reconstructing the Financial History of the Matador Land and Cattle Company, 1883–1920," *Journal of the Economic and Business History Society* 35, no. 2 (2017), 1–25.

39. Dale, *Range Cattle Industry*, 81–83.

40. Jimmy Snodgrass, "Cherokee Strip Live Stock Association," in *Encyclopedia of Oklahoma History and Culture*, accessed August 21, 2015, http://www.okhistory.org/publications/enc/entry.php?entry=CH025; William W. Savage Jr., "Of Cattle and Corporations: The Rise, Progress, and Termination of the Cherokee Strip Live Stock Association," *Chronicles of Oklahoma* 71, no. 2 (Summer 1993): 138–53.

41. Untitled article, *Evening Star*, July 2, 1884.

42. Dale, *Range Cattle Industry*, 84–89.

43. Agent quoted in H. Craig Miner, "The Dream of a Native Cattle Industry in Indian Territory," in Skaggs, *Ranch and Range*, 27.

44. William W. Savage Jr., "The Rock Falls Raid: An Analysis of the Documentary Evidence," *Chronicles of Oklahoma* 49, no. 1 (Spring 1971): 75.

45. Price, "Prairie Policemen," 55–56.

46. Ibid.

47. Dyer quoted in Miner, "Dream of a Native Cattle Industry," 25.

48. Untitled article, *Cheyenne Transporter*, December 26, 1882.

49. "Official Brevities," *National Republican*, August 14, 1884.

50. "Cattle-Growers Convention," *Indian Chieftain*, November 20, 1884.

51. Pope quoted in Ellis, "General John Pope and the Southern Plains Indians," 165.

52. Shelli Rae Freeman, "Miles, John DeBras (1832–1926)," in *Encyclopedia of Oklahoma History and Culture*, accessed August 21, 2015, http://www.okhistory. org/publications/enc/entry.php?entry=MI019; Berthrong, "Cattlemen on the Cheyenne and Arapaho Reservation, 1883–1885," 6–7; Price, "Prairie Policemen," 55.

53. "Notice to Stockmen!" *Cheyenne Transporter*, August 10, 1882.

54. Berthrong, "Cattlemen on the Cheyenne and Arapaho Reservation, 1883–1885," 10.

55. "The Territory Cattle Question," *Barbour County (Kans.) Index*, January 12, 1883.

56. Campbell quoted in McCallum, *Wire That Fenced the West*, 168.

57. Ibid., 12, 190.

58. Untitled article, *Dodge City Times*, January 11, 1883.

59. "A Congress Cow Pasture," *New York Sun*, August 31, 1884.

60. Dale, *Range Cattle Industry*, 89.

61. Christopher Ketcham, "The Great Republican Land Heist: Clive Bundy and the Politicians Who Are Plundering the West," *Harpers* 330, no. 1977 (February 2015): 25.

62. McCallum, *Wire That Fenced the West*, 175.

63. Jackson and Cole, *Oklahoma!* 48–49.

64. Ibid., 54.

CHAPTER FIVE

Epigraph. "Local Items," *Cheyenne Transporter*, February 10, 1881.

1. Hoig, *David L. Payne*, x; Savage, "Rock Falls Raid," 76; Johnson, *Chickasaw Rancher*, 172.

2. "Story of Oklahoma."

3. "The Oklahoma Boys," *Wichita City Eagle*, January 6, 1881.

4. Ibid.; "The Oklahoma Boomers Turned Government Freighters," *Cherokee Advocate*, January 26, 1881.

5. Untitled article, *Cheyenne Transporter*, January 10, 1881; untitled article, *Emporia News*, January 21, 1881.

6. United States v. D. L. Payne, District Court of the United States for the Western District of Arkansas, May session, 1881, doc # 30778, box 23, Creek Nation Foreign Relations Collection. See also microfilm roll CRN 37–2.

7. Rister, *Land Hunger*, 94; "The Trial of Payne," *Cherokee Advocate*, March 16, 1881. This article was published earlier in the *Indian Journal*.

8. "What G. W. Stidham Thinks of Vest's Oklahoma Bill," *Indian Journal*, January 29, 1880; Warde, *When the Wolf Came*, 267.

9. "Trial of Payne."

10. S. K. Kirkwood to Samuel Checote, April 23, 1881, doc # 30775, box 23, Creek Nation Foreign Relations Collection.

11. United States v. Payne; "Decision of District Judge I. C. Parker," *Cherokee Advocate*, June 1, 1881. See also "Judge Parker's Decision on the Oklahoma Invasion," *Cheyenne Transporter*, May 25, 1881.

12. "The Boomers in Council," *Wichita City Eagle*, May 5, 1881; Hoig, "Boomer Movement."

13. "Decline of the Boom," *Cheyenne Transporter*, May 10, 1881.

14. Grayson to the National Council of the Muskogee Nation, October 1881, doc # 30780, box 23, Creek Nation Foreign Relations Collection.

15. Kenneth Marvin Hamilton, *Black Towns and Profit: Promotion and Development in the Trans-Appalachian West, 1877–1915* (Urbana: University of Illinois Press, 1991), 99; "Decline of the Boom."

16. "Decline of the Boom." The General Land Office was an independent agency operating under the purview of the U.S. government, and it was responsible for public domain land. It was created in 1812 and merged with the U.S. Grazing Service in 1946 to become the Bureau of Land Management. The commissioner of the General Land Office was appointed by the president and confirmed by the Senate.

17. "Denison," *Dallas Weekly Herald*, July 7, 1881; Hoig, "Old Payne Trail," 155; Hoig, *David L. Payne*, x; "Late News Items," *Iola Register*, September 9, 1881.

18. "Editorial Notes," *(Austin) Weekly Democratic Statesman*, September 15, 1881.

19. "Denison," *Dallas Daily Herald*, November 30, 1881; Hoig, "Old Payne Trail," 155; Hoig, *David L. Payne*, x.

20. William H. Osburn, "Tribute to Capt. D. L. Payne," pt. 2, *Chronicles of Oklahoma* 7, no. 4 (December 1929): 378–79. Osburn had been elected as the colony's secretary at an organizational meeting in Wichita in October 1881. Yet he did not learn of his good fortune until mail was delivered from Denison on November 28, 1881.

21. Untitled article, *Dallas Daily Herald*, December 4, 1881; "Texas Facts and Fancies," *Weekly Democratic Statesman*, December 15, 1881.

22. "Editorial Notes," *Butler (Mo.) Weekly Times*, January 4, 1882.

23. Hoig, "Old Payne Trail," 155; Hoig, *David L. Payne*, x.

24. "Indian Lands," *Cheyenne Transporter*, April 10, 1882. The *Cheyenne Transporter* mistakenly dated the act to June 30, 1854. See Rister, *Land Hunger*, 94.

25. "Oklahoma Tactics," *Cheyenne Transporter*, April 10, 1882.

26. The *Leavenworth Weekly Times*' story was published in "A Talk with General Pope in Regard to It," *Weekly Kansas Chief*, May 25, 1882.

27. "The Oklahoma Boom," *Weekly Kansas Chief*, May 25, 1882.

28. "Boomed Boomers," *Cheyenne Transporter*, June 10, 1882.

29. Untitled articles, *Evening Star*, July 7, 14, 1882; Hoig, "Old Payne Trail," 156; Hoig, *David L. Payne*, x; W. H. Osburn, "Tribute to Captain D. L. Payne," pt. 3, *Chronicles of Oklahoma* 8, no. 1 (March 1930): 20.

30. "Payne and Gould," *Wichita City Eagle*, September 28, 1882.

31. "Oklahoma," *Cherokee Advocate*, January 27, 1882.

32. Untitled article, *Cheyenne Transporter*, November 25, 1882; "Railroad Council," *Cheyenne Transporter*, September 26, 1882.

33. "Payne and Gould."

34. "The Indian Territory," *New York Sun*, February 23, 1883.

35. "Major George M. Randall," *Cheyenne Transporter*, August 25, 1882; Mrs. N. L. Phillips, "Fort Reno," unpublished manuscript, August 3, 1938, Fort Reno History, Vertical Files, Research Division, Oklahoma Historical Society, Oklahoma City.

36. "Oklahoma Payne in Prison," *Cherokee Advocate*, September 8, 1882.

37. Untitled articles, *Oklahoma War Chief*, January 19, 1883. See also Linda D. Wilson, "*Oklahoma War Chief*," in *Encyclopedia of Oklahoma History and Culture*, accessed August 21, 2015, http://www.okhistory.org/publications/enc/entry. php?entry=OK087; and Carter, *Story of Oklahoma Newspapers*, 16–17.

38. "Answers to Inquiries," *Oklahoma War Chief*, January 19, 1883.

39. "Gen. Pope's Idea," *Oklahoma War Chief*, January 19, 1883.

40. "Capt. Payne in the Courts," *Oklahoma War Chief*, January 19, 1883.

41. Michael W. Lovegrove, "Couch, William Lewis (1850–1890)," in *Encyclopedia of Oklahoma History and Culture*, accessed August 25, 2015, http://www.okhistory. org/publications/enc/entry.php?entry=CO070.

42. "The Ewing Town Company," *Oklahoma War Chief*, January 26, 1883.

43. *Augusta (Kans.) Republican* cited in "A Cattle Monopoly," *Oklahoma War Chief*, February 2, 1883.

44. Hoig, *David L. Payne*, x.

45. "Beware of Him!" *New York Sun*, February 3, 1883.

46. Eugene Couch, interview by Mildred B. McFarland, October 27, 1937, vol. 21, 112–15, IPP online.

47. David Payne Diary, February 1–20, 1883, folder 18, box 1, Payne Papers.

48. Ibid.

49. C. P. Wickmiller, "C. P. Wickmiller's Recollections of David L. Payne as Official Photographer in the Expedition of 1883," address delivered at the annual meeting of the Oklahoma Historical Society, *Chronicles of Oklahoma* 14, no. 2 (June 1936): 242. In the third installment of his published tribute to Payne, W. H. Osburn mentions several of Wickmiller's photos by name, including *Captain Payne Crossing the Line Going to Oklahoma*, *Bridging the Deep Fork*, *Crossing from the Deep Fork to the Canadian*, *Camp Alice*, *Payne's Last Camp*, and *Payne Crossing the Line Going Home*. See Osburn, "Tribute to Captain D. L. Payne," pt. 3, 23–26.

50. "The Invasion of Oklahoma," *New York Tribune*, February 7, 1883. Robert Todd Lincoln, who served under Presidents James A. Garfield and Chester A. Arthur, was the first son of Abraham and Mary Todd Lincoln.

51. Osburn, "Tribute to Captain D. L. Payne," pt. 3, 24; David Payne Diary, February 1–20, 1883.

52. "March of the Five Hundred," *Oklahoma War Chief*, March 9, 1883; Osburn, "Tribute to Captain D. L. Payne," pt. 3, 24–25; "C. P. Wickmiller's Recollections," 242–43.

53. David Payne Diary, February 1–20, 1883; "C. P. Wickmiller's Recollections," 243.

54. "C. P. Wickmiller's Recollections," 243.

55. David Payne Diary, February 1–20, 1883.

56. "Oklahoma Notes," *Cheyenne Transporter*, February 26, 1883.

57. "The Oklahoma Lands," *Oklahoma War Chief*, March 2, 1883.

58. Ibid. Turner, whose frontier thesis has long since been discredited by more sophisticated theories and research methodologies, introduced his frontier thesis at the American Historical Association's meeting in Chicago in 1893. See Frederick Jackson Turner, *The Frontier in American History* (Franklin Center, Penn.: Franklin Library, 1977). See also Richard Hofstadter and Seymour Martin Lipset, eds., *Turner and the Sociology of the Frontier* (New York: Basic Books, 1968); Wilbur R. Jacobs, *On Turner's Trail: 100 Years of Writing Western History* (Lawrence: University Press of Kansas, 1994).

59. "Oklahoma Lands."

60. Untitled article, *Oklahoma War Chief*, March 2, 1883.

61. "March of the Five Hundred," *Oklahoma War Chief*, March 2 and 9, 1883.

62. "Oklahoma," *Oklahoma War Chief*, March 2, 1883.

63. Couch quoted in "March of the Five Hundred"; "The Gallant Five Hundred," *Oklahoma War Chief*, March 9, 1883.

64. "Oklahoma Again," *Oklahoma War Chief*, March 9, 1883; Rister, *Land Hunger*, 121; Hoig, *David L. Payne*, 143, 151–52.

65. "Oklahoma Again."

66. Untitled article, *New York Sun*, June 30, 1883; "The Indian Territory," ibid., February 23, 1883.

67. "Oklahoma Payne Again," *Emporia (Kans.) Weekly News*, July 5, 1883.

68. Hoig, *David L. Payne*, x.

69. "Obliged to Capitulate," *Cheyenne Transporter*, August 28, 1883; Hoig, "Old Payne Trail," 157.

70. W. L. C. to Capt. [Payne], August 22, 1883, folder 8, box 6, Edna Mae Couch Collection, Research Division, Oklahoma Historical Society, Oklahoma City (hereafter cited as Edna Mae Couch Collection).

71. W. L. Couch to Capt. D. L. Payne, August 27, 1883, folder 8, box 6, Edna Mae Couch Collection.

72. "Obliged to Capitulate."

73. Untitled article, *Indian Chieftain*, September 21, 1883.

74. "The Invasion of Oklahoma," *New York Tribune*, October 20, 1883; untitled article, *San Antonio Light*, October 20, 1883.

75. "Prattling Payne," *Emporia Weekly News*, October 25, 1883.

76. Colcord, *Autobiography*, 102.

77. "The Indian Beef Issue," *Cheyenne Transporter*, February 10, 1883; "Cattlemen in Oklahoma," *Iola Register*, February 13, 1885.

CHAPTER SIX

Epigraph. "Wichita Branch Colony," *Oklahoma War-Chief*, December 4, 1884.

1. "Oklahoma to Be Opened," *Emporia Weekly News*, April 17, 1884.

2. "The Oklahoma Payne Case," *Emporia Weekly News*, April 24, 1884; "Oklahoma," *Emporia Weekly News*, May 1, 1884; Rister, *Land Hunger*, 143–51; Hoig, *David L. Payne*, x.

3. Rister, *Land Hunger*, 146.

4. "Troublesome Boomers" and untitled article excerpted from *Caldwell Journal*, *Indian Chieftain*, May 29, 1884.

5. Savage, "Rock Falls Raid," 77; Hoig, *David L. Payne*, x; John S. Koller, "Pioneer Experiences with Capt. Payne," in 89ers Association, *Oklahoma: The Beautiful Land*, 9–12.

6. Jenness, "Fight of Payne and the Boomers," 23; "The New Oklahoma City," *Oklahoma Chief*, June 14, 1884. During its location at Rock Falls, the boomer newspaper was published as the *Oklahoma Chief*.

7. The complete account of Harris's tenure as the *Oklahoma Chief* printer at Rock Falls is published in Grant Harris, "Publishing a Newspaper in a 'Boomer' Camp," *Chronicles of Oklahoma* 5, no. 4 (December 1927): 363–70.

8. Harris, "Publishing a Newspaper in a 'Boomer' Camp," 365–66. See also Carolyn Thomas Foreman, *Oklahoma Imprints, 1835–1907: A History of Printing in Oklahoma before Statehood* (Norman: University of Oklahoma Press, 1936), 395; Carter, *Story of Oklahoma Newspapers*, 16–17.

9. Wilson, "*Oklahoma War Chief*."

10. "Story of Oklahoma"; Harris, "Publishing a Newspaper in a 'Boomer' Camp," 366–67.

11. Harris, "Publishing a Newspaper in a 'Boomer' Camp," 366–67.

12. "Intruders on Indian Lands."

13. Savage, "Rock Falls Raid," 76–77; "Another Invasion," *Indian Chieftain*, November 13, 1884.

14. Hoig, *David L. Payne*, x.

15. "Intruders on Indian Lands."

16. Harris, "Publishing a Newspaper in a 'Boomer' Camp," 368–70.

17. "Bounced Boomers," *Wichita Daily Eagle*, August 8, 1884; "Payne's Pilgrim's Paradise," *Oklahoma War-Chief*, April 29, 1886.

18. Hightower, *Banking in Oklahoma Before Statehood*, 152; James M. Smallwood, *An Oklahoma Adventure of Banks and Bankers* (Norman: University of Oklahoma Press, 1979), 13.

19. Harris, "Publishing a Newspaper in a 'Boomer' Camp," 369–70.
20. "Bounced Boomers."
21. Unpublished and undated manuscript beginning, "There was considerable colony money," folder 9, box 6, Edna Mae Couch Collection.
22. Savage, "Rock Falls Raid," 77.
23. "Bounced Boomers"; "The Boomers Removed," *Cheyenne Transporter*, August 15, 1884; Harris, "Publishing a Newspaper in a 'Boomer' Camp," 368–69; unpublished and undated manuscript beginning, "There was considerable colony money." This manuscript lists the prisoners as D. L. Payne, J. B. Cooper, D. G. Greathouse, T. W. Echelberger, and S. L. Mosley.
24. John F. Lyons to D. W. Bushyhead, November 19, 1884, Indian Archives Collection, Cherokee Nation Records, folder 2, box 125, Research Division, Oklahoma Historical Society, Oklahoma City. One official estimated there were 150 people (including women and children) in Rock Falls. Other estimates ran as high as 800. See Savage, "Rock Falls Raid," 79n15.
25. Harris, "Publishing a Newspaper in a 'Boomer' Camp," 368–69.
26. "Bounced Boomers."
27. Lyons to Bushyhead, November 19, 1884.
28. "The Arrested Oklahoma 'Boomers'—Statement by Captain Payne," *Sacramento Daily Record-Union*, August 28, 1884; "Payne's Pilgrim's Paradise"; "Story of Oklahoma."
29. Unpublished and undated manuscript beginning, "There was considerable colony money."
30. "Payne's Pilgrim's Paradise."
31. Harris, "Publishing a Newspaper in a 'Boomer' Camp," 369.
32. "Rock Falls to Fort Smith, August 7–19, 30, 1884," item 1, folder 22, box 1, Payne Papers; "The Arrested Oklahoma 'Boomers'—Statement by Captain Payne."
33. "Rock Falls to Fort Smith"; Hoig, "Boomer Movement"; News brief, *Indian Chieftain*, August 28, 1884.
34. "Payne's Arrival," *Wichita Daily Eagle*, September 13, 1884.
35. "Rock Falls to Fort Smith."
36. The President of the United States of America to the Marshal of the Western District of Arkansas, Court Summons for D. L. Payne, September 8, 1884, item 2, folder 13, box 2, Payne Papers.
37. "Oklahoma Payne Released," *National Republican*, September 9, 1884.
38. Untitled article, *Oklahoma War-Chief*, October 30, 1884.
39. Harris, "Publishing a Newspaper in a 'Boomer' Camp," 369.
40. Wilson, *"Oklahoma War Chief."* Payne's arrest at Rock Falls and subsequent trip to Fort Smith, during which he was "chained to a wagon and forced to foot it a greater part of the distance," are described in Jenness, "Fight of Payne and the Boomers," 24.
41. Buffalo Bill Cody, *Buffalo Bill's Wild West; America's National Entertainment* (Hartford, Conn.: Calhoun Printing, 1884), in "Collecting America: How a

Friendship Enriched Our Understanding of American Culture," Digital Resources, Newberry Library, Chicago, http://publications.newberry.org/digitalexhibitions/exhibits/show/collectingamerica/life/item/425; Hoig, *David L. Payne*, 170.

42. "Oklahoma Payne Released"; "Payne's Arrival"; untitled article, *Evening Star*, September 12, 1884; untitled article, *Indian Chieftain*, September 18, 1884.

43. Untitled article, *Oklahoma War-Chief*, October 30, 1884.

44. "Payne's Arrival." For the lyrics sung by Professor Arbuckle, see Rister, *Land Hunger*, 174–75. See also "Denouncing the Government," *Evening Star*, September 13, 1884.

45. "Payne's Arrival." McCoy's reference was to William Shakespeare, *Hamlet*, act 1, scene 4.

46. "Payne's Arrival."

47. Harris, "Publishing a Newspaper in a 'Boomer' Camp," 369–70.

48. Chapman, "Oklahoma City, from Public Land to Private Property," pt. 1, 213; Sibyl Lupton, "History," unpublished manuscript, dated by hand September 30, 1940, folder 12, box 78, Federal Writers Project, Transportation, Research Division, Oklahoma Historical Society, Oklahoma City (hereafter cited as FWP Transportation Collection).

49. Lynch quoted in Chapman, "Oklahoma City, from Public Land to Private Property," pt. 1, 214. According to the 1871 *Report of the Commissioner of the General Land Office*, an initial point was arbitrarily selected about one mile south of Fort Arbuckle and about six miles west of present-day Davis in Murray County. From this initial point, a north-south line called the "Indian Meridian" and an east-west line called the "Indian Base Line" became the bases for surveys across present-day Oklahoma, excluding the Panhandle. After 1866, the portion of the Indian Meridian between the Cimarron and Canadian Rivers became the eastern border of Oklahoma Proper, and it formed one of the boundary lines for the Run of '89. See Dianna Everett, "Indian Meridian (and Indian Base Line)," in *Encyclopedia of Oklahoma History and Culture*, accessed November 21, 2017, http://www.okhistory.org/publications/enc/entry.php?entryname=INDIAN%20 MERIDIAN%20(AND%20INDIAN%20BASE%20LINE).

50. Untitled articles, *Oklahoma War-Chief*, October 30, 1884.

51. Untitled article and "Not a Party Question," *Oklahoma War-Chief*, October 30, 1884.

52. "The Public Lands," *Oklahoma War-Chief*, November 20, 1884.

53. "Glory! Hallelujah!" *Oklahoma War-Chief*, November 20, 1884.

54. "Early Oklahoma History, The Hardships of D. L. Payne, the 'Original Boomer,'" unsourced newspaper article, December 3, 1903, Scrapbook, September 20, 1903–January 9, 1904, box 40, vol. 11, 50, Barde Collection; Harris, "Publishing a Newspaper in a 'Boomer' Camp," 370.

55. "Early Oklahoma History."

56. Harris, "Publishing a Newspaper in a 'Boomer' Camp," 370; "Our Sorrow," *Oklahoma Chief*, December 4, 1884; Fred Sutton, "April 22, 1889–April 22, 1929," 18; Wilson, "*Oklahoma War Chief*."

57. "Our Sorrow"; "Story of Oklahoma."

58. "Wichita Branch Colony."

59. "Oklahoma Payne Dead," *Cheyenne Transporter*, December 5, 1884.

60. Koller, "Pioneer Experiences with Capt. Payne," 12; Hoig, *David L. Payne*, 168–73, 185, 214–15.

61. "Story of Oklahoma"; Hoig, *David L. Payne*, x.

62. "Return of the Colony," "Speech of Capt. Couch at the Oklahoma Convention," *Oklahoma Chief*, February 10, 1885; I. N. Terrill, "The Boomers' Last Raid," *Sturm's Oklahoma Magazine* 8, no. 2 (April 1909): 39–40.

63. *Chicago Tribune* article of January 21, 1885 quoted in "Not One Drop of Blood!" *Oklahoma Chief*, February 3, 1885.

64. Open letter, *Oklahoma Chief*, February 3, 1885.

65. "Capt. Couch's Answer," *Oklahoma Chief*, February 3, 1885. See also W. L. Couch to Maj. Gen. Edward Hatch, January 21, 1885, folder 8, box 6, Edna Mae Couch Collection.

66. "Boomers Must Go," *Emporia Weekly News*, January 22, 1885.

67. "City Negro Trooper in Early Days," unsourced and undated newspaper article, folder 10, box 6, Edna Mae Couch Collection.

68. "Speech of Capt. Couch at the Oklahoma Convention," *Oklahoma Chief*, February 10, 1885; "Glorious Achievement!" *Oklahoma Chief*, February 3, 1885. S. J. Zerger served as editor from December 1884 to June 1885. See Wilson, "*Oklahoma War Chief*."

69. "Story of Oklahoma."

70. "Speech of Capt. Couch at the Oklahoma Convention," and "March 5 Is the Day," *Oklahoma Boomer*, January 21, 1885, Santa Fe Railroad, Vertical Files, Research Division, Oklahoma Historical Society, Oklahoma City (hereafter cited as Santa Fe Railroad Vertical Files). The *Oklahoma Boomer* was published briefly in Coffeyville, Kansas. For a thorough account of the boomer convention in Topeka on February 2–3, 1885, see Wood, *Boomer*, 79–83.

71. "Cattlemen in Oklahoma," *Iola Register*, February 13, 1885.

72. "Will Congress Act?" *Oklahoma Chief*, February 17, 1885.

73. Dan W. Peery, "Colonel Crocker and the Boomer Movement," *Chronicles of Oklahoma* 13, no. 3 (September 1935): 273–78, 296.

74. Crocker quoted in Fred Sutton, "April 22, 1889–April 22, 1929," 21. Samuel Crocker bought the newspaper in June 1885 and served as editor until it suspended publication on August 12, 1886. See also Peery, "Colonel Crocker and the Boomer Movement," 276n2; and Wilson, "*Oklahoma War Chief*."

CHAPTER SEVEN

Epigraph. "Concerning Oklahoma," *Oklahoma Chief*, March 31, 1885.

1. Unpublished collection of letters and articles beginning with handwritten heading, "Cleveland in the White House and Cattle in the Promised Land," n.d., folder 9, box 6, Edna Mae Couch Collection.

2. Sidney Clarke to Capt. Couch, March 31, 1885, *Oklahoma Chief*, April 7, 1885.

3. "The Senate Sub Committee—Fraudulent Investigation—Illegal Occupancy of Oklahoma," *Oklahoma War-Chief*, June 18, 1885; "Gaining in Numbers!" *Oklahoma Chief*, April 7, 1885.

4. "Senate Sub Committee." The *Oklahoma War-Chief*'s article attributes Senator Vest's comments to Senator Samuel B. Maxey of Texas. Boomer leader William L. Couch consulted the *Congressional Record* to discover that Vest was the one who claimed ignorance about surveying, sectioning, and subdividing the Oklahoma country. See Jackson and Cole, *Oklahoma!* 134.

5. "Senate Sub Committee"; Treaty between the United States of America and the Seminole Nation of Indians, Barrett Collection. See chapter one, "Antecedents," for a detailed description of Seminole land cessions to the U.S. government.

6. For the full text of President Cleveland's Proclamation of March 13, 1885, see "The Oklahoma Difficulty—Proclamation by the President," *Sacramento Daily Record-Union*, March 14, 1885.

7. "Story of Oklahoma."

8. "Bad Boomers," *Sedalia (Mo.) Weekly Bazoo*, March 17, 1885.

9. Couch's interview was published in the *Wichita Beacon* on February 26, 1885; the *St. Louis Globe-Democrat* on March 5, 1885; and the *Kansas City Times* on March 6, 1885. See also Jackson and Cole, *Oklahoma!* 134–42; unpublished collection of letters and articles, folder 9, box 6, Edna Mae Couch Collection.

10. Jackson and Cole, *Oklahoma!* 134–37.

11. "Story of Oklahoma."

12. Jackson and Cole, *Oklahoma!* 139–42.

13. Untitled article, *Oklahoma Chief*, June 11, 1885. See also untitled article, *Evening Star*, August 18, 1885.

14. "Couch Court's Inquiry," *Oklahoma War-Chief*, June 18, 1885.

15. "Senate Sub Committee"; "Oklahoma," *Oklahoma War-Chief*, June 25, 1885.

16. "President's Proclamation Effecting the Removal of Cattle from the Entire Indian Territory and all other Government Lands," *Oklahoma War-Chief*, August 13, 1885. See also McCallum, *Wire That Fenced the West*, 177–78.

17. "Must Go: The Cattlemen Must Evacuate the Indian Territory," *Iola Register*, July 31, 1885.

18. Untitled article, *Oklahoma Chief*, June 11, 1885.

19. "An Act to Provide for the Allotment of Lands in Severalty to Indians on the Various Reservations, and to Extend the Protection of the Laws of the United States and the Territories over the Indians, and for Other Purposes," February 8, 1887, Avalon Project, http://avalon.law.yale.edu/19th_century/dawes.asp (accessed December 28, 2015); Wickett, *Contested Territory*, 51.

20. "Story, Hitherto Untold, about Moving of Troops to Ft. Reno to Pacify Indians Is Related," *El Reno Daily Tribune*, April 22, 1934.

21. "Must Go."

22. Unpublished manuscript beginning, "The boomer movement was dying fast," n.d., folder 9, box 6, Edna Mae Couch Collection. Although the document is incomplete and unsigned, it was clearly written by a boomer leader.

23. "Crocker on his Road and in his Cell in the Cowley County Jail," *Oklahoma War-Chief*, July 23, 1885. S. C. Smith and his son bought the newspaper from S. J. Zerger. In their first issue on June 18, 1885, they returned the newspaper to its original and more bellicose name and announced that Samuel Crocker would serve as its new editor. See "Salutation," and "Our Connection with the *Oklahoma War-Chief*," *Oklahoma War-Chief*, June 18, 1885.

24. "Cowley County Jail," *Oklahoma War Chief*, August 27, 1885.

25. "Captain Couch on Trial for Treason," *Oklahoma War-Chief*, September 10, 1885"; Hoig, *David L. Payne*, x.

26. "Concerning Oklahoma."

27. "Running Out the Cow Boys," *Evening Star*, August 1, 1885.

28. Untitled article, *Washington (D.C.) Critic*, July 27, 1885.

29. "Oklahoma," *Indian Chieftain*, February 12, 1885; "Oklahoma," *Indian Chieftain*, July 16, 1885.

30. Dale, *Range Cattle Industry*, 91–93.

31. Skaggs, "Cattle Trails in Oklahoma," 17.

32. *Kansas City Indicator* referenced in untitled article, *Indian Chieftain*, August 27, 1885.

33. "Cattle-Growers Convention"; "St. Louis Convention," *Barbour County (Kans.) Index*, December 4, 1885.

34. McCallum, *Wire That Fenced the West*, 128–39 (ranch foreman quoted on 133).

35. "Angry Bucks," *Emporia Weekly News*, December 17, 1885.

36. "The Oklahoma Boomers: Secretary Lamar Accuses Them of Bad Faith," *Evening Star*, November 18, 1885; "The Boomers Bad Faith," *National Republican*, November 19, 1885; "Only Obeyed in Part," *Evening Star*, December 12, 1885.

37. "Important Inquiries Answered," *Oklahoma War-Chief*, February 4, 1886.

38. "History of the State of Oklahoma," unpublished manuscript, n.d., folder 9, box 6; "Information sent by family after nomination, June 23, 1937," letter dated by hand June 23, 1937, folder 8, box 6, both in Edna Mae Couch Collection.

39. "The Oklahoma Bills," *Evening Star*, January 18, 1886.

40. W. L. Couch to Mr. A. E. Stinson, January 2, 1886, folder 8, box 6, Edna Mae Couch Collection; "Opposed to the Oklahoma Bills," *Washington Critic*, February 18, 1886; "The House," *National Republican*, March 12, 1886.

41. W. L. Couch to Mr. A. E. Stinson, February 17 and 20, 1886, folder 8, box 6, Edna Mae Couch Collection.

42. "Oklahoma," *Washington Critic*, March 26, 1886.

43. W. L. Couch to Mr. A. E. Stinson, April 8, 1886, folder 8, box 6, Edna Mae Couch Collection.

44. Untitled article, "A Fresh Oklahoma Bill," *Indian Chieftain*, April 8, 1886.

45. W. L. Couch to Mr. A. E. Stinson, May 8, 1886, folder 8, box 6, Edna Mae Couch Collection.

46. W. L. Couch to Mr. A. E. Stinson, June 16, 1886, folder 8, box 6, Edna Mae Couch Collection.

47. W. L. Couch to Mr. A. E. Stinson, January 28; February 4; March 13 and 24; April 2, 12, 19, 22, and 27; May 2, 5, and 15; June 6, and 30; July 20, 1886, folder 8, box 6, Edna Mae Couch Collection.

48. "Another Amusing Scene," *Evening Star*, June 29, 1886; "The House," *National Republican*, June 30, 1886; "The Work of Congress," *(Washington, D.C.) National Tribune*, August 12, 1886.

49. "A Worthless Congress," *Oklahoma War-Chief*, August 12, 1886.

50. Ibid.; "Couch," *Oklahoma War-Chief*, August 12, 1886.

51. "Moving Oklahoma Boomers," *National Republican*, November 24, 1886.

52. "Oklahoma Lands," *National Republican*, December 11, 1886.

53. Frank J. Best, "Early Day Account Santa Fe Railway in Oklahoma," unpublished manuscript, 1949, folder 14, box 26, Berlin B. Chapman Collection, Research Division, Oklahoma Historical Society, Oklahoma City (hereafter cited as Chapman Collection); Chapman, "Oklahoma City, from Public Land to Private Property," pt. 1, 215.

54. "Oklahoma War-Chief Suspended," *Oklahoma War-Chief*, August 12, 1886.

55. E. H. Kelley, "When Oklahoma City Was Seymour and Verbeck," *Chronicles of Oklahoma* 27, no. 4 (winter 1949): 350–52; "A Bit of History," *Norman Transcript*, May 3, 1890.

56. Best, "Early Day Account Santa Fe Railway in Oklahoma."

57. Jenny Robertson, interview by Jimmie Birdwell, June 14, 1937, vol. 77, 36–38, IPP online.

58. Dale, *Range Cattle Industry*, 96–97; "Santa Fe Built South and Area Was Born," *Guthrie Daily Leader*, April 16, 1961, Santa Fe Railroad Vertical Files; A. B. Griggs, "Sketch of Construction and Early Operation of Santa Fe Line Across Oklahoma from Arkansas City, Kansas to Gainesville, Texas," folder 18, box 78, FWP Transportation Collection.

59. Colcord, *Autobiography*, 126–27; McCallum, *Wire That Fenced the West*, 128–39.

60. Kelley, "When Oklahoma City Was Seymour and Verbeck," 350.

61. Griggs, "Sketch of Construction and Early Operation of Santa Fe Line"; Griggs, unpublished paper presented to the Guthrie Rotary Club, February 20, 1939, folder 1, box 1, Santa Fe Railroad Collection.

62. C. J. Turpin to Mr. Nedry, April 19, 1938, folder 29, box 78; untitled manuscript, n.d., folder 10, box 78, FWP Transportation Collection.

63. Dale, *Range Cattle Industry*, 96–97; Chapman, "Oklahoma City, from Public Land to Private Property," pt. 1, 215; Kelley, "When Oklahoma City was Seymour and Verbeck," 352–53.

64. "And There Oklahoma City Stands," unsourced newspaper article, December 26, 1900, Scrapbook, September 1, 1900–March 22, 1901, box 38, vol. 6, 108, Barde Collection.

65. R. F. Vanderford, "Building Santa Fe Depots," interview by Mary Hopkins, 1936, folder 18, box 78, FWP Transportation Collection.

66. "Guthrie Carpenter Still Has Tools He Used in Building Oklahoma City Depot in '87," unsourced newspaper article, April 18, 1940, folder 1, box 7, Fred L.

Wenner Collection, University of Oklahoma Western History Collections, Norman (hereafter cited as Wenner Collection).

67. Chapman, "Oklahoma City, from Public Land to Private Property," pt. 1, 216; Frank J. Best, "The Santa Fe Railway as an Oklahoma Pioneer," unpublished manuscript, 1951, folder 14, box 26, Chapman Collection; Frank J. Best, "Pioneer Railroader," interview by Fred L. Wenner, 1936, folder 9, box 78, FWP Transportation Collection; Frank J. Best, interview by Harry M. Dreyer, March 4, 1937, vol. 7, 450–61, IPP online.

68. Chapman, "Oklahoma City, from Public Land to Private Property," pt. 1, 216. Chapman cites the Santa Fe's July 1887 timetable as an early reference to "Oklahoma."

69. George J. Haas, interview by Don Moon Jr., February 26, 1938, vol. 37, 2–6, IPP online; George J. Haas, interview by Ruth Moon, "Personal Story of George Haas, Pioneer Railway Engineer," unpublished manuscript, n.d., folder 9, box 78, FWP Transportation Collection.

70. "When Oklahoma Was Wild: A. R. Glazier Ran the First Train across the Territory," unsourced newspaper article, March 25, 1910, Scrapbook, August 1, 1909–February 9, 1911, box 45, vol. 22, 107, Barde Collection.

71. Ibid.; George H. Shirk, "First Post Offices within the Boundaries of Oklahoma," *Chronicles of Oklahoma* 30, no. 1 (Spring 1952): 38–104.

72. Chapman, "Oklahoma City, from Public Land to Private Property," pt. 1, 218n14.

73. A. W. Dunham, "A Pioneer Railroad Agent," *Chronicles of Oklahoma* 2, no. 1 (March 1924): 48–62; A. W. Dunham, "Oklahoma City before the Run of 1889," *Chronicles of Oklahoma* 36, no. 1 (Spring 1958): 72–73; Louise Skelton, "Oklahoma Station—On the Santa Fe," unpublished manuscript, n.d., folder 24, box 78, FWP Transportation Collection.

74. Miller, *Oklahoma Populism*, 16–21.

75. "The Industrial Party," *National Republican*, February 24, 1887; "The Platform of the Industrial Party," *Evening Star*, February 26, 1887.

76. W. L. Couch to Mr. A. E. Stinson, March 27, 1887, folder 8, box 6, Edna Mae Couch Collection.

77. Colcord, *Autobiography*, 133.

78. Ibid., 134–35.

79. "Oklahoma Boomers," *Evening Star*, August 8, 1887.

80. W. L. Couch to A. E. Stinson, September 3, 1887, folder 8, box 6, Edna Mae Couch Collection.

81. "Another Oklahoma Raid," *National Republican*, December 16, 1887.

82. Jackson and Cole, *Oklahoma!* Jackson and Cole's polemic on behalf of settlement closes with an advertisement for E. C. Cole & Co. The ad concludes, "We shall open an office in the Oklahoma Country, as soon as it is Opened up to Settlement."

83. "The New Oklahoma Crusade," *Evening Star*, December 17, 1887.

84. Best, "The Santa Fe Railway as an Oklahoma Pioneer." See also Best, "Early Day Account Santa Fe Railway in Oklahoma."

85. "Sidney Clark's [sic] Oklahoma Scheme," *Evening Star*, December 6, 1887.

CHAPTER EIGHT

Epigraph. Colcord, *Autobiography*, 136.

1. "A Flood of Bills," *Iron County (Mo.) Register*, January 12, 1888; "Measures of Interest," *Indian Chieftain*, January 12, 1888. See also A Bill to Extend the Laws of the United States over Certain Unorganized Territory South of the State of Kansas, H.R. 1447, 50th Cong., 1st sess., January 4, 1888, folder 9, box 6; A Bill to Protect Lands Belonging to Indians from Unlawful Grazing, and for Other Purposes, H.R. 4922, 50th Cong., 1st sess., January 16, 1888, folder 7, box 6, both in Clarke Collection.

2. "Sanguine Springer," *Los Angeles Times*, April 22, 1889.

3. "Measures of Interest"; "Flood of Bills"; "Story of Oklahoma"; Stan Hoig, *The Oklahoma Land Rush of 1889* (Oklahoma City: Oklahoma Historical Society, 1984), 7.

4. W. L. Couch to A. E. Stinson, January 25, 1888, folder 8, box 6, Edna Mae Couch Collection.

5. W. L. Couch to Honorable Sidney Clarke, January 27, 1888, folder 7, box 6, Clarke Collection.

6. "The Springer Bill," *Richmond (Mo.) Democrat*, February 2, 1888.

7. George T. Barnes, "Oklahoma," Views of the Minority, For the Organization of the Territory of Oklahoma, H.R. 1277, 50th Cong., 1st sess., n.d., folder 12, box 6, Clarke Collection.

8. Charles S. Baker, Additional Views of Mr. Charles S. Baker, addendum, "Oklahoma," Views of the Minority, For the Organization of the Territory of Oklahoma, H.R. 1277, 50th Cong., 1st sess., n.d., folder 12, box 6, Clarke Collection.

9. "The Oklahoma Question," *Washington Critic*, February 25, 1888.

10. Peery, "Colonel Crocker and the Boomer Movement," 280–83.

11. W. L. Couch to A. E. Stinson, March 22, 1888, folder 8, box 6, Edna Mae Couch Collection.

12. "Ejecting the Settlers," *National Republican*, February 17, 1888.

13. *Topeka American Citizen* article of March 1, 1888, quoted in Hamilton, *Black Towns and Profit*, 99–100.

14. "Objects to Springer's Bill," *Indian Chieftain*, April 5, 1888.

15. Dunham, "Oklahoma City before the Run of 1889," 72–78; Skelton, "Oklahoma Station."

16. Dunham, "Oklahoma City before the Run of 1889," 76.

17. "Contest over the Oklahoma Bill," *Evening Star*, September 14, 1888.

18. Untitled article, *Indian Chieftain*, September 27, 1888; Hoig, *Land Rush*, 12.

19. "Monster Oklahoma Convention," editorial advertisement, folder 14, box 6, Clarke Collection; "Monster Oklahoma Convention," *Wichita Eagle*, November 20, 1888.

20. J. M. Springer to Sidney Clarke, November 14, 1888, folder 14, box 6, Clarke Collection.

21. C. H. Mansur to Sidney Clarke, November 17, 1888 (two letters), folder 14, box 6, Clarke Collection.

22. Springer quoted in Hoig, *Land Rush*, 11–12; "Opening Oklahoma," (*Washington, D.C.*) *Evening Post*, November 23, 1888.

23. Samuel Crocker to Hon. Sidney Clarke, November 21, 1888, folder 14, box 6, Clarke Collection.

24. H. L. Pierce memo, November 26, 1888, folder 14, box 6, Clarke Collection.

25. Julian speech, "Our Land Policy." See also chapter one, "Antecedents."

26. Wickett, *Contested Territory*, 138. For a sample of unsourced articles in Clarke's collection of crime clippings, see "A Shootist Shot," December 24, 1888; "Revolting Murder of Two Women," December 24, 1888; "A Sensational Killing," December 24, 1888; "The Trouble in the Chickasaw Nation," December 26, 1888; "Efforts to Capture a Daring Desperado," December 28, 1888; and untitled newspaper article referenced and dated by hand as *Arkansas City Democrat*, December 28, 1888, all in folder 3, box 6, Clarke Collection.

27. "Crime Holds Carnival: Deplorable State of Affairs in the Indian Territory," unsourced newspaper article, November 17, 1888, folder 3, box 6, Clarke Collection.

28. Shirk, "First Post Offices within the Boundaries of Oklahoma," 83; Chapman, "Oklahoma City, from Public Land to Private Property," pt. 1, 216. The post office was designated as "Oklahoma" until July 1, 1923, when it was changed to "Oklahoma City."

29. "Up Again: The Oklahoma Colonists Reorganized," *Wichita Eagle*, December 23, 1888.

30. Handwritten chronology of William L. Couch and the boomer movement, folder 3, box 6, Edna Mae Couch Collection. In all likelihood, Samuel Crocker was the author of this handwritten chronology.

31. Ibid.; Erin Glanville Brown, "Pawnee Bill (Gordon William Lillie)," in *Encyclopedia of Oklahoma History and Culture*, accessed February 4, 2016, http://www.okhistory.org/publications/enc/entry.php?entry=pa024.

32. "Up Again: The Oklahoma Colonists Reorganized."

33. Untitled article, *Emporia Weekly News*, December 27, 1888.

34. *Washington Post* cited in untitled article, *Wichita Eagle*, December 30, 1888.

35. Irving Geffs (a.k.a. Bunky), *The First Eight Months of Oklahoma City* (Oklahoma City: McMasters, 1890; repr. Quantum Forms, 1988), 99–100; Carter, *Story of Oklahoma Newspapers*, 43–44.

36. "Oklahoma," *Oklahoma City Times*, December 29, 1888.

37. "A Farmer in Oklahoma"; and "Oklahoma Colony," *Oklahoma City Times*, December 29, 1888.

38. "Letters by the Bushel"; and "Cattle at Fort Reno," *Oklahoma City Times*, December 29, 1888.

39. "Room for All," *Oklahoma City Times*, December 29, 1888.

40. Atchison, Topeka and Santa Fe Railroad stockholders' report quoted in Chapman, "Oklahoma City, from Public Land to Private Property," pt. 1, 217.

41. Geffs, *First Eight Months of Oklahoma City*, 100.

42. Fred L. Wenner, *The Story of Oklahoma and the Eighty-Niners, Retold on the Golden Anniversary* (Guthrie, Okla.: Co-operative Publishing, 1939), 8; "Story of Oklahoma"; Baldwin, *89ers*, 10–11.

43. Wenner, *Story of Oklahoma*, 8; Baldwin, *89ers*, 10. See also chapter six, "Our Sorrow."

44. "Springer Hopeful," *Barton County (Kans.) Democrat*, January 3, 1889.

45. "Mayes on Oklahoma," *Dodge City Times*, January 31, 1889.

46. Hoig, *Land Rush*, 13–14.

47. Ibid.; Wenner, *Story of Oklahoma*, 8–9.

48. "The Oklahoma Bill Defeated," *Phillipsburg (Kans.) Herald*, March 8, 1889; "About Jumping to Conclusions," *Wichita Eagle*, March 1, 1889.

49. "The Oklahoma Invasion," *Phillipsburg Herald*, February 15, 1889.

50. Hoig, *Land Rush*, 14–15.

51. Peery, "Colonel Crocker and the Boomer Movement," 285–86.

52. Best, "The Santa Fe Railway as an Oklahoma Pioneer"; Best, "Early Day Account Santa Fe Railway in Oklahoma"; Peery, "Colonel Crocker and the Boomer Movement," 286; McReynolds, *Oklahoma: A History*, 287–89; Baldwin, *89ers*, 12–13; Hoig, *Land Rush*, 14–15.

53. Dan W. Peery, "The First Two Years," pt. 1, *Chronicles of Oklahoma* 7, no. 3 (September 1929): 283. For an introduction to Peery's three-part account of Oklahoma City's beginnings, see Dan W. Peery, "Introduction: The First Two Years," *Chronicles of Oklahoma* 7, no. 3 (September 1929): 278–80. See also Wenner, *Story of Oklahoma*, 9; and Baldwin, *89ers*, 14.

54. "Wild with Joy," *Wichita Eagle*, March 7, 1889; "Washington Notes," *Iola Register*, March 15, 1889.

55. Dispatch from *Purcell Register* published in "Oklahoma Leaders," *Oklahoma City Times*, March 13, 1889. See also Peery, "Colonel Crocker and the Boomer Movement," 287.

56. "Oklahoma: Conditions of Settlement," *Oklahoma City Times*, March 13, 1889; "Oklahoma," *Abilene (Kans.) Weekly Reflector*, March 21, 1889.

57. "The New Public Domain," *Oklahoma City Times*, March 13, 1889.

58. "Gov. Glick in the Soup," *Wichita Eagle*, March 23, 1889.

59. *Washington (D.C.) City Post* cited in "The Oklahoma Evictions," *Wichita Eagle*, March 23, 1889.

60. Peery, "First Two Years," pt. 1, 283–84.

61. Wenner, *Story of Oklahoma*, 12; Peery, "First Two Years," pt. 1, 283–84.

62. "The Boomers Rejoicing," *Indian Journal*, April 4, 1889.

63. For a succinct account of the Chickasaw freedmen's precarious existence from 1866 to the 1890s, see Parthena Louise James, "Reconstruction in the Chickasaw Nation: The Freedman Problem," *Chronicles of Oklahoma* 45, no. 1 (Spring 1967): 44–57.

64. Ronald James Webb, "Oklahoma City's Historic Sandtown Neighborhood," privately published online (January 2013), http://www.dougloudenback.com/

okchistory/sandtown_ronald_j_webb_2005.pdf (accessed February 15, 2016). For a thorough history of Sandtown, see Phelicia Ann Morton, "Home Is Where the People Are: Sandtown, Oklahoma" (master's thesis, Cornell University, 1999). Celebrations of Sandtown continued well into the 1990s. See "Sandtown Celebration," *Daily Oklahoman/Oklahoma City Times*, September 15, 1995, Oklahoma City—Sandtown Vertical Files, Research Division, Oklahoma Historical Society, Oklahoma City. Thanks go to independent historian Sam Stalcup of Oklahoma City for bringing Webb's article and Morton's thesis to the author's attention at the Oklahoma Historical Society's annual conference in Sulphur in April 2015.

65. "Boomers Rejoicing"; "Southern Kansas Wild," and "Fatal Fight over a Claim," *Evening Star*, March 28, 1889.

66. Carol H. Welsh, "Deadly Games: The Struggle for a Quarter-Section of Land," *Chronicles of Oklahoma* 52, no. 1 (Spring 1994): 37.

67. Glen V. McIntyre, "Kingfisher," in *Encyclopedia of Oklahoma History and Culture*, accessed February 8, 2016, http://www.okhistory.org/publications/enc/entry.php?entry=KI010. For various distances between key locations in the Oklahoma country, see "The Oklahoma Country," *New York Times*, April 22, 1889.

68. "The Oklahoma Land Office," *Wichita Eagle*, March 27, 1889.

69. Best, "The Santa Fe Railway as an Oklahoma Pioneer"; Best, "Early Day Account Santa Fe Railway in Oklahoma."

70. "Fred Wenner, Land Rush Pioneer, Still Civic Leader in Adopted State," *Denver Post*, April 30, 1950, folder 2, box 7, Wenner Collection; "Fred L. Wenner: City Treasurer and Police Judge, Guthrie, Okla.," folder 3, box 1, Wenner Collection.

71. Fred L. Wenner, "On the Border," unpublished manuscript, folder 12, box 1, Wenner Collection.

72. Wenner, *Story of Oklahoma*, 12.

73. Colcord, *Autobiography*, 135–36. Colcord referred to his campsite as "Bullfoot Spring." He might have confused Bull Foot Station, which was 4.5 miles south of the Unassigned Lands' northern boundary, with Buffalo Springs, which was located about a mile north of present-day Bison in Garfield County.

74. Best, Wenner interview.

75. Haas, Don Moon Jr. interview; Haas, Ruth Moon interview.

CHAPTER NINE

Epigraph. Dunham, "Pioneer Railroad Agent," 56–57.

1. Wenner, *Story of Oklahoma*, 9.

2. Chapman, "Oklahoma City, from Public Land to Private Property," pt. 1, 218–19.

3. Oklahoma Capital City Townsites and Improvement Company official quoted in ibid., 219.

4. Ibid., 218n14.

5. John Holzapfel, "The Kansas Oklahoma Colony," in 89ers Association, *Oklahoma: The Beautiful Land*, 35–36; James L. Brown, "Early and Important Litigations," *Sturm's Oklahoma Magazine* 8, no. 2 (April 1909): 26–30; Hoig, *Land Rush*, 188; Welsh, "Deadly Games," 37.

6. John Holzapfel, "The Kansas Oklahoma Colony," in 89ers Association, *Oklahoma: The Beautiful Land*, 33–39.

7. Chapman, "Oklahoma City, from Public Land to Private Property," pt. 1, 220; "Information from Oklahoma," *Oklahoma City Daily Times*, December 11, 1889. The newspaper account of the filing identifies J. C. rather than J. W. Wilson.

8. "Fred Wenner, Land Rush Pioneer"; Linda D. Wilson, "Greer, Frank Hilton (1862–1933)," in *Encyclopedia of Oklahoma History and Culture*, accessed August 5, 2016, http://www.okhistory.org/publications/enc/entry.php?entry=GR026; George O. Carne, "Flynn, Dennis Thomas," in *Encyclopedia of Oklahoma History and Culture*, accessed August 5, 2016, http://www.okhistory.org/publications/enc/entry.php?entry=FL006; Victor Murdock, "Dennis T. Flynn," *Chronicles of Oklahoma* 18, no. 2 (June 1940): 109–10; Miller, *Oklahoma Populism*, 66. For background on Victor Murdock, see Dan W. Peery, "The First Two Years," pt. 3, *Chronicles of Oklahoma* 8, no. 3 (March 1930): 97.

9. Hamilton S. Wicks, "The Opening of Oklahoma," *Cosmopolitan Magazine* 7, no. 5 (September 1889): 460–61.

10. Ibid., 461, 464. See also "The Boomers Take Up their Assault from Arkansas City," *Chicago Tribune*, April 19, 1889.

11. Wicks, "Opening of Oklahoma," 464–65.

12. T. M. Richardson Jr., interview by Harry M. Dreyer, April 6, 1937, vol. 76, 6–12, IPP online; Hightower, *Banking in Oklahoma Before Statehood*, 157–62; Max Nichols and David R. "Dusty" Martin, *Continuing an Oklahoma Banking Tradition* (Oklahoma City: First Interstate Bank of Oklahoma, N.A., 1989), 3–4.

13. Andrew Jackson Burton, interview by James Russell Gray, April 26, 1938, vol. 13, 383–92, IPP online.

14. Joseph W. Bouse, interview by Arnold N. Aronson, n.d., vol. 9, 474–93, IPP online.

15. Geffs, *First Eight Months of Oklahoma City*, 8.

16. "Movement of Cattle Called Key to Opening Oklahoma," *Oklahoma Journal*, March 9, 1967, Couch Family Vertical Files, Research Division, Oklahoma Historical Society, Oklahoma City (hereafter cited as Couch Family Vertical Files). See also "Civic Center Built on Accursed Acres," *Oklahoma News*, February 14, 1937, Couch Family Vertical Files. This article includes comments by William Couch's son, Eugene. For a map of the quarter section where Couch staked his claim, see Welsh, "Deadly Games," 40. See also Peery, "Colonel Crocker and the Boomer Movement," 289.

17. McClure, "The First Legal Settler in Oklahoma City," 76–77; Peery, "Colonel Crocker and the Boomer Movement," 290–91; Lester, "William J. McClure and the McClure Ranch," 301–2.

18. "A History of Two Weeks," *Oklahoma Times*, May 9, 1889; Linda D. Wilson, "Seminole Town and Improvement Company," in *Encyclopedia of Oklahoma History and Culture*, accessed February 27, 2016, http://www.okhistory.org/publications/enc/entry.php?entry=SE016; Angelo C. Scott, *Story of Oklahoma City* (Oklahoma City: Times-Journal Publishing, 1939), 13.

19. Holzapfel, "Kansas Oklahoma Colony," 37.

20. Geffs, *First Eight Months of Oklahoma City*, 9.

21. Charles M. Purdum, questionnaire, n.d., roll 25, vol. 76, 380, IPP microfilm. The author (b. 1955) grew up at the corner of NW Fifteenth Street and Walker Avenue in Oklahoma City. The house was built in 1905 by his great-grandparents, Frank P. and Aida Johnson, and remained in the family until 2001.

22. Holzapfel, "Kansas Oklahoma Colony," 37; Scott, *Story of Oklahoma City*, 14; Albert McRill, *And Satan Came Also: An Inside Story of a City's Social and Political History* (Oklahoma City: Britton Publishing, 1955), 2; Albert L. McRill, Questionnaire, n.d., roll 25, vol. 76, 156, IPP microfilm.

23. Scott, *Story of Oklahoma City*, 15–16.

24. J. A. Ryan, interview by Harry M. Dreyer, April 5, 1937, roll 3, vol. 9, 135–38, IPP microfilm. See also McRill, *And Satan Came Also*, 2.

25. McRill, *And Satan Came Also*, 2–4.

26. Scott, *Story of Oklahoma City*, 14.

27. Holzapfel, "Kansas Oklahoma Colony," 37; Geffs, *First Eight Months of Oklahoma City*, 9–10.

28. Burton, Gray interview; McRill, *And Satan Came Also*, 2.

29. Brown, "Pawnee Bill."

30. Colcord, *Autobiography*, 136–37.

31. Haas, Ruth Moon interview.

32. Best, Wenner interview. For the Commercial National Bank of Guthrie's sudden demise in November 1890, see "Gone to the Wall," unsourced newspaper article, November 21, 1890, folder 26, box 2, Barde Collection; Hightower, *Banking in Oklahoma Before Statehood*, 177; and Smallwood, *Oklahoma Adventure of Banks and Bankers*, 16–17.

33. Richardson, Dreyer interview.

34. Nichols and Martin, *Continuing an Oklahoma Banking Tradition*, 4.

35. McRill, *And Satan Came Also*, 35.

36. Nichols and Martin, *Continuing an Oklahoma Banking Tradition*, 4; John Cecil Brown, "Early Days of the First National: A Bank as Old as the City It Serves," in *Fifty Years Forward: The First National Bank and Trust Company of Oklahoma City, 1889–1939* (Oklahoma City: First National Bank and Trust Company of Oklahoma City, 1939), 47–48; Mary Marsh, ed., "Our First Seventy-Five Years," in *Bank Life: 1889/1964—Our First 75* (Oklahoma City: First National Bank and Trust Company, April 1964), 2–3; Hightower, *Banking in Oklahoma Before Statehood*, 158–62.

37. Brown, "Early Days of the First National," 48–49; Richardson, Dreyer interview; "Where's Jo?" *Oklahoma Chief* (mistakenly titled *Pioneer* in early edition), May 11, 1889. For the newspaper's mistaken masthead in early editions, see "Not 'Pioneer' but 'Chief,'" *Oklahoma Chief*, n.d. For more on the slogan, "Oh Joe, here's your mule!" see Frank McMaster, "An '89er, How He Rushed and What For," *Sturm's Oklahoma Magazine* 8, no. 2 (April 1909): 47–48.

38. Howard L. Meredith and George H. Shirk, "Oklahoma City: Growth and Recon-struction, 1889–1939," *Chronicles of Oklahoma* 55, no. 3 (Fall 1977): 293; "History of Two Weeks."

39. Mrs. H. Robert Wood, "Virgil Andrew Wood, M.D.," *Chronicles of Oklahoma* 34, no. 3 (Fall 1956): 305–6.

40. "They Arrived Too Late," *Oklahoma City Times*, April 29, 1889.

41. "A Brighter View," *Los Angeles Times*, April 24, 1889.

42. "History of Two Weeks"; Chapman, "Oklahoma City, from Public Land to Private Property," pt. 1, 221.

43. "History of Two Weeks"; Scott, *Story of Oklahoma City*, 17–21; Roy P. Stewart, *Born Grown: An Oklahoma City History* (Oklahoma City: Fidelity Bank National Association, 1974), 14–15.

44. "Kind Words," *Oklahoma Times*, May 9, 1889.

45. Scott, *Story of Oklahoma City*, 20; Carolyn G. Hanneman, "Scott, Angelo Cyrus," in *Encyclopedia of Oklahoma History and Culture*, accessed February 15, 2016, http://www.okhistory.org/publications/enc/entry.php?entry=SC008.

46. "History of Two Weeks"; Holzapfel, "Kansas Oklahoma Colony," 37.

47. Colcord, *Autobiography*, 138.

48. Ibid., 139–40; Scott, *Story of Oklahoma City*, 20–21.

49. Holzapfel, "Kansas Oklahoma Colony," 37.

50. Stewart, *Born Grown*, 26, 331; Geffs, *First Eight Months of Oklahoma City*, 20.

51. Bouse, Aronson interview.

52. Ibid.

53. Jana Hausburg, "First Election Day—May 1, 1889," Oklahoma Images, Ron Norick Public Library, Oklahoma City, http://cybermarsx.mls.lib.ok.us/okimages/okimages.asp?WCI=ViewEssay&WCU=000000109 (accessed March 23, 2016).

54. Ibid.; "History of Two Weeks."

55. Scott, *Story of Oklahoma City*, 25.

56. "History of Two Weeks"; Holzapfel, "Kansas Oklahoma Colony," 37; Geffs, *First Eight Months of Oklahoma City*, 14–16.

CHAPTER TEN

Epigraph. McMaster, "'89er," 46.

1. "Boomers, Names which were in this country after second of March and before 22nd of Apr. 1889," handwritten roster signed by M. (or W.) T. Kay, n.d.; "Sooners: Names of Persons found in Oklahoma, I.T., prior to 12 o'clock, M. April 22, 1889," typed list submitted by Captain Forbush, Lieut. A'dair, and the noncommissioned officers, Troop L, Fifth Cavalry, and 2nd Lieut. J. M. Carson Jr., Fifth Cavalry, folder 5, box 2, both in William F. Harn Collection, 1890–1930, Research Division, Oklahoma Historical Society, Oklahoma City (hereafter cited as Harn Collection).

2. "History of Two Weeks"; Geffs, *First Eight Months of Oklahoma City*, 16–18.

3. Scott, *Story of Oklahoma City*, 29.

4. Holzapfel, "Kansas Oklahoma Colony," 38.

5. Ibid.

6. "History of Two Weeks."

7. Ibid.; Geffs, *First Eight Months of Oklahoma City*, 18–19; McMaster, "'89er," 46; Scott, *Story of Oklahoma City*, 29–31.

8. "The Beautiful Land," *Oklahoma Chief*, May 11, 1889. For the mistaken newspaper heading, see "Not 'Pioneer,' but 'Chief,'" *Oklahoma Chief*, n.d.

9. Geffs, *First Eight Months of Oklahoma City*, 19–20.

10. "History of Two Weeks."

11. "In the Soup," and "A Word of Greeting," *Oklahoma Chief*, n.d.; Geffs, *First Eight Months of Oklahoma City*, 63.

12. Untitled articles, *Oklahoma Chief*, n.d.

13. "Busy as Bees," *Oklahoma Chief*, May 11, 1889; "Water at Four Feet," untitled articles, *Oklahoma Chief*, n.d.

14. "All about Town," *Oklahoma Chief*, n.d.; Fred R. Young, "My First Three Months in Oklahoma City," in 89ers, *Oklahoma: The Beautiful Land*, 264.

15. L. L. Land, interview by Amelia F. Harris, January 17, 1938, vol. 52, 229–36, IPP online.

16. Untitled article, *Oklahoma Chief*, n.d.

17. Oklahoma Bank advertisement, *Oklahoma Times*, May 9, 1889.

18. McMaster, "'89er," 46; Suzzanne Kelley, "McMaster's Oklahoma Magazine," in *Encyclopedia of Oklahoma History and Culture*, accessed March 29, 2016, http://www.okhistory.org/publications/enc/entry.php?entry=MC037. From May 21 to July 23, 1889, the newspaper was published as the *Oklahoma Gazette*. Without notice, McMaster rechristened his paper as the *Evening Gazette* on July 24, even though he kept the same format. See Berlin B. Chapman, "Oklahoma City, from Public Land to Private Property: The Provisional Government," pt. 2, *Chronicles of Oklahoma* 37, no. 3 (Fall 1959): 333n11.

19. Berlin B. Chapman, "Oklahoma City, from Public Land to Private Property: The Day in Court," pt. 3, *Chronicles of Oklahoma* 37, no. 4 (Winter 1959–60): 444, 444n9.

20. News brief, *Oklahoma Gazette*, May 24, 1889.

21. "California Ave.," *Oklahoma Gazette*, May 23, 1889.

22. Geffs, *First Eight Months of Oklahoma City*, 64.

23. Colcord, *Autobiography*, 143–44; Stewart, *Born Grown*, 25–26; Dianna Everett, "Overholser, Henry," in *Encyclopedia of Oklahoma History and Culture*, accessed February 16, 2016, http://www.okhistory.org/publications/enc/entry.php?entry=OV003.

24. E. E. Brown, interview by Amelia F. Harris, August 13, 1937, vol. 12, 34–42, IPP online.

25. For a sociology of frontier business, see Norman L. Crockett, "The Opening of Oklahoma: A Businessman's Frontier," *Chronicles of Oklahoma* 56, no. 1 (Spring 1978): 85–95.

26. Untitled news briefs, *Oklahoma Chief*, n.d.

27. Untitled article, *Oklahoma Chief*, n.d.
28. "Ordinance No. 1," *Oklahoma Chief*, n.d.
29. "Ordinance No. 2," untitled articles, *Oklahoma Chief*, n.d.
30. News brief, *Oklahoma Times*, May 9, 1889; Carter, *Story of Oklahoma Newspapers*, 44.
31. "Ordinance No. 3," *Oklahoma Gazette*, May 24, 1889.
32. "How Many Town Lots One Person May Lawfully Hold," *Oklahoma Gazette*, May 23, 1889.
33. Untitled article, *Oklahoma Chief*, n.d.
34. "Claim Jumpers," *Oklahoma Chief*, May 11, 1889.
35. Peery, "First Two Years," pt. 1, 299; *Kansas City Times* cited in Geffs, *First Eight Months of Oklahoma City*, 97–98. See also Lara J. Wilson, "Daniel F. Stiles—Captain," unpublished biographical sketch, November 17, 1937, Stiles, Daniel F., Vertical Files, Research Division, Oklahoma Historical Society, Oklahoma City (hereafter cited as Stiles Vertical Files).
36. "A High Handed Outrage," *Oklahoma Chief*, n.d.
37. "After the Marshals," *Oklahoma Chief*, May 11, 1889.
38. Earl Conway, interview by Jimmie Birdwell, January 24, 1938, roll 33, vol. 100, 189–90, IPP microfilm; Mrs. Edith Barrows, interview by Harry M. Dreyer, May 17, 1937, vol. 79, 204–10, IPP online.
39. Colcord, *Autobiography*, 172–73.
40. McRill, *And Satan Came Also*, 6, 27–32; Scott, *Story of Oklahoma City*, 38; Stewart, *Born Grown*, 20.
41. Colcord, *Autobiography*, 140–46.
42. C. S. "Bud" Peniston, interview by Warren D. Morse, April 14, 1937, roll 3, vol. 8, 152–55, IPP microfilm.
43. S. L. Dunham, interview by W. T. Holland, June 24, 1937, vol. 26, 281–87, IPP online. Frank J. Hightower (1923–2000) was the author's father. As of this writing, the Hightower Building at 105 North Hudson remained in the Hightower family with the author's brother, G. P. Johnson Hightower, as manager.
44. Ibid.
45. Thomas H. Jordan, interview by Charline M. Culbertson, January 1, 1938, vol. 49, 445–48, IPP online.
46. "Right You Are, Jake," untitled article, *Oklahoma Chief*, May 11, 1889.
47. Best, "The Santa Fe Railway as an Okla. Pioneer," Chapman Collection.
48. Untitled article, *Oklahoma Chief*, n.d.
49. "Further Organization," *Oklahoma Chief*, May 11, 1889.
50. "Sour Grapes," *Oklahoma Chief*, n.d.
51. Mrs. E. G. Remmers, interview by Harry M. Dreyer, May 20, 1937, vol. 75, 209–19, IPP online.
52. Ibid.; Geffs, *First Eight Months of Oklahoma City*, 57–59; Stewart, *Born Grown*, 33.

53. July 4, 1889 poster, Research Division, Oklahoma Historical Society, Oklahoma City; "Back & 4th," *Oklahoman*, July 4, 2013; "Fourth of July," *Oklahoma Gazette*, June 7, 1889.

54. Etta Dale, interview by Nora L. Lorrin, March 28, 1938, vol. 23, 33–43, IPP online; Lester, "William J. McClure and the McClure Ranch," 302–3.

55. Geffs, *First Eight Months of Oklahoma City*, 27–32; Peery, "First Two Years," pt. 1, 306–8; Scott, *Story of Oklahoma City*, 48–51.

56. McMaster, "'89er," 46.

CHAPTER ELEVEN

Epigraph. Untitled article, *Evening Gazette*, December 28, 1889.

1. Jim Simpson, interview by Grace Kelley, April 20, 1938, vol. 83, 414–35, IPP online.

2. Alfred Smith, interview by Harry M. Dreyer, n.d., vol. 84, 307–10, IPP online. For a similar example of Indian hospitality, involving puppies as a delicacy, see Osburn, "Tribute to Capt. D. L. Payne," pt. 2, 382.

3. Mary Ellen Carver, interview by Amelia F. Harris, March 29, 1937, vol. 16, 260–64, IPP online; Samuel Curleon, interview by Nannie Lee Burns, March 14, 1938, vol. 22, 452–56, IPP online.

4. Barrows, Dreyer interview.

5. Ibid.

6. Jeff D. Randolph, interview by Harry M. Dreyer, n.d., vol. 74, 235–38, IPP online.

7. Johnson, *Chickasaw Rancher*, 90.

8. Clarence E. Trosper, interview by Amelia F. Harris, May 13, 1937, vol. 92, 100–15, IPP online; questionnaire, n.d., roll 24, vol. 73, 228–31, IPP microfilm.

9. Land, Harris interview. For listings for Sheppard's meat market and other businesses that were in full operation in 1889, see R. W. McAdam and S. E. Levi, comps., *The City Directory—1889, Oklahoma City, Oklahoma Territory* (Oklahoma City, I.T., August 22, 1889).

10. Untitled article, *Oklahoma City Daily Times*, September 7, 1889.

11. Land, Harris interview; Young, "My First Three Months in Oklahoma City," 264.

12. Mrs. Flora Ragon, interview by Amelia F. Harris, July 12, 1937, vol. 74, 106–10, IPP online; Ella Brownlee Leach, "Knowledge That Couldn't Be Learned from Books," in 89ers Association, *Oklahoma: The Beautiful Land*, 209–12. Leach's article was previously published in the April 22, 1929, edition of the *Kingfisher Free Press*.

13. Dale, Lorrin interview; "Pioneer Teacher Accorded Honor," *El Reno Daily Tribune*, May 2, 1937.

14. South Oklahoma Mayor T. J. Fagan and Oklahoma mayor W. L. Couch issued separate summons in announcements under the same heading, "Call for Primary Convention," *Oklahoma Gazette*, July 12, 1889. See also Scott, *Story of Oklahoma City*, 48; and Peery, "First Two Years," pt. 1, 306–8.

15. Scott, *Story of Oklahoma City*, 48–51; Geffs, *First Eight Months of Oklahoma City*, 27–28.

16. Geffs, *First Eight Months of Oklahoma City,* 27–32.

17. "The Guthrie Convention"; "The Guthrie Convention Adjourns Sine Die"; untitled article; "Call for a Delegate Convention"; and "Anti-Convention Meeting," all in *Oklahoma News,* August 30, 1889.

18. "Frisco Convention," *Oklahoma City Daily Times,* September 11, 1889.

19. Mrs. J. B. Harrell, interview by Amelia Harris, April 20, 1937, vol. 39, 170–75, IPP online.

20. Mrs. A. W. White, "Oklahoma City's First School—The Teacher, Mrs. North," in 89ers Association, *Oklahoma: The Beautiful Land,* 187–89; untitled article, *Oklahoma City Daily Times,* August 27, 1889.

21. Untitled article, *Oklahoma City Daily Times,* September 5, 1889.

22. Alice Biteman [*sic*] Heaney, interview by Amelia F. Harris, October 18, 1937, vol. 41, 17–26, IPP online; Mrs. A. S. Heaney, interview by Harry M. Dreyer, March 5 , 1937, roll 2, vol. 4, 493–96, IPP microfilm; Mrs. A. S. Heaney, "How a Woman Took a Claim," in 89ers Association, *Oklahoma: The Beautiful Land,* 183–86. See also Ragon, Harris interview.

23. Mrs. Fred Sutton, "Schools of '89 and their Development," *Sturm's Oklahoma Magazine* 8, no. 2 (April 1909): 41–42; Sutton, "Schools of '89 and their Development," in 89ers Association, *Oklahoma: The Beautiful Land,* 155.

24. Untitled article, *Oklahoma City Daily Times,* September 6, 1889; "That Right of Way," and "The Latest Choctaw News," *Oklahoma City Daily Times,*" September 7, 1889; "Not True," *Oklahoma City Daily Times,* September 9, 1889.

25. "Railway Meeting," *Oklahoma City Daily Times,* September 9, 1889.

26. "Czar Stiles," *Oklahoma City Daily Times,* September 9, 1889.

27. Wilson, "Daniel F. Stiles—Captain."

28. Untitled news brief, *Oklahoma Gazette,* July 12, 1889.

29. "A Vote on the Citizens' Charter," *Oklahoma City Daily Times,* September 14, 1889; "Citizens' Charter," *Oklahoma City Daily Times,* September 16, 1889; untitled article, *Oklahoma City Daily Times,* November 18, 1889.

30. Untitled article, *Oklahoma City Daily Times,* September 10, 1889.

31. "Welcome to Oklahoma City," *Oklahoma City Daily Times,* September 17, 1889.

32. Untitled article, *Oklahoma City Daily Times,* September 18, 1889.

33. "Oklahoma City's Welcome," *Oklahoma City Daily Times,* September 18, 1889; Geffs, *First Eight Months of Oklahoma City,* 84–85.

34. "Oklahoma City's Welcome"; Geffs, *First Eight Months of Oklahoma City,* 85–88.

35. Untitled article, *Oklahoma City Daily Times,* September 18, 1889; "Couch's and Clark's [*sic*] Graveyards," and "To the Rescue!" *Oklahoma City Daily Times,* September 19, 1889.

36. "Dog in the Manger," *Oklahoma City Daily Times,* September 19, 1889.

37. Scott, *Story of Oklahoma City,* 65.

38. Untitled article, *Oklahoma City Daily Times,* September 19, 1889.

39. Scott, *Story of Oklahoma City,* 65.

40. "Times Editor Jailed," *Oklahoma City Daily Times,* September 21, 1889.

41. Roscoe Bell, interview by Amelia F. Harris, January 4, 1938, vol. 7, 46–53, IPP online. Bell quotes President Harrison's telegram in his interview.

42. "Bayonets and Blood," *Oklahoma City Daily Times*, September 21, 1889.

43. "Voices from South Oklahoma," *Oklahoma City Daily Times*, September 21, 1889.

44. Untitled article, *Evening Gazette*, September 24, 1889.

45. Stewart, *Born Grown*, 16.

46. "Robbery," *Oklahoma City Daily Times*, September 30, 1889.

47. "Captain Stiles Exhonerated [sic]," *Oklahoma City Daily Times*, September 26, 1889.

48. *St. Louis Republic* cited in "Stiles, Not Styles, Once More to the Front," *Oklahoma City Daily Times*, September 27, 1889.

49. "The Cowardly Couches," *Oklahoma City Daily Times*, September 29, 1889.

50. Untitled article, *Oklahoma City Daily Times*, October 14, 1889. There were too many Mitchells listed in Oklahoma City's first directory to identify the man who came to Overstreet's aid. See McAdam and Levi, *City Directory—1889*.

51. Trosper, Harris interview; questionnaire, IPP microfilm. The term "lot jumping" was used to describe a range of nefarious activities that boiled down to theft of another person's lot. Lot jumpers joined sooners in the eighty-niner generation's gallery of rogues.

52. Best, Dreyer interview.

53. Untitled article, *Oklahoma City Daily Times*, Oct 15, 1889.

54. Untitled article, *Oklahoma Chief*, December 22, 1889.

55. The legal description of the disputed area is the southwest corner of section 33, township 12 north, range 3 west. See Welsh, "Deadly Games," 40. See also "Movement of Cattle Called Key to Opening Oklahoma."

56. Geffs, *First Eight Months of Oklahoma City*, 55; "Mayor Couch Resigns," *Oklahoma City Daily Times*, November 12, 1889.

57. Biography of Andrew Jackson Beale, Genealogy Trails History Group, Oklahoma Genealogy Trails, http://genealogytrails.com/oka/oklahoma/Beale.html; Andrew J. Beale Biography, ancestry.com.

58. Geffs, *First Eight Months of Oklahoma City*, 60–63.

59. Colcord, *Autobiography*, 140.

60. Untitled article, *Evening Gazette*, November 25, 1889.

61. Geffs, *First Eight Months of Oklahoma City*, 56; "Mayor Beale to Be Seated," *Oklahoma City Daily Times*, November 30, 1889.

62. Colcord, *Autobiography*, 149.

63. "Beale's Manifesto," *Oklahoma City Daily Times*, December 3, 1889; Untitled article, *Evening Gazette*, December 3, 1889.

64. "Beale's Manifesto."

65. Scott, *Story of Oklahoma City*, 80; Aaron Bachhofer, "Forgotten Founder: Charles G. 'Gristmill' Jones and the Growth of Oklahoma City, 1889–1911," *Chronicles of Oklahoma* 80, no. 1 (Spring 2002): 44–61.

66. "Food for Thought," *Oklahoma City Daily Times*, October 5, 1889.

67. Wenner, *Story of Oklahoma*, 39–40.

68. Scott, *Story of Oklahoma City*, 78.

69. Untitled article, *Oklahoma Chief*, December 22, 1889.

70. Geffs, *First Eight Months of Oklahoma City*, 67.

71. "An Appeal for Law and Order," *Evening Gazette*, December 23, 1889.

72. Chapman, "Oklahoma City, from Public Land to Private Property," pt. 2, 344–45.

73. Untitled article, *Evening Gazette*, December 28, 1889.

CHAPTER TWELVE

Epigraph. Mamie Page, interview by Amelia F. Harris, January 12, 1938, vol. 69, 26–32, IPP online.

1. Edna M. Couch, untitled manuscript beginning, "The problems that confronted William L. Couch," n.d., folder 6, box 10; and "How We Lived in Oklahoma Territory," unpublished manuscript, n.d., folder 6, box 10, both in Edna Mae Couch Collection; Eugene Couch, McFarland interview; Welsh, "Deadly Games," 36–42.

2. "Information sent by family after nomination, June 23, 1937"; Edna Mae Couch, "Problems that confronted William L. Couch"; Hill, "Civic Center Built on Accursed Acres."

3. "J. C. Adams," *Oklahoma Pioneer*, n.d.; Albert Columbus Couch, interview by Mildred B. McFarland, October 12, 1937, roll 7, vol. 21, 17–22, IPP microfilm; Bill Tharp, "Open Invitation to Gangrene," *Oklahoma Journal*, dated by hand May 6, 1970, Couch Family Vertical Files.

4. Tharp, "Open Invitation to Gangrene"; Hill, "Civic Center Built on Accursed Acres."

5. Scott, *Story of Oklahoma City*, 107–8.

6. Edna Mae Couch, "The problems that confronted William L. Couch"; "Movement of Cattle Called Key to Opening Oklahoma."

7. "Civic Center Built on Accursed Acres"; Scott, *Story of Oklahoma City*, 107–8; "J. C. Adams."

8. "Names of Colcord and Couch Recommended for Civic Drives," unsourced newspaper article, dated by hand June 19, 1937, Couch, Capt. William L., Vertical Files, Research Division, Oklahoma Historical Society, Oklahoma City.

9. William Cronon, George Miles, and Jay Gitlin, "Becoming West: Toward a New Meaning for Western History," in *Under an Open Sky: Rethinking America's Western Past*, ed. William Cronon, George Miles, and Jay Gitlin (New York: W. W. Norton, 1992), 17; McReynolds, *Oklahoma*, 292n28.

10. "Jubilation in Oklahoma," *Evening Star*, May 3, 1890.

11. "New Appointees," *National Tribune*, May 15, 1890; Scott, *Story of Oklahoma City*, 109–11; LeRoy H. Fischer, "Oklahoma Territory, 1890–1907," *Chronicles of Oklahoma* 53, no. 1 (Spring 1975): 4.

12. "Oklahoma Officials Commissioned," *Evening Star*, May 16, 1890.

13. Dan W. Peery, "The First Two Years," pt. 2, *Chronicles of Oklahoma* 7, no. 4 (December 1929): 426.

14. Scott, *Story of Oklahoma City*, 109–14; Fischer, "Oklahoma Territory, 1890–1907," 3–8; McReynolds, *Oklahoma: A History*, 292–97. For an account of Old Greer County's anomalous status until the U.S. Supreme Court placed it in Oklahoma Territory in 1896, see Hightower, "Businessman's Frontier."

15. Fischer, "Oklahoma Territory, 1890–1907," 4–5.

16. "Oklahoma's Governor," *Indian Chieftain*, May 29, 1890; Peery, "First Two Years," pt. 2, 425–26.

17. Scott, *Story of Oklahoma City*, 111–12.

18. Peery, "First Two Years," pt. 2, 431.

19. Ibid., 428.

20. "Oklahoma's First Legislature," *Oklahoma Journal*, March 28, 1890.

21. "How Do You Stand!" *Oklahoma Journal*, March 28, 1890.

22. Rhoda Morris, interview by Ruth E. Moon, July 30, 1937, vol. 65, 77–86, IPP online.

23. Miller, *Oklahoma Populism*, 44.

24. McReynolds, *Oklahoma: A History*, 292–97; Peery, "First Two Years," pt. 2, 432–33; Scott, *Story of Oklahoma City*, 113.

25. Peery, "First Two Years," pt. 2, 453–56.

26. "Delegate Election," *Oklahoma Daily Journal*, October 16, 1890.

27. Peery, "First Two Years," pt. 3, 100–101. Council Bill No. 7, known simply as "the capital bill," was published in its entirety in the press. See "The Capital Bill," *Oklahoma Daily Journal*, October 3, 1890.

28. Peery, "First Two Years," pt. 3, 99–100. An invitation to the legislative banquet on September 10, 1890, survives in folder 96, box 7, Clarke Collection.

29. Scott, *Story of Oklahoma City*, 114.

30. Peery, "First Two Years," pt. 3, 102–4.

31. Ibid., 110–11; "Inflamatory [*sic*]," *Guthrie (O.T.) Democrat*, October 4, 1890; "Chased by a Legislature," *Daily Critic*, October 3, 1890. For a slightly difference version of incident, see Trosper, Harris interview.

32. "Notes" and "Dastardly!" *Oklahoma Daily Journal*, October 3, 1890.

33. "Inflamatory."

34. "Capital Fight," and "Kingfisher's Methods," *Guthrie Democrat*, October 6, 1890.

35. "Guthrie and Oklahoma City Both Determined to Have 'Fair Play,'" *Evening Star*, October 4, 1890.

36. Peery, "First Two Years," pt. 3, 114–15.

37. "Guthrie and Oklahoma City," and untitled article, *Oklahoma Daily Journal*, October 16, 1890; "On to Kingfisher!" and untitled article, *Oklahoma Daily Journal*, October 17, 1890.

38. "The Capitol Bill!" November 12, 1890; and "Disgraceful Scenes," December 12, 1890, both in *Oklahoma Daily Journal*.

39. Scott, *Story of Oklahoma City*, 111.

40. News brief, *Oklahoma Daily Journal*, October 19, 1890; untitled article, *Oklahoma Journal*, December 26, 1890.

41. "Harvey Is His Name," *Oklahoma Daily Journal*, October 19, 1890; Fischer, "Oklahoma Territory," 4; Miller, *Oklahoma Populism*, 52.

42. Sutton, "Schools of '89," *Sturm's Oklahoma Magazine*, 43–45, and in 89ers Association, *Oklahoma: The Beautiful Land*, 156–58; Trosper, Harris interview; Heaney, Harris interview; Heaney, Dreyer interview. Alice Beitman married A. S. Heaney.

43. Jno. H. Burford to Hon. Jno. W. Noble, Sect. of Interior, November 22, 1890, folder 2, box 2, Harn Collection.

44. John Sherman to Hon. John W. Noble, Secretary of the Interior, April 25, 1889, folder 1, box 2; and E. W. Halford, private secretary to President Benjamin Harrison, to Hon. John Sherman, July 14, 1890, folder 1, box 2, both in Harn Collection. The spelling of Halford's name and his position in the Executive Mansion in Washington, D.C., are inferred from his letter.

45. Secretary John W. Noble to Hon. John Sherman, December 2, 1890, folder 1, box 2; and Instructions Governing Traveling Expenses and Other Allowances and Preparation of Weekly Reports and Accounts for Inspectors, Special Agents, and Others of the General Land Office, issued May 10, 1890 (Washington: Government Printing Office, 1890), folder 15, box 2, both in Harn Collection.

46. Don Green, "Harn, William Freemont," in *Encyclopedia of Oklahoma History and Culture*, accessed July 16, 2016, http://www.okhistory.org/publications/enc/entry.php?entry=HA027. The author's mother, Dannie Bea Hightower, was instrumental in preserving the Harn Homestead so that all of us, young and old alike, can catch a glimpse of Old Oklahoma.

47. George Turner, interview by Anna R. Barry, July 21, 1937, vol. 92, 360–68, IPP online.

48. Carver, Harris interview. See also Barney P. Curry, interview by Robert H. Boatman, December 27, 1937, vol. 22, 469–71, IPP online.

49. Mrs. I. C. Renfro, interview by John F. Daugherty, March 11, 1938, vol. 75, 221–32, IPP online.

50. Land, Harris interview.

51. Page, Harris interview.

52. Land, Harris interview.

53. Henry J. Stevenson, interview by Nora L. Lorrin, March 18, 1938, vol. 87, 297–306, IPP online.

54. For in-depth studies of African Americans in early Oklahoma history, see Jimmie Lewis Franklin, *Journey toward Hope: A History of Blacks in Oklahoma* (Norman: University of Oklahoma Press, 1982), and *The Blacks in Oklahoma* (Norman: University of Oklahoma Press, 1980). For a statistical analysis of African American participation in the Run of 1889 and subsequent settlement in Oklahoma Proper, see John Womack, comp., *Blacks, the First Year in Oklahoma; Blacks Who Were Land Claimants in Oklahoma Territory as of June, 1890, Who Came There in April 1889* (Oklahoma Historical Society: unpublished report, 1981).

55. Winifred M. Clark, Immigration of Negroes, September 20, 1938, vol. 103, 467–71, IPP online; Winifred M. Clark, Early Day Negro Settlers, October 12, 1938, vol. 103, 473–79, IPP online.
56. David Humphrey Miller, *Ghost Dance* (Lincoln: University of Nebraska Press, 1959), 24–28.
57. Ibid., 34.
58. Ibid., 108–9.
59. Kicking Bear quoted in ibid., 80.
60. Ibid., 140.
61. "Indians Massing," *Evening Gazette*, November 28, 1890; "The Ghost Dance," *Indian Chieftain*, November 27, 1890.
62. Harrison quoted in Miller, *Ghost Dance*, 128.
63. Johnson, *Chickasaw Rancher*, 241–44.
64. "The Southern Indians," *Evening Gazette*, November 29, 1890.
65. Heaney, Dreyer interview.
66. Myrtle Hill Allen, interviewer unknown, n.d., roll 26, vol. 77, 24–25, IPP microfilm; C. A. McNabb, "Oklahoma City's Indian Scare," *Chronicles of Oklahoma* 2, no. 4 (December 1924): 395–97; Richardson, Dreyer interview; Heaney, Dreyer interview.

POSTSCRIPT

Epigraph. Untitled article, *Oklahoma Journal*, December 26, 1890.
1. Michael P. Conzen, "Understanding Great Plains Urbanization through the Lens of South Dakota Townscapes," *Journal of Geography* 109, no. 1 (January–February 2010): 3–17. To explore the similarities and differences between urban development in Great Plains in the late nineteenth century and patterns of city building in the early federal period, see Richard C. Wade, *The Urban Frontier: The Rise of Western Cities, 1790–1830* (Urbana: University of Illinois Press, 1996).
2. Scott, *Story of Oklahoma City*, 20.
3. Turner, *Frontier in American History*, 3.
4. Angie Debo, *Prairie City: The Story of an American Community* (Tulsa: Council Oak Books, 1985), 3.
5. Scott, *Story of Oklahoma City*, 114.
6. Untitled article, *Oklahoma Journal*, December 26, 1890. See also O. P. Sturm, "Great Fortunes Made in Oklahoma City Real Estate," *Sturm's Oklahoma Magazine* 8, no. 3 (May 1909): 16.
7. Brown, "Early and Important Litigations," 26–30.
8. On April 22, 1913, a century chest was buried in the basement of the First English Lutheran Church (later, the First Lutheran Church of Oklahoma City) at 1300 North Robinson. After it was unearthed on April 22, 2013, the artifacts were catalogued and put on display at the Oklahoma History Center. To learn more about this remarkable collection, visit the Oklahoma History Center or experience it online at Oklahoma Historical Society, Century Chest, 1913–2013, http://www.okhistory.org/centurychest/.

9. O'Dell, "Clarke, Sidney."

10. Peery, "Colonel Crocker and the Boomer Movement," 293–96; Worth Robert Miller, "Crocker, Samuel," in *Encyclopedia of Oklahoma History and Culture*, accessed August 24, 2016, http://www.okhistory.org/publications/enc/entry.php?entryname=SAMUEL%20CROCKER.

11. David C. Peters, "Friends in High Places: The United States Presidential Election of 1892, Political Patronage and Oklahoma's First Land Grant College," *State* 12, no. 1 (Fall 2016): 125.

12. Brown, "Pawnee Bill."

13. Linda D. Wilson, "Colcord, Charles Francis," in *Encyclopedia of Oklahoma History and Culture*, accessed August 24, 2016, http://www.okhistory.org/publications/enc/entry.php?entry=CO020.

14. Larry O'Dell, "Richardson, Thomas Meriwether," in *Encyclopedia of Oklahoma History and Culture*, accessed August 24, 2016, http://www.okhistory.org/publications/enc/entry.php?entry=RI001. For various episodes in the history of the First National Bank and Trust Company of Oklahoma City and its predecessors, see Hightower, "Brother Bankers"; *Banking in Oklahoma Before Statehood*; and *Banking in Oklahoma, 1907–2000* (Norman: University of Oklahoma Press, 2014).

15. Dianna Everett, "Overholser, Henry," in *Encyclopedia of Oklahoma History and Culture*, accessed August 24, 2016, http://www.okhistory.org/publications/enc/entry.php?entryname=HENRY%20OVERHOLSER.

16. The author and his brother, G. P. Johnson Hightower, were born to Frank J. and Dannie Bea Hightower and were raised in the Johnson-Hightower home at 439 Northwest Fifteenth Street. The house was built by the author's great-grandfather, pioneer banker Frank P. Johnson, cofounder with his brother, Hugh, of the First National Bank and Trust Company of Oklahoma City. Frank and his wife, Aida, of Kosciusko, Mississippi, relocated to Oklahoma Territory in 1895.

17. "Oklahoma Pioneer Dies in Kentucky," *Oklahoman*, January 5, 1909; "Adopt Resolutions: Condone Death of Oklahoma City's Mayor, Dr. Beale," *Oklahoman*, January 22, 1909.

18. For a thorough biography of Charles "Gristmill" Jones, see Bachhofer, "Forgotten Founder," 44–61.

19. "The Incredible Court-Martial of Capt. Stiles," *Daily Oklahoman*, April 22, 1979, Stiles Vertical Files.

20. Hanneman, "Scott, Angelo Cyrus."

21. The Ewing townsite is mislocated on most early-day Indian Territory maps, possibly because Jackson and Cole got it wrong in their 1885 book, *Oklahoma! Politically and Topographically Described*. The site is designated in United States v. Payne, where Payne specifies his homestead claim as section 14, township 11 north, range 3 West. The township he originally sought to establish is bounded by present-day Fifteenth, High, Fifty-Ninth, and Bryant Streets. See Hoig, "Old Payne Trail," 153–54.

Bibliography

Archival, Corporate, Personal, and Vertical File Collections

Frederick. S. Barde Collection, 1890–1916. Research Division, Oklahoma Historical Society, Oklahoma City.

T. H. Barrett Collection. Research Division, Oklahoma Historical Society, Oklahoma City.

Boomer Literature Collection. Western History Collections, Norman, Oklahoma.

Berlin B. Chapman Collection. Research Division, Oklahoma Historical Society, Oklahoma City.

Sidney Clarke Collection. Research Division, Oklahoma Historical Society, Oklahoma City.

Couch Family Vertical Files. Research Division, Oklahoma Historical Society, Oklahoma City.

Edna Mae Couch Collection. Research Division, Oklahoma Historical Society, Oklahoma City.

Creek Nation Foreign Relations Collection (D. L. Payne, 1880–81). Research Division, Oklahoma Historical Society, Oklahoma City.

Federal Writers Project Transportation Collection. Research Division, Oklahoma Historical Society, Oklahoma City.

William F. Harn Collection. Research Division, Oklahoma Historical Society, Oklahoma City.

Indian Archives. Research Division, Oklahoma Historical Society, Oklahoma City.

Indian-Pioneer Papers. Research Division, Oklahoma Historical Society, Oklahoma City.

Indian-Pioneer Papers. Western History Collections, University of Oklahoma, Norman, Oklahoma.

Oklahoma City–Sandtown Vertical Files. Research Division, Oklahoma Historical Society, Oklahoma City.

Oklahoma Territorial Museum Collection. Guthrie, Oklahoma.

David Payne Papers, 1877–1884. Research Division, Oklahoma Historical Society, Oklahoma City.

Santa Fe Railroad Collection. Research Division, Oklahoma Historical Society, Oklahoma City.

Santa Fe Railroad Vertical Files. Research Division, Oklahoma Historical Society, Oklahoma City.

Stiles, Daniel F., Vertical Files. Research Division, Oklahoma Historical Society, Oklahoma City.

Fred L. Wenner Collection. University of Oklahoma Western History Collections, Norman.

Newspapers and Magazines

Abilene (Kans.) Weekly Reflector
Barbour County (Kans.) Index
Barton County (Kans.) Democrat
Butler (Mo.) Weekly Times
(Tahlequah, Cherokee Nation, I.T.) Cherokee Advocate
(Darlington Indian Agency, I.T.) Cheyenne Transporter
Chicago Tribune
(Washington, D.C.) Daily National Republican
Daily Oklahoman
Dallas Daily Herald
Dallas Weekly Herald
Dodge City (Kans.) Times
El Reno (Okla.) American
El Reno (Okla.) Daily Tribune
Emporia (Kans.) News
Emporia (Kans.) Weekly News
(Washington, D.C.) Evening Post
(Washington, D.C.) Evening Star
Guthrie (O.T.) Democrat
(Vinita, Cherokee Nation, I.T.) Indian Chieftain
(Muskogee, later, Eufaula, Creek Nation, I.T.) Indian Journal
Iola (Kans.) Register
Iron County (Mo.) Register
Leavenworth (Kans.) Weekly Times
Los Angeles Times
(Washington, D.C.) National Republican
(Washington, D.C.) National Tribune
New York Sun
New York Times
New York Tribune
Norman (Okla.) Transcript
Oklahoma Chief (mistakenly printed as *Oklahoma Pioneer* in early editions)

Oklahoma City Times
Oklahoma City Daily Times
Oklahoma Daily Journal
Oklahoma (later, Evening) Gazette
Oklahoma News
Oklahoma Times (later, Journal)
Oklahoma War Chief/Chief/War-Chief (various border towns, Kans.; later, I.T.)
Phillipsburg (Kans.) Herald
Richmond (Mo.) Democrat
Sacramento Daily Record-Union
San Antonio Light
Sedalia (Mo.) Weekly Bazoo
Washington (D.C.) Critic
(Austin, Tex.) Weekly Democratic Statesman
Weekly (Troy) Kansas Chief
White Cloud (Kans.) Chief
Wichita City Eagle
Wichita Daily Eagle
Wichita Eagle

Books and Theses

Abbott, E. C. ("Teddy Blue"), and Helena Huntington Smith. *We Pointed Them North: Reminiscences of a Cow Puncher*. New York: Farrar and Rinehart, 1939.

Adams, Andy. *The Log of a Cowboy: A Narrative of the Old Trail Days*. Illustrated by E. Boyd Smith. Boston: Houghton, Mifflin, 1903.

Baldwin, Kathlyn. *The 89ers: Oklahoma Land Rush of 1889*. Oklahoma City: Western Heritage Books, 1981.

Barker, Carolyn. *Fort Reno: The Military Post*. El Reno, Okla.: privately printed, 1993.

Bellesiles, Michael A. *1877: America's Year of Living Violently*. New York: New Press, 2010.

Boorstin, Daniel J. *The Americans: The Democratic Experience*. New York: Random House, 1974.

Brands, H. W. *American Colossus: The Triumph of Capitalism, 1865–1900*. New York: Anchor Books, 2010.

Brown, Dee. *The American West*. New York: Simon and Schuster, 1995.

Brown, John Cecil. "Early Days of the First National: A Bank as Old as the City It Serves." In *Fifty Years Forward: The First National Bank and Trust Company of Oklahoma City, 1889–1939*. Oklahoma City: First National Bank and Trust Company of Oklahoma City, 1939.

Carter, L. Edward. *The Story of Oklahoma Newspapers*. Oklahoma City: Western Heritage Books, 1984.

Colcord, Charles Francis. *Autobiography of Charles Francis Colcord, 1859–1934*. Tulsa: privately printed, 1970.

Cronon, William, George Miles, and Jay Gitlin, eds. *Under an Open Sky: Rethinking America's Western Past*. New York: W. W. Norton, 1992.

Dale, Edward Everett. *Cow Country*. Norman: University of Oklahoma Press, 1945.

———. *The Range Cattle Industry: Ranching on the Great Plains from 1865 to 1925*. Norman: University of Oklahoma Press, 1960.

Debo, Angie. *A History of the Indians of the United States*. Norman: University of Oklahoma Press, 1970.

———. *Prairie City: The Story of an American Community*. Tulsa: Council Oak Books, 1985.

89ers Association. *Oklahoma: The Beautiful Land*. Oklahoma City: Times-Journal Publishing, 1943.

Ellis, Joseph J. *The Quartet: Orchestrating the Second American Revolution, 1783–1789*. New York: Knopf, 2015.

Foreman, Carolyn Thomas. *Oklahoma Imprints, 1835–1907: A History of Printing in Oklahoma before Statehood*. Norman: University of Oklahoma Press, 1936.

Foreman, Grant. *The Five Civilized Tribes: Cherokee, Chickasaw, Choctaw, Creek, Seminole*. Norman: University of Oklahoma Press, 1934.

———, ed. *A Traveler in Indian Territory: The Journal of Ethan Allen Hitchcock*. Norman: University of Oklahoma Press, 1996.

Franklin, Jimmie Lewis. *The Blacks in Oklahoma*. Norman: University of Oklahoma Press, 1980.

———. *Journey toward Hope: A History of Blacks in Oklahoma*. Norman: University of Oklahoma Press, 1982.

Geffs, Irving (a.k.a. Bunky). *The First Eight Months of Oklahoma City*. Oklahoma City: McMasters, 1890. Reprint, Oklahoma City: Quantum Forms, 1988.

Gwynne, S. C. *Empire of the Summer Moon: Quanah Parker and the Rise and Fall of the Comanches, the Most Powerful Indian Tribe in American History*. New York: Scribner, 2010.

Hamilton, Kenneth Marvin. *Black Towns and Profit: Promotion and Development in the Trans-Appalachian West, 1877–1915*. Urbana: University of Illinois Press, 1991.

Hightower, Michael J. *Banking in Oklahoma Before Statehood*. Norman: University of Oklahoma Press, 2013.

———. *Banking in Oklahoma, 1907–2000*. Norman: University of Oklahoma Press, 2014.

Hofstadter, Richard, and Seymour Martin Lipset, eds. *Turner and the Sociology of the Frontier*. New York: Basic Books, 1968.

Hoig, Stan. *David L. Payne: The Oklahoma Boomer*. Oklahoma City: Western Heritage Books, 1980.

———. *The Oklahoma Land Rush of 1889*. Oklahoma City: Oklahoma Historical Society, 1984.

Jackson, A. P., and E. C. Cole. *Oklahoma! Politically and Topographically Described—History and Guide to the Indian Territory*. Kansas City, Mo.: Ramsey, Millett and Hudson, 1885.

Jacobs, Wilbur R. *On Turner's Trail: 100 Years of Writing Western History*. Lawrence: University Press of Kansas, 1994.

Johnson, Neil R. *The Chickasaw Rancher*. Rev. ed. Edited by C. Neil Kingsley. Boulder: University Press of Colorado, 2001.

La Vere, David. *Contrary Neighbors: Southern Plains and Removed Indians in Indian Territory*. Norman: University of Oklahoma Press, 2000.

Larkin, Jack. *The Reshaping of Everyday Life, 1790–1840*. New York: HarperCollins, 1989.

Leckie, William H. *The Buffalo Soldiers: A Narrative of the Negro Cavalry in the West*. Norman: University of Oklahoma Press, 1967.

Liu, Joanne S. *Barbed Wire: The Fence That Changed the West*. Missoula, Mont.: Mountain Press, 2009.

McAdam, R. W., and S. E. Levi, comps. *The City Directory—1889, Oklahoma City, Oklahoma Territory*. Oklahoma City, I.T., August 22, 1889.

McCallum, Henry D., and Frances T. *The Wire That Fenced the West*. Norman: University of Oklahoma Press, 1965.

McPherson, James M. *Battle Cry of Freedom: The Civil War Era*. New York: Ballantine Books, 1988.

McReynolds, Edwin C. *Oklahoma: A History of the Sooner State*. Norman: University of Oklahoma Press, 1954.

McRill, Albert. *And Satan Came Also: An Inside Story of a City's Social and Political History*. Oklahoma City: Britton Publishing, 1955.

Miller, David Humphrey. *Ghost Dance*. Lincoln: University of Nebraska Press, 1959.

Miller, Worth Robert. *Oklahoma Populism: A History of the People's Party in the Oklahoma Territory*. Norman: University of Oklahoma Press, 1987.

Morton, Phelicia Ann. "Home Is Where the People Are: Sandtown, Oklahoma." Master's thesis, Cornell University, 1999.

Nichols, Max, and David R. "Dusty" Martin. *Continuing an Oklahoma Banking Tradition*. Oklahoma City: First Interstate Bank of Oklahoma, N.A., 1989.

Nichols, Roger L. *American Indians in U.S. History*. Norman: University of Oklahoma Press, 2003.

Remini, Robert V. *The Life of Andrew Jackson*. New York: HarperCollins, 2009.

Rister, Carl Coke. *Land Hunger: David L. Payne and the Oklahoma Boomers*. New York: Arno Press, 1975.

Scott, Angelo C. *The Story of Oklahoma City*. Oklahoma City: Times-Journal Publishing, 1939.

Skaggs, Jimmy M., ed. *Ranch and Range in Oklahoma*. Oklahoma City: Oklahoma Historical Society, 1978.

Smallwood, James M. *An Oklahoma Adventure of Banks and Bankers*. Norman: University of Oklahoma Press, 1979.

Stewart, Roy P. *Born Grown: An Oklahoma City History*. Oklahoma City: Fidelity Bank National Association, 1974.

Turner, Frederick Jackson. *The Frontier in American History*. Franklin Center, Penn.: Franklin Library, 1977.

Varley, Molly K. *Americans Recaptured: Progressive Era Memory of Frontier Captivity.* Norman: University of Oklahoma Press, 2014.

Wade, Richard C. *The Urban Frontier: The Rise of Western Cities, 1790–1830.* Urbana: University of Illinois Press, 1996.

Walker, Henry Pickering. *The Wagonmasters: High Plains Freighting from the Earliest Days of the Santa Fe Trail to 1880.* Norman: University of Oklahoma Press, 1966.

Warde, Mary Jane. *When the Wolf Came: The Civil War and the Indian Territory.* Fayetteville: University of Arkansas Press, 2013.

Webb, Walter Prescott. *The Great Plains.* Boston: Ginn, 1931.

Wenner, Fred L. *The Story of Oklahoma and the Eighty-Niners, Retold on the Golden Anniversary.* Guthrie, Okla.: Co-Operative Publishing, 1939.

Wickett, Murray R. *Contested Territory: Whites, Native Americans, and African Americans in Oklahoma, 1865–1907.* Baton Rouge: Louisiana State University Press, 2000.

Winchester, Simon.*The Men Who United the States: America's Explorers, Inventors, Eccentrics, and Mavericks, and the Creation of One Nation, Indivisible.* New York: HarperCollins, 2013.

Wood, S. N. *The Boomer: The True Story of Oklahoma, or the Beautiful Land.* Topeka: Bond and Neill, 1885.

Articles, Book Chapters, and Unpublished Reports

Asplin, Ray. "A History of Council Grove in Oklahoma." *Chronicles of Oklahoma* 45, no. 4 (Winter 1967–68): 433–50.

Bachhofer, Aaron. "Forgotten Founder: Charles G. 'Gristmill' Jones and the Growth of Oklahoma City, 1889–1911." *Chronicles of Oklahoma* 80, no. 1 (Spring 2002): 44–61.

Berthrong, Donald J. "Cattlemen on the Cheyenne and Arapaho Reservation, 1883–1885." *Arizona and the West* 13, no. 1 (Spring 1971): 5–32.

Billiot, Mary Jo, Randy McFerrin, and Douglas Wills. "Returns in the Western Range Cattle Industry: Reconstructing the Financial History of the Matador Land and Cattle Company, 1883–1920." *Journal of the Economic and Business History Society* 35, no. 2 (2017): 1–25.

Brown, James L. "Early and Important Litigations." *Sturm's Oklahoma Magazine* 8, no. 2 (April 1909): 26–30.

Carmichael, John B. "Fort Supply, Indian Territory." *Oklahoma Magazine* 2, no. 1 (Spring–Summer 1997): 17–24.

Chapman, Berlin B. "Oklahoma City, from Public Land to Private Property: Surveying the Townsite." Pt. 1. *Chronicles of Oklahoma* 37, no. 2 (Summer 1959): 211–37.

———. "Oklahoma City, from Public Land to Private Property: The Provisional Government." Pt. 2. *Chronicles of Oklahoma* 37, no. 3 (Fall 1959): 330–53.

———. "Oklahoma City, from Public Land to Private Property: The Day in Court." Pt. 3. *Chronicles of Oklahoma* 37, no. 4 (Winter 1959–60): 440–78.

Clarke, Sidney. "At the Grave of Capt. D. L. Payne: An Address Delivered on Decoration Day, 1885." In 89ers Association, *Oklahoma: The Beautiful Land*, 26–31.

Conzen, Michael P. "Understanding Great Plains Urbanization through the Lens of South Dakota Townscapes." *Journal of Geography* 109, no. 1 (January–February 2010): 3–17.

Crockett, Norman L. "The Opening of Oklahoma: A Businessman's Frontier." *Chronicles of Oklahoma* 56, no. 1 (Spring 1978): 85–95.

Cronon, William, George Miles, and Jay Gitlin. "Becoming West: Toward a New Meaning for Western History." In *Under an Open Sky: Rethinking America's Western Past*, edited by William Cronon, George Miles, and Jay Gitlin, 3–27. New York: W. W. Norton, 1992.

Dale, Edward Everett. "The Cherokee Strip Live Stock Association." *Chronicles of Oklahoma* 5, no. 1 (March 1927): 58–78.

Dunham, Arthur W. "Oklahoma City before the Run of 1889." *Chronicles of Oklahoma* 36, no. 1 (Spring 1958): 72–78.

———. "A Pioneer Railroad Agent." *Chronicles of Oklahoma* 2, no. 1 (March 1924): 48–62.

Ellis, Richard N. "General John Pope and the Southern Plains Indians, 1875–1883." *Southwestern Historical Quarterly* 72, no. 2 (October 1968): 152–69.

Fischer, LeRoy H. "Oklahoma Territory, 1890–1907." *Chronicles of Oklahoma* 53, no. 1 (Spring 1975): 3–8.

Gibson, Arrell M. "The Homesteader's Last Frontier." *American Scene* 4 (1962): 27–69.

Harris, Grant. "Publishing a Newspaper in a 'Boomer' Camp." *Chronicles of Oklahoma* 5, no. 4 (December 1927): 363–70.

Heaney, Mrs. A. S. "How a Woman Took a Claim." In 89ers Association, *Oklahoma: The Beautiful Land*, 183–86.

Hightower, Michael J. "Brother Bankers: Frank P. and Hugh M. Johnson, Founders of the First National Bank and Trust Company of Oklahoma City." *Chronicles of Oklahoma* 88, no. 4 (Winter 2010–11): 388–415.

———. "The Businessman's Frontier: C. C. Hightower, Commerce, and Old Greer County, 1891–1903." *Chronicles of Oklahoma* 86, no. 1 (Spring 2008): 4–31.

Hoig, Stan. "Jesse Chisholm: Peace-Maker, Trader, Forgotten Frontiersman." *Chronicles of Oklahoma* 66, no. 4 (Winter 1988): 350–73.

———. "The Old Payne Trail and the Boomer Colony Sites." *Chronicles of Oklahoma* 58, no. 2 (Summer 1980): 150–59.

Holzapfel, John. "The Kansas Oklahoma Colony." In 89ers Association, *Oklahoma: The Beautiful Land*, 33–39.

Hoogenboom, Ari. "Spoilsmen and Reformers: Civil Service Reform and Public Morality." In *The Gilded Age: A Reappraisal*, edited by H. Wayne Morgan, 69–90. Syracuse: Syracuse University Press, 1963.

James, Parthena Louise. "Reconstruction in the Chickasaw Nation: The Freedman Problem." *Chronicles of Oklahoma* 45, no. 1 (Spring 1967): 44–57.

Jenness, Captain George B. "Fight of Payne and the Boomers." *Sturm's Oklahoma Magazine* 8, no. 2 (April 1909): 19–26.

Kelley, E. H. "When Oklahoma City Was Seymour and Verbeck." *Chronicles of Oklahoma* 27, no. 4 (winter 1949): 347–53.

Ketcham, Christopher. "The Great Republican Land Heist: Clive Bundy and the Politicians Who Are Plundering the West." *Harpers* 330, no. 1977 (February 2015): 23–31.

Koller, John S. "Pioneer Experiences with Capt. Payne." In 89ers Association, *Oklahoma: The Beautiful Land*, 9–12.

Kraisinger, Gary, and Margaret Kraisinger. "The Early Chisholm Trail to Abilene, Kansas, 1867–71." *Chronicles of Oklahoma* 93, no. 2 (Summer 2015): 150–81.

Leach, Ella Brownlee. "Knowledge That Couldn't Be Learned from Books." In 89ers Association, *Oklahoma: The Beautiful Land*, 209–12.

Lester, Patricia. "William J. McClure and the McClure Ranch." *Chronicles of Oklahoma* 58, no. 3 (Fall 1980): 296–307.

LeVan, Sandra W. "The Quaker Agents at Darlington." *Chronicles of Oklahoma* 51, no. 1 (Spring 1973): 92–99.

Malcolm, J. C. "Notes on Silver City by J. C. Malcolm." *Chronicles of Oklahoma* 36, no. 2 (Summer 1958): 210–13.

Marsh, Mary, ed. "Our First Seventy-Five Years." In *Bank Life: 1889/1964—Our First 75*. Oklahoma City: First National Bank and Trust Company, April 1964.

McClure, William J. "The First Legal Settler in Oklahoma City." In 89ers Association, *Oklahoma: The Beautiful Land*, 72–77.

McMaster, Frank. "An '89er, How He Rushed and What For." *Sturm's Oklahoma Magazine* 8, no. 2 (April 1909): 45–48.

McNabb, C. A. "Oklahoma City's Indian Scare." *Chronicles of Oklahoma* 2, no. 4 (December 1924): 395–97.

Meredith, Howard L., and George H. Shirk. "Oklahoma City: Growth and Reconstruction, 1889–1939." *Chronicles of Oklahoma* 55, no. 3 (Fall 1977): 293–308.

Miner, H. Craig. "The Dream of a Native Cattle Industry in Indian Territory." In Skaggs, *Ranch and Range in Oklahoma*, 18–29.

Murdock, Victor. "Dennis T. Flynn." *Chronicles of Oklahoma* 18, no. 2 (June 1940): 107–13.

Ortiz, Roxanne Dunbar. "Land Reform and Indian Survival in the United States." In *Land Reform, American Style*, edited by Charles C. Geisler and Frank J. Popper, 151–87. Totowa, N.J.: Rowman and Allanheld, 1984.

Osburn, William H. "A Tribute to Captain D. L. Payne by his Private Secretary, W. H. Osburn, Also Colony Secretary during the Fourth Raid." Pt. 1. *Chronicles of Oklahoma* 7, no. 3 (September 1929): 266–77.

———. "Tribute to Capt. D. L. Payne." Pt. 2. *Chronicles of Oklahoma* 7, no. 4 (December 1929): 375–87.

———. "Tribute to Captain D. L. Payne," Pt. 3. *Chronicles of Oklahoma* 8, no. 1 (March 1930): 13–34.

Peery, Dan W. "Captain David L. Payne." *Chronicles of Oklahoma* 13, no. 4 (December 1935): 438–56.

———. "Colonel Crocker and the Boomer Movement." *Chronicles of Oklahoma* 13, no. 3 (September 1935): 273–96.

———. "The First Two Years." Pt. 1. *Chronicles of Oklahoma* 7, no. 3 (September 1929): 281–322.

———. "The First Two Years." Pt. 2. *Chronicles of Oklahoma* 7, no. 4 (December 1929): 419–57.

———. "The First Two Years." Pt. 3. *Chronicles of Oklahoma* 8, no. 3 (March 1930): 94–128.

———. "Introduction: The First Two Years." *Chronicles of Oklahoma* 7, no. 3 (September 1929): 278–80.

Peters, David C. "Friends in High Places: The United States Presidential Election of 1892, Political Patronage and Oklahoma's First Land Grant College." *State* 12, no. 1 (Fall 2016): 124–27.

Peterson, Susan. "Fort Supply: Isolated Outpost." In *Early Military Forts and Posts in Oklahoma*, edited by Odie B. Faulk, Kenny A. Franks, and Paul F. Lambert, 78–89. Oklahoma City: Oklahoma Historical Society, 1978.

Price, B. Byron. "Prairie Policemen: The United States Army's Relationship to the Cattle Industry in Indian Territory, 1866–1893." In Skaggs, *Ranch and Range in Oklahoma*, 45–60.

Riddleberger, Patrick W. "George W. Julian: Abolitionist Land Reformer." *Agricultural History* 29, no. 3 (July 1955): 108–15.

Savage, William W. Jr. "Of Cattle and Corporations: The Rise, Progress, and Termination of the Cherokee Strip Live Stock Association." *Chronicles of Oklahoma* 71, no. 2 (Summer 1993): 138–53.

———. "The Rock Falls Raid: An Analysis of the Documentary Evidence." *Chronicles of Oklahoma* 49, no. 1 (Spring 1971): 75–82.

Shirk, George H. "First Post Offices within the Boundaries of Oklahoma." *Chronicles of Oklahoma* 30, no. 1 (Spring 1952): 38–104.

Skaggs, Jimmy M. "Cattle Trails in Oklahoma." In Skaggs, *Ranch and Range in Oklahoma*, 7–17.

Sturm, O. P. "Great Fortunes Made in Oklahoma City Real Estate." *Sturm's Oklahoma Magazine* 8, no. 3 (May 1909): 16–17.

Sutton, Fred E. "April 22, 1889–April 22, 1929." In 89ers Association, *Oklahoma: The Beautiful Land*, 17–21.

Sutton, Mrs. Fred. "Schools of '89 and Their Development." *Sturm's Oklahoma Magazine* 8, no. 2 (April 1909): 41–45.

———. "Schools of '89 and Their Development." In 89ers Association, *Oklahoma: The Beautiful Land*, 153–58.

Tennant, H. S. "Two Cattle Trails." *Chronicles of Oklahoma* 14, no. 1 (March 1936): 84–121.

Terrill, I. N. "The Boomers' Last Raid." *Sturm's Oklahoma Magazine* 8, no. 2 (April 1909): 39–40.

Townsend, Jesse R. "Camp Supply 40 Years Ago." *Sturm's Oklahoma Magazine* 12, no. 1 (March 1911): 9–10.

————. "Grant's Peace Policy." *Sturm's Oklahoma Magazine* 11, nos. 5 and 6 (January–February 1911): 5–7.

Welsh, Carol H. "Deadly Games: The Struggle for a Quarter-Section of Land." *Chronicles of Oklahoma* 52, no. 1 (Spring 1994): 36–51.

White, Mrs. A. W. "Oklahoma City's First School—The Teacher, Mrs. North." In 89ers Association, *Oklahoma: The Beautiful Land,* 187–89.

White, Wayne A. "'This Faithfulness Destroyed Them': The Failure of Grant's Peace Policy among the Kiowas and Comanches." *Chronicles of Oklahoma* 93, no. 2 (Summer 2015): 182–99.

Wickmiller, C. P. "C. P. Wickmiller's Recollections of David L. Payne as Official Photographer in the Expedition of 1883: Address delivered at the annual meeting of the Oklahoma Historical Society." *Chronicles of Oklahoma* 14, no. 2 (June 1936): 241–43.

Wicks, Hamilton S. "The Opening of Oklahoma." *Cosmopolitan Magazine* 7, no. 5 (September 1889): 460–70.

Womack, John, comp. "Blacks, the First Year in Oklahoma; Blacks who were Land Claimants in Oklahoma Territory as of June, 1890, who Came There in April 1889." Unpublished report, Oklahoma Historical Society, Oklahoma City, 1981.

Wood, Mrs. H. Robert. "Virgil Andrew Wood, M.D." *Chronicles of Oklahoma* 34, no. 3 (Fall 1956): 302–14.

Young, Fred R. "My First Three Months in Oklahoma City." In 89ers Association, *Oklahoma: The Beautiful Land,* 264.

Index

Abilene, Kans., 58–59

A'dair, Lt. (stationed at Oklahoma depot), 291n1

Ackley, E. N., 88

Adams, John C., 219, 227–28, 259

Admire, Receiver, 199

Adobe Walls, Tex., 25

Albuquerque, N.Mex., 81

Alfred (later Mulhall), Ind. Terr., 156, 206

Allen, John M., 211–12

Allen, Maj. (stationed at Oklahoma City), 215

Allen, Myrtle Hill, 245

American National Bank (Oklahoma City), 168, 254

American War of Independence, 3, 13

Antioch Baptist Church (Sandtown; later Oklahoma City), 155

Apache Wars, 32

Appomattox Courthouse, Va., 6, 36

Arbuckle Trail, 41, 60–62

Arizona Territory, 20, 30, 132, 136

Arkansas City, Kans., 33, 38, 41–44, 50–51, 84, 96, 109–12, 118, 131–36, 156, 160, 167, 230

Arkansas River, 67, 81, 134

Arkansas Territory, 3

Army of the Frontier, 35

Army of Virginia, 31

Arthur, Chester A., 98–99, 106–10

Arthur (African American settler), 242

Atchison, Topeka, and Santa Fe Railroad Co., 33, 38, 41, 64, 81–82, 130–34, 137, 142, 148–51, 155–59, 165–71, 174, 196, 198–201, 209, 219, 236, 257–58

Atkins, John DeWitt Clinton, 117–18, 130

Atlantic and Pacific Railroad Co., 10–11, 19, 27, 38, 81, 121

Augusta (Kans.) Republican, 84

Baker, Charles S., 140, 150, 211–12

Baltimore Investment Company, 254

Bank of Oklahoma City, 184

Barbour County (Kans.) Index, 70–71, 127

Barnes, George T., 140–41, 150

Barney, M. V., 178

Barrows, Edith, 195, 204

Barrows Crossing (on South Canadian River), 161, 168

Bass Pro Shop (Oklahoma City), 259

Bates, John C., 255

Battle of the Washita, 21–22, 25, 37

Battle Row (Oklahoma City), 196

Baxter Springs, Kans., 58, 153; Board of Trade, 45

Beale, Andrew Jackson, 220, 224–25; death of, 254; election as mayor, 220–22; Kickapoo Council, sachem of, 220, 224; manifesto of, 222; status quo order, recipient of, 225

Beatty, M. M., 178

Beaver Co., No Man's Land (later Oklahoma Panhandle), 228–32 beef issues, 23–25, 68–70, 91–93, 127, 134, 205–6, 208, 241, 248

Beidler, G. A., 186

Beitman, Alice (later Mrs. A. S. Heaney), 208, 237, 245; Charles (brother), 208; William (brother), 208

Bell, Roscoe, 215; father of, 215

Bennington, C. E., 133

Best, Frank J., 133, 137, 156–57, 166, 171, 199, 219

Bethany, Okla., 44, 258

Bickford Springs, Ind. Terr., 196–97

Bird, Mrs. Tom (William Couch's daughter), 227

bison, 40, 57, 93, 243; conservation of, 253; slaughter of, 23–25, 59–62

Bixler, Mort, 215, 218

Black Bear Creek, 41

Blackburn, John A., 185, 190–92, 196, 221

Black Hills, 30

Blaine, James G., 117

Blair, Henry W., 78

Blue Front Butcher Shop (Oklahoma City), 204

Blue Front Restaurant (Oklahoma City), 175

Boathouse District (Oklahoma City), 259

Boles, J. W., 233

Bone McKinnon Building (Oklahoma City), 212

boomer movement, 34, 50, 73, 78, 84–85, 94, 97, 101–6, 111–14, 124, 128–29, 135–38, 146, 161, 166, 179, 183, 222, 248–51, 266n44, 266n48; opposition to, 46–50, 54–56, 75–77; origins of, 40; railroad support for, 45

Borrows, J. A., 233

Boudinot, Elias C., 7, 28–33, 38

Bouse, Joseph W., 165, 176–77

Britton, Ind. Terr., 156, 208

Broadhead, Krum, and Phillips law firm (St. Louis, Mo.), 54

Broadhurst, W., 51

Broadway Ave. (Oklahoma City), 133, 169, 172–79, 183–84, 187–89, 193–200, 204–5, 208–9, 214–15, 241

Brown, E. E., 189

Brown, Jack, 62

Brown, James L., 232–33, 251–52

Brown, Lou, 101; father of, 101

Bryan, William Jennings, 253

Buffalo Bill's Wild West show, 104. See also Cody, William F. (Buffalo Bill)

buffalo soldiers, 20, 59–60, 87, 99–103, 109, 141–42, 154–55. See also Ninth U.S. Cavalry; Tenth U.S. Cavalry

Bull Foot Station, Ind. Terr., 157, 288n73

Bureau of Land Management, 274n16

Burford, John H., 237–38, 251

Burke, C. M., 232

Burnes, James Nelson, 125

Burton, Andrew Jackson, 165

Bushyhead, D. W., 46–47, 100–101, 128

C., J. T. (contributor to Indian Chieftain), 141–42

Caldwell, Kans., 50–54, 60, 67, 75, 86, 100–102, 114, 124, 128–30, 135, 152, 157

Caldwell (Kans.) Journal, 96

Caldwell (Kans.) Standard, 97

California Ave. (Oklahoma City), 184, 187–89, 196, 204, 209, 218, 259

Camp Alice, Ind. Terr., 85–88, 95, 257

Campbell, B. H., 71, 93, 112

Campbell, W. P., 48–50

Camp Supply (later, Fort Supply), Ind. Terr., 21–23, 37, 92. See also Fort Supply (formerly, Camp Supply), Ind. Terr.

Camp Wood, Ind. Terr., 75

Canadian Co., Okla. Terr., 60, 206, 232

Carnegie, Andrew, 8

Carpenter, Charles C., 30–34, 40

Carrol, Henry, 80, 90

Carson, J. M., Jr., 291n1

Carver, Mary Ellen, 240

Casey's Infantry Tactics (1862), 215

cattle industry, 38, 55–73, 81–86, 89, 92–94, 97, 100–109, 112–14, 117–26, 130–35, 139–44, 148–50, 154–57, 187, 256, 271n14, 271n21, 272n38; demise of, 126–28; origins and evolution of, 55–59. *See also* Cherokee Strip Live Stock Association

Cellar Restaurant (Oklahoma City), 198

Chaddick, Maj. (Choctaw Road official), 224

Chamberlin, Charles, 185

Checote, Samuel, 47, 77

Cherokee Advocate, 44, 53–54, 76, 82

Cherokee Indians/Nation, 27, 31, 46, 58–59, 67, 70–72, 100, 103; boomer movement, opposition to, 128, 149; Indian Territory, settlement in, 3–5

Cherokee Outlet, Ind. Terr., 29, 66–72, 87, 97, 104, 136, 149, 187; conduit for participants in the Run of '89, 160, 163–64; opening to non-Indian settlement, 254. *See also* Cherokee Strip Live Stock Association; Rock Falls settlement, Ind. Terr.

Cherokee Strip, 107

Cherokee Strip Live Stock Association, 67, 100, 104–6, 127

Chesapeake Arena (Oklahoma City), 258–59

Cheyenne and Arapaho Reservation, 19, 24–26, 29, 47, 61–62, 70, 92–93, 112, 123–27, 131–32, 155, 245

Cheyenne Indians, 20–23, 26, 59, 68–69, 81–82, 130, 147–48, 187–89, 244–45, 248

Cheyenne Transporter, 54, 70, 75, 78–80, 86, 108

Chicago, Ill., 24, 81, 156, 242

Chicago Times, 28–29, 33, 188

Chicago Tribune, 109

Chickasaw Indians/Nation, 29, 60–66, 106, 130, 133, 141, 154–55; Ind. Terr., settlement in, 3–5

Chikaskia River, 41, 96, 151

Childs, Dr. (townsite claimant), 193

Chisholm, Bill (son), 63–64

Chisholm, Jesse, 59–64, 258

Chisholm Trail, 41, 60–64, 157, 256

Choctaw Coal and Railway Co. (Choctaw Road), 185, 209–10, 217, 224, 236

Choctaw Indians/Nation, 10, 58, 65, 209, 247; Ind. Terr., settlement in, 3–5

Chop House (Oklahoma City), 189

Chup-Co, John, 10

Cimarron Co., Okla., 228

Cimarron River, 41, 60, 88–90, 96, 102–4, 109, 134, 279

Cincinnati, Ohio, 135, 156, 193

Citizens' Bank (Oklahoma City), 188, 198

Civil War, 3, 18–20, 76, 83–84, 112–14, 124, 130, 215, 230, 248; Battle of Chickamauga, Ga., 87; Battle of Murfreesboro, Tenn., 220; Battle of Prairie Grove, Ark., 35; Battle of Second Bull Run/Manassas, Va., 31–32; Battle of South Mountain/ Boonsboro Gap, Md., 25–26; Battle of Stones River, Tenn., 87; Battle of the Wilderness, Va., 87; Five Tribes affected by, 6–9, 140; homestead laws pertaining to Union veterans of, 152; Payne, David L., service during, 35–38; range cattle industry following, 55–60. *See also* Reconstruction Treaties (1866)

Clark, John F., 229

Clark, Winifred and family, 242

Clarke, Sidney, 12, 58, 170, 174, 234, 251–53; and boomer convention (Topeka), 111–12, 117–18; congressional delegation, welcoming speech delivered to, 212; death of, 253; at Frisco Convention, 206; and Interstate Oklahoma Convention (Wichita), 143–45; as Oklahoma City provisional mayor, 219–21; Okla. Terr., coauthor of bills to create, 128–30, 136–41; as Oklahoma

Clarke, Sidney (*continued*)
    townsite first ward councilman, 185;
    School Reservation Bill, lobbyist
    for, 237; and Seminole Town and
    Improvement Company, 161, 169–70
Clarke St. (later, Grand Ave., Sheridan
    Ave.; Oklahoma City), 171, 183–84
Cleveland, Stephen Grover, 112, 119–25,
    130, 148, 184, 208, 230; boomer
    leaders, meeting with, 141; Indian
    Appropriation Bill, signing of, 151–52;
    proclamations pertaining to grazing
    and settlement in Oklahoma Proper,
    118, 123–28; as U.S. president, 117,
    239
Cleveland Co., Okla. Terr., 232
Cobb, Stephen A., 28
Cody, William F. (Buffalo Bill), 30, 104,
    146, 253. *See also* Buffalo Bill's Wild
    West show
Coffeyville, Kans., 30–34, 39–40, 46, 50
Colbert's Ferry (on Red River), 58
Colcord, Charles F. "Charley," 38, 136,
    175–76, 220, 228; as cowboy, 92–93,
    132; death of, 254; Oklahoma City
    police chief, appointments and
    experiences as, 195–99, 221–22,
    232–34; Run of '89, preparation for
    and participation in, 157, 170
Colcord, William R. (father), 38, 136
Colcord Building (Oklahoma City), 254
Cole, Coleman, 65
Cole, E. C., 73, 136
Cole, George W., 194, 198
Colfax, Schuyler, 23
Commercial National Bank (Guthrie),
    163, 171
Confederation Congress (1783–89),
    13–14, 228
Conrad, George, 110
Cook's Saloon (Oklahoma City), 197
Cooley, Dennis N., 6
Cooper, George, 95
Cooper, J. B., 98–100, 108
Coppinger, J. J., 51

Cosmopolitan Magazine, 162
Cottonwood Creek, 158, 190
Couch, William L. "Bill," 100, 107, 118–
    21, 124–25, 128–30, 135–36, 183, 192,
    196, 209, 223; in boomer movement,
    83–85; Camp Alice expedition, wagon
    master of, 85–88, 95; congressional
    delegation, welcome of, 212; death
    of, 227–28, 252–53, 259; and election
    of September 21, 1889, 214–17; and
    Interstate Oklahoma Convention
    (Wichita), 143–44, 147; as Oklahoma
    City provisional mayor, 178, 185,
    217–20, 226; and Oklahoma
    Interstate Convention (Kansas City),
    140–41; Payne's Crossing expeditions,
    leadership of, 90, 95–99; and Seminole
    Town and Improvement Company,
    161, 166–67; Stillwater Creek
    expedition, leadership of, 109–12
Couch family: Abe (brother), 217; Edna
    Mae (granddaughter), 227; Eugene
    (son), 227; Ira (son), 227; Meshach
    (father), 96
Council Bill No. 7 (capital relocation
    bill), 233–35, 251
Council Grove, Ind. Terr., 44, 60, 63–64,
    204, 258
Council Rd. (Oklahoma City), 64
Courtney, Rebekah, 62
Cox Convention Center (Oklahoma
    City), 215, 258–59
Craddock, T. D., 39
Crandall, L. H., 161
Crawford, Samuel J., 20, 36–37
Creek Indians/Nation, 31, 46–47, 52, 60,
    64, 69, 76, 103, 143, 204; Ind. Terr.,
    settlement in, 3–6; Reconstruction
    Treaties (1866), provisions pertaining
    to, 9–11, 29, 121, 126, 150–52. *See
    also* Muskogee Creek Nation
Crittenden, Thomas T., 153
Crocker, Samuel, 128–31, 135–36,
    166, 183–85, 251–53; arrest and
    imprisonment of, 124–25; in boomer

movement, 113–14; death of, 253; Indian Appropriation Bill, presence at signing, 151; and Interstate Oklahoma Convention (Wichita), 143–46; and Oklahoma Interstate Convention (Kansas City), 140–41; as *Oklahoma War Chief* editor, 114
Crossroads Mall (Oklahoma City), 95–96
Crutcho Creek/Ranch, 41–42
Cunningham, William, 97
Curtis, C. H., 132
Custer, George Armstrong, 20–21, 37

Daily State Capital, 162
Dakota Territory, 15, 61, 132, 243
Dale, Etta, 202, 205–6
Dallas, Tex., 51, 75, 79, 164
Dallas Daily Herald, 79
Daniels, Arthur N., 234
Daniels, C. W., 45
Darlington, Brinton, 23, 26
Darlington Indian Agency, 24–26, 54, 61, 69–70, 80–81, 127, 131, 134, 142, 187, 259; beef issues at, 91–93, 205–8, 241, 257; ghost dance held near, 243–44
Darwin, Charles, 49. *See also* Social Darwinism
Davis, Jefferson, 5, 114
Davis, Robert A., 184
Dawes, Henry L., Mass. senator, 121–23
Dawes Severalty Act (General Allotment Act, 1887), 123–24, 132
Dawson, John M., 219
Day, M. W., 96, 102, 109–10
Dead Man's Crossing, 204
Decker, William S., 131–32
Deep Fork River, 79, 81
Delaney, L. R., 156
Delano, Columbus, 27
Del City, Okla., 41
Delmonico Restaurant (Oklahoma City), 189
Denison, Tex., 27, 50, 78
Devens, Charles, 45

Devon Tower (Oklahoma City), 198, 259
Diamond Link Ranch, 63
Dodge City Times, 32–33, 43
Doniphan Co., Kans., 54
Douglas, Selwyn, 255
Douglass, Kans., 161
Dunham, A. W., 142–43, 198; as Oklahoma depot stationmaster, 134–35; witnesses Run of '89, 165–67
Dunham, S. L., 198
Dwyer, Frank, 63
Dyer, D. B., 69, 163

East Guthrie, Ind. Terr., 213
Echelberger, T. W., 278n23
Edmond, Okla. Terr., 133–34, 156
89ers Association, 228
89ers Circle (Oklahoma City), 228
Elliott, William, 140, 150
El Reno, Okla., 60, 206, 229–30, 236, 241, 256
Elterman, E. E., 172
Emporia, Kans., 46, 90
Emporia (Kans.) News, 24, 27, 30, 46, 51, 54
Emporia (Kans.) Weekly News, 146
Endicott, William C., 117
Epworth University (later, Oklahoma City University), 256
Etta Dale Junior High School (El Reno, Okla.), 206
Eufaula, Ind. Terr., 47–48, 52, 76, 132
Ewing, Thomas, Jr., 37–38
Ewing settlement, Ind. Terr., 18, 34, 42–46, 53, 183, 258, 301n21
Ewing Town Co., 83–84

Fagan, T. J., 206
Fall Creek camp, 52–53, 75
Farmers Alliance, 231
Farmers National Bank (Oklahoma City), 184
Faulkenstein, John, 39
Federalist Papers, 220
Fifth Street (Oklahoma City), 218

Fifth U.S. Cavalry, 136, 244
Fifty-First Congress (1889–91), 149
First English Lutheran Church (later,
    First Lutheran Church of Oklahoma
    City), 300n8
First National Bank and Trust Co.
    (formerly, Oklahoma Bank; Oklahoma
    City), 172, 200, 208, 245, 254,
    301n14, 301n16
First Street (Oklahoma City), 208
Flynn, Dennis T., 162, 236–37
Forbush, Capt. (officer stationed at
    Oklahoma depot), 291n1
Fort Arbuckle, Ind. Terr., 60–62, 279n49
Fort Dodge, Kans., 20
Fort Gibson, Ind. Terr., 58, 100, 132
Fort Leavenworth, Kans., 36–37, 51, 83,
    193
Fort Reno, Ind. Terr., 25–26, 42–43, 61,
    75, 80–82, 86, 90–92, 109, 121, 124,
    127, 131, 134, 141–42, 155, 160,
    187–89, 193, 205, 216, 244, 256–59
Fort Scott and Gulf Railroad Co., 82
Fort Sill, Ind. Terr., 24–25, 60; Indian
    Agency, 24
Fort Smith, Ark., 4–7, 50; U.S. district
    court in, 45–47, 75–77, 82, 100–104,
    144–45
Fort Sully, S.Dak., 243–44
Fort Supply (formerly, Camp Supply),
    Ind. Terr., 21–26, 37, 68, 92
Fort Washita, Ind. Terr., 58
Foster, Judge C. G., 104, 107–10, 149
Fourth of July, 162, 201–2, 205, 258
Fourth St. (Oklahoma City), 166, 195,
    201, 255
Fourth U.S. Cavalry, 26, 51
freedmen, 10–11, 76–79, 121, 126, 150,
    248; Chickasaw, 62, 154–55, 258,
    287n63
Freedmen's Oklahoma Association, 78
Friday (land run participant), 165, 176
Frisco, Ind. Terr., 206–7
Frisco Convention, 206

Front St. (later, Santa Fe Ave.; Oklahoma
    City), 196

Gainesville, Tex., 79, 156, 198
Gainesville Town Company, 168
Gale, G. H. G., 43
Galveston, Tex., 106, 130
Garfield, James A., 79
Garland, Augustus H., 118
Gates, John W. "Bet-a-Million," 57
Gault, William J., 232–34
Geary, James, 163, 188–90
Geffs, Irving "Bunky," 165–68, 212–13,
    221
General Land Office (GLO), 14, 72, 78,
    100, 107, 159, 226, 239, 252, 274n16
George, J. B., 214, 217
ghost dance, 243–44
Gibbs, D. W., 232
Gillpatrick, J. H., 144–45
Gilpin and Frick (Oklahoma City), 189,
    245
Glazier, Albert R., 134
Gleason, H. W., 81
Glick, George W., 153
Glidden, Joseph F., 57
Goodrich, C., 41–42
Gould, Jay, 8, 69, 81–82
Grainger, Rev. (El Reno minister), 241
Grand Ave. (Oklahoma City), 133, 171,
    176, 184, 187–90, 195–97, 215, 233,
    241, 254
Grand Saline River, 58
Grant, Ulysses S., 27, 230; Ninth and
    Tenth U.S. Cavalry, formation of,
    20; peace policy of, 23–24, 66, 70,
    264n20, 265n23
Gray, Lon and Lucinda, 63
Grayson, G. W., 52, 78
Greathouse, D. G., 278n23
Greeley (Run of '89 participant), 161
Green, Edward B., 229
Greenlee, R. B., 39
Greer, Frank H., 162
Grierson, Benjamin, 20
Griffenstein family, 64

Grimes, William, 234
Gulf, Colorado and Santa Fe Railway Co.
    (Gulf and Colorado), 106, 130, 133
Guthrie, Ind. Terr., 41, 131–33, 154–63,
    166, 170–73, 211–13, 229–31, 237,
    257; depot, 160, 171, 199; Deer Creek
    (former name), 85, 131; Oklahoma
    City, rivalry with, 173, 190, 209,
    215, 218–19, 231, 235–36, 250; as
    territorial capital, 230–32, 235–36,
    239; territorial convention held
    in, 206–7; Territorial Executive
    Committee formed in, 202; territorial
    legislature meeting in, 233–35
Guthrie, John, 163
Guthrie, Ledru, 185, 216
Guthrie Democrat, 235

Haas, George J., 133–34, 158, 170
Haines, Rachel Anna, 108
Hallowell, J. R., 104
Hambly, H. C., 80
Hancock, Winfield Scott, 36
Harn, William F., 238–39, 251
Harn Homestead (Oklahoma City), 239,
    299n46
Harrington, B. R., 147–49, 192
Harris, A. W., 82–83, 87
Harris, Grant, 97–102, 105–8
Harrison, Benjamin, 152–55, 160, 168,
    211, 215, 236; ghost dance, response
    to, 244; and Organic Act (May 2,
    1890), 228–29; proclamation of
    March 23, 1889, 154, 160, 183, 238,
    251; status quo order, 225, 237
Harrison, James H., 168
Harrison, William Henry, 152
Harvey, David A., 236–37
Harvey Ave. (Oklahoma City), 166, 171,
    176, 200–201, 215
Haskell, Charles N., 239
Hatch, Edward, 20, 51–52, 99, 102, 105,
    109–11
Hayes, Jack, 244
Hayes, Rutherford B., 17, 51, 54, 75, 81;
    proclamations prohibiting settlement

in Oklahoma Proper, 31–32, 40,
    44–46, 98
Heaney, Mrs. A. S. (formerly, Alice
    Beitman). *See* Beitman, Alice (later,
    Mrs. A. S. Heaney)
Hell's Half Acre (Oklahoma City),
    194–97, 204, 226, 258–59
Hembree, Charles C., 179
Hennessey, Ind. Terr., 60, 170
Hensley, T. F., 241
Herman (or Harmon), Vicey, 63
Herskowitz Building (Oklahoma City),
    215
Higgins, Dr. Robert W., 219
Hightower Building (Oklahoma City),
    198, 228, 293n43
Hightower family: Dannie Bea (author's
    mother), 299n46, 301n16; Frank J.
    (author's father), 198, 293n43,
    301n16; G. P. Johnson (author's
    brother), 293n43, 301n16
Hill, Harry L., 38–43, 51–52
Hill, William D., 129
Hitchcock, Ethan Allen, 3–5
Hog's Back Trail, 40
Holzapfel, John, 160–61, 168, 176, 184
Homestead Act: of 1862, 8, 12; of 1879,
    section 2239, 121
Homestead and Town Site Co. of Okla.,
    153
Hotel de Barnard (Wellington, Kans.),
    107–8
Howard, J. W., 232
Hudson, F. G., 185
Hudson, J. A., 161
Hudson Ave. (Oklahoma City), 176, 198,
    254
Hunnewell, Kans., 51, 96–101, 105,
    150–51
Hunt, P. B., 70
Hutchison, W. B., 39

Indian Appropriation Bill: of 1879, 29; of
    1889, 151–52, 159
Indian Appropriations Act (1871), 21–22

Indian Chieftain, 141–43
Indian country, 4–7, 17, 20, 24, 45, 55,
  77, 80–83, 88–89, 103, 118–19
Indian Journal, 46–47, 65
Indian Meridian, 106, 279n49
Indian Removal Act (1830), 4–6, 9
Indian Territory, 12, 19–21, 25–27,
  35–40, 44–51, 54, 74–82, 85–94,
  111–13, 117, 123, 129–30, 135–37,
  141–43, 148–49, 156, 159, 162,
  185–87, 203, 209–11, 238–39, 244,
  247–49, 254, 257–58, 263n4, 266n44;
  Atlantic and Pacific Railroad, survey
  and tracklaying through, 11, 38,
  81–82; Boudinot, Elias C., vision for,
  28–32, 38; Coffeeville expedition to,
  30–33, 46; and Ewing settlement,
  18, 40–43; Five Tribes' occupation
  of, 3–6; formation of, 4; and
  Indian Appropriation Bill, 151–52;
  lawlessness in, 144–45; Organic
  Act (May 2, 1890), separation from
  Okla. Terr., 230–32; Reconstruction
  Treaties (1866), provisions pertaining
  to, 7–11, 46; Red River War fought
  in, 25; Rock Falls settlement in,
  96–107; Springer bill pertaining to,
  128–30, 139–44, 149–53, 211–12.
  See also Cherokee Outlet, Ind. Terr.;
  Oklahoma country; Oklahoma Proper;
  Unassigned Lands
Indiana House (Oklahoma City), 200
Indianapolis, Ind., 42
Ingalls, John J., 28, 67, 106, 118
Interstate Oklahoma Convention
  (Wichita, 1888), 143–46
Interstate 35, 41–42, 258
Interstate 40, 41, 258
Iola, Kans., 256
Iola (Kans.) Register, 112, 174

Jackson, Andrew, 4–6, 251
Jackson, A. P., 73, 136
Jefferson, Thomas, 12–14, 93, 249–51

Jenkins Ford (on South Canadian River),
  161
Jenness, George B., 38–39
Jerome, David H., 230
J. H. Wedemeyer and Co. (later,
  Wedemeyer, Clay and Co.), 172
Johnson, Andrew, 10
Johnson, Charles B. (Montford's father),
  62
Johnson, Frank P., 254, 290n21, 301n16,
  Aida (wife), 290n21, 301n16; Hugh
  (brother), 301n16
Johnson, Montford T., 62–64, 74, 155,
  244, 256
Johnson, Neil (Montford's grandson), 74
Johnson Grove. *See* Council Grove, Ind.
  Terr.
Jones, Charles Gasham "Gristmill,"
  222–24, 232–34; death of, 255
Jones, J. E., 185, 224
Jones, Okla., 81, 86, 255–57
Jordan, Thomas H., 198
Julian, George W., 12–16, 56, 144,
  262n22
Jumper, John, 6

Kansa (Kaw) Reservation, Ind. Terr., 65
Kansas City, Mo., 81, 88, 140–42, 179,
  194
Kansas City Star, 103
Kansas City Times, 31–34, 43, 83, 87,
  140–41, 193, 199
Kansas Oklahoma Colony, 160, 168–70,
  184
Kansas Pacific Railway, 58
Kansas Volunteer Cavalry, 20, 37
Kay, M. (or W.) T., 291n1
Keith (Oklahoma Proper farmer), 148
Kickapoo Council, 220, 224
Kickapoo: faction (Oklahoma City),
  168, 175, 185, 188, 193, 206, 212–17,
  221–22; city charter, 210
Kickapoo Indians, 204–5, 248;
  reservation, 29, 64, 166

Kicking Bear (Minneconjou Sioux), 243
Kincaid, Robert, 184
Kingfisher Co. Ind. Terr., 190, 199,
   205–6, 213, 230, 235–36, 242; Okla.
   Terr., 60, 232
Kingfisher Creek, 155
Kingman, Kans., 73, 136
Kiowa, Comanche, and Apache
   Reservation, 19, 24, 29, 59–61
Kiowa Indians/Tribe, 19, 69–70, 130,
   204–5, 244, 263n4
Kirkwood, Samuel J., 77–79
Knights of Labor, 135
Knights of Pythias, 199
Koller, John S., 108

Lake Overholser (Oklahoma City), 44
Lamar, Lucius Quintus Cincinnatus,
   117–18, 128
Land, L. L., 187, 190, 204–5, 240
Land Ordinance (1785), 13
Lawton, Ind. Terr., 198
Leach, Ella Brownlee, 205
Leavenworth, Kans., 90–91
Leavenworth (Kans.) Weekly Times, 28,
   32, 80
Lillie, Gordon William "Pawnee Bill,"
   146–47, 150–51, 170; death of, 253
Lincoln, Abraham, 169, 251
Lincoln, Robert Todd, 85, 89, 107, 112,
   120, 276n50
Lisbon, Ind. Terr., 206–7
Little River, 242
Little Rock and Fort Smith Railroad Co.,
   82
Little Wichita River, 79
Logan Co., Okla. Terr., 232–35
Los Angeles Times, 173
Louisiana Purchase (1803), 9, 78–80
Love, John E. "Jack," 214, 217
Lowe, David P., 28
Lurty, Warren, 229
Lynch, Michael L., 106
Lyons, John F., 100–101

MacArthur Blvd. (Oklahoma City), 63
Maidt, Hill M., 51
Main St. (Oklahoma City), 167–69,
   172–74, 177–79, 183–89, 196–200,
   204, 214–15, 240–41
Mansfield (Ohio) Herald, 238–39
Mansur, Charles H., 141, 144, 211–12
March of the Five Hundred, 87
Martin, John Frank, 228
Martin, Robert, 229–30
Mason, S. A., 51
Maxey, Samuel B., 281n4
Mayes, Joel B., 149
Maywood Addition (Oklahoma City),
   166, 201
McAdam, R. W., 186–92
McAlester, Choctaw Nation, 209, 236
McCartney, James H., 184
McClure, William J. "Bill," 64, 74, 155,
   166, 187, 201–2, 256; Dave (son),
   202, 258; William J. (grandson), 166
McCoy, Joseph G., 58–61, 105
McDonald, J. Wade, 104, 128
McFarland, Noah C., 107
McKennon Opera House (Guthrie), 233
McLain, C. R., 163, 171
McMaster, Frank, 172, 188, 192, 202,
   215, 222, 225, 292n18
McNabb, C. A., 189–90, 245
McNabb's Oklahoma Flour and Feed
   Depot, 189
McNeal, John, 30
McPherson, Alice, 85–86
McRill, Albert, 196
Medicine Lodge, Kans., 59, 70–71
Medicine Lodge Creek Treaty, 18–21
Mendota (later, Perry), Ind. Terr., 131
Merritt, Wesley, 225
Methodist Episcopal Church (Oklahoma
   City), 179
Methodist Episcopal Church
   (Wellington, Kans.), 108
Mexican-American War (1846–48), 56
Midwest City, Okla., 41
Miles, John DeBras, 26, 70, 82

Miles, Nelson A., 124
Military Division of the Missouri, 18, 20,
    24, 31–32
Military Plaza (San Antonio), 57
Military Reservation (Oklahoma City),
    160, 168, 215, 218, 237
Miller, Ben S., 104–6, 185
Miller, M. N., 232–33
Miller, M. S., 232
Miller, William Henry Harrison, 194
Mills, Roger Q., 29
Mississippi River, 3–6, 15
Missouri, Kansas and Texas Railway Co.
    (Katy), 27, 46, 106
Missouri Pacific Railroad Co., 82
Mitchell, H. B., 232–34
Mitchell (Oklahoma City resident), 218,
    296n50
Mizner, John K., 26
Monroe, W. W., 209–10
Moore, Okla., 131, 156
Morgan, John Tyler, 118
Mormon War, 35
Mosley, S. L., 278n23
Munford, Morrison, 34, 140–41
Murdock, Marsh, 162; Victor (son), 162
Murray, Rev. James, 168, 179, 185, 212
Muskogee, Creek Nation, 46–47, 64, 100,
    103, 132
Muskogee Creek Nation, 47, 52, 76–78
Myriad Gardens (Oklahoma City), 247,
    258

National Council of the Muskogee
    Nation (1881), 52, 78
National Hotel (Washington, D.C.), 128,
    135, 140–41
National Indian Defense Association, 128
National Industrial Convention
    (Cincinnati, 1887), 135
Neal, Moses, 178
Needham and McDonald photography
    (Oklahoma City), 188–89
Newton, Kans., 134, 156

New York Sun, 11, 28, 39, 42, 71, 82–84,
    199
New York Times, 101
New York Tribune, 30
Nine Mile Flats (near Oklahoma
    townsite), 200
Nineteenth Amendment to U.S.
    Constitution, 237
Nineteenth Kansas Volunteer Cavalry,
    20, 37
Ninth Regiment, Kentucky Mounted
    Infantry, 220
Ninth U.S. Cavalry, 20, 59, 90, 100, 110,
    121. See also buffalo soldiers
Noble, John W., 155, 159–60, 224–25,
    238–39, 251
Noble, Okla., 60, 156, 206
Noble Hotel (Guthrie), 234
Non-Intercourse Act (aka Indian
    Intercourse Act, Indian Non-
    Intercourse Act; 1834), 45, 75, 80
Norman, Ind. Terr., 133, 156, 206, 230
North, Lyman Hoyt, 207; wife, 207–8
North Canadian River (North Fork), 18,
    23, 30, 40–44, 60, 64, 79, 86, 95–96,
    121, 131–33, 154, 187, 222–23
Northwest Ordinance (1787), 228

Odd Fellows: Oklahoma City, 199;
    Topeka, 111
Odell, D. J., 121
O.K. Bus and Baggage Company
    (Oklahoma City), 184
Oklahoma (later, Evening) Gazette, 168,
    188, 202, 215, 221–22, 225, 244,
    292n18
Oklahoma A&M College (later,
    Oklahoma State University), 256
Oklahoma Bank (later, First National
    Bank and Trust Co.; Oklahoma City),
    172, 188–89
Oklahoma Capital City Townsites and
    Improvement Co. (Topeka), 159, 168
Oklahoma Chief, 185–94, 199–200, 219,
    224, 290n37, 292n8

Oklahoma City, 12, 18, 23, 26, 63–66, 84, 87–88, 92, 95–96, 125, 131, 136, 154–55, 166, 172, 184–86, 194, 198, 202, 207, 212–13, 222–31, 237–39, 247–59; Art Museum, 228; Board of Trade (later, Chamber of Commerce), 187–89, 209; Bricktown/Canal, 160, 204, 247, 258–59; City Hall, 187, 196, 220, 228; Civic Center, 228, 259; designation as, 211; elections held in, 213–17, 220–22, 232–34; Guthrie, rivalry with, 173, 190, 209, 215, 218–19, 231, 235–36, 250; Indian scare (December 1890), 243–45; July 4, 1889, celebration in, 201–2; National Memorial and Museum, 166, 258; Organic Act (May 2, 1890), pertaining to, 230–32; Payne's Springs located in, 41–42, 79; pioneers' descriptions of, 195–97, 203–5, 240–41; railroad depot, 133; Seymour, former name, 131–33; Thunder (NBA team), 258–59; Verbeck, former name, 131–33. See also Oklahoma depot; Oklahoma Station; Oklahoma townsite

Oklahoma City (Daily) Times, 147–49, 152–53, 173, 192, 209–19

Oklahoma City streets: NE Fourth, 255; NW Fourth, 166, 195, 201; NW Tenth, 63–64; NW Fifteenth, 254, 290n21, 301n16, 301n21. See also individual names of streets

Oklahoma Co., Okla., 64, 79–81, 86, 184, 233–35, 255–57

Oklahoma country, 18, 38–39, 48, 52–53, 74, 78–79, 89–91, 105, 111, 118, 124–26, 130–36, 141–43, 148, 199, 222. See also Oklahoma Proper; Unassigned Lands

Oklahoma Daily Journal, 234–35

Oklahoma depot, 133–35, 142, 154–56, 160–61, 164–71, 176, 186–89, 199–200, 205, 211, 223, 237, 248, 258.

See also Oklahoma City; Oklahoma Station; Oklahoma townsite

Oklahoma Dry Goods Co. (Oklahoma City), 189

Oklahoma Historical Society (Oklahoma City), 254

Oklahoma History Center (Oklahoma City), 252, 300n8

Oklahoma Interstate Convention, 140–41

Oklahoma land run, 156, 162–73, 184

Oklahoma News, 207

Oklahoma Panhandle (formerly No Man's Land, public land strip), 136–39, 189, 202, 228, 232, 279n49

Oklahoma Proper, 5, 12, 20, 26, 32–33, 45, 52–54, 66–67, 71–79, 82–84, 91–96, 106, 114, 156–62, 190, 199, 202, 208, 212, 228, 246–48, 252, 257–58, 279n49; agricultural activity in before opening, 63–65, 148; black migration to, 78, 299n54; Boudinot's letter pertaining to, 28–30; cattle trails through, 55–56, 60; grazing leases in, 68, 84; Indian Appropriation Bill pertaining to, 151–53; legal status of, 75–78, 88–89, 103–4, 107–11, 117–19, 128–31, 134–38, 144–50; President Cleveland's proclamations pertaining to, 123–24; President Harrison's proclamation for opening to settlement, 154–55, 238; Reconstruction Treaties (1866), provisions pertaining to, 9–12, 126, 150–54; Red River War in, 25. See also Oklahoma country; Unassigned Lands

Oklahoma River, 258

Oklahoma State Highway 81, 60

Oklahoma State Highway Dept., 61

Oklahoma Station, 64, 131–35, 142, 250; shortened to "Oklahoma," 146. See also Oklahoma City; Oklahoma depot; Oklahoma townsite

Oklahoma Territory, 66, 111, 128–29, 162, 231–33, 236, 239–41, 247,

Oklahoma Territory (*continued*)
    250–52, 255; black migration to, 242,
    248–49; ghost dance held in, 243–44;
    Organic Act (May 2, 1890), created
    by, 228–30; Springer bill pertaining to,
    128–30, 139–44, 149–53, 211–12
Oklahoma Times (later, *Journal*), 173–75,
    178, 186–88, 192, 231–32, 250
Oklahoma Town Co. (later,
    Southwestern Colonization Society),
    39–40, 51, 54, 268n17
Oklahoma townsite, 43, 155, 166, 173–
    77, 185, 189–90, 198, 206–9, 258. *See
    also* Oklahoma City; Oklahoma depot;
    Oklahoma Station
Oklahoma War Chief/Chief/War-Chief,
    82–84, 97–99, 101–3, 106–8, 111–14,
    123–25, 128–30, 135, 185, 277n6,
    277n7, 280n74, 281n4, 282n23
Old Greer Co., Okla. Terr., 66, 230,
    266n51, 298n14
Organic Act (May 2, 1890), 228–33
Orlando, Ind. Terr., 156
Osburn, William H., 79, 86, 274n20,
    275n49
Overholser, Henry, 189–90, 220–21,
    254–55; Anna (wife), 254; death of,
    254
Overholser & Avey Insurance Co.
    (Oklahoma City), 184
Overholser: block, 206; mansion, 254–55;
    opera house, 254; theater, 254
Overstreet, R. L., 218, 296n50
Overton, B. F., 65

Pack, Sam D., 232
Page, Mamie, 240
Palace Clothing House (Oklahoma City),
    189
Palace Hotel (Guthrie), 234
Pardee, J. H., 43
Parker, Isaac C., 46–47, 75–80, 88–90,
    103–4, 145
Parker, Quanah, 18, 25
Parsons, Kans., 27, 78–80

Patrick, George W., 175–77
Payne, David Lewis, 34–39, 45–48,
    71, 74, 78–84, 87–91, 95–96,
    104–8, 111–12, 185, 258; Camp Alice,
    expedition to, 84–86; death of, 108–9,
    113–14, 252; Deep Fork, expeditions
    to, 79–81; Ewing, first expedition to,
    40–43, 183; Ewing, second expedition
    to, and Council Grove, 44–45, 59–60,
    63; Fall Creek camp, expedition
    to, 50–54; Jones (present-day),
    expedition to, 81; military service of,
    35–37; Payne's Ranch, 37; Payne's
    Springs, expeditions to, 79; Rock
    Falls, expedition to, 96–104; Texas,
    expeditions from, 78–79; in U.S.
    District Court in Fort Smith, 75–78,
    103–4
Payne, Jack (David's brother), 35
Payne Co., Okla., 53, 109, 232
Payne's Crossing, 41, 90, 95, 99
Payne's Oklahoma Colony, 39, 44, 50, 79,
    82, 95–97, 108–10, 118–19, 128–29,
    135, 268n17
Payne's Springs, 41, 79
Payson, Lewis E., 149
Peel, Samuel W., 151
Peery, Dan W., 232–34
Penateka (Silver Brooch; Comanche), 18
Peniston, C. S. "Bud," 198
Pennsylvania Ave. (Oklahoma City), 154
Perkins, Bishop W., 129, 151, 211–12
Perry (formerly, Mendota), Ind. Terr.,
    131, 254
Peters, Samuel R., 211–12
Pettee, W. J., 245
Peyton, C. A., 232–33
Philadelphia, Penn., 146, 165
Phillips, D. M., and O.K. Cab Company,
    184
Pierce, H. L., 144
Pittman, L. G., 232
Plumb, Preston B., 67, 90–91, 106, 150
Polecat Creek, 43–45
Ponca (later, White Eagle), Ind. Terr., 131

Ponca Indians, 51, 65, 200
Pope, John, 24, 31–32, 45, 51, 69–70, 80, 83–85, 89
Preemption Act (1841), 8
Price, S., 108
Proctor, Redfield, 160
Public land strip, 136–37. *See also* No Man's Land; Oklahoma Panhandle
Public lands/domain, 8, 11–15, 28–29, 32, 38, 43, 54–57, 63, 67–68, 72, 76–79, 83–84, 87–94, 106–13, 123–25, 135–36, 139, 144, 149, 152, 155, 158–59, 192, 222, 249–52, 274n16
Purcell (formerly, Walnut Creek), Chickasaw Nation, 60, 131–34, 148, 154–56, 160–61, 164–67, 173, 176, 189, 200, 257. *See also* Walnut Creek (later, Purcell), Chickasaw Nation

Quinn, Henry, 133
Quinton, M. C., 185
Quong, Sam, 187

Radebaugh, Samuel H., 134, 146, 186
Ragon, Flora Gilpin, 205, 208
Ragsdale, J. M., 163, 171
Ramsey, Alexander, 45
Randall, George M., 82
Randolph, Jeff, 204
Rastus (Guthrie resident), 234
Reconstruction Treaties (1866), 7–9, 29, 46, 67, 77, 118, 126, 140, 150–54
Red Fork Ranch, 60
Red River, 3–5, 60–61, 66–68, 78–79, 198, 230
Red River War (1874–75), 25, 32, 61–62, 66
Red Rock, Ind. Terr., 132
Red Rock Creek, 41
Regan, J. A., 232–33
Remmers, Mrs. E. G., 200
Reno, Jesse L., 25–26
Reno Ave. (Oklahoma City), 154, 166–68, 174–76, 187–89, 226–27, 259

Reno City, Ind. Terr., 206, 213
Reno Trail, 189
Republic of Texas, 56
Richardson, T. M., Jr., 164–65, 171–72; father (T. M. Sr.), 164–65, 171–72, 188–90, 245, 301n14; death of, 254
Richardson, W. T., 185
Robberts, Margaret, 205
Robertson, Jenny, 131, 134
Robinson, Thomas B., 45
Robinson Ave. (Oklahoma City), 176, 184, 190, 200, 208, 233, 300n8
Rock Falls settlement, Ind. Terr., 96–107, 151, 278n24, 278n40
Romick, John C., 232–33
Round Grove (Oklahoma City), 212
Ryan, Thomas, 151

Sandtown, Ind. Terr., 154–55, 249, 258, 287–88n64
Santa Fe depot (Guthrie). *See under* Guthrie, Ind. Terr.
Santa Fe depot (Oklahoma City). *See* Oklahoma depot
Santa Fe Trail, 5, 36
Satanta (White Bear; Kiowa), 18–19
Saunders (Oklahoma City businessman), 193–94
Sawyer, Hamlin Whitmore, 147–49, 192, 210, 215–18
Sayre, Warren G., 230
Scallan, N. F., 200–201
School Reservation Bill, 237
Schurz, Carl, 31–32, 266n51
Scott, Angelo C., 168, 174–75, 178, 184–86, 192, 206, 214, 223, 227, 233–36, 247, 250, 255–56; and Century Chest, 252; death of, 256
Scott, C. T., 178, 185
Scott, W. W. (Angelo's brother), 174, 186, 192
Seay, Abraham J., 229
Second Ave. (Oklahoma City), 200
Second U.S. Infantry, 255

Seminole faction, 168–69, 175, 183–85, 188, 193, 206, 209–11, 220–25, 231. *See also* Seminole Town and Improvement Co.

Seminole Indians/Nation, 3–6, 118, 150–52; Reconstruction Treaties (1866), provisions pertaining to, 9–11, 29, 118, 121, 126, 152, 266n44

Seminole Town and Improvement Co., 161–62, 166–69, 175, 178, 185, 188, 192–93, 220–22. *See also* Seminole faction

Seminole Wars, 6

7C Ranch, 64, 166

Seventh St. (Oklahoma City), 174

Seventh U.S. Cavalry, 20, 37

Severs, F. B., 69

Shartel Ave. (Oklahoma City), 227

Shaw, W. P., 178–79

Shawnee Indians, 60, 248; reservation, 29

Shawnee Trail, 58, 64

Sheppard, J. P., meat market (Oklahoma City), 188–90, 204

Sheridan, Philip, 20–21, 24, 37, 124–25

Sheridan Ave. (Oklahoma City), 171

Sherman, John, 238–39

Sherman, Victor, 189

Sherman, William Tecumseh, 18–20, 89

Shoefly Creek, 41

Shuman, W. A., 39

Silver City, Chickasaw Nation, 63

Simpson, Jim, 203

Sitting Bull (Arapaho), 243–44

Sitting Bull (Hunkpapa Sioux), 243

Sixth U.S. Infantry, 60

Skirvin Hotel (Oklahoma City), 258

Smith, Alfred, 203

Smith, C. H., 51

Smith, S. C., 282n23

Snyder, Bill, 119

Social Darwinism, 49, 154, 248

Society of Friends, 23

Sorosis Club (Oklahoma City), 245

South Canadian River, 63, 88, 161

Southern Kansas Railway Co., 82, 106, 130–31

South Oklahoma, Ind. Terr., 176–77, 206, 213–15

Southwest Colony Town and Mining Co., 39–40

Sparks, William A. J., 72

Speed, Horace, 229

Spencer, Herbert, 49. *See also* Social Darwinism

Springer, William M., 128, 211; bill to create Okla. Terr., 128–30, 139–44, 149–53, 211–12

Stacey, W. A., 97

Stafford, Harry, 40, 183

Standard Oil Cattle Co., 72

Standing Rock Reservation, S.Dak., 243

Starr, T. J., 189

Star Restaurant (Oklahoma City), 198, 259

Steele, George W., 229–36

Steele, J. M., 54

Stevens, Lt. (Ninth U.S. Cavalry), 121

Stevenson, Henry J., art gallery (Oklahoma City; later El Reno), 241

Stidham, George W., 76–77

Stiles, Daniel F., 193–94, 210–18, 237, 244; death of, 255

Stillwater, Ind. Terr., 110, 230

Stillwater Creek, 109–11, 124

Stinson, A. E., 129, 135, 140–41

St. Joseph's Church (Oklahoma City), 201

St. Louis, Mo., 47, 54, 64, 69, 78, 81, 127, 144

St. Louis Globe-Democrat, 32

St. Louis Republic, 216

St. Louis–San Francisco Railroad Co. (Frisco), 10–11, 38–39, 81–82

Stone Calf (Cheyenne), 124

Story of Oklahoma City (Scott; 1939), 256. *See also* Scott, Angelo C.

Sully, Alfred B., 20–21

Sumner, William Graham, 49. *See also* Social Darwinism

Sutton, Mrs. Fred, 208

Tecumseh, Ind. Terr., 242–43
Teller, Henry M., 68–71, 80–81, 90–91,
  97, 102, 107, 112
Ten Bears (Comanche), 18
Tennant, H. S., 61
Tenth St. (Oklahoma City), 63–64
Tenth U.S. Cavalry, 20, 59–60. See also
  buffalo soldiers
Tenth U.S. Infantry, 193
Territorial Executive Committee
  (Guthrie), 202
Texas (Spanish) fever, 58, 64, 69
Texas Panhandle, 3, 25, 37
Topeka, Kans., 37, 111–13, 117, 156,
  159–61, 194; U.S. district court in, 95,
  104, 107
Topeka American Citizen, 78, 141
Topeka Commonwealth, 30, 43
Townsend, Jesse R., 23
Townshend, Richard W., 128–29
Treaty of Guadalupe Hidalgo (1848), 56
Treaty of Paris (1783), 13
Trosper, Clarence, 218; Hugh G. (father),
  218, 232
Tulsa, Creek Nation, 81, 203
Turkey Track Ranch, 64
Turner, Frederick Jackson, 87, 276n58
Turner, George, 240
Tuttle, Okla., 63
Twin Territories (Okla. and Ind. Terr.),
  50, 236, 253
Two Johns Saloon (Oklahoma City), 196

Umholtz, F. H., 208
Unassigned Lands, 160–62, 165–66, 170,
  176, 179, 183, 186, 194–96, 207–9,
  225, 228–32, 250, 288n73. See also
  Oklahoma country; Oklahoma Proper
Union Agency (U.S. Bureau of Indian
  Affairs, Muskogee, Creek Nation),
  100
Union Pacific Railway Co., 58

University of Oklahoma, 158, 227;
  Health Sciences Complex, 41, 96
Upshaw, T. M., 232
U.S. Constitution, 28–29, 73, 123, 220,
  228, 237
U.S. Grazing Service, 274n16
U.S. House of Representatives: Bill 370,
  12; Committee on Indian Affairs, 12,
  151; Committee on Public Lands, 12,
  149, 237; Committee on Territories,
  128–29, 139–41, 149
U.S. Post Office Dept., 132, 146
U.S. Senate: Committee on Indian
  Affairs, 121; Committee on
  Territories, 27, 149
U.S. War Department, 5, 45, 51, 66, 74,
  80, 89

Vanderford, R. F., 133
Van Wyck, Charles H., 128
Vendome (Oklahoma City), 196
Vest, George Graham, 76–77, 118–20,
  281n4
Vilas, William F., 149
Vinita, Cherokee Nation, 27
Violet, O. H., 185, 192
Voss, John T., 178

Wade, Col. (officer stationed at
  Oklahoma depot), 194
Walden, B. S., 112
Walden, Kans. Colony, 88
Walker, C. P., 168, 178, 184–85; Delos
  (brother), 184, 237
Walker Ave. (Oklahoma City), 166,
  174–76, 184, 226, 290n21
Wallace, Eugene, 184
Wallace, John, 178, 184–85
Walnut Creek (later, Purcell), Chickasaw
  Nation, 130–33, 141. See also Purcell
  (formerly, Walnut Creek), Chickasaw
  Nation
Walnut Creek Ranch, 62–63
Walnut Valley (Kans.) Times, 86–87

Walters (German miner), 165

Wantland, Lewis Cass, 41–42, 53, 63–64, 74, 155, 256

Warr Acres, Okla., 44, 258

Washington, D.C., 4, 7–9, 21–22, 26–28, 31–32, 38, 42, 53–54, 66–71, 75, 78, 81, 95, 100, 111–12, 117–21, 126–30, 135–41, 144–50, 153–55, 186, 225–26, 252

Washington, D.C., newspapers: *City Post*, 153–54; *Critic*, 101; *Evening Star*, 99, 229; *Post*, 147

Washita River, 20–21, 60

Waynick, Sarah A., 219

Weaver, James B., 113, 117–18, 128–29, 144, 151, 169–70, 174, 178, 251; death of, 253

Weekly (Troy) Kansas Chief, 54

Weekly Democratic Statesman (Austin, Tex.), 79

Welcome, E. S., 112

Wells, W. C., 185, 224

Wenner, Fred L., 156, 162–63, 223

Western Ave. (Oklahoma City), 166

Western Lumber Co. (Oklahoma City), 254

West Guthrie, Ind. Terr., 213

Wheeler, James B., 184

White, William Allen, 162

White Caps (las Gorras Blancas), 216

Wichita, Kans., 33, 37–40, 47, 51, 54, 75–77, 82, 88, 102–4, 136, 141–48, 156–57, 228; Board of Trade, 38, 143, 150, 170; Payne's Oklahoma Colony, branch in, 47, 50, 108; U.S. district court in, 103–4

Wichita Indians, 69, 130, 244

Wichita Mountains/National Wildlife Refuge, 37, 253

Wichita newspapers: *City Eagle*, 44, 48, 75–78, 81, 105; *Daily Eagle*, 99–103; *Eagle*, 143, 146, 152–53, 162; *Times*, 82–83

Wickmiller, C. P., 85–86, 275n49

Wicks, Hamilton S., 162–65

Wiley Post Airport (Oklahoma City), 44

Wilson, Alfred M., 230

Wilson, J. C./J. W., 161, 289n7

Wilson, J. S., 87

Wilson, Robert, 51–53, 75

Wilson, Woodrow, 117

Wind River Reservation, Wyo., 243

Winfield, Kans., 104, 162, 215

Witten, W. W., 232

Wood, Samuel N., 112, 117

Wood, Virgil Andrew, 173

Woodford, J. F., 185

Woods, M. H., 174

Woodson, Maj. (Fort Reno), 205

Wounded Knee, S.Dak., 244

Wovoka (the Cutter), 243

Wright, Allen, 9–10, 247

Wright, R. T., 187–90, 204–5

Wynn, "Big Anne," 196

XYZ Ranch, 72

Young Ladies Seminary (Oklahoma City), 208

Yukon, Okla. Terr., 245

Zerger, S. J., 111, 280n68, 282n23